YA MANGA BABY
Ragawa, Marimo.
Baby & me. Vol. 1

8/06

D1292288

Shojo Beat

Baby & Me™

Vol. 1

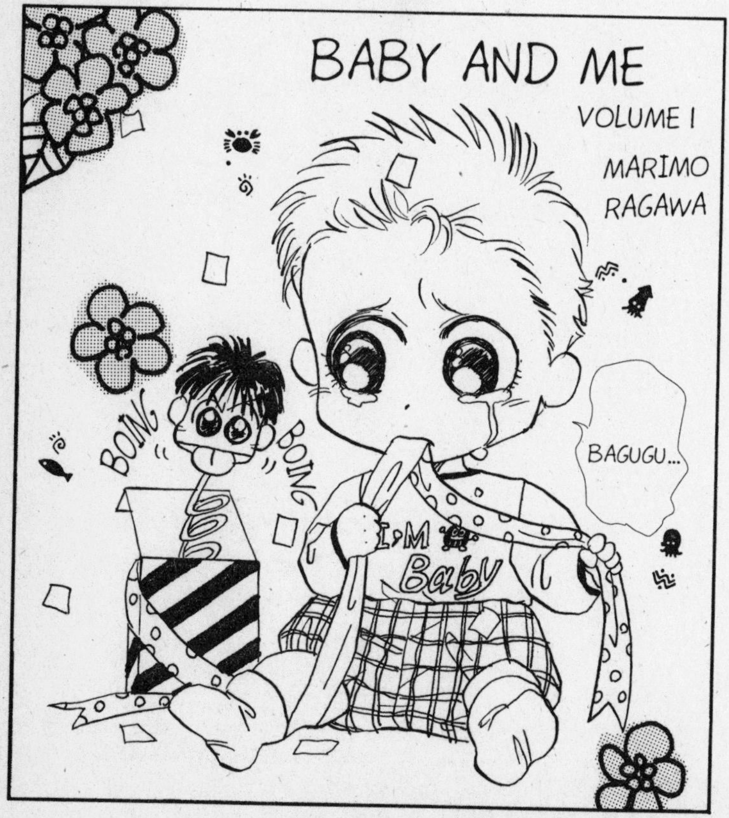
BABY AND ME
VOLUME 1
MARIMO RAGAWA
BOING
BOING
BAGUGU...
I'M Baby

Story & Art by Marimo Ragawa

Baby & Me™ Table of Contents

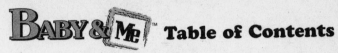

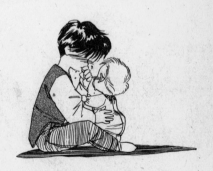

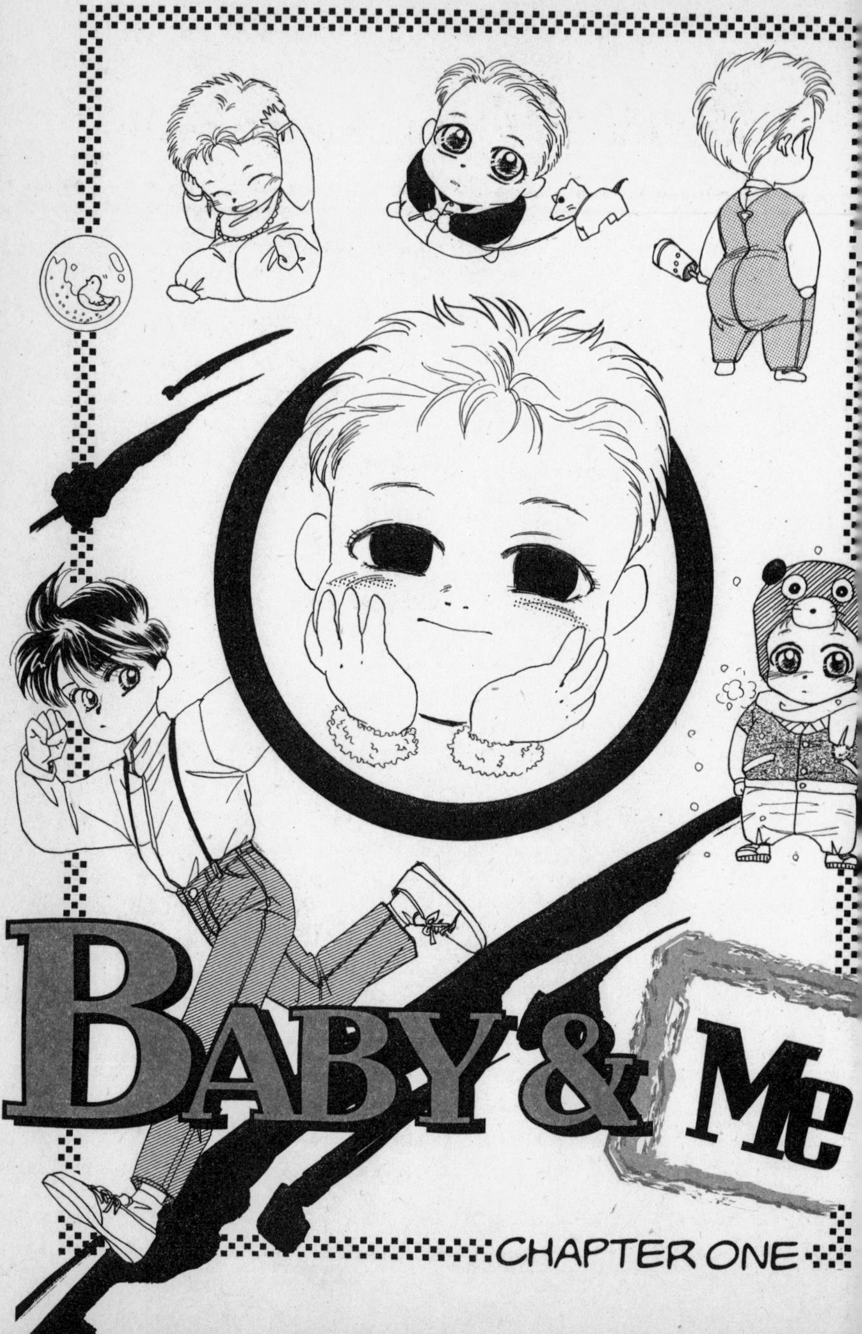
BABY & ME
CHAPTER ONE

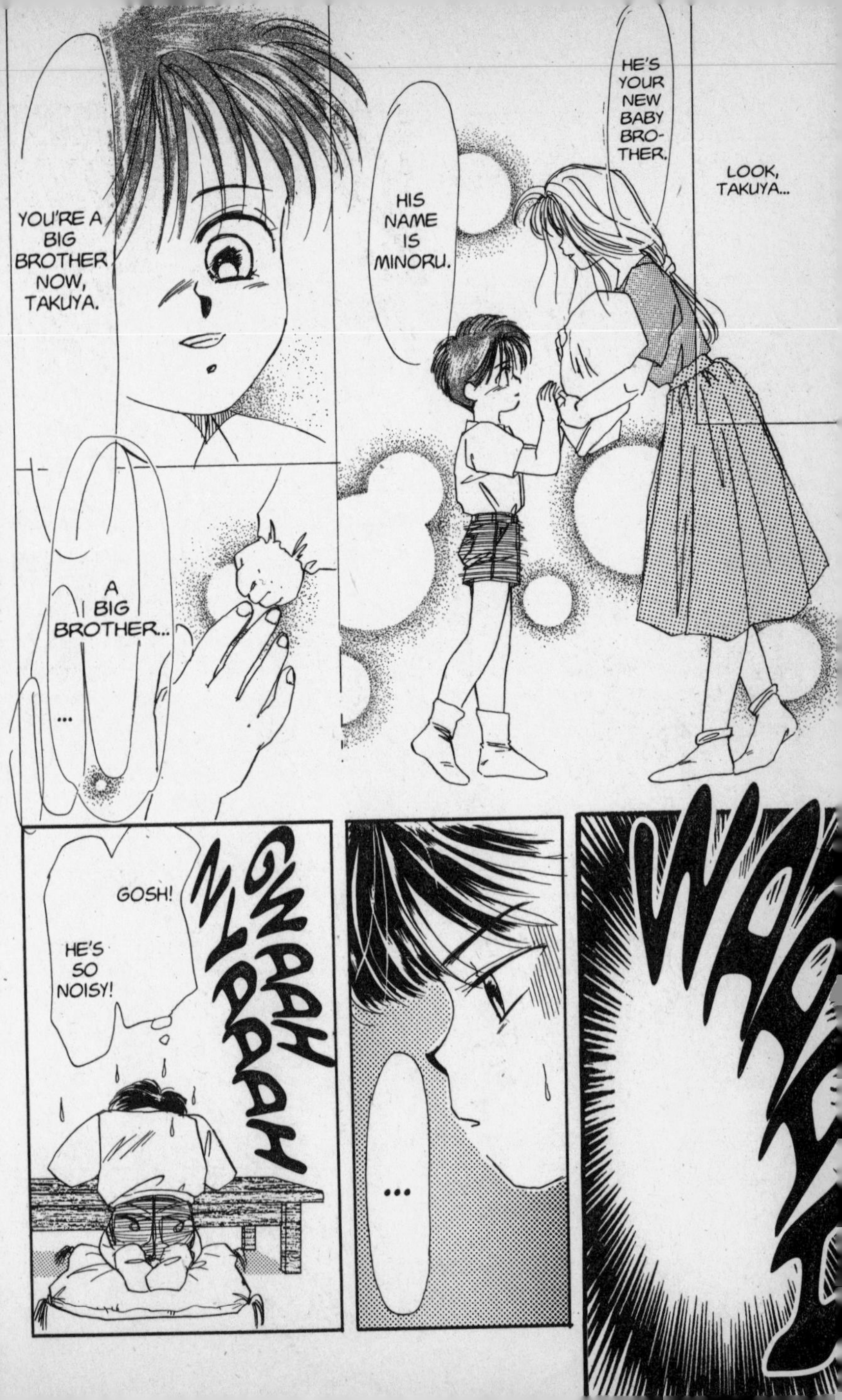
LOOK, TAKUYA...
HE'S YOUR NEW BABY BRO-THER.
HIS NAME IS MINORU.
YOU'RE A BIG BROTHER NOW, TAKUYA.
A BIG BROTHER...
...
...
GWAAH
NYAAAH
GOSH!
HE'S SO NOISY!

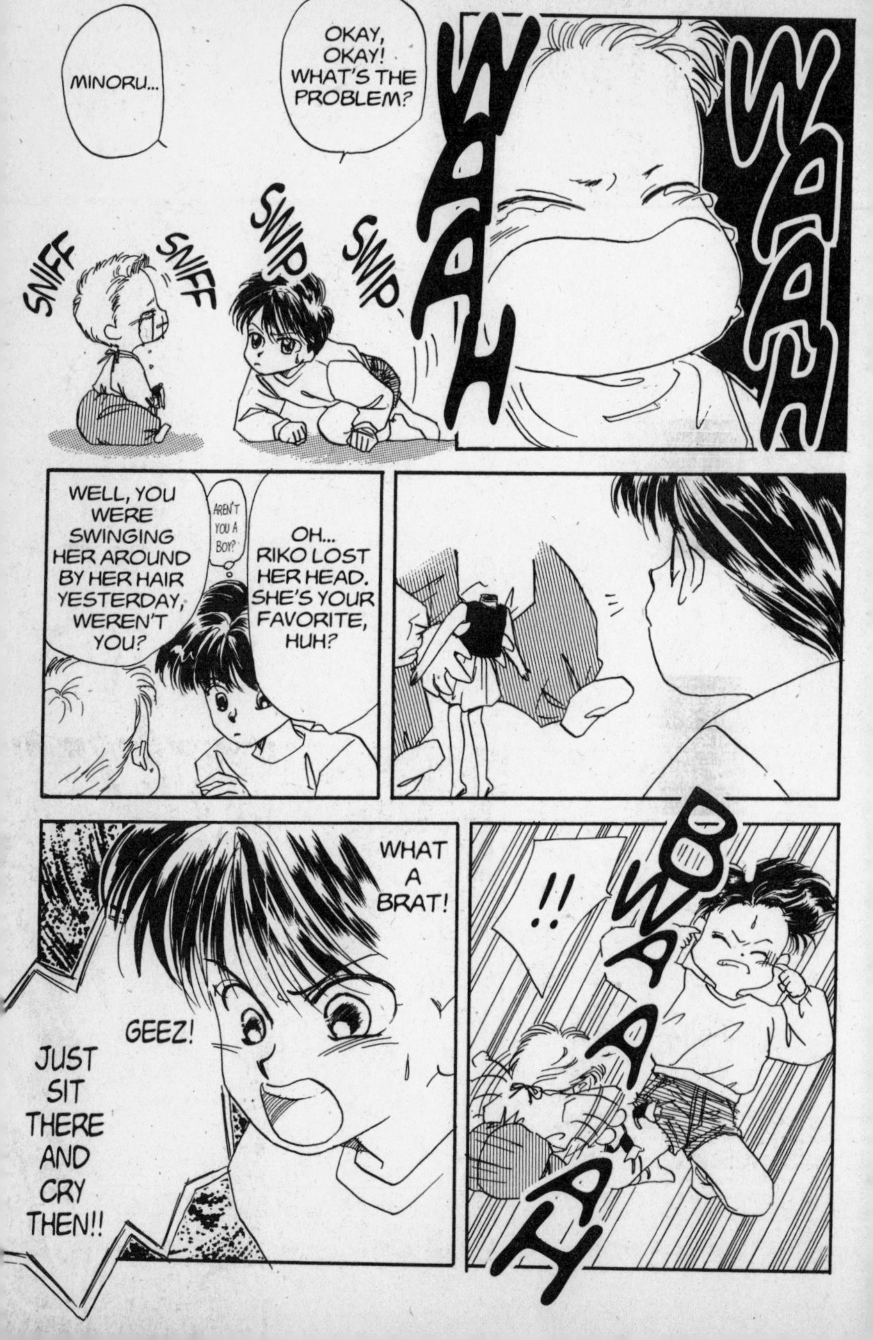
WAAAH
WAAH
OKAY, OKAY! WHAT'S THE PROBLEM?
SWIP
SWIP
MINORU...
SNIFF
SNIFF
OH... RIKO LOST HER HEAD. SHE'S YOUR FAVORITE, HUH?
AREN'T YOU A BOY?
WELL, YOU WERE SWINGING HER AROUND BY HER HAIR YESTERDAY, WEREN'T YOU?
BWAAAH
!!
WHAT A BRAT!
GEEZ!
JUST SIT THERE AND CRY THEN!!

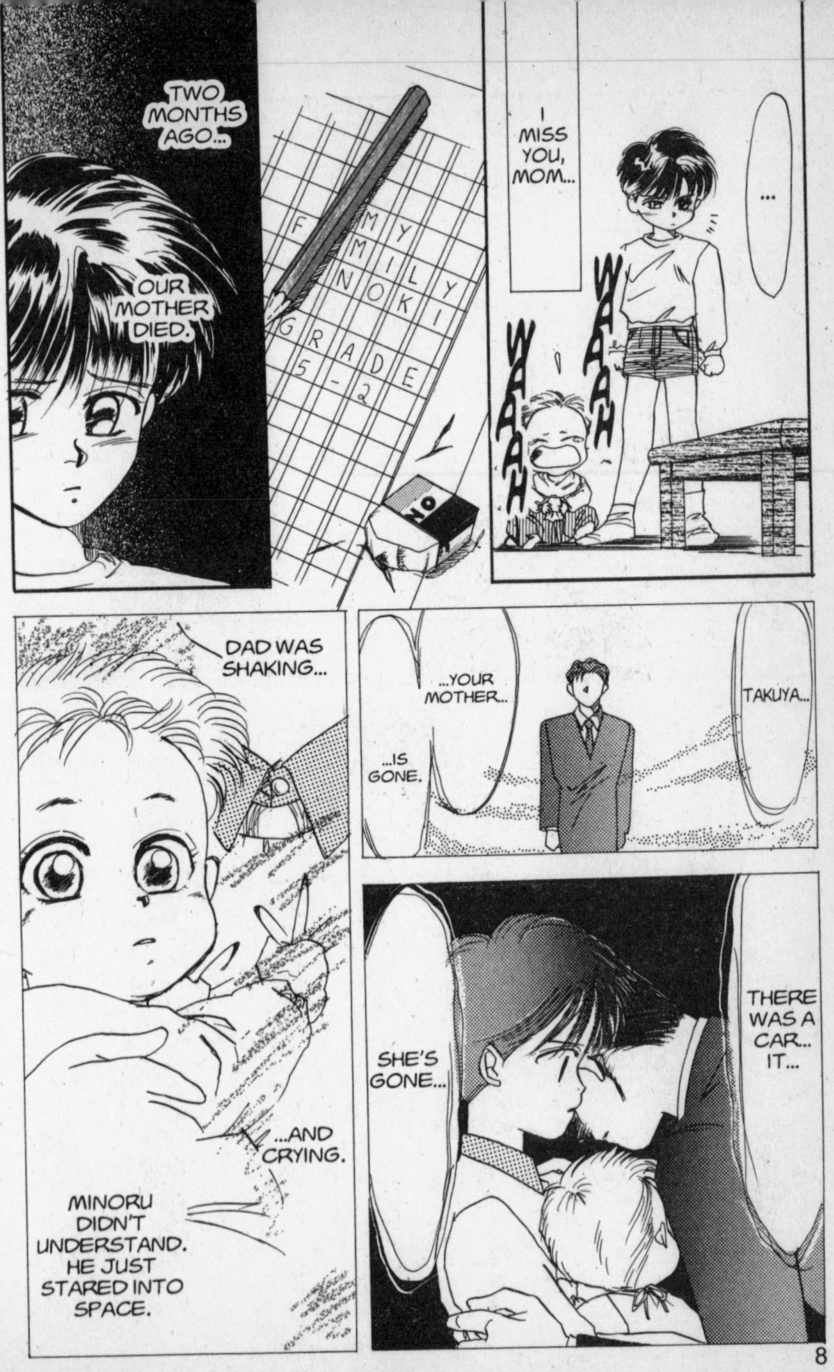
...
I MISS YOU, MOM...
WAAAH
WAAAH
GRADE 5-2
TWO MONTHS AGO...
OUR MOTHER DIED.
TAKUYA...
...YOUR MOTHER...
...IS GONE.
THERE WAS A CAR... IT...
SHE'S GONE...
DAD WAS SHAKING...
...AND CRYING.
MINORU DIDN'T UNDERSTAND. HE JUST STARED INTO SPACE.

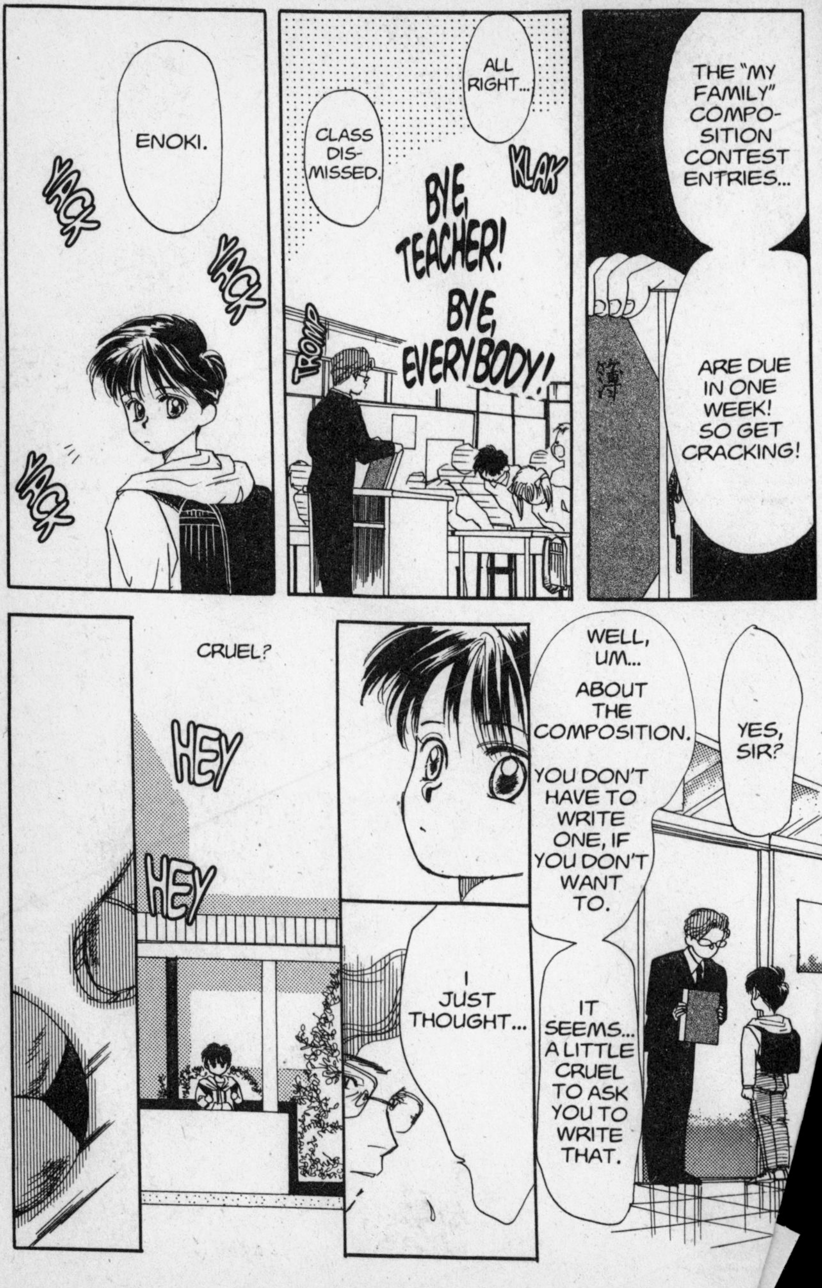
THE "MY FAMILY" COMPOSITION CONTEST ENTRIES...
ARE DUE IN ONE WEEK! SO GET CRACKING!
ALL RIGHT...
CLASS DISMISSED.
KLAK
BYE, TEACHER!
BYE, EVERYBODY!
TROMP
ENOKI.
YACK
YACK
YACK
YES, SIR?
WELL, UM...
ABOUT THE COMPOSITION.
YOU DON'T HAVE TO WRITE ONE, IF YOU DON'T WANT TO.
I JUST THOUGHT...
IT SEEMS... A LITTLE CRUEL TO ASK YOU TO WRITE THAT.
CRUEL?
HEY
HEY

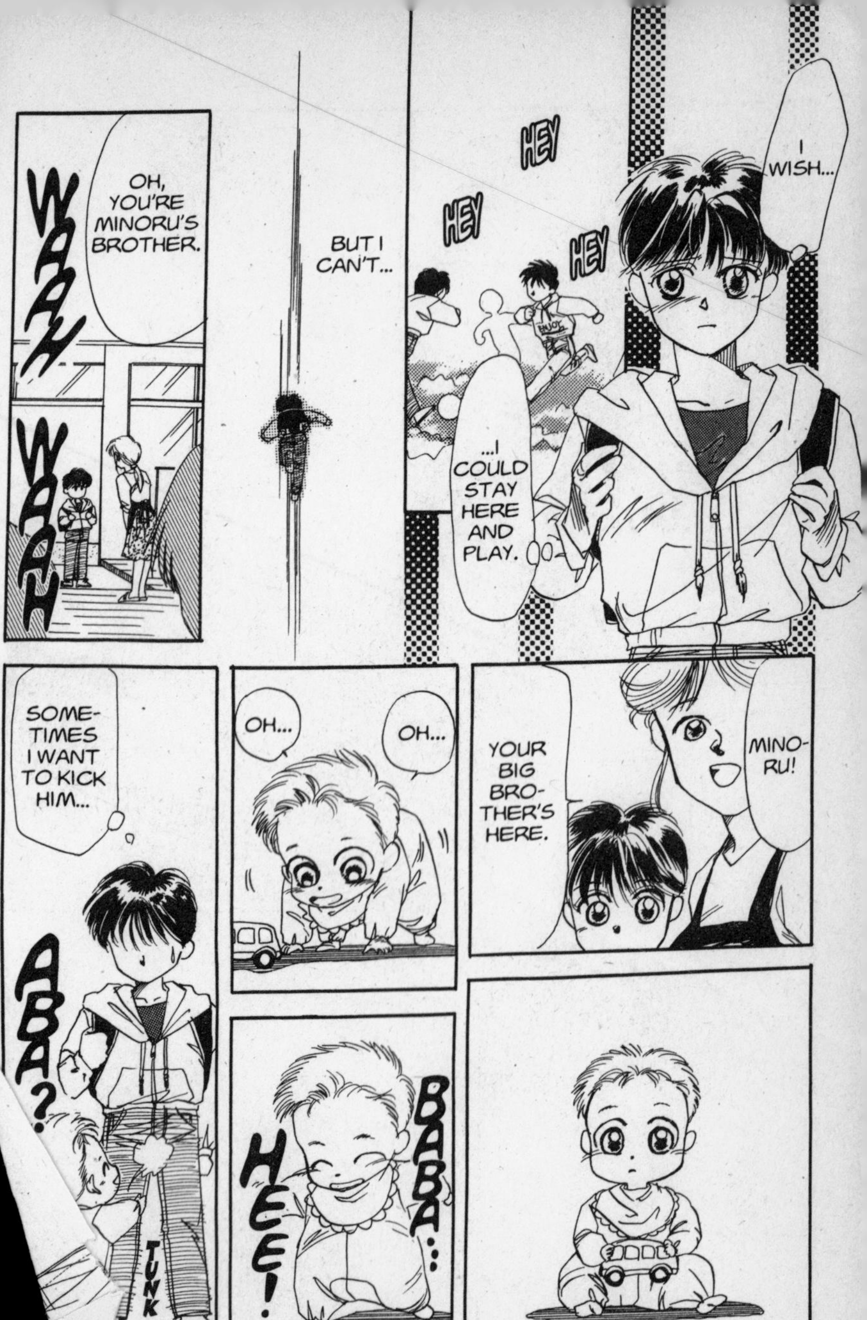
I WISH...
HEY
HEY
HEY
...I COULD STAY HERE AND PLAY.
BUT I CAN'T...
OH, YOU'RE MINORU'S BROTHER.
WAAH...
WAAH
MINO-RU!
YOUR BIG BRO-THER'S HERE.
OH...
OH...
BABA...
HEE!
SOME-TIMES I WANT TO KICK HIM...
ABA?
TUNK

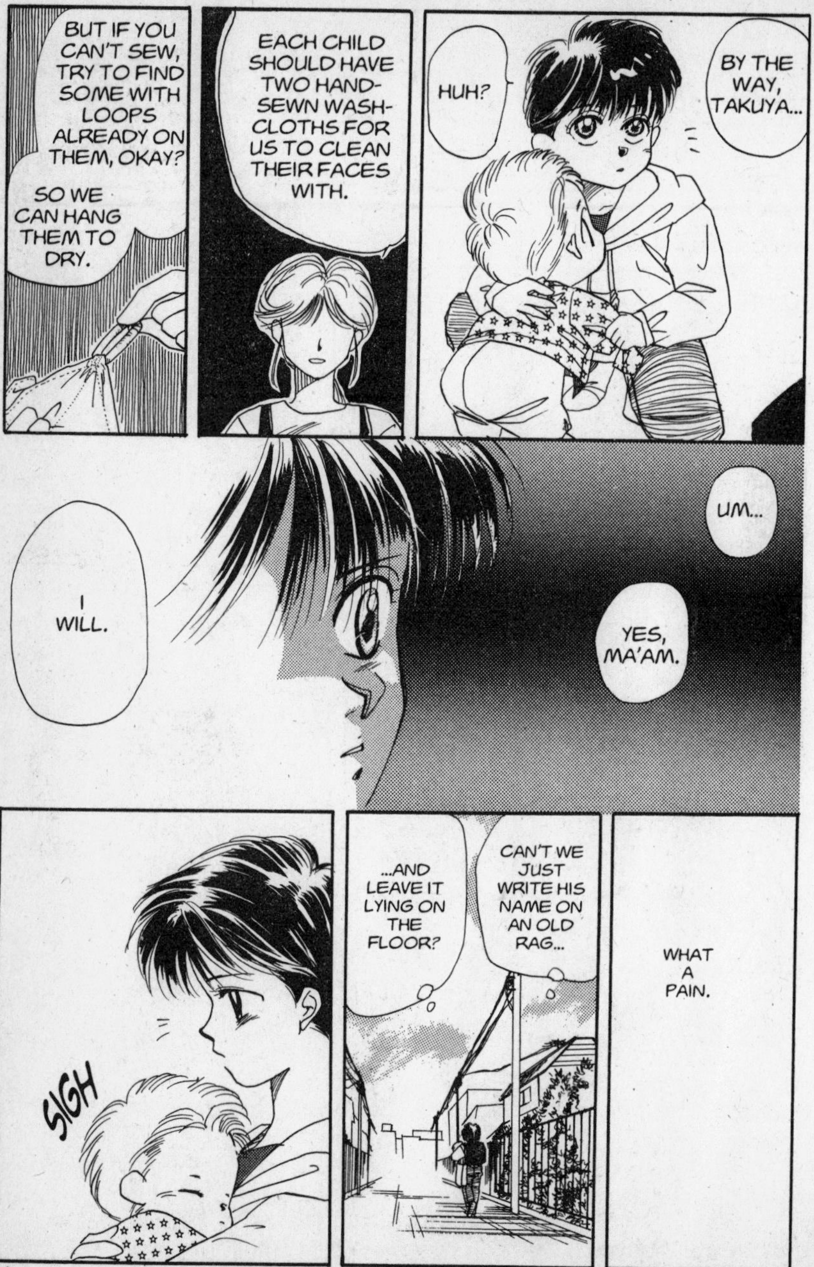
BY THE WAY, TAKUYA...
HUH?
EACH CHILD SHOULD HAVE TWO HAND-SEWN WASH-CLOTHS FOR US TO CLEAN THEIR FACES WITH.
BUT IF YOU CAN'T SEW, TRY TO FIND SOME WITH LOOPS ALREADY ON THEM, OKAY?
SO WE CAN HANG THEM TO DRY.
UM...
YES, MA'AM.
I WILL.
WHAT A PAIN.
CAN'T WE JUST WRITE HIS NAME ON AN OLD RAG...
...AND LEAVE IT LYING ON THE FLOOR?
SIGH

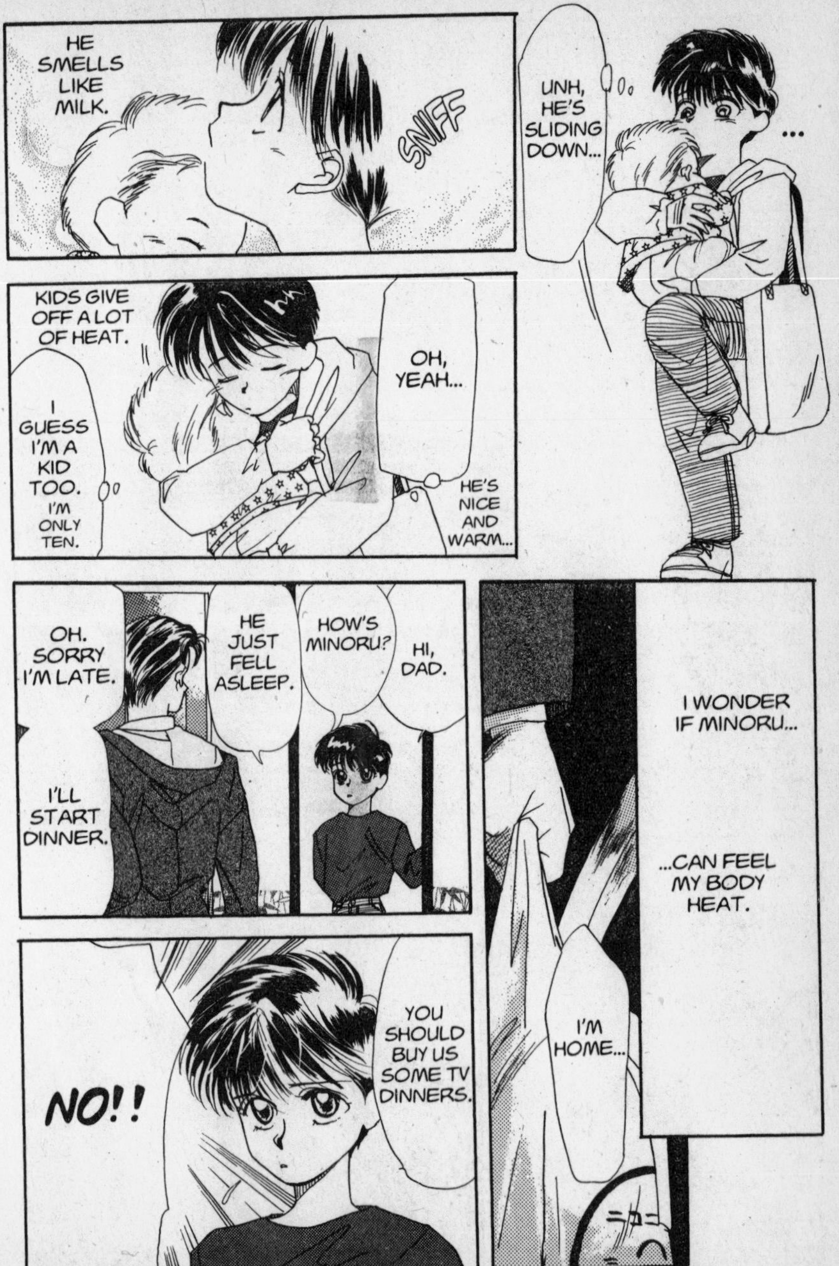
UNH, HE'S SLIDING DOWN...
...
HE SMELLS LIKE MILK.
SNIFF
OH, YEAH...
HE'S NICE AND WARM...
KIDS GIVE OFF A LOT OF HEAT.
I GUESS I'M A KID TOO.
I'M ONLY TEN.
I WONDER IF MINORU...
...CAN FEEL MY BODY HEAT.
I'M HOME...
HI, DAD.
HOW'S MINORU?
HE JUST FELL ASLEEP.
OH. SORRY I'M LATE.
I'LL START DINNER.
YOU SHOULD BUY US SOME TV DINNERS.
NO!!

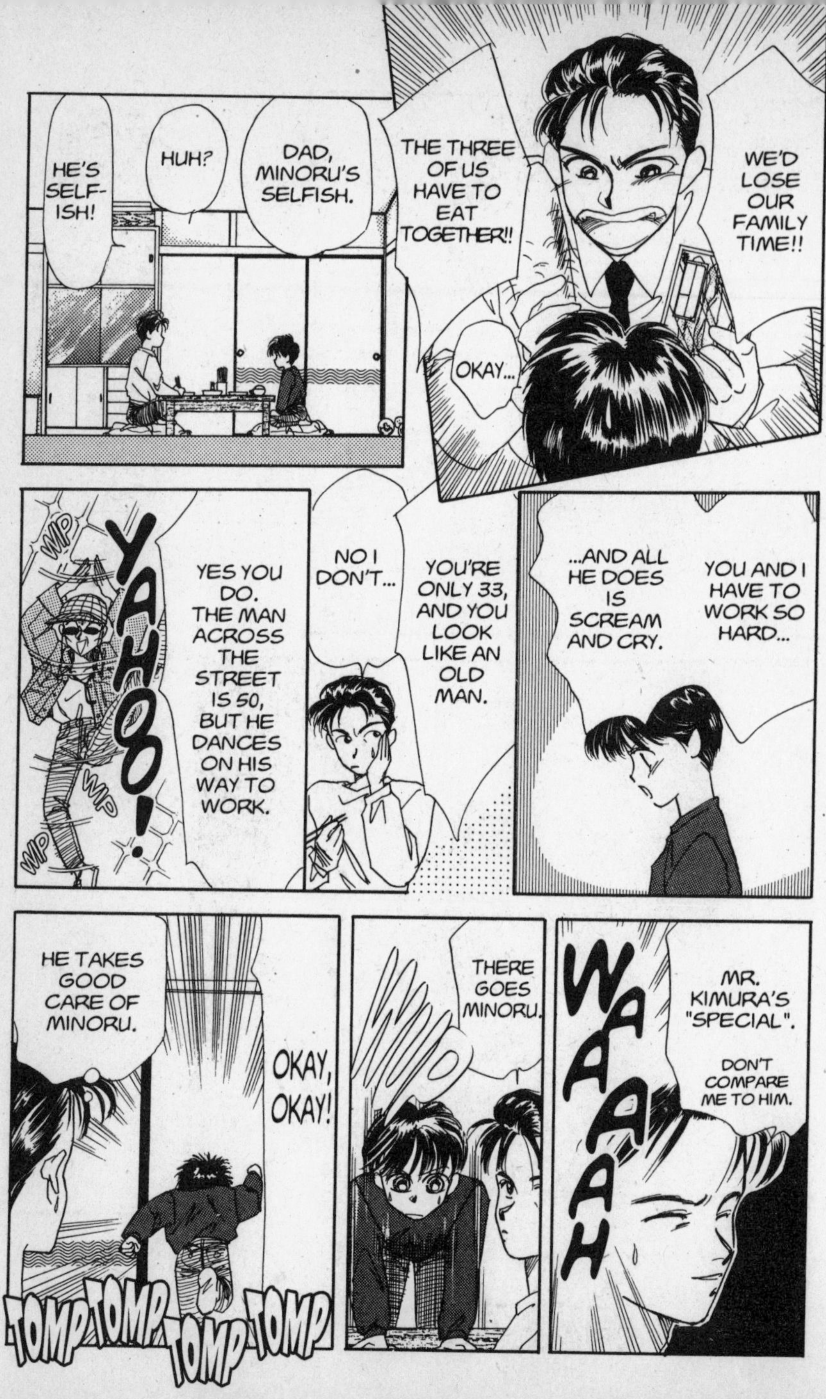
WE'D LOSE OUR FAMILY TIME!!
THE THREE OF US HAVE TO EAT TOGETHER!!
OKAY...
DAD, MINORU'S SELFISH.
HUH?
HE'S SELF-ISH!
YOU AND I HAVE TO WORK SO HARD...
...AND ALL HE DOES IS SCREAM AND CRY.
YOU'RE ONLY 33, AND YOU LOOK LIKE AN OLD MAN.
NO I DON'T...
YES YOU DO. THE MAN ACROSS THE STREET IS 50, BUT HE DANCES ON HIS WAY TO WORK.
YAHOO!
WIP
WIP
WIP
MR. KIMURA'S "SPECIAL".
DON'T COMPARE ME TO HIM.
WAAAAH
THERE GOES MINORU.
HE TAKES GOOD CARE OF MINORU.
OKAY, OKAY!
TOMP TOMP TOMP TOMP

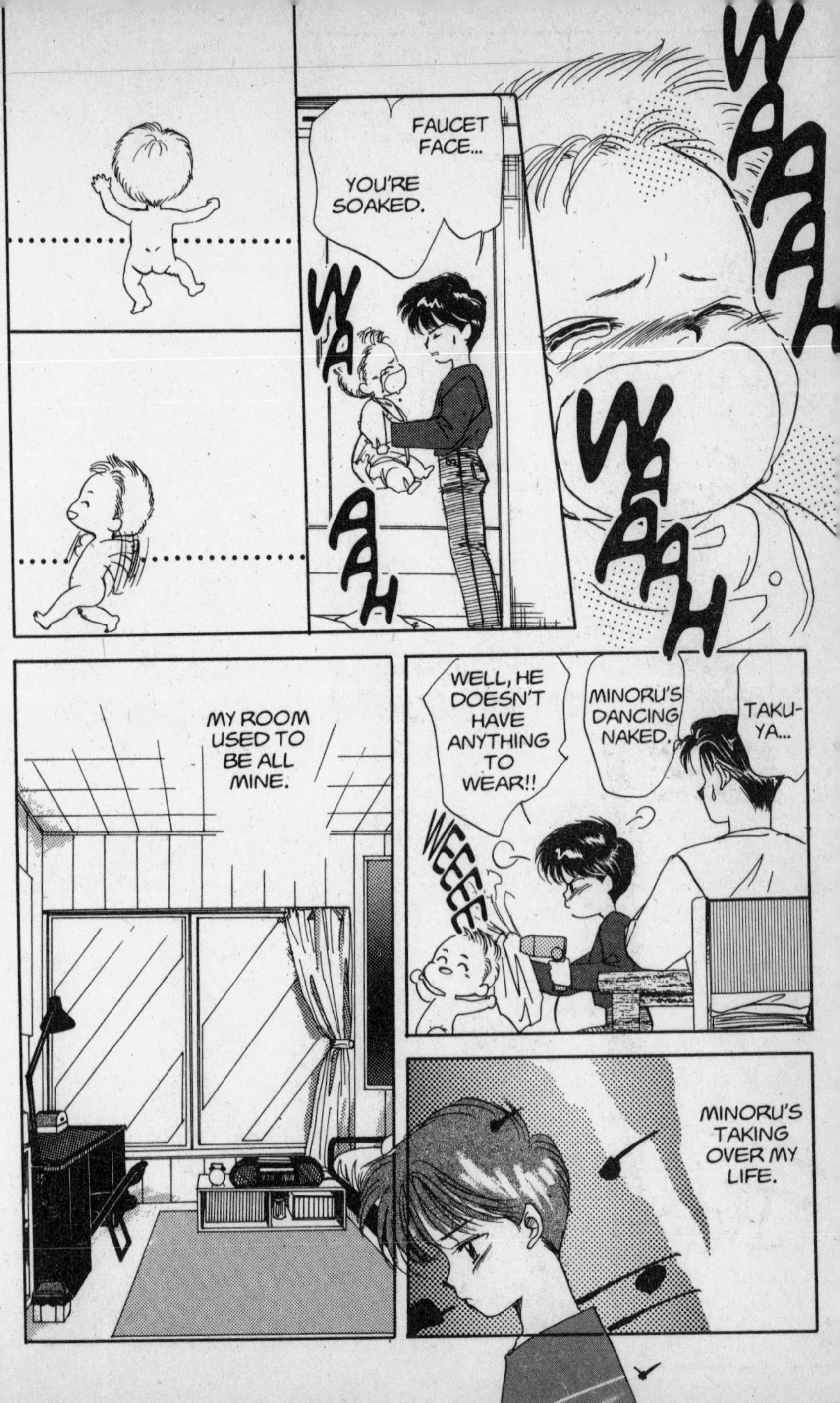
WAAAH
WAAAH
FAUCET FACE...
YOU'RE SOAKED.
WAAAH
TAKU-YA...
MINORU'S DANCING NAKED.
WELL, HE DOESN'T HAVE ANYTHING TO WEAR!!
WEEEE
MINORU'S TAKING OVER MY LIFE.
MY ROOM USED TO BE ALL MINE.

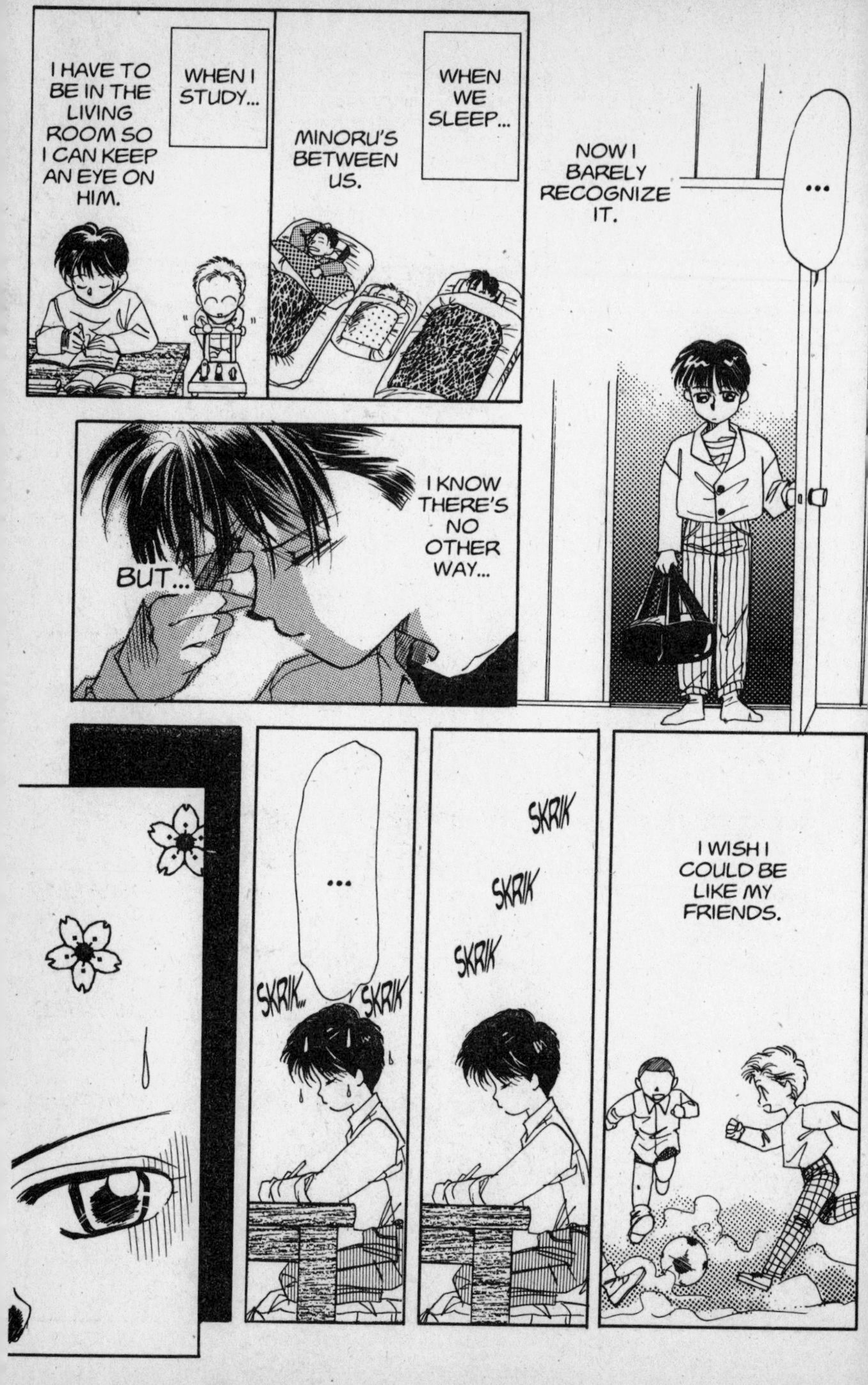
...
NOW I BARELY RECOGNIZE IT.
WHEN WE SLEEP...
MINORU'S BETWEEN US.
WHEN I STUDY...
I HAVE TO BE IN THE LIVING ROOM SO I CAN KEEP AN EYE ON HIM.
I KNOW THERE'S NO OTHER WAY...
BUT...
I WISH I COULD BE LIKE MY FRIENDS.
SKRIK
SKRIK
SKRIK
...
SKRIK
SKRIK...

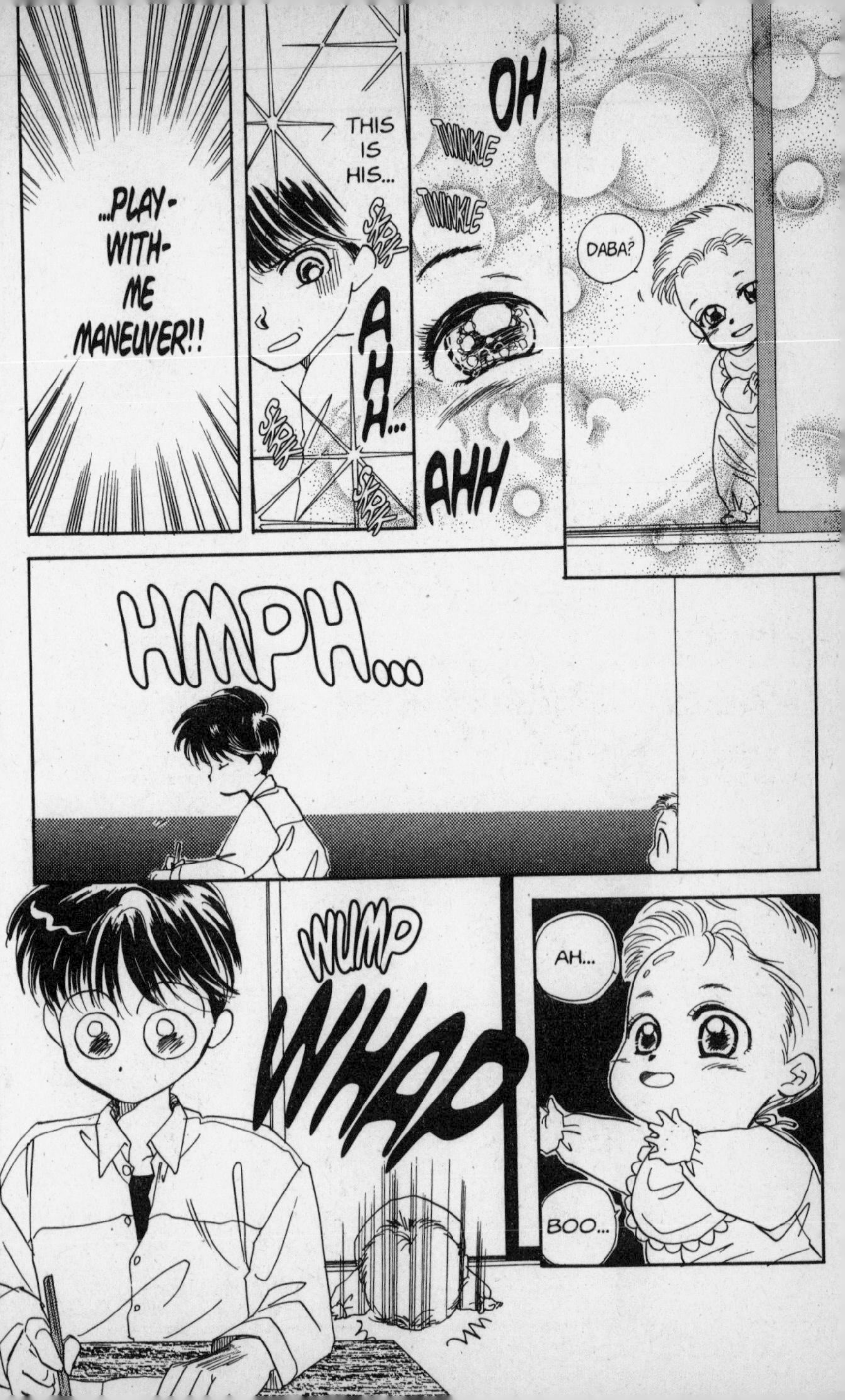
DABA?
OH
TWINKLE
TWINKLE
AHH
THIS IS HIS...
SKRK
AHH...
SKRK
SKRK
...PLAY-WITH-ME MANEUVER!!
HMPH...
AH...
BOO...
WUMP
WHAP

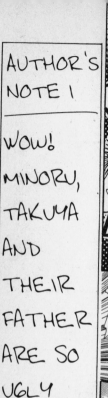

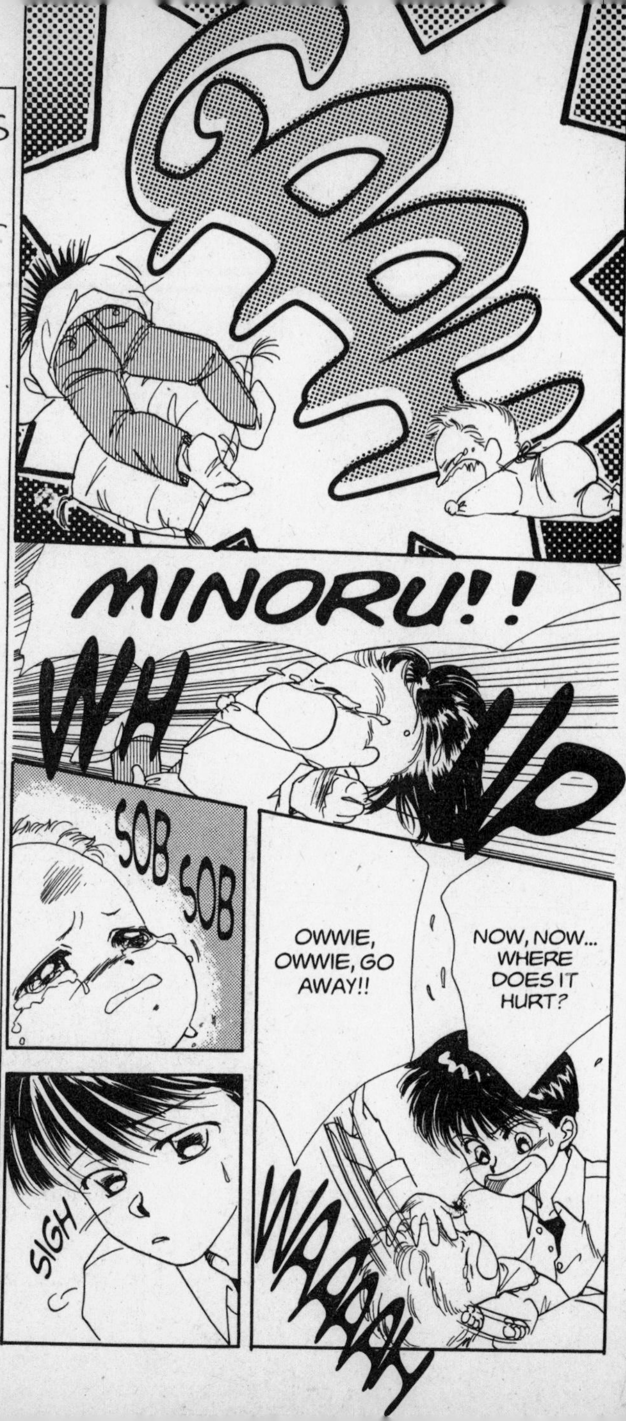
MINORU!!
NOW, NOW... WHERE DOES IT HURT?
OWWIE, OWWIE, GO AWAY!!
SOB SOB
SIGH

AUTHOR'S NOTE 1

WOW! MINORU, TAKUYA AND THEIR FATHER ARE SO UGLY COMPARED TO MY LATER DRAWINGS!

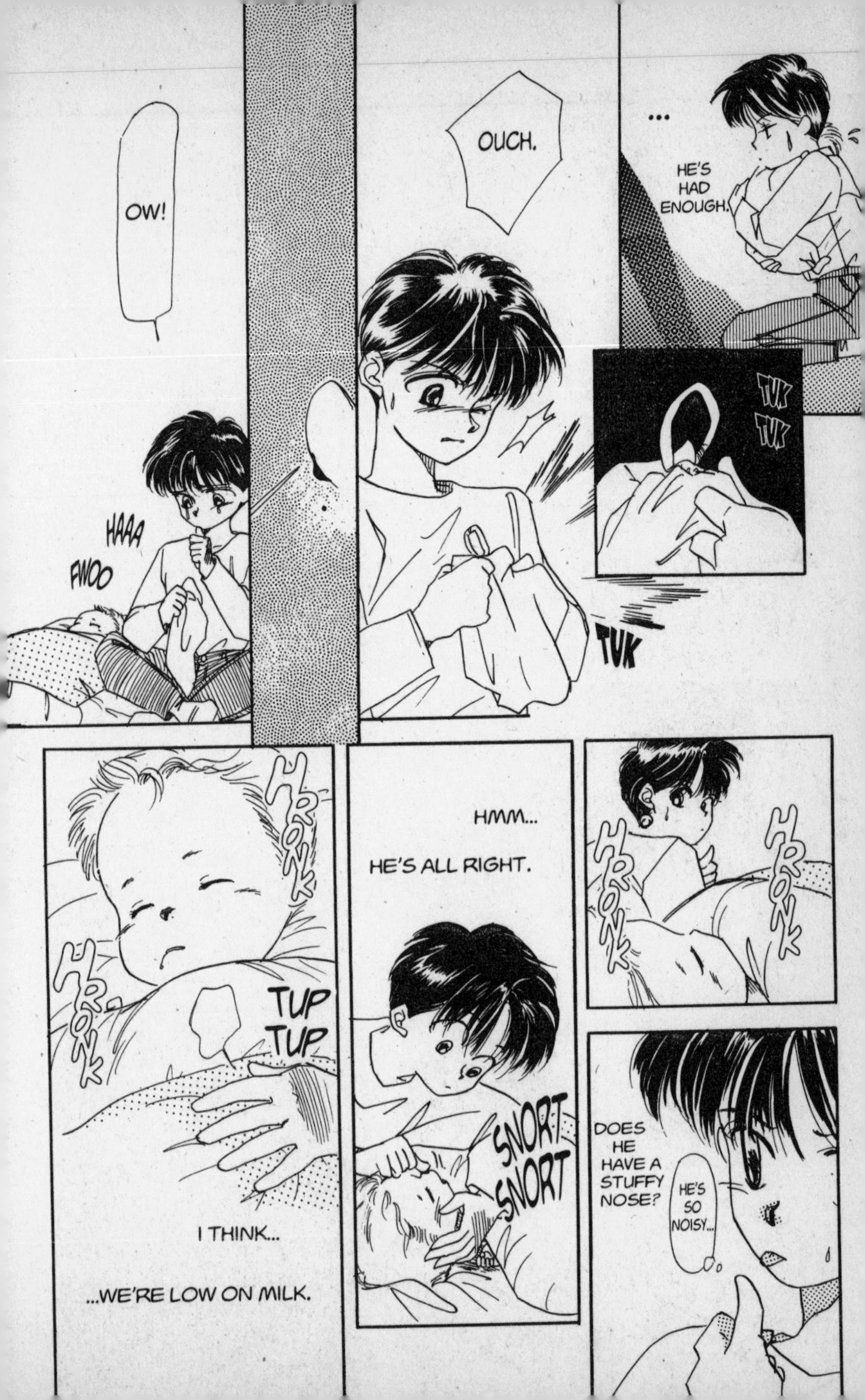
...
HE'S HAD ENOUGH.
TUK TUK
OUCH.
TUK
OW!
HAAA FWOO
HRONK
HRONK
DOES HE HAVE A STUFFY NOSE?
HE'S SO NOISY...
HMM...
HE'S ALL RIGHT.
SNORT SNORT
HRONK
HRONK
TUP TUP
I THINK...
...WE'RE LOW ON MILK.

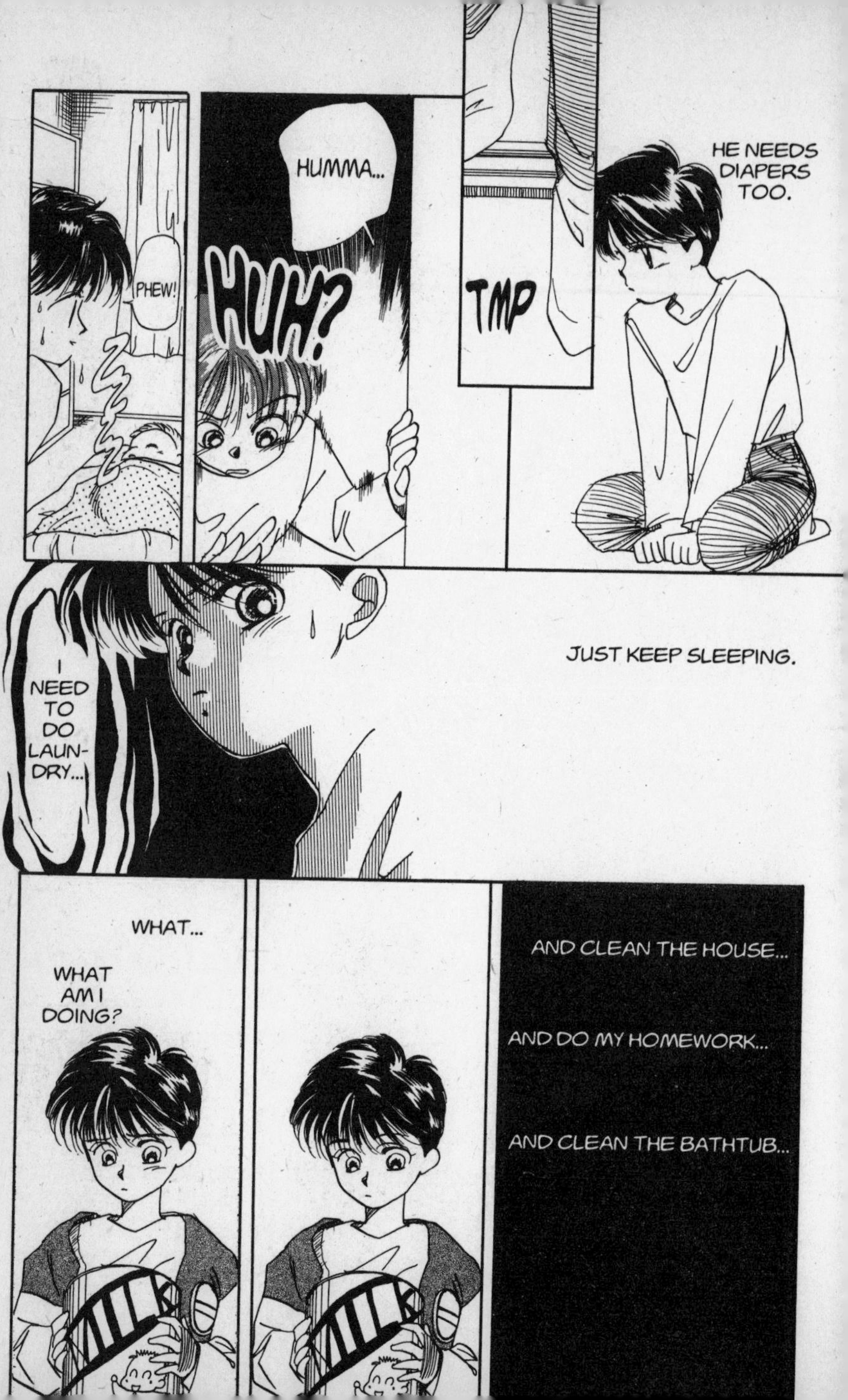

HE NEEDS DIAPERS TOO.
TMP
HUMMA...
HUH?
PHEW!
JUST KEEP SLEEPING.
I NEED TO DO LAUN-DRY...
AND CLEAN THE HOUSE...
AND DO MY HOMEWORK...
AND CLEAN THE BATHTUB...
WHAT...
WHAT AM I DOING?

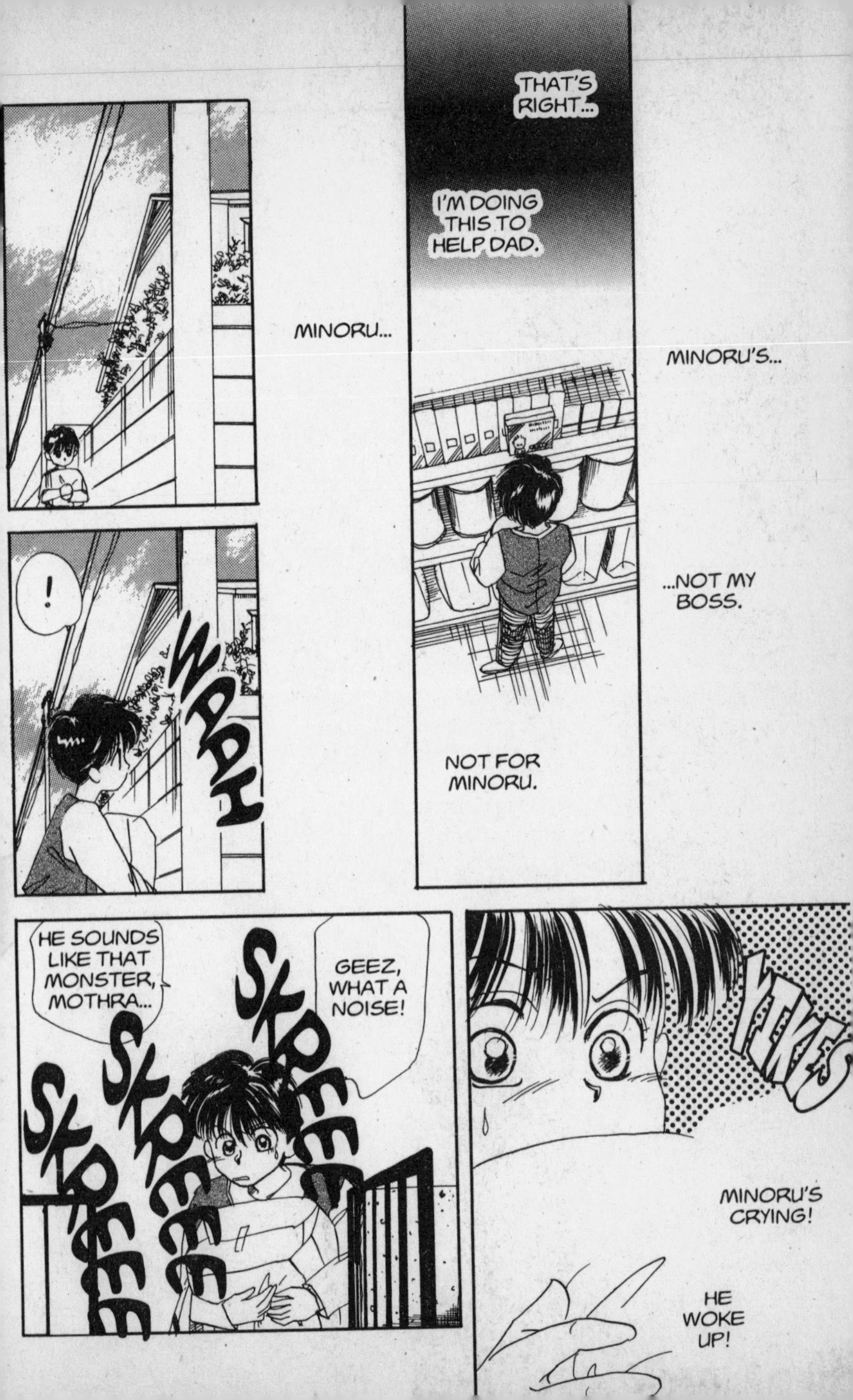
THAT'S RIGHT...
I'M DOING THIS TO HELP DAD.
NOT FOR MINORU.
MINORU'S...
...NOT MY BOSS.
MINORU...
!
WAAH
YIKES
MINORU'S CRYING!
HE WOKE UP!
GEEZ, WHAT A NOISE!
HE SOUNDS LIKE THAT MONSTER, MOTHRA...
SKREEE
SKREEE
SKREEE

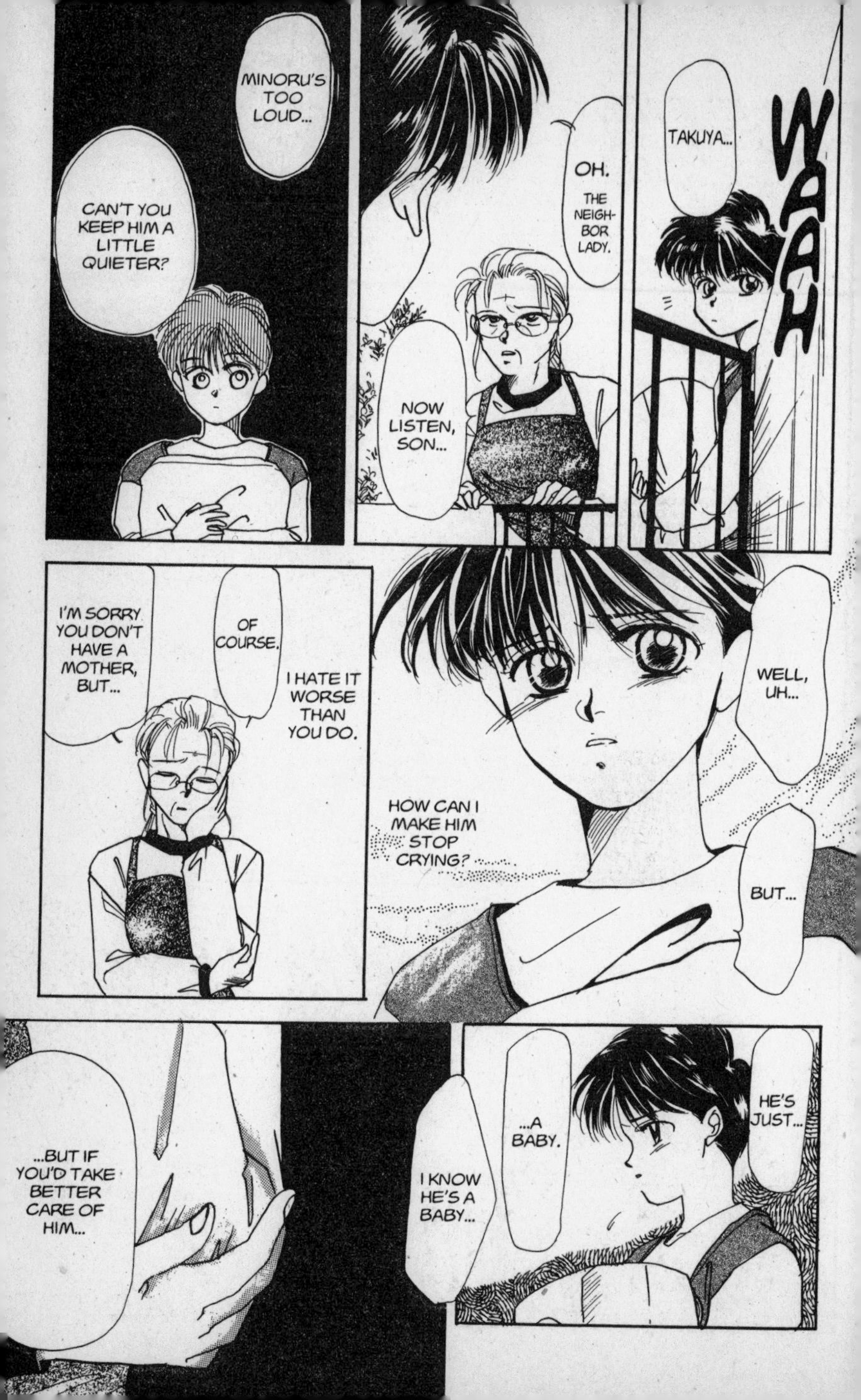
WAAH
TAKUYA...
OH.
THE NEIGHBOR LADY.
NOW LISTEN, SON...
MINORU'S TOO LOUD...
CAN'T YOU KEEP HIM A LITTLE QUIETER?
WELL, UH...
BUT...
HOW CAN I MAKE HIM STOP CRYING?
OF COURSE.
I HATE IT WORSE THAN YOU DO.
I'M SORRY YOU DON'T HAVE A MOTHER, BUT...
HE'S JUST...
...A BABY.
I KNOW HE'S A BABY...
...BUT IF YOU'D TAKE BETTER CARE OF HIM...

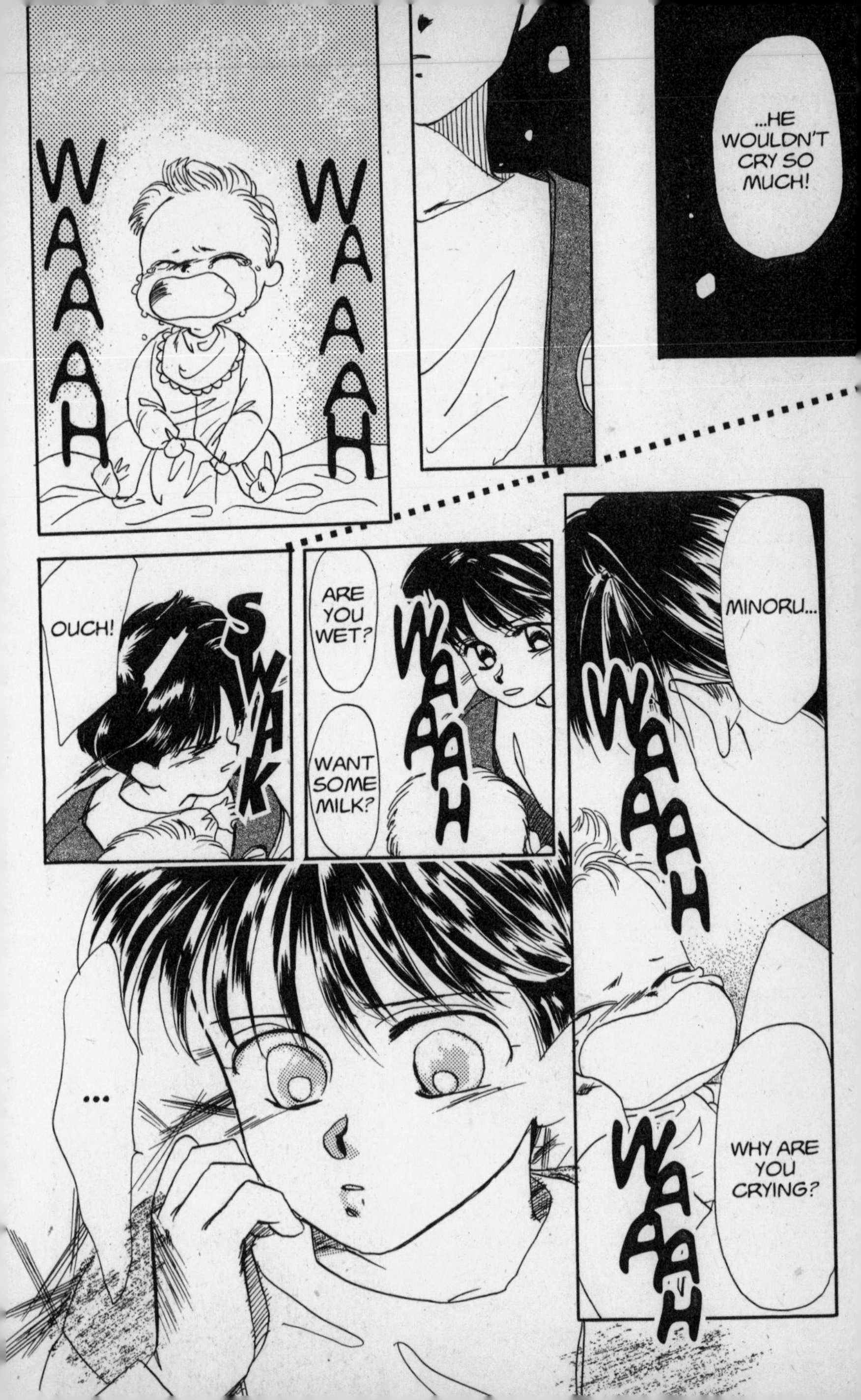
...HE WOULDN'T CRY SO MUCH!
WAAAAH
WAAAAH
MINORU...
WAAAAH
WHY ARE YOU CRYING?
WAAAAH
ARE YOU WET?
WAAAH
WANT SOME MILK?
OUCH!
SWAK
...

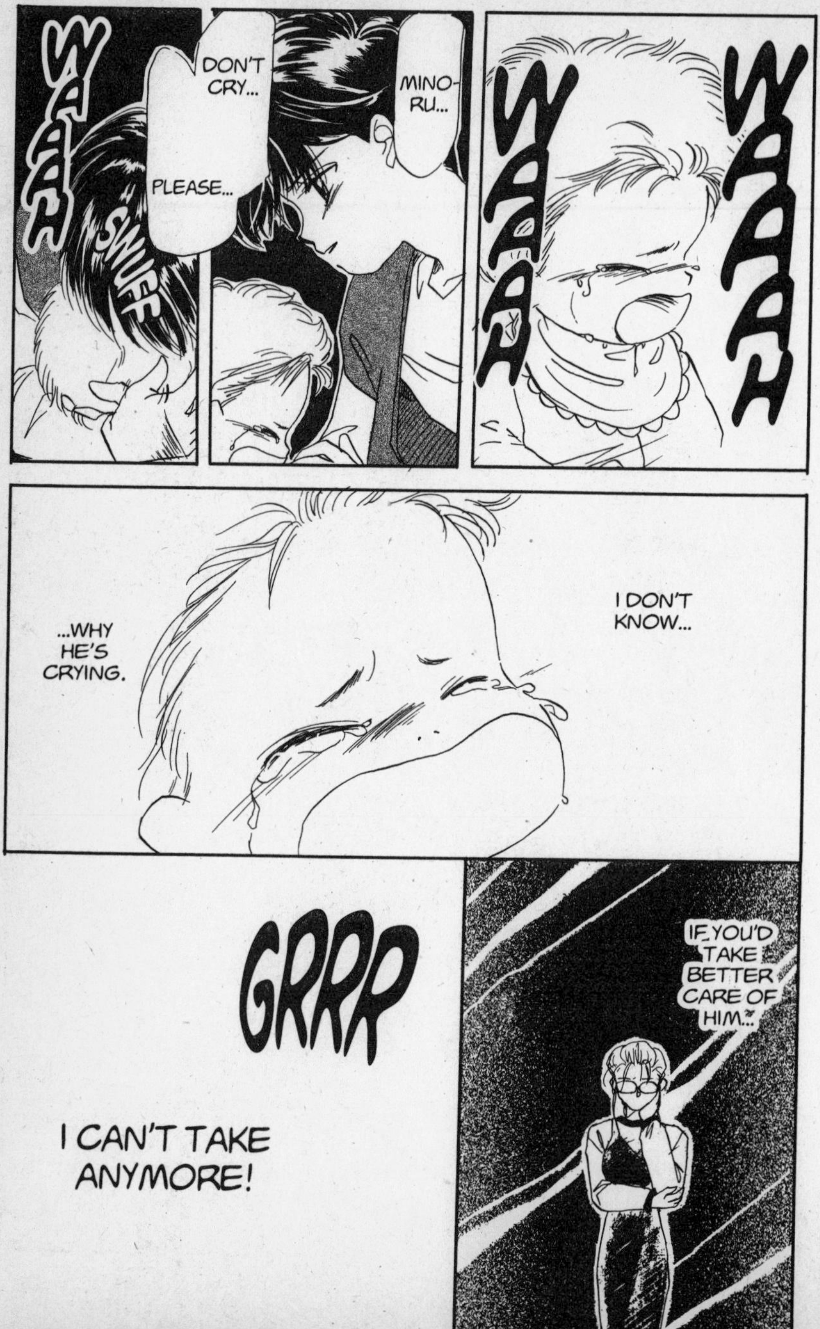
WAAAAH
WAAAAH
MINO-RU...
DON'T CRY...
PLEASE...
WAAAH
SNIFF
I DON'T KNOW...
...WHY HE'S CRYING.
IF YOU'D TAKE BETTER CARE OF HIM...
GRRR
I CAN'T TAKE ANYMORE!

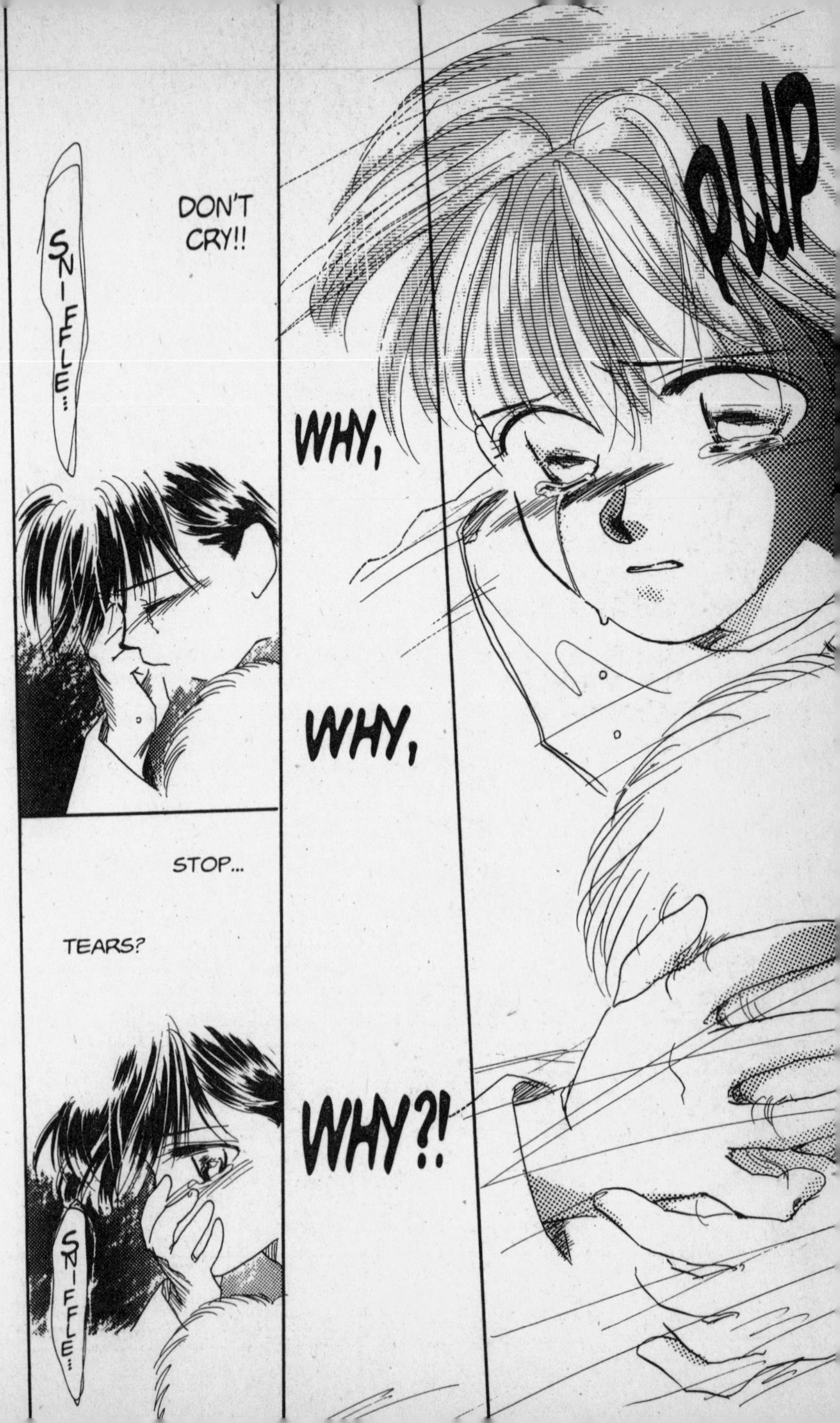
GULP
WHY,
WHY,
WHY?!
DON'T CRY!!
SNIFFLE...
STOP...
TEARS?
SNIFFLE...

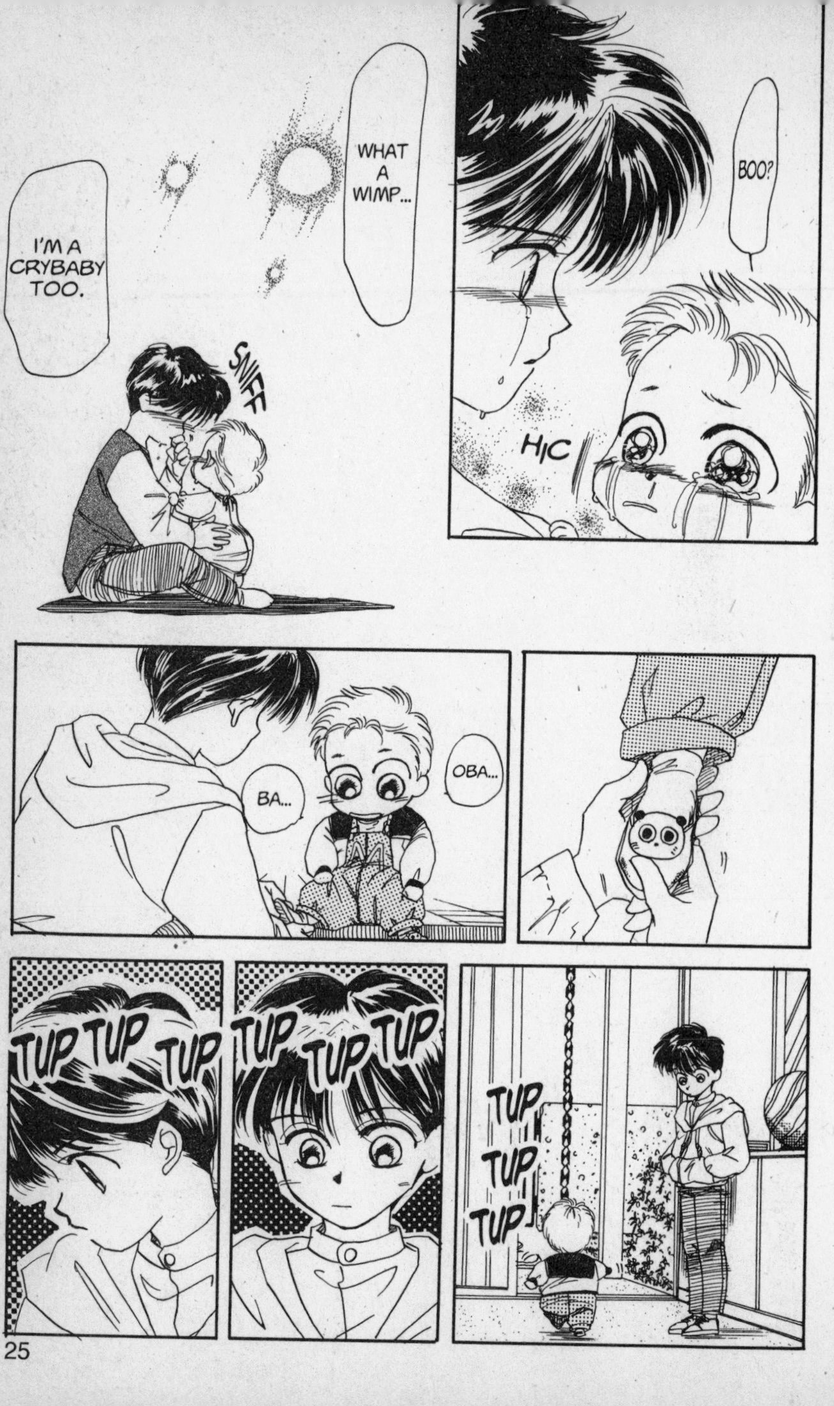
BOO?
HIC
WHAT A WIMP...
I'M A CRYBABY TOO.
SNIFF
OBA...
BA...
TUP
TUP
TUP
TUP TUP TUP
TUP TUP TUP

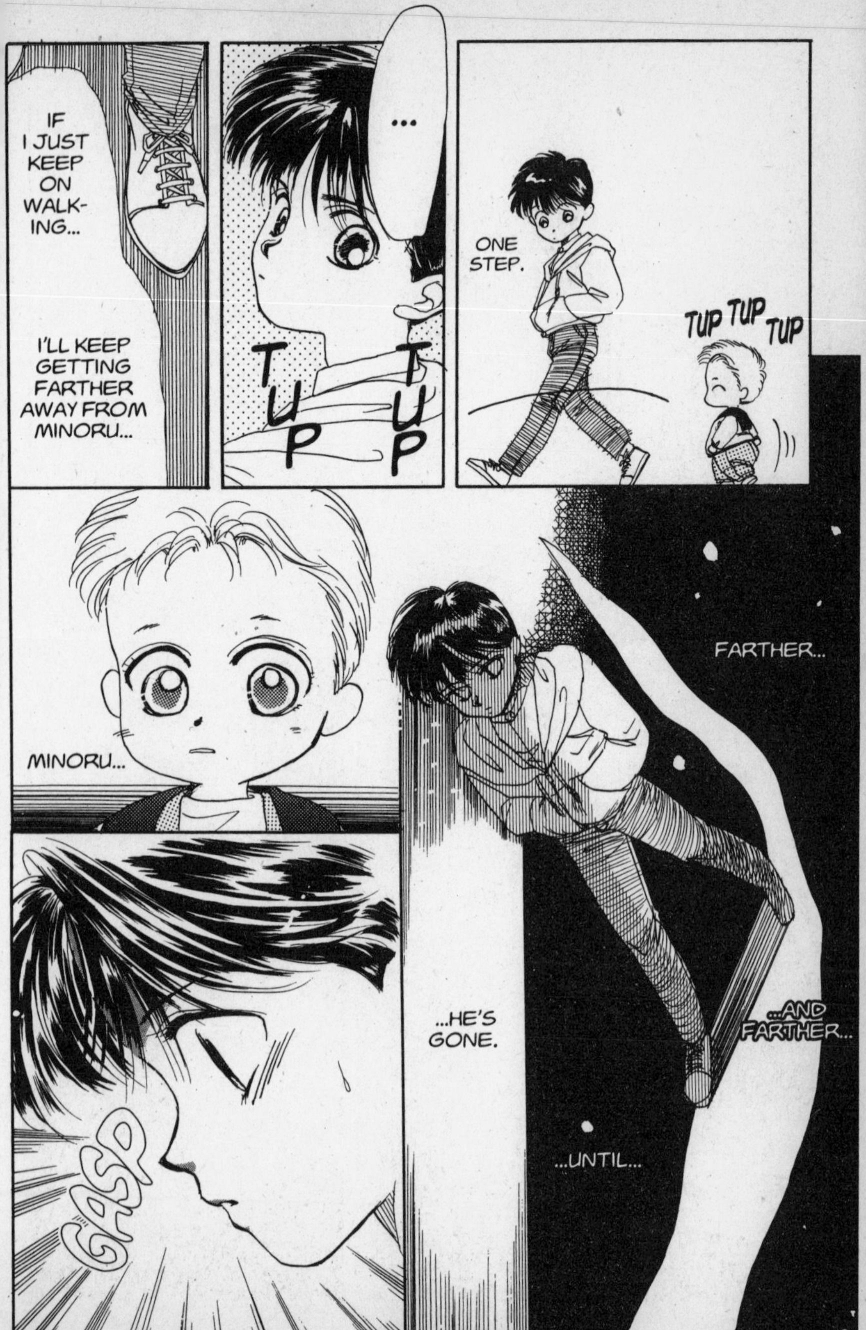
ONE STEP.
TUP TUP TUP
...
TUP
TUP
IF I JUST KEEP ON WALKING...
I'LL KEEP GETTING FARTHER AWAY FROM MINORU...
FARTHER...
...AND FARTHER...
...UNTIL...
...HE'S GONE.
MINORU...
GASP

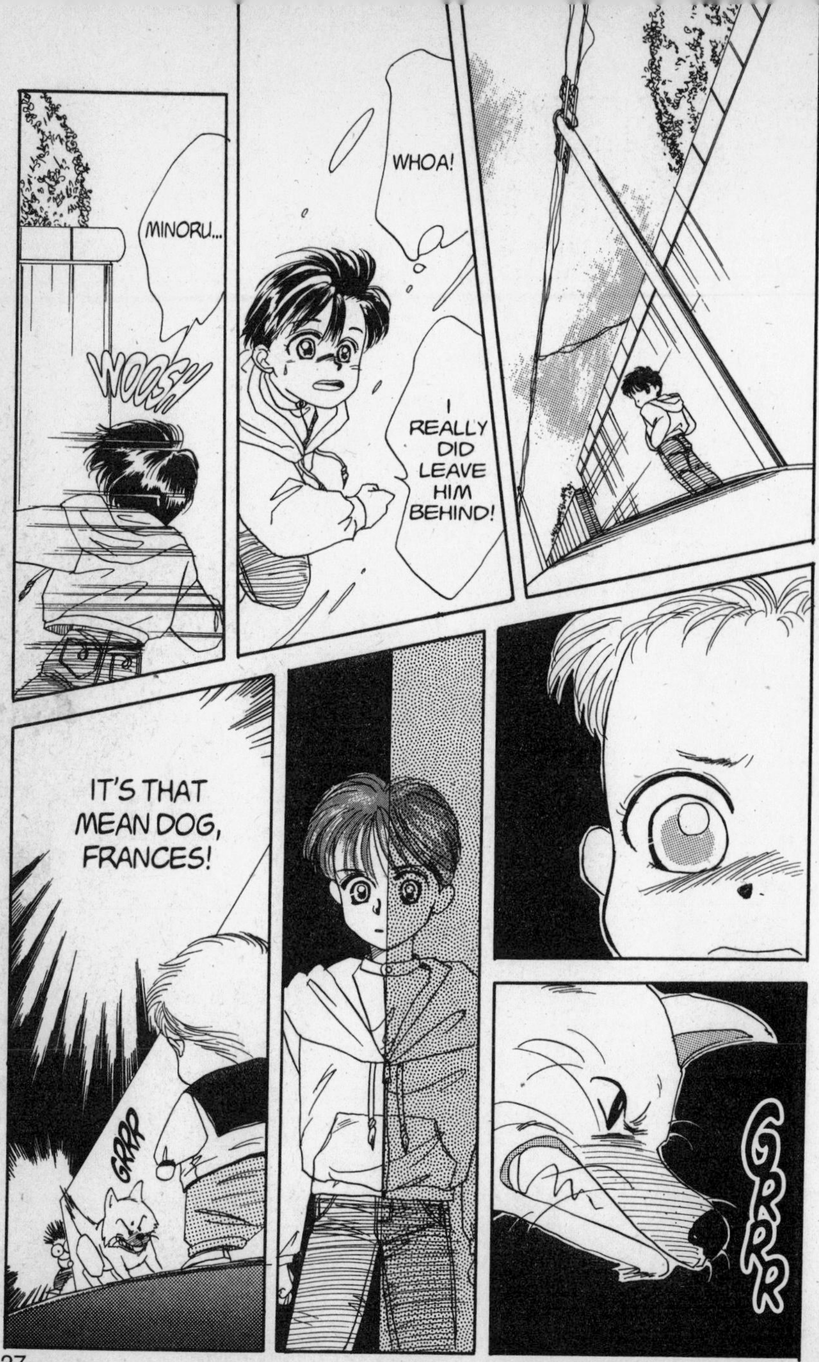
WHOA!
I REALLY DID LEAVE HIM BEHIND!
MINORU...
WOOSH
GRRRR
IT'S THAT MEAN DOG, FRANCES!
GRRR

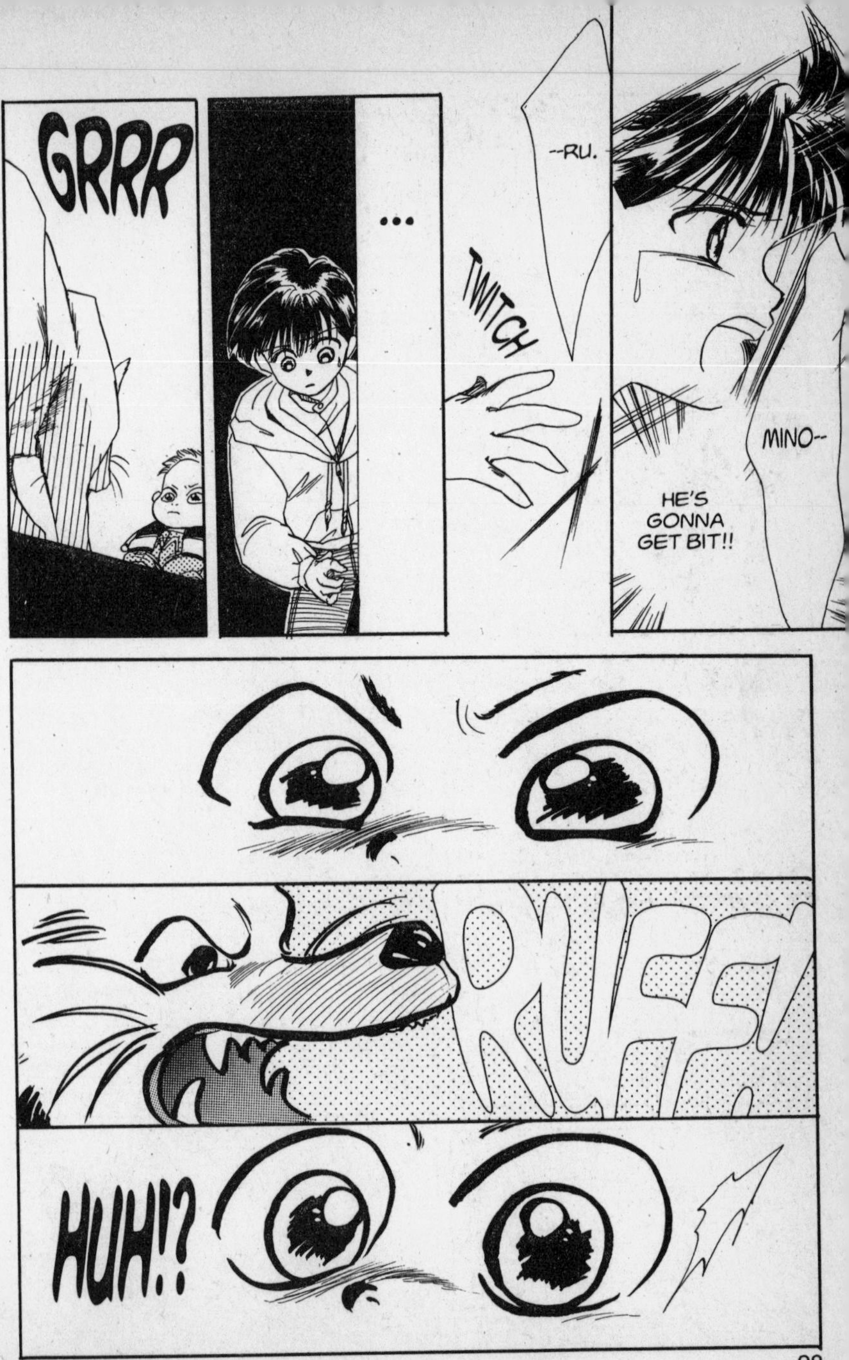
MINO--
HE'S GONNA GET BIT!!
--RU.
TWITCH
...
GRRR
RUFF
HUH!?

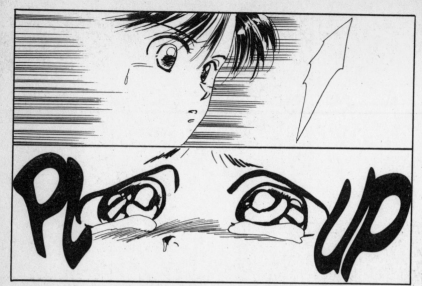

MI--

--NO--

--RU!!!

RUFF

RUFF

STUPID?

PUBBI...

RUFF

TOMP

29

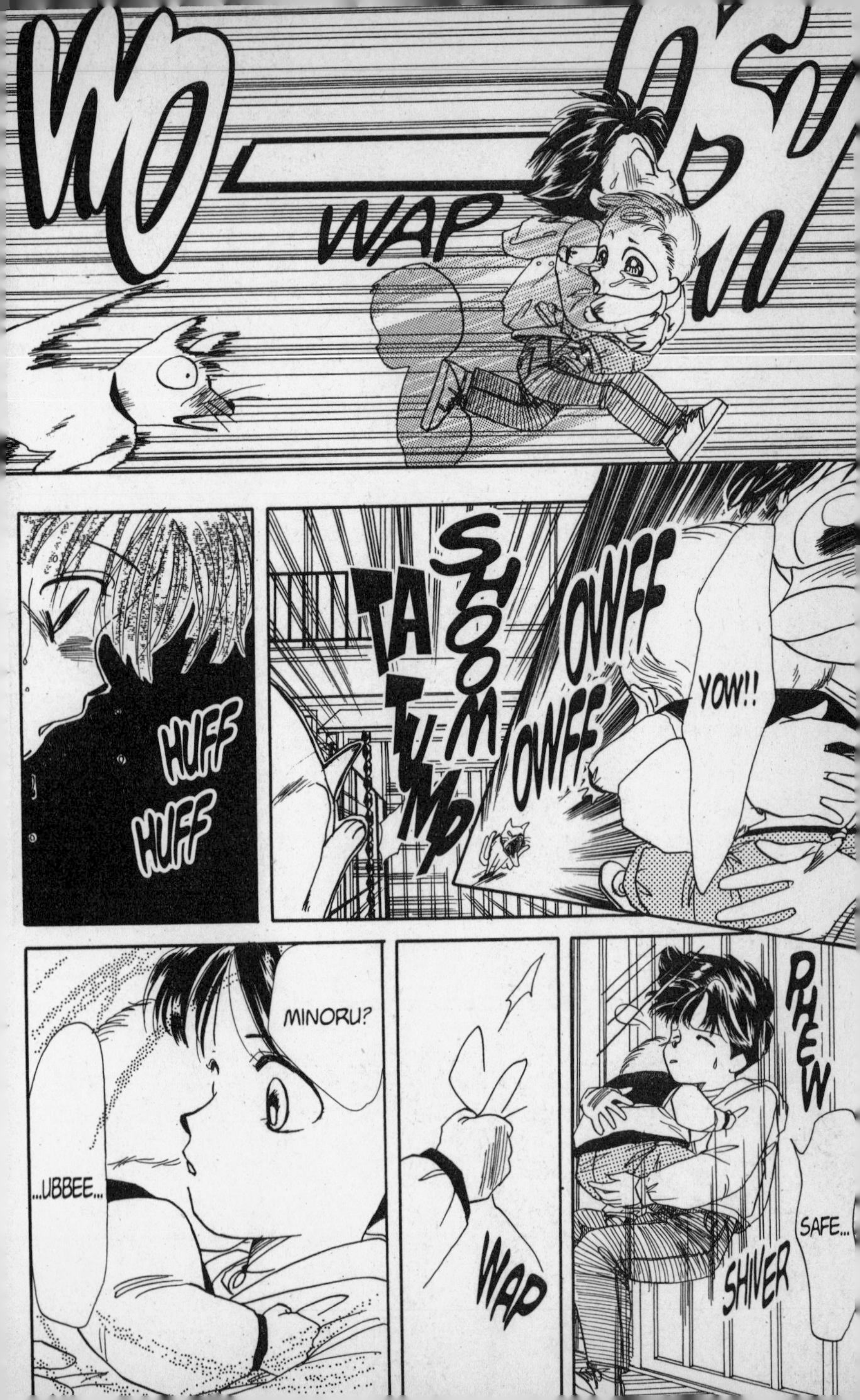
WAP
YOW!!
ONFF
ONFF
SHOOM
TA TUMP
HUFF
HUFF
PHEW
SAFE...
SHIVER
WAP
MINORU?
...UBBEE...

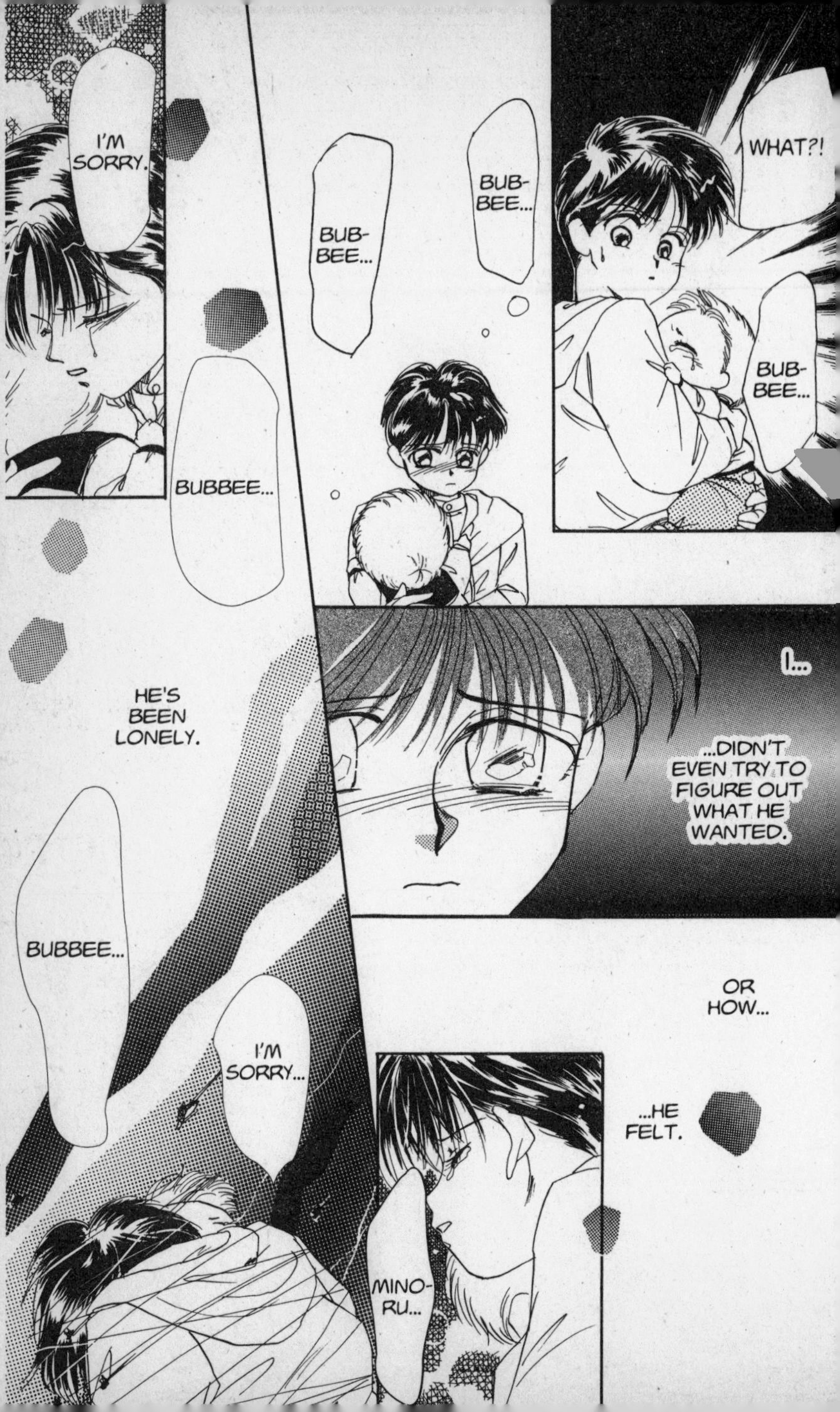
WHAT?!
BUB-BEE...
BUB-BEE...
BUB-BEE...
I'M SORRY.
BUBBEE...
I...
...DIDN'T EVEN TRY TO FIGURE OUT WHAT HE WANTED.
OR HOW...
...HE FELT.
MINO-RU...
HE'S BEEN LONELY.
BUBBEE...
I'M SORRY...

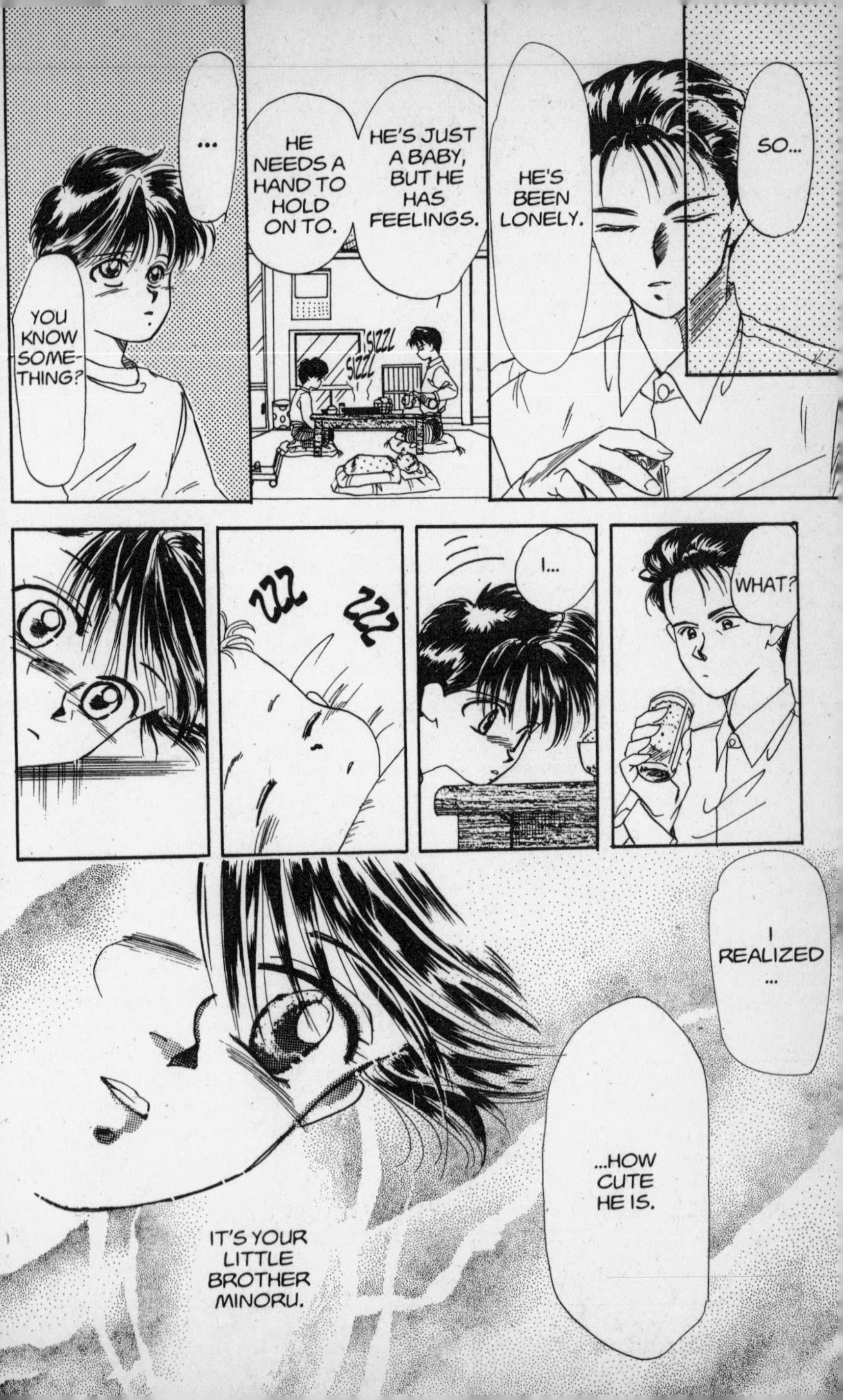
SO...
HE'S BEEN LONELY.
HE'S JUST A BABY, BUT HE HAS FEELINGS.
HE NEEDS A HAND TO HOLD ON TO.
SIZZZ SIZZZ
...
YOU KNOW SOME-THING?
WHAT?
I...
ZZZ
ZZZ
I REALIZED...
...HOW CUTE HE IS.
IT'S YOUR LITTLE BROTHER MINORU.

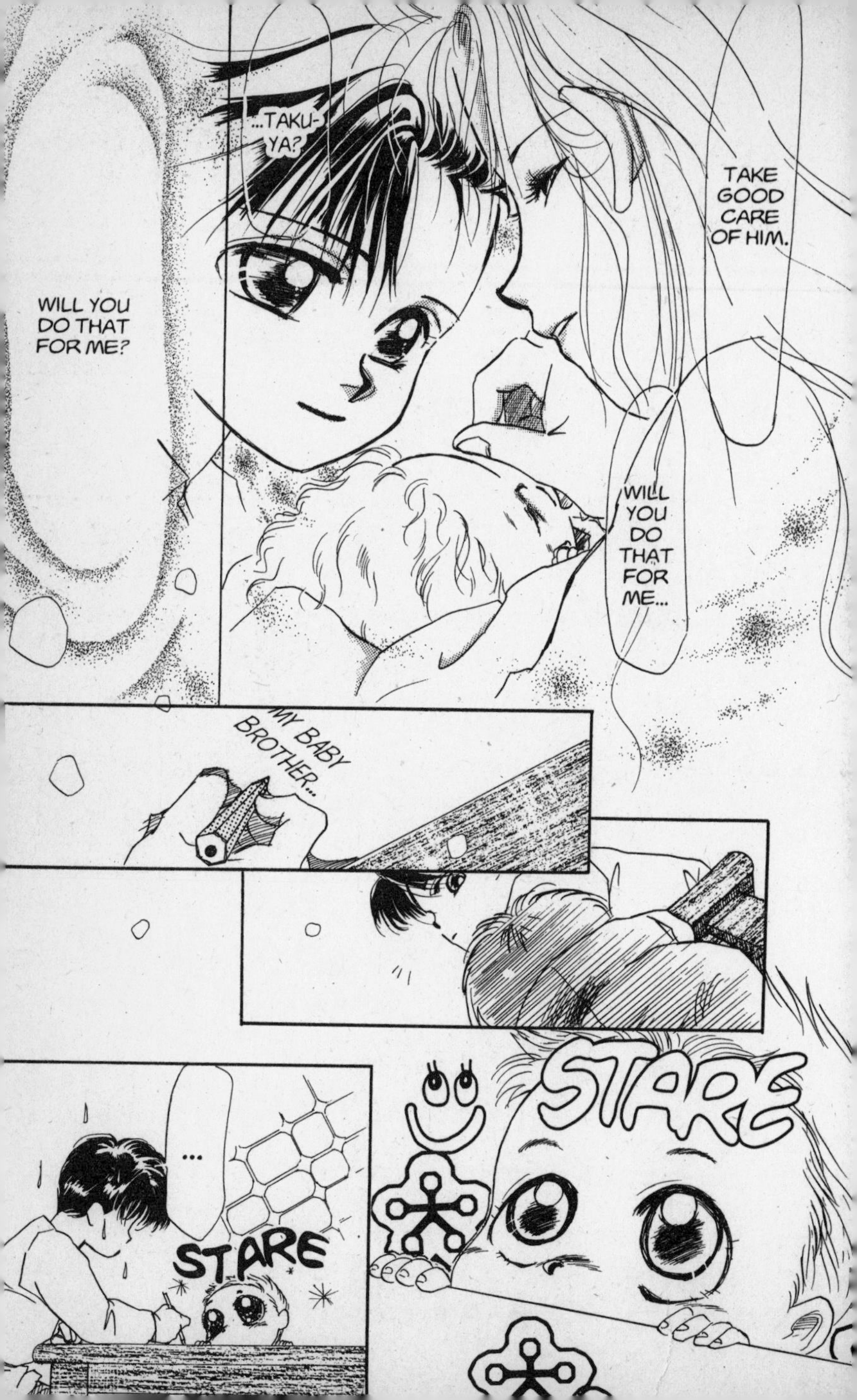
...TAKU-YA?
TAKE GOOD CARE OF HIM.
WILL YOU DO THAT FOR ME...
WILL YOU DO THAT FOR ME?
MY BABY BROTHER...
STARE
...
STARE

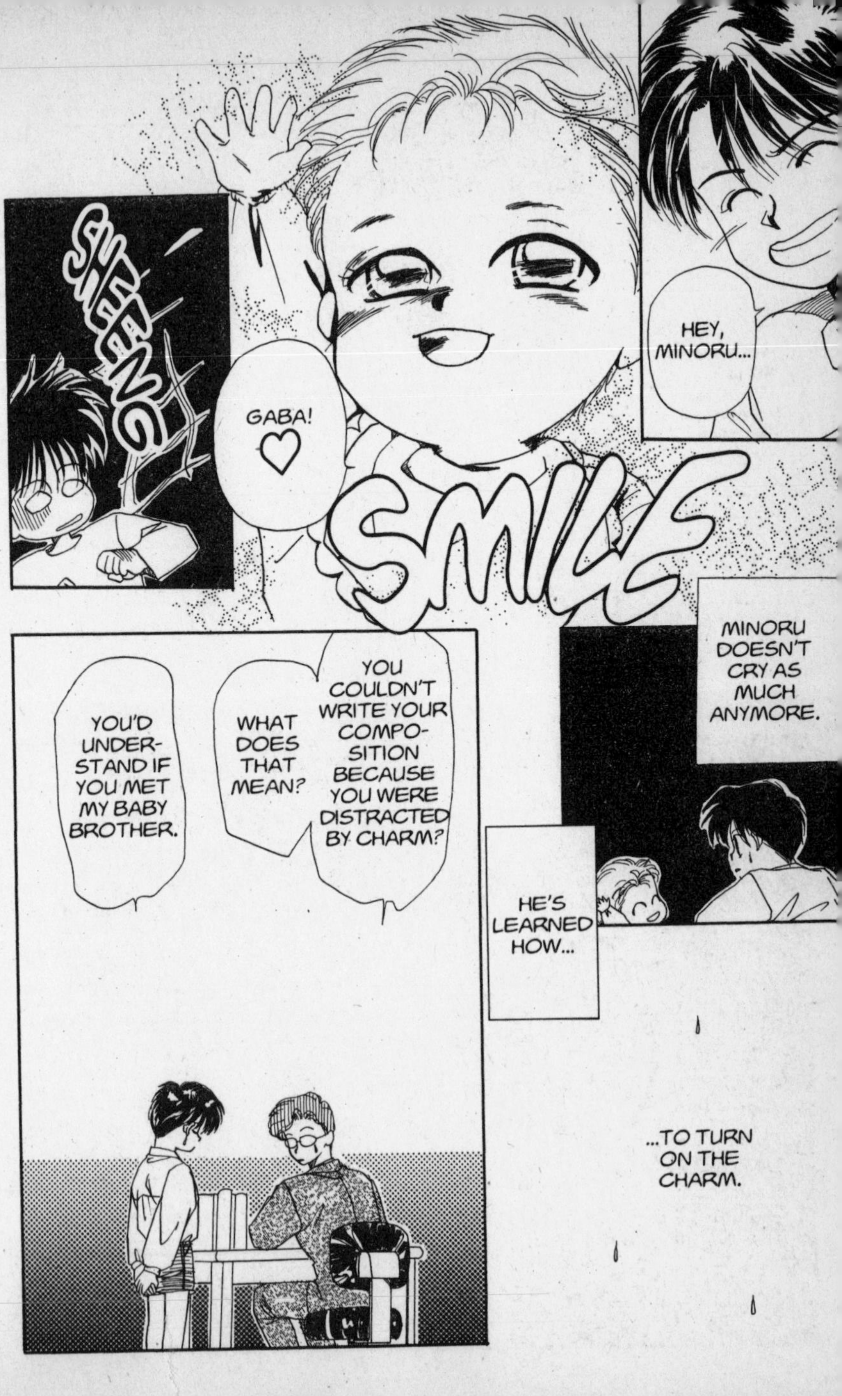
HEY, MINORU...
GABA! ♥
SMILE
SHEENG
MINORU DOESN'T CRY AS MUCH ANYMORE.
HE'S LEARNED HOW...
...TO TURN ON THE CHARM.
YOU COULDN'T WRITE YOUR COMPOSITION BECAUSE YOU WERE DISTRACTED BY CHARM?
WHAT DOES THAT MEAN?
YOU'D UNDERSTAND IF YOU MET MY BABY BROTHER.

I'M A BIG BROTHER

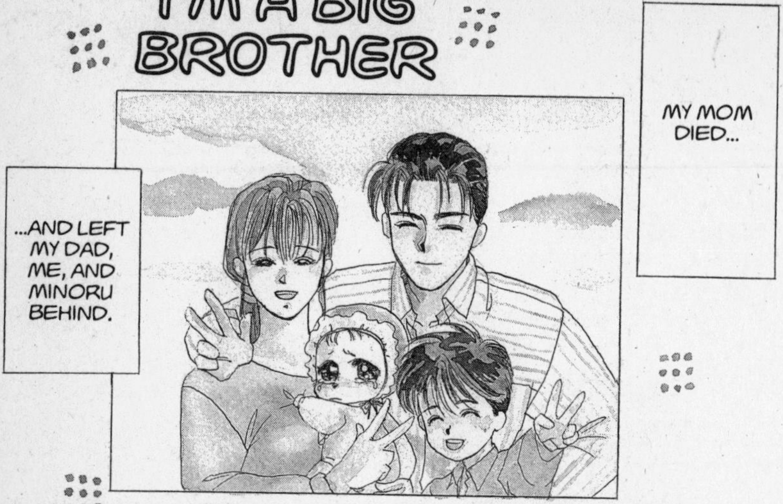
MY MOM DIED...
...AND LEFT MY DAD, ME, AND MINORU BEHIND.

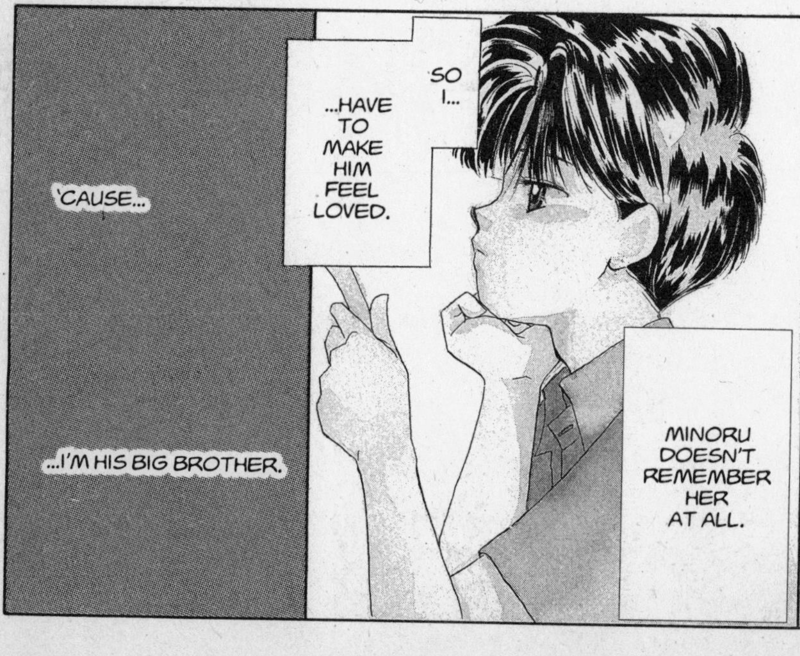
MINORU DOESN'T REMEMBER HER AT ALL.
SO I...
...HAVE TO MAKE HIM FEEL LOVED.
'CAUSE...
...I'M HIS BIG BROTHER.

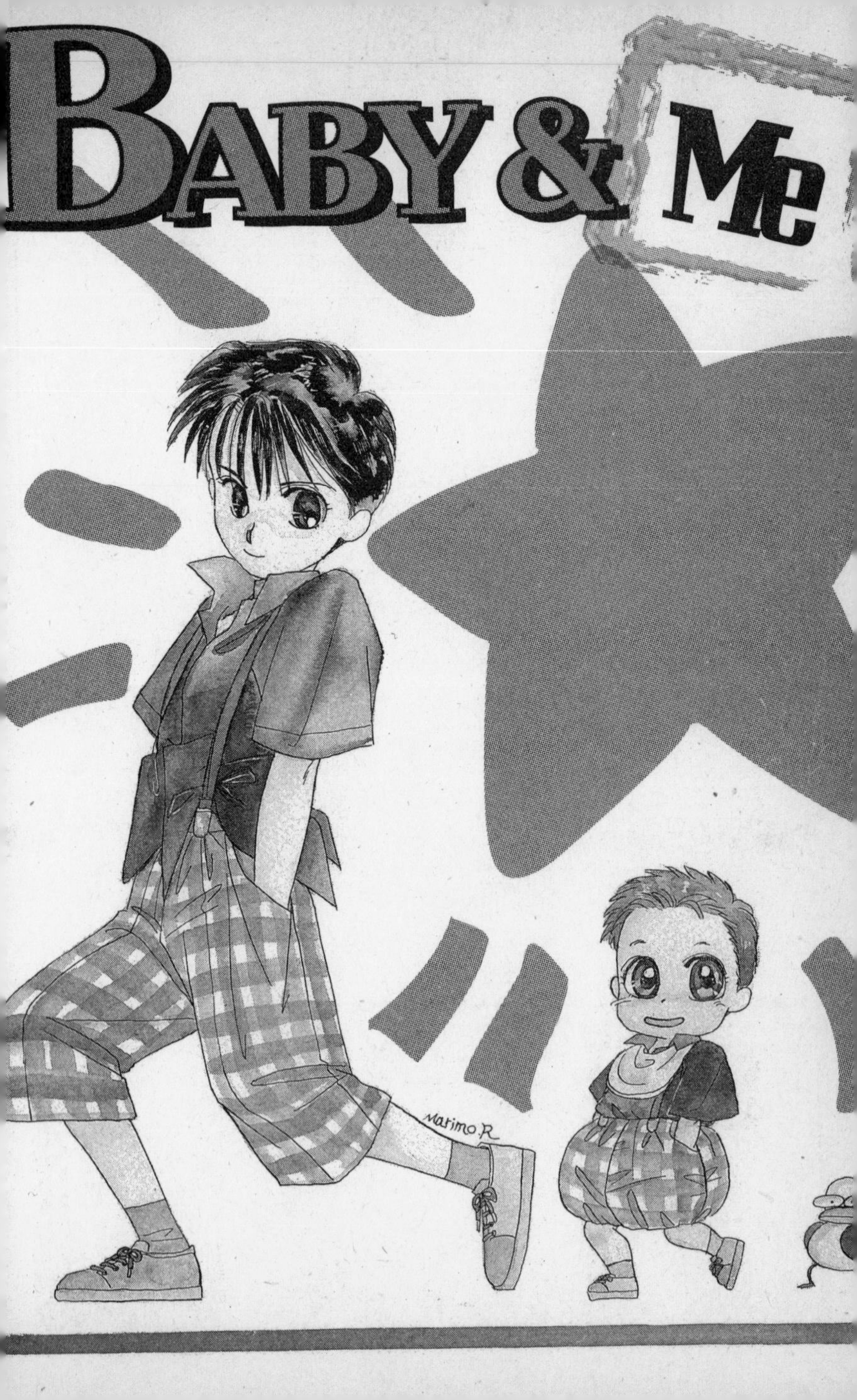
BABY & Me
Marimo.R

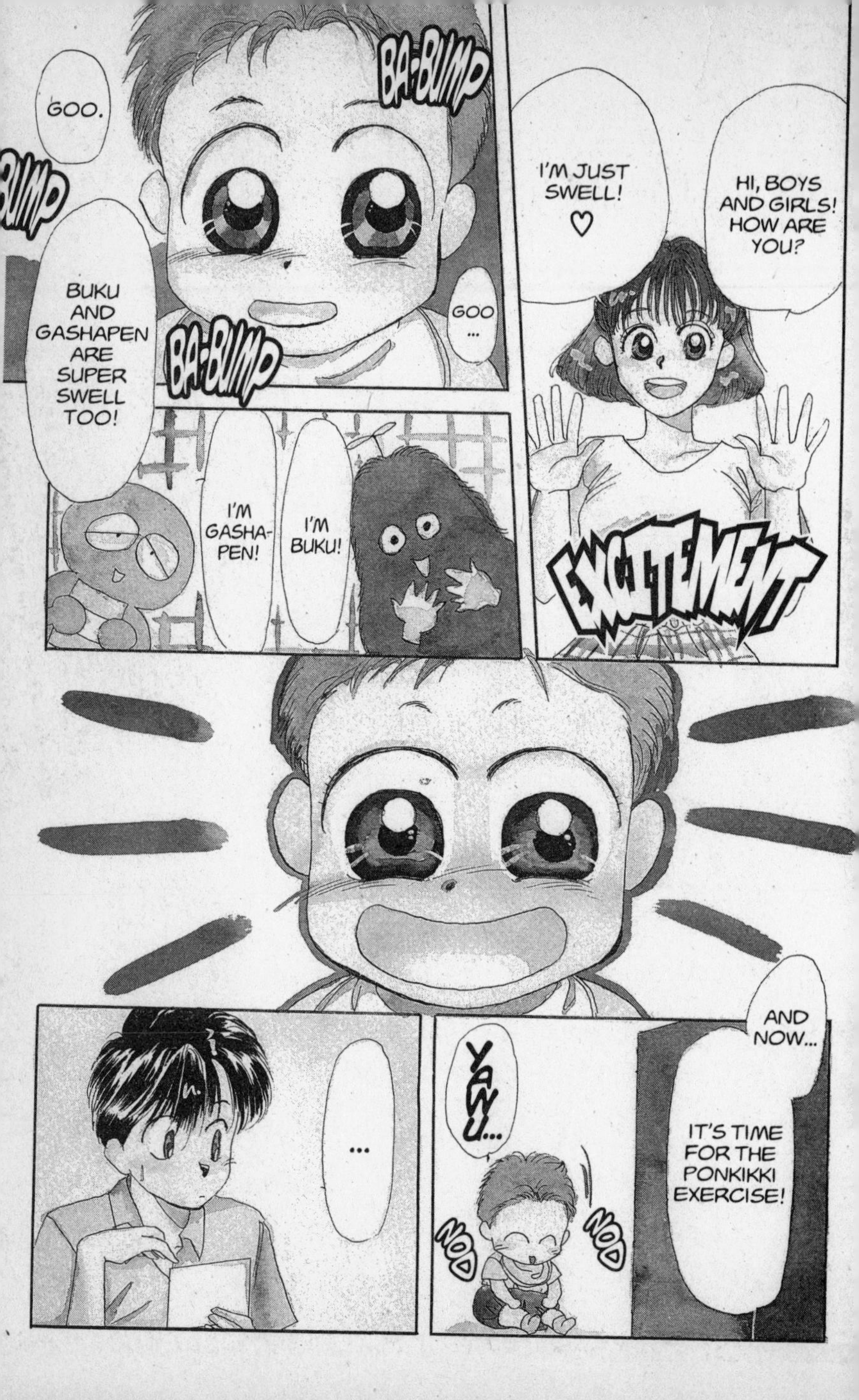
HI, BOYS AND GIRLS! HOW ARE YOU?
I'M JUST SWELL! ♡
EXCITEMENT
BA-BUMP
GOO.
BUMP
GOO ...
BA-BUMP
I'M BUKU!
I'M GASHA-PEN!
BUKU AND GASHAPEN ARE SUPER SWELL TOO!
AND NOW...
IT'S TIME FOR THE PONKIKKI EXERCISE!
YAWU...
NOD
NOD
...

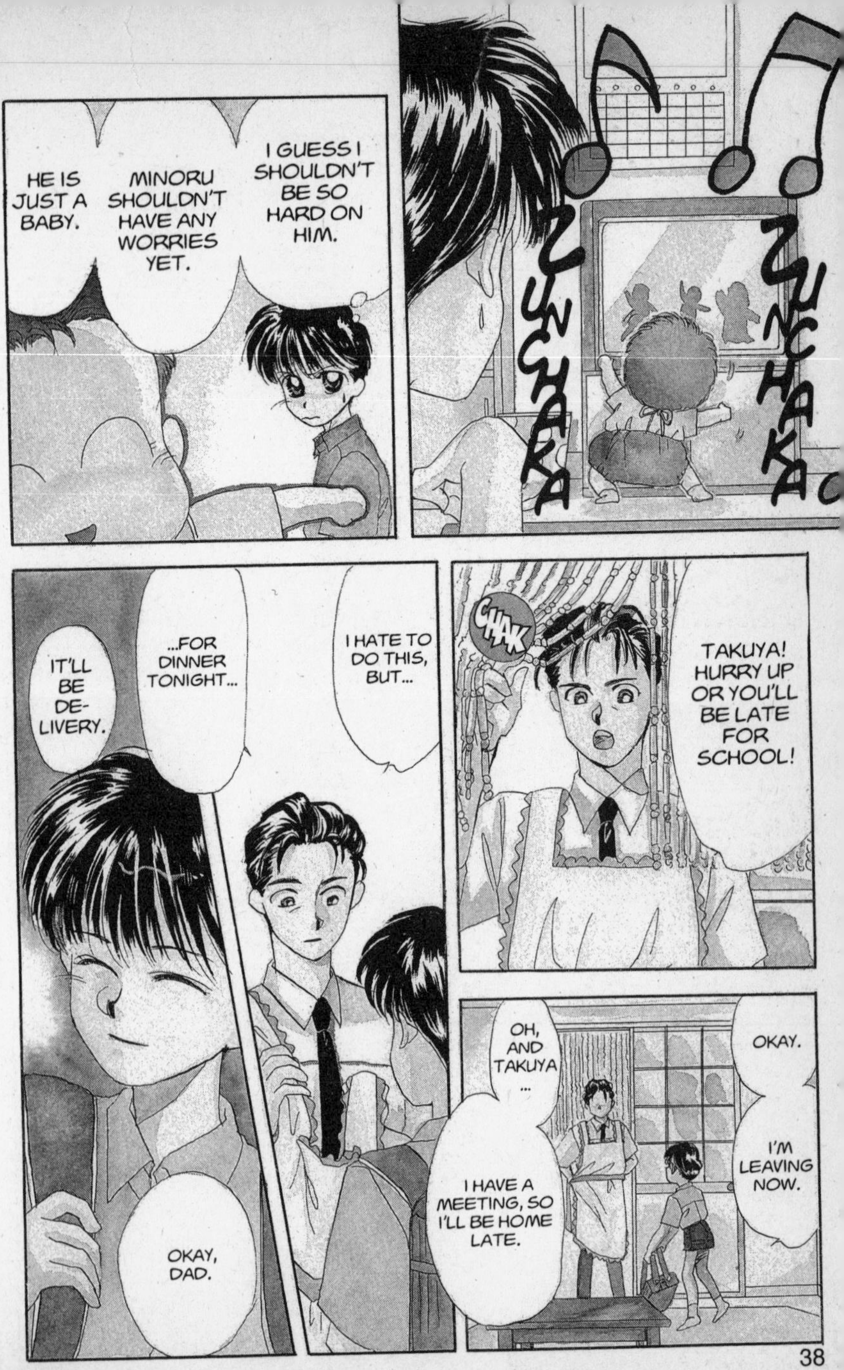
ZUNCHAKA
ZUNCHAKA
I GUESS I SHOULDN'T BE SO HARD ON HIM.
MINORU SHOULDN'T HAVE ANY WORRIES YET.
HE IS JUST A BABY.
CHAK
TAKUYA! HURRY UP OR YOU'LL BE LATE FOR SCHOOL!
OKAY.
I'M LEAVING NOW.
OH, AND TAKUYA...
I HAVE A MEETING, SO I'LL BE HOME LATE.
I HATE TO DO THIS, BUT...
...FOR DINNER TONIGHT...
IT'LL BE DE-LIVERY.
OKAY, DAD.

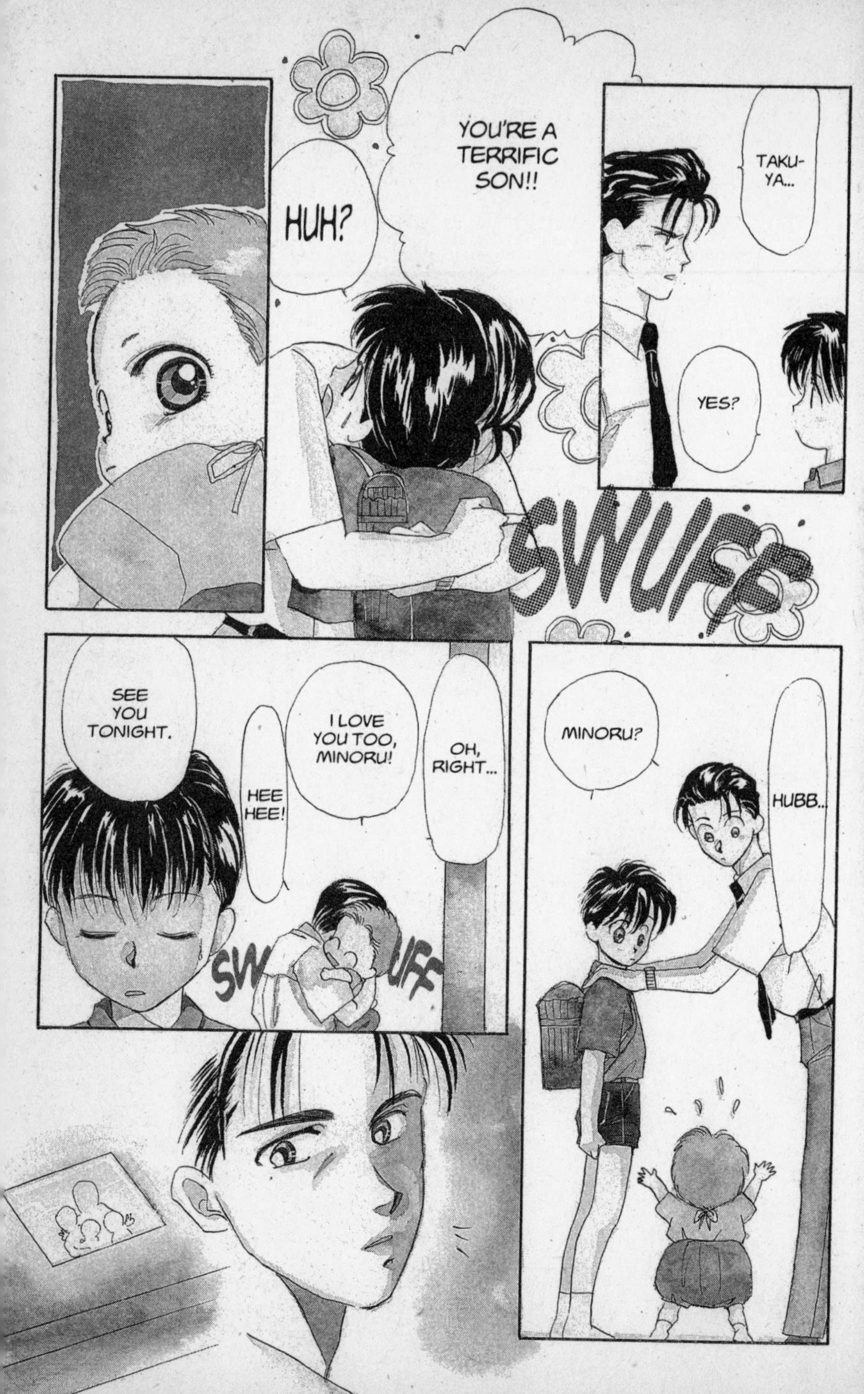
TAKU-YA...
YES?
YOU'RE A TERRIFIC SON!!
HUH?
SWUFF
HUBB...
MINORU?
OH, RIGHT...
I LOVE YOU TOO, MINORU!
HEE HEE!
SEE YOU TONIGHT.
SWUFF

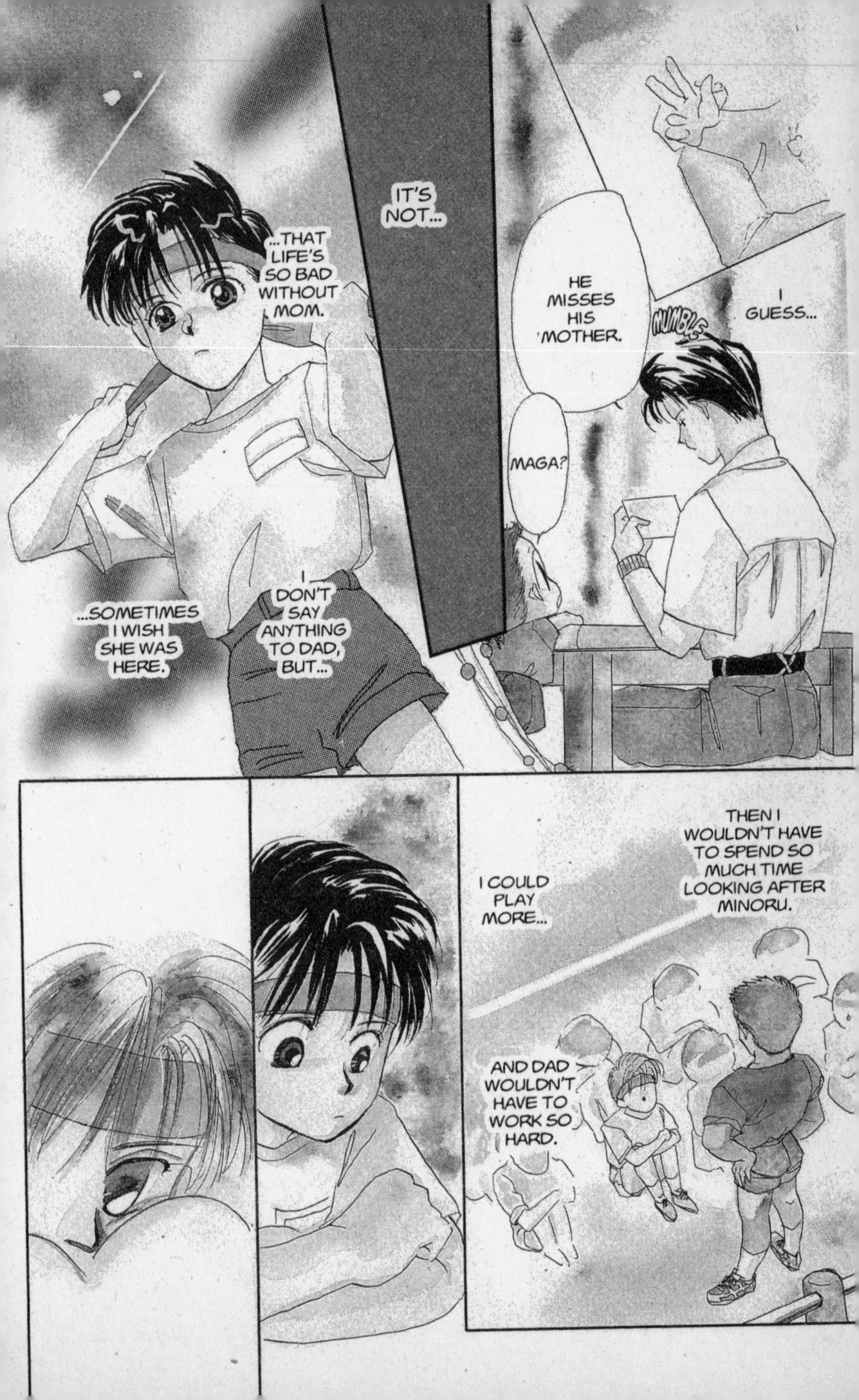
HE MISSES HIS MOTHER.
I GUESS...
MUMBLE
MAGA?
IT'S NOT...
...THAT LIFE'S SO BAD WITHOUT MOM.
I DON'T SAY ANYTHING TO DAD, BUT...
...SOMETIMES I WISH SHE WAS HERE.
THEN I WOULDN'T HAVE TO SPEND SO MUCH TIME LOOKING AFTER MINORU.
I COULD PLAY MORE...
AND DAD WOULDN'T HAVE TO WORK SO HARD.

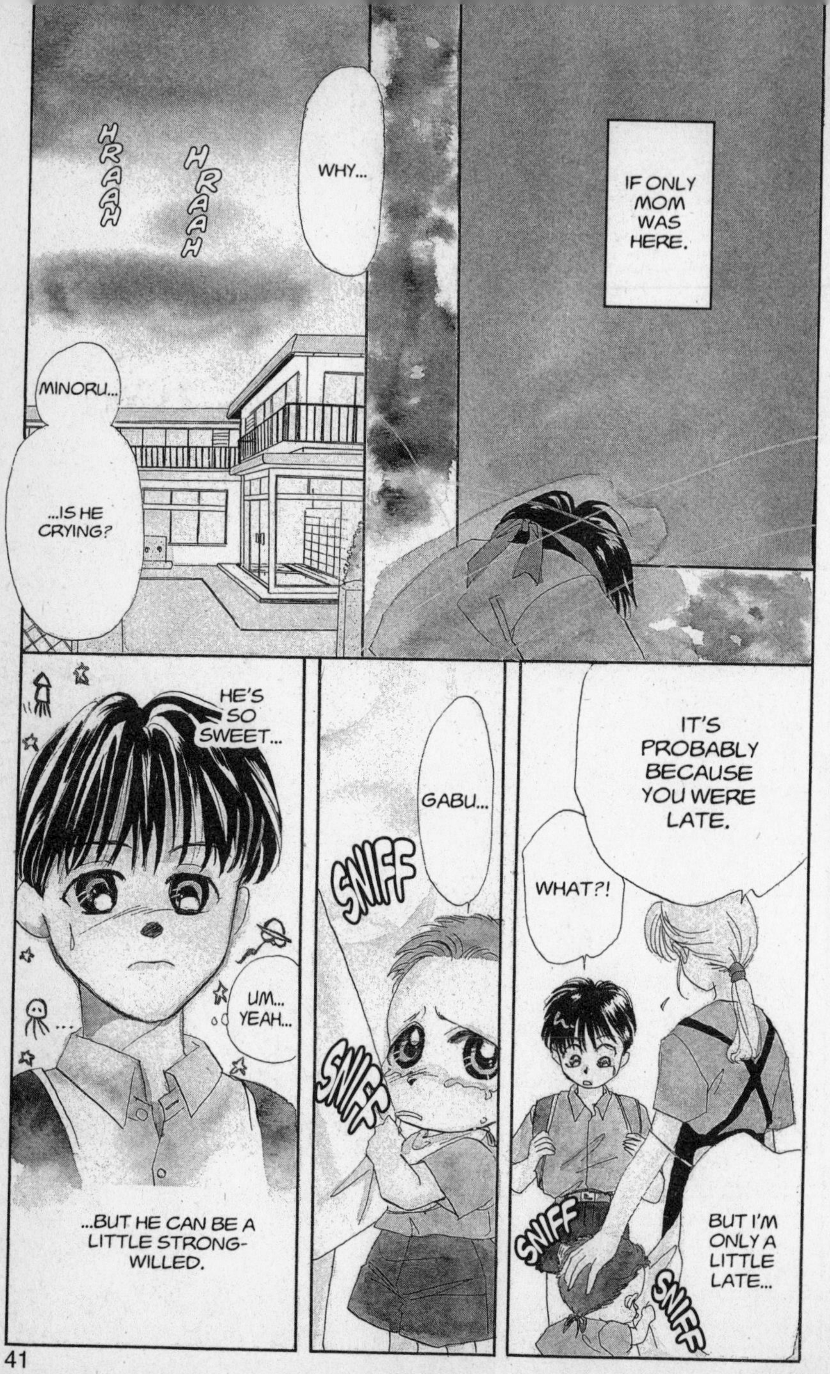
IF ONLY MOM WAS HERE.
WHY...
HRAAAH
HRAAAH
MINORU...
...IS HE CRYING?
IT'S PROBABLY BECAUSE YOU WERE LATE.
WHAT?!
BUT I'M ONLY A LITTLE LATE...
SNIFF
SNIFF
GABU...
SNIFF
SNIFF
HE'S SO SWEET...
UM... YEAH...
...
...BUT HE CAN BE A LITTLE STRONG-WILLED.

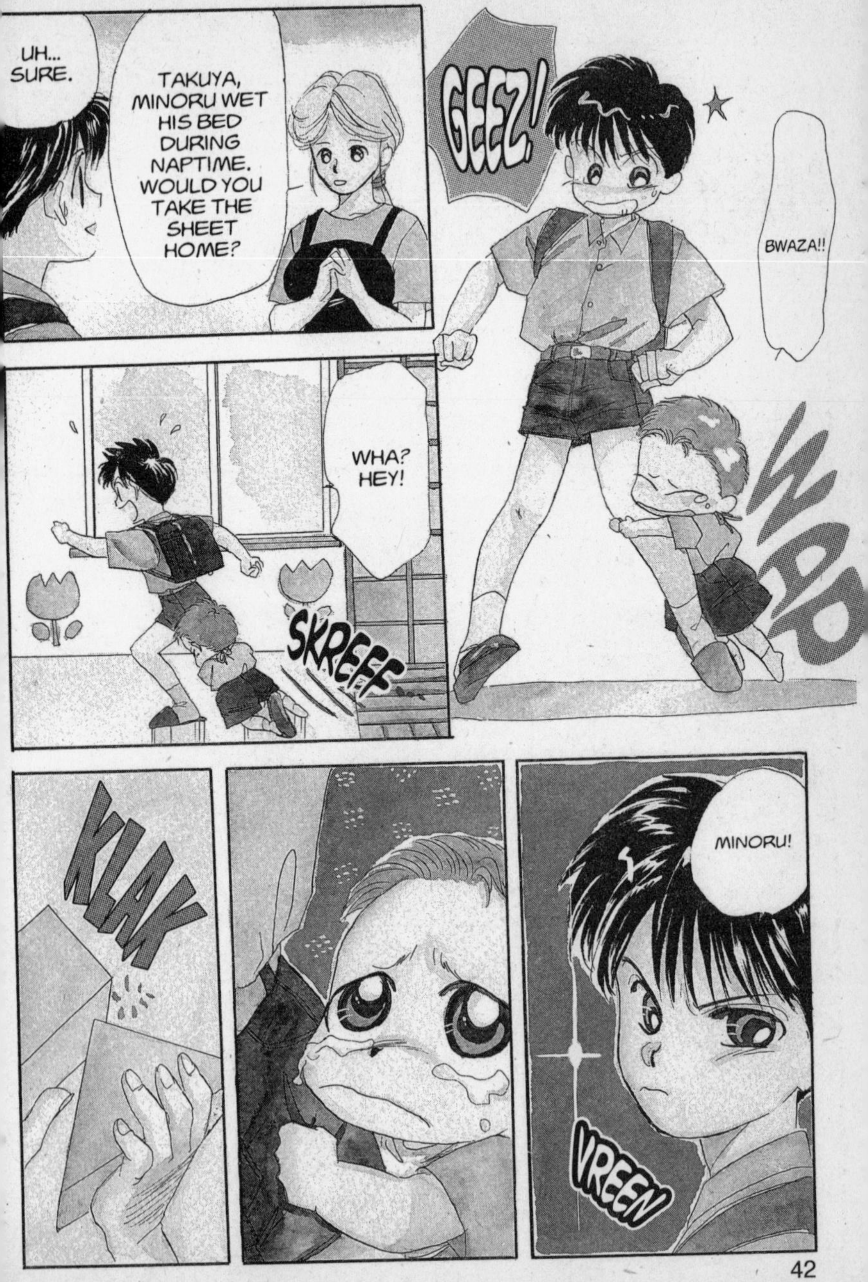
GEEZ!
BWAZA!!
WAP
TAKUYA, MINORU WET HIS BED DURING NAPTIME. WOULD YOU TAKE THE SHEET HOME?
UH... SURE.
WHA? HEY!
SKREFF
MINORU!
VREEN
KLAK

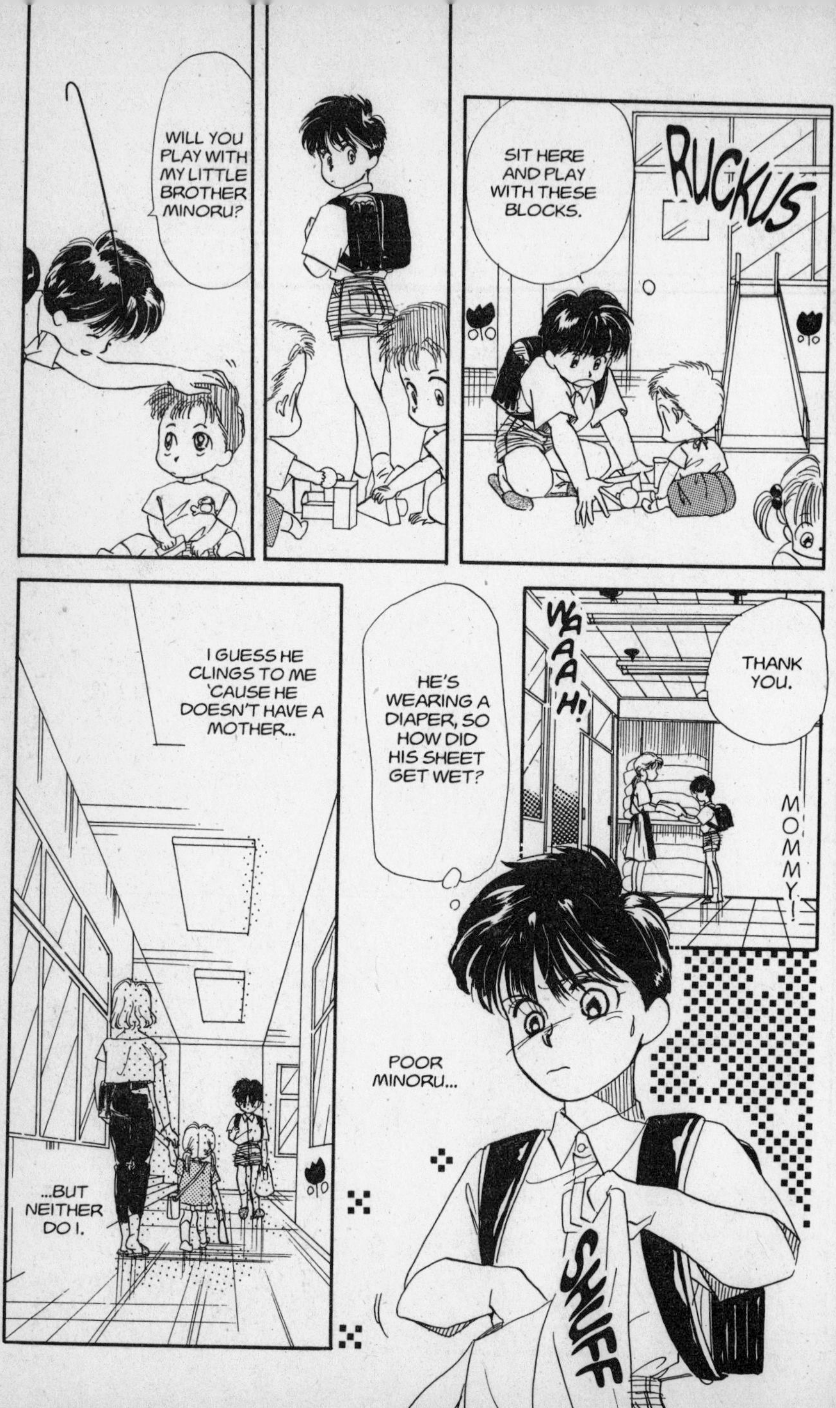
RUCKUS
SIT HERE AND PLAY WITH THESE BLOCKS.
WILL YOU PLAY WITH MY LITTLE BROTHER MINORU?
THANK YOU.
MOMMY!
WAAAH!
HE'S WEARING A DIAPER, SO HOW DID HIS SHEET GET WET?
POOR MINORU...
SHUFF
I GUESS HE CLINGS TO ME 'CAUSE HE DOESN'T HAVE A MOTHER...
...BUT NEITHER DO I.

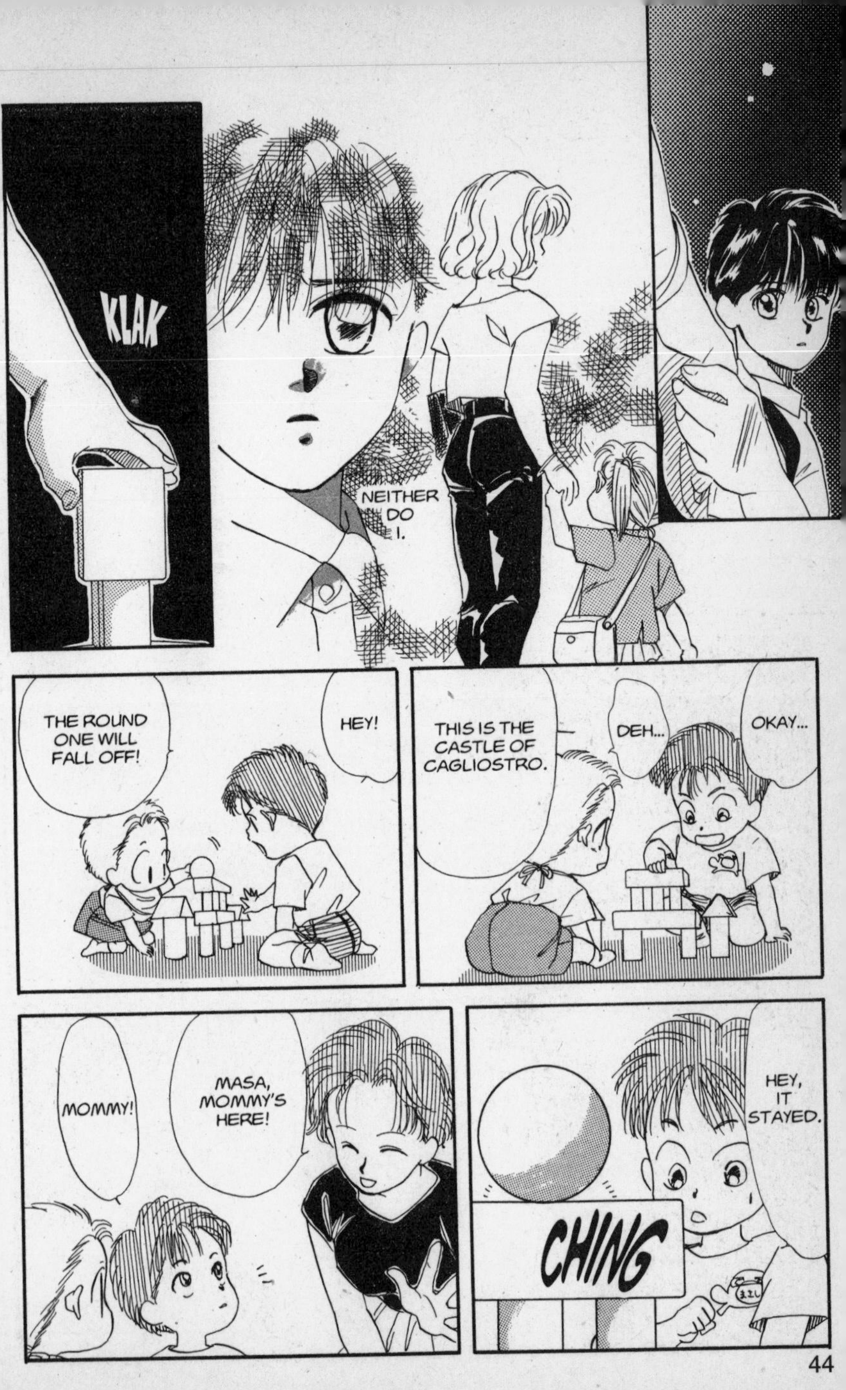
NEITHER DO I.
KLAK
OKAY...
DEH...
THIS IS THE CASTLE OF CAGLIOSTRO.
HEY!
THE ROUND ONE WILL FALL OFF!
HEY, IT STAYED.
CHING
MASA, MOMMY'S HERE!
MOMMY!

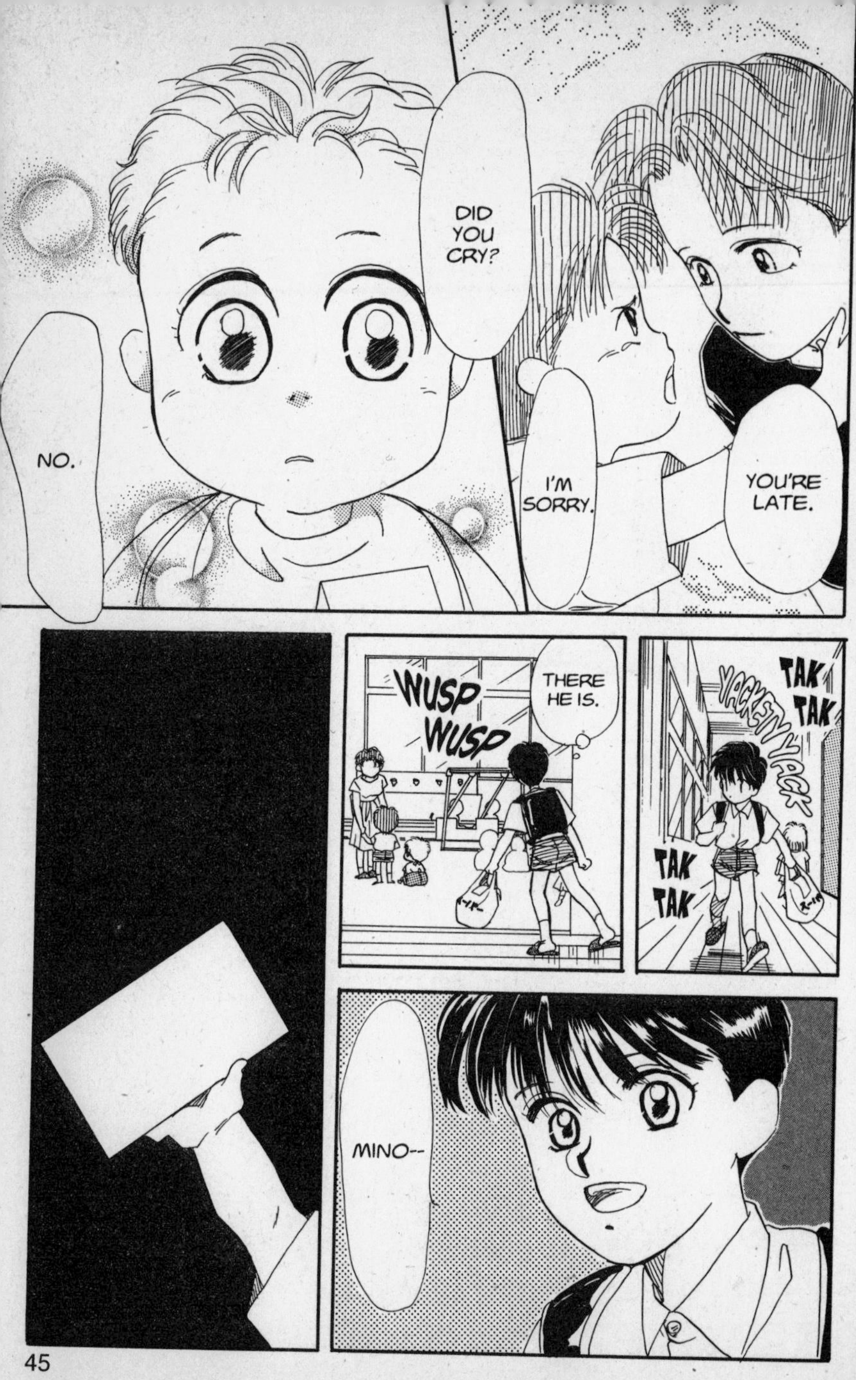
YOU'RE LATE.
I'M SORRY.
DID YOU CRY?
NO.
TAK TAK
YACKETY YACK
TAK TAK
WUSP WUSP
THERE HE IS.
MINO--

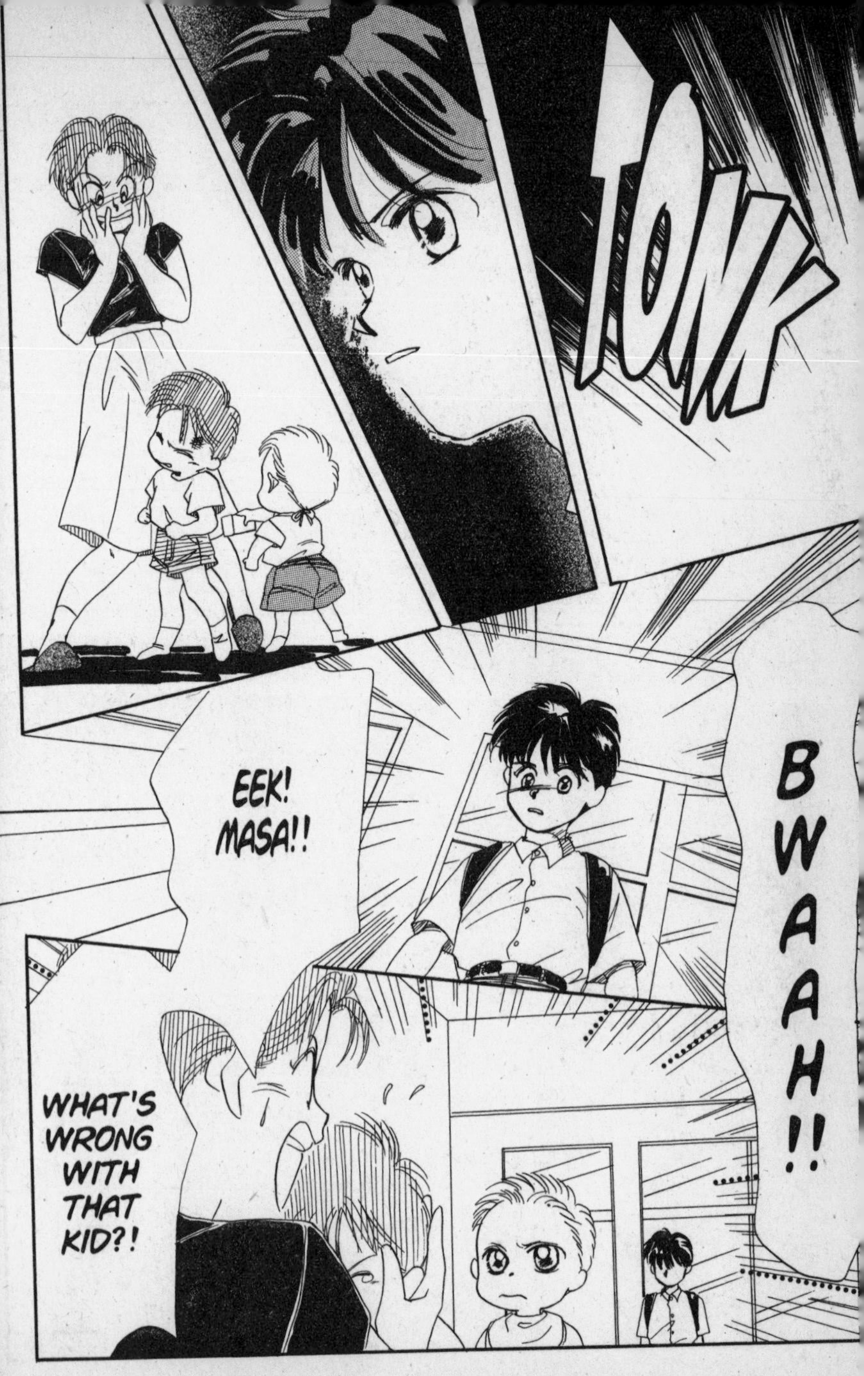
TONK
BWAAAH!!
EEK! MASA!!
WHAT'S WRONG WITH THAT KID?!

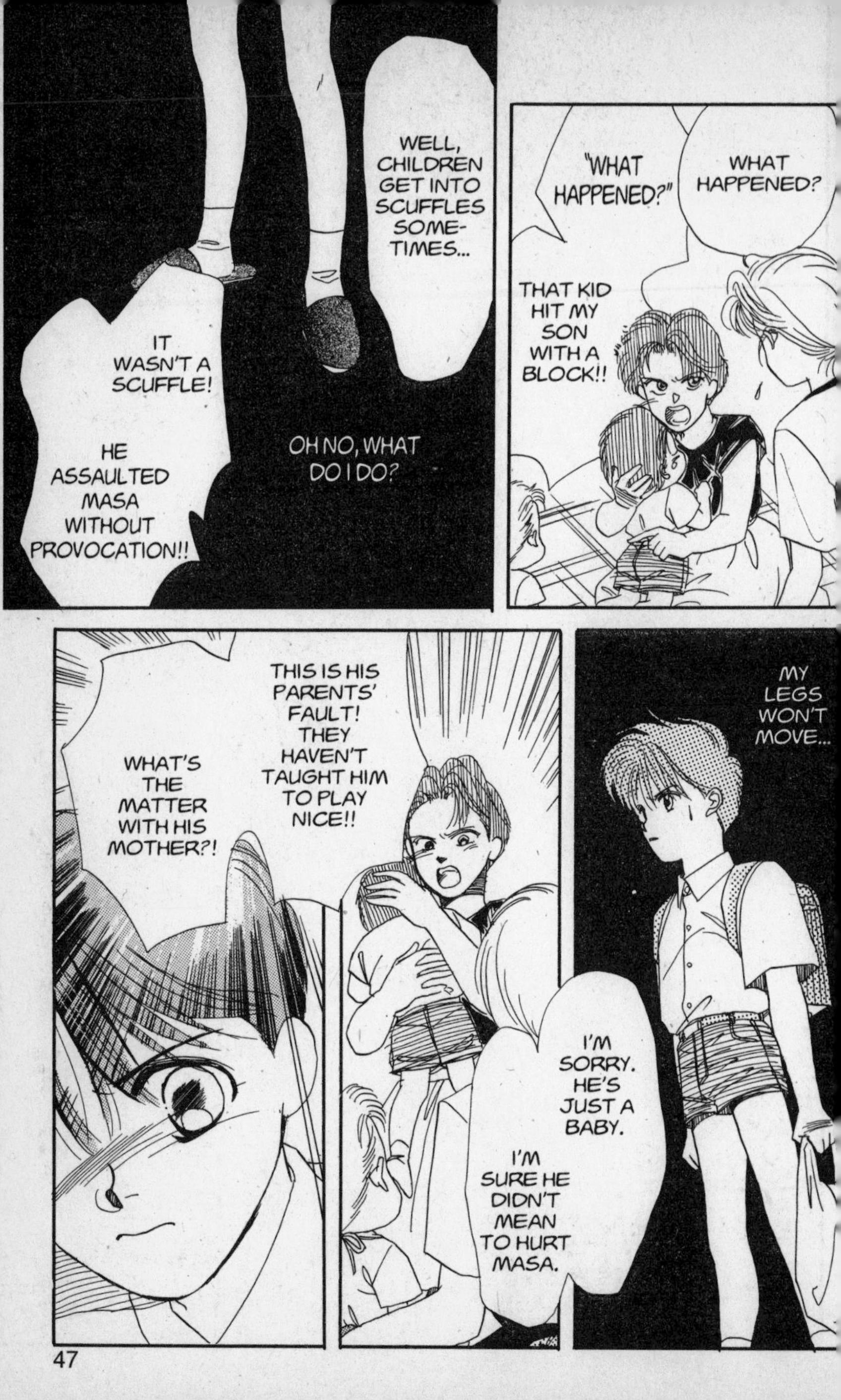
WHAT HAPPENED?
"WHAT HAPPENED?"
THAT KID HIT MY SON WITH A BLOCK!!
WELL, CHILDREN GET INTO SCUFFLES SOME-TIMES...
OH NO, WHAT DO I DO?
IT WASN'T A SCUFFLE!
HE ASSAULTED MASA WITHOUT PROVOCATION!!
MY LEGS WON'T MOVE...
THIS IS HIS PARENTS' FAULT! THEY HAVEN'T TAUGHT HIM TO PLAY NICE!!
I'M SORRY. HE'S JUST A BABY.
I'M SURE HE DIDN'T MEAN TO HURT MASA.
WHAT'S THE MATTER WITH HIS MOTHER?!

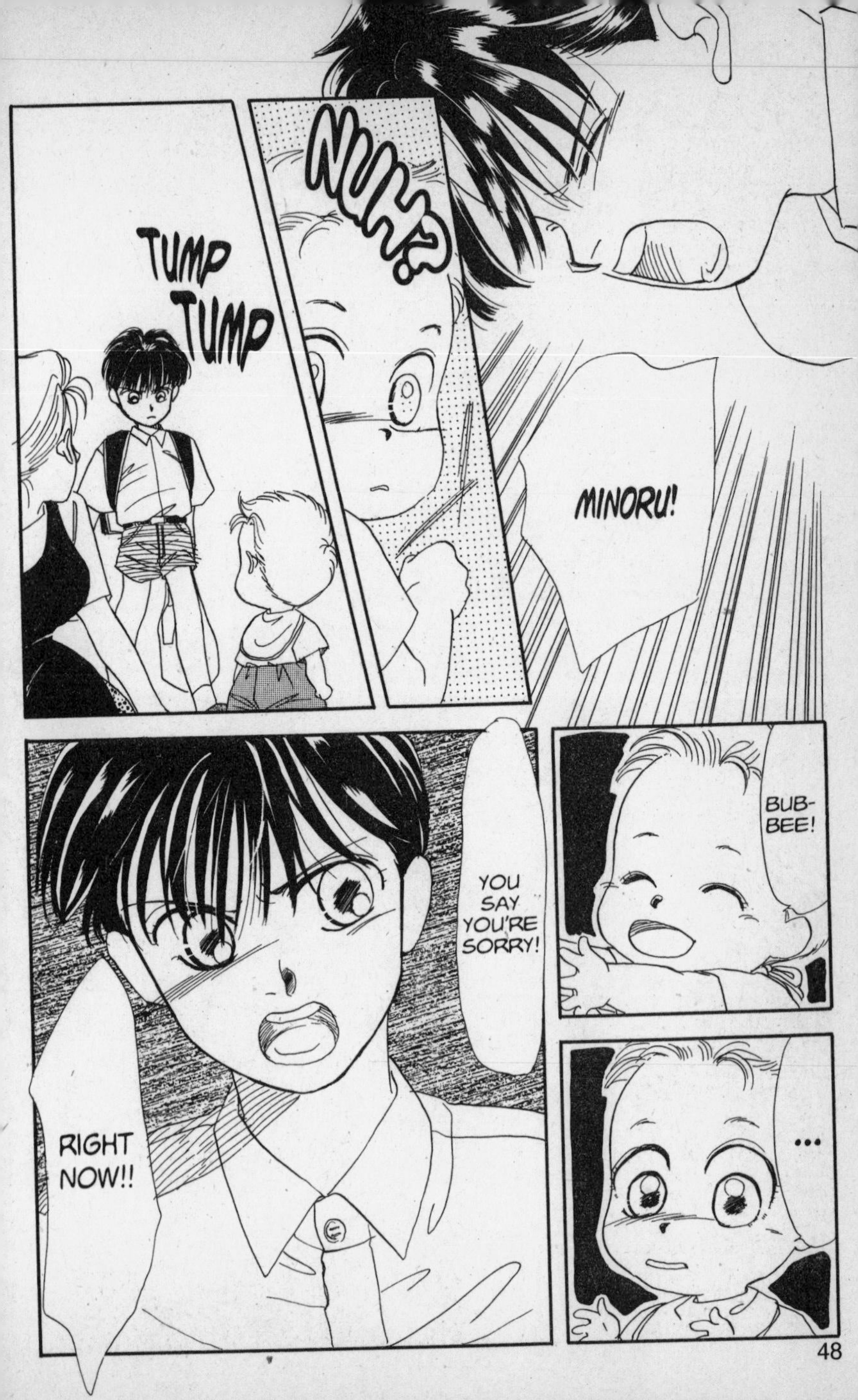
MINORU!
NUH?!
TUMP TUMP
BUB-BEE!
...
YOU SAY YOU'RE SORRY!
RIGHT NOW!!

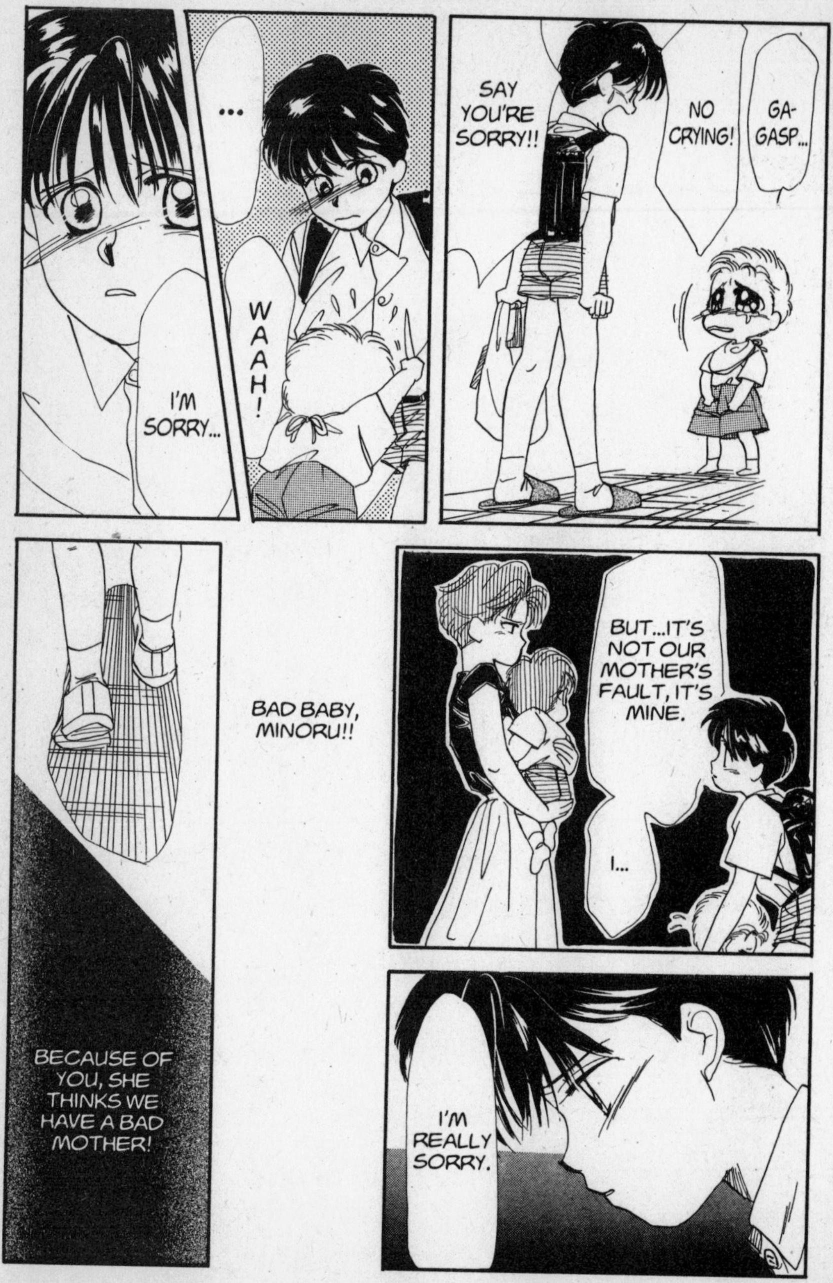
GA-GASP...
NO CRYING!
SAY YOU'RE SORRY!!
...
WAAAH!
I'M SORRY...
BUT...IT'S NOT OUR MOTHER'S FAULT, IT'S MINE.
I...
I'M REALLY SORRY.
BAD BABY, MINORU!!
BECAUSE OF YOU, SHE THINKS WE HAVE A BAD MOTHER!

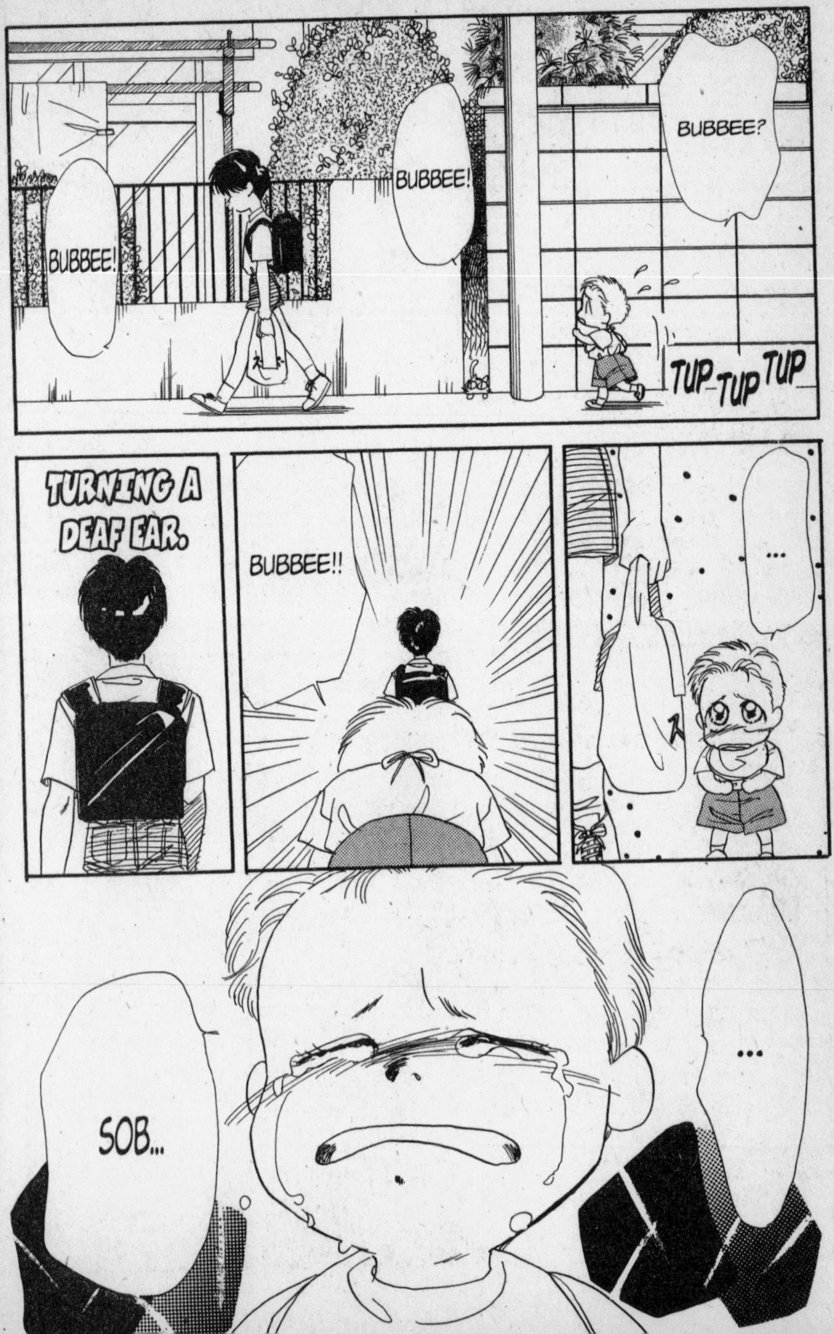
BUBBEE?
TUP-TUP TUP
BUBBEE!
BUBBEE!
...
BUBBEE!!
TURNING A DEAF EAR.
...
SOB...

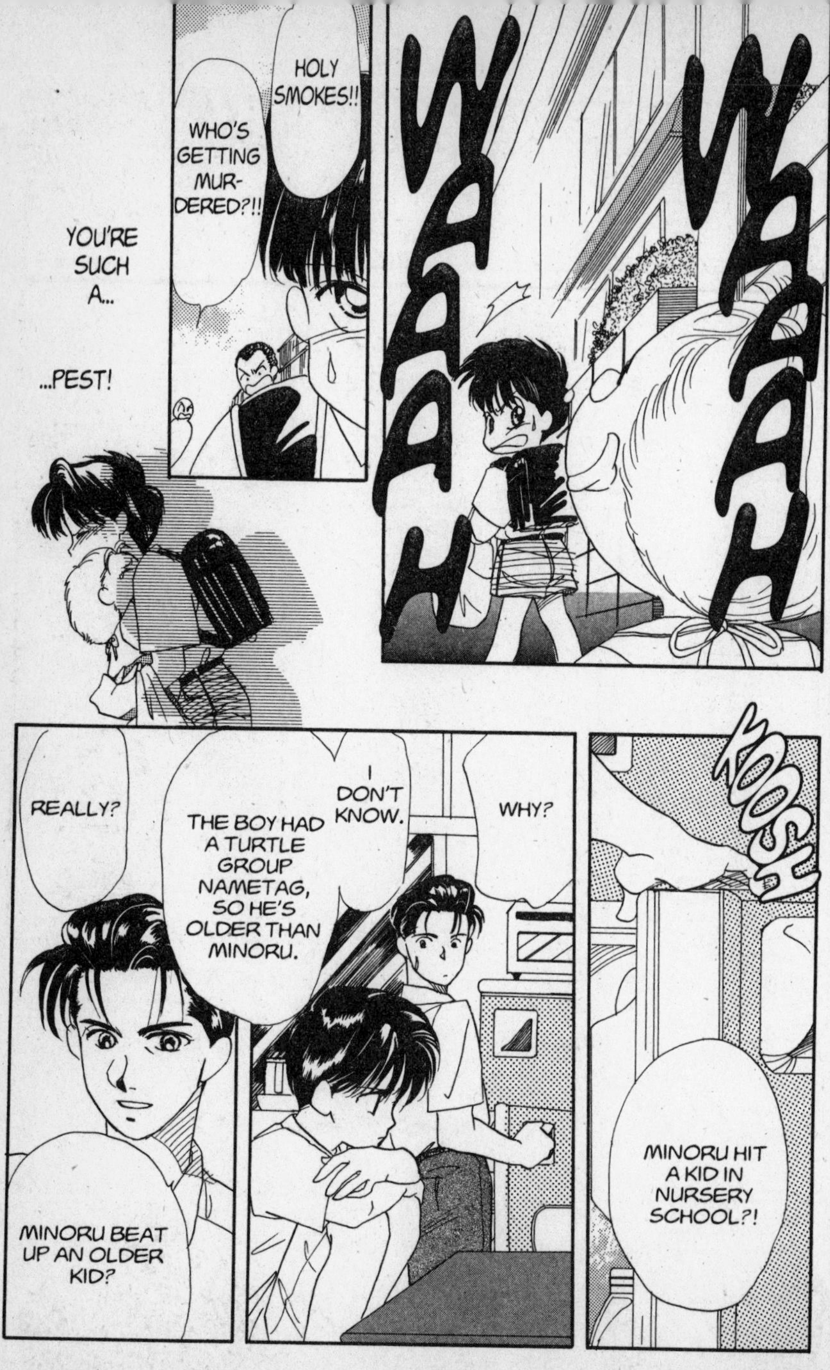
WAAAAAH
WAAAAH
HOLY SMOKES!!
WHO'S GETTING MUR-DERED?!!
YOU'RE SUCH A...
...PEST!
KOOSH
MINORU HIT A KID IN NURSERY SCHOOL?!
WHY?
I DON'T KNOW.
THE BOY HAD A TURTLE GROUP NAMETAG, SO HE'S OLDER THAN MINORU.
REALLY?
MINORU BEAT UP AN OLDER KID?

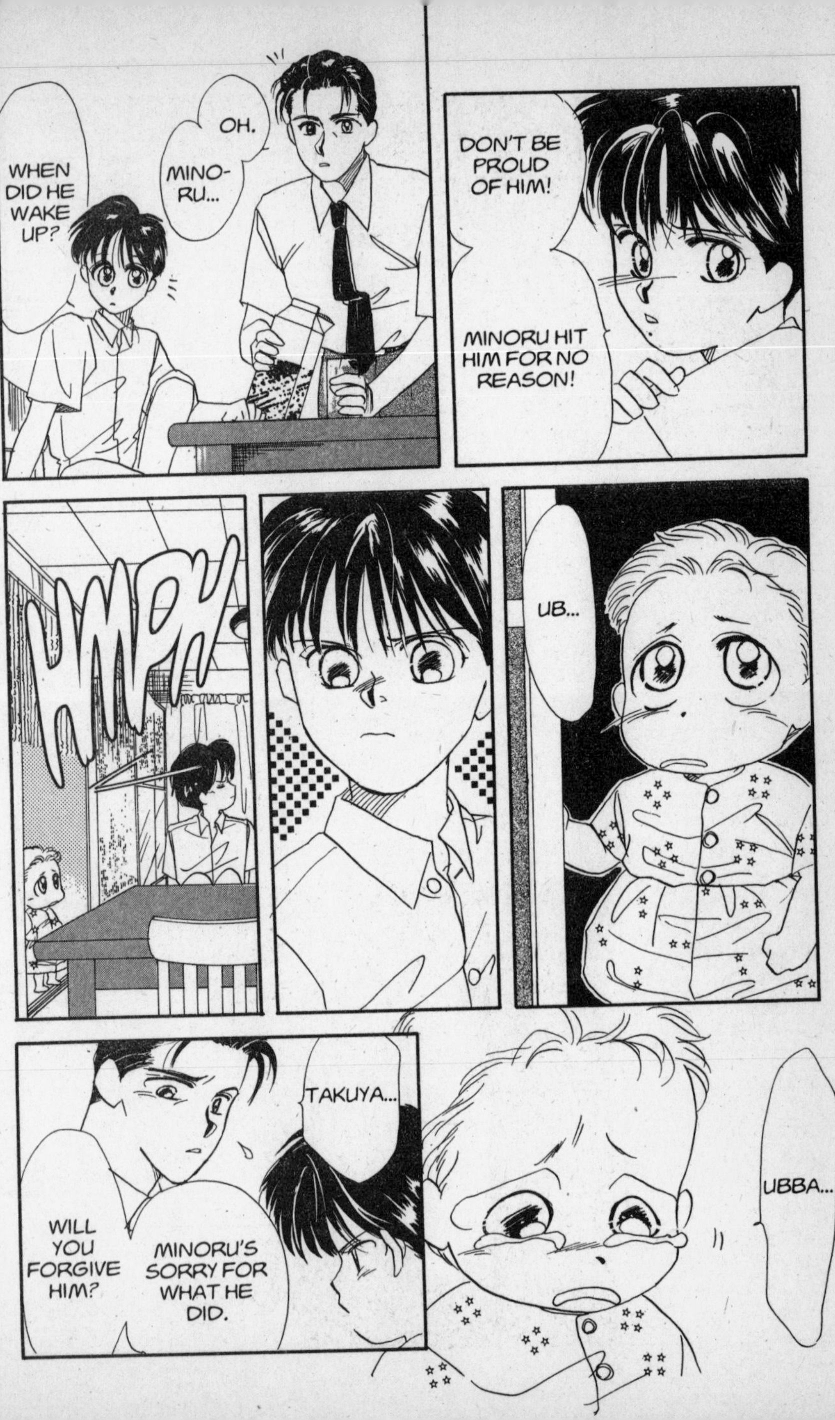
DON'T BE PROUD OF HIM!
MINORU HIT HIM FOR NO REASON!
OH.
MINO-RU...
WHEN DID HE WAKE UP?
UB...
HMPH
UBBA...
TAKUYA...
MINORU'S SORRY FOR WHAT HE DID.
WILL YOU FORGIVE HIM?

Author's Note 2

I'd like to thank all of you who bought my book. This is my very first comic.

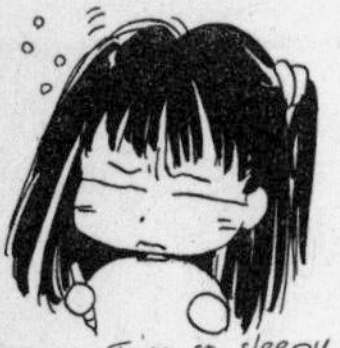
I'm so sleepy...

I was excited to be writing my first author's note, but I don't normally take a good look at my work. So, when I reviewed it, I started to wonder if it was really fit to be published.

Especially Chapter 1.

I worked on Chapter 2 when I was in a slump. For every chapter that I completed, I think it took me 3 or 4 tries.

In the beginning, I made all of my deadlines, but with each succeeding chapter, I grew bolder, and soon I was missing deadlines all the time.

Apologies to my editor.

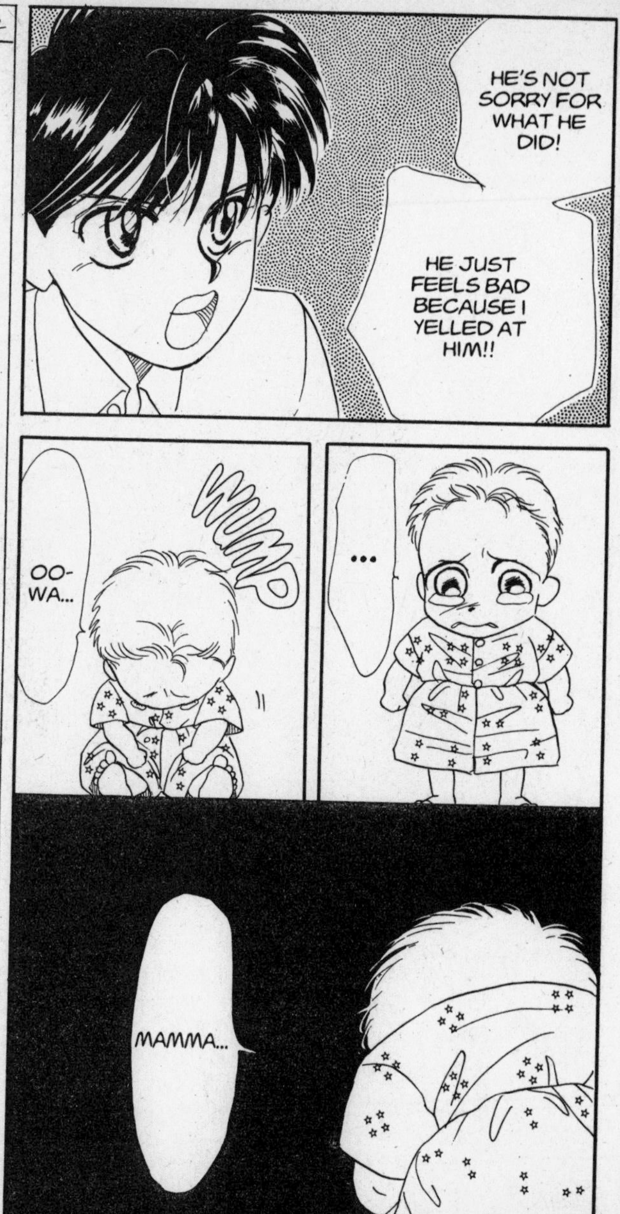
HE'S NOT SORRY FOR WHAT HE DID!
HE JUST FEELS BAD BECAUSE I YELLED AT HIM!!
...
WUMP
OO-WA...
MAMMA...

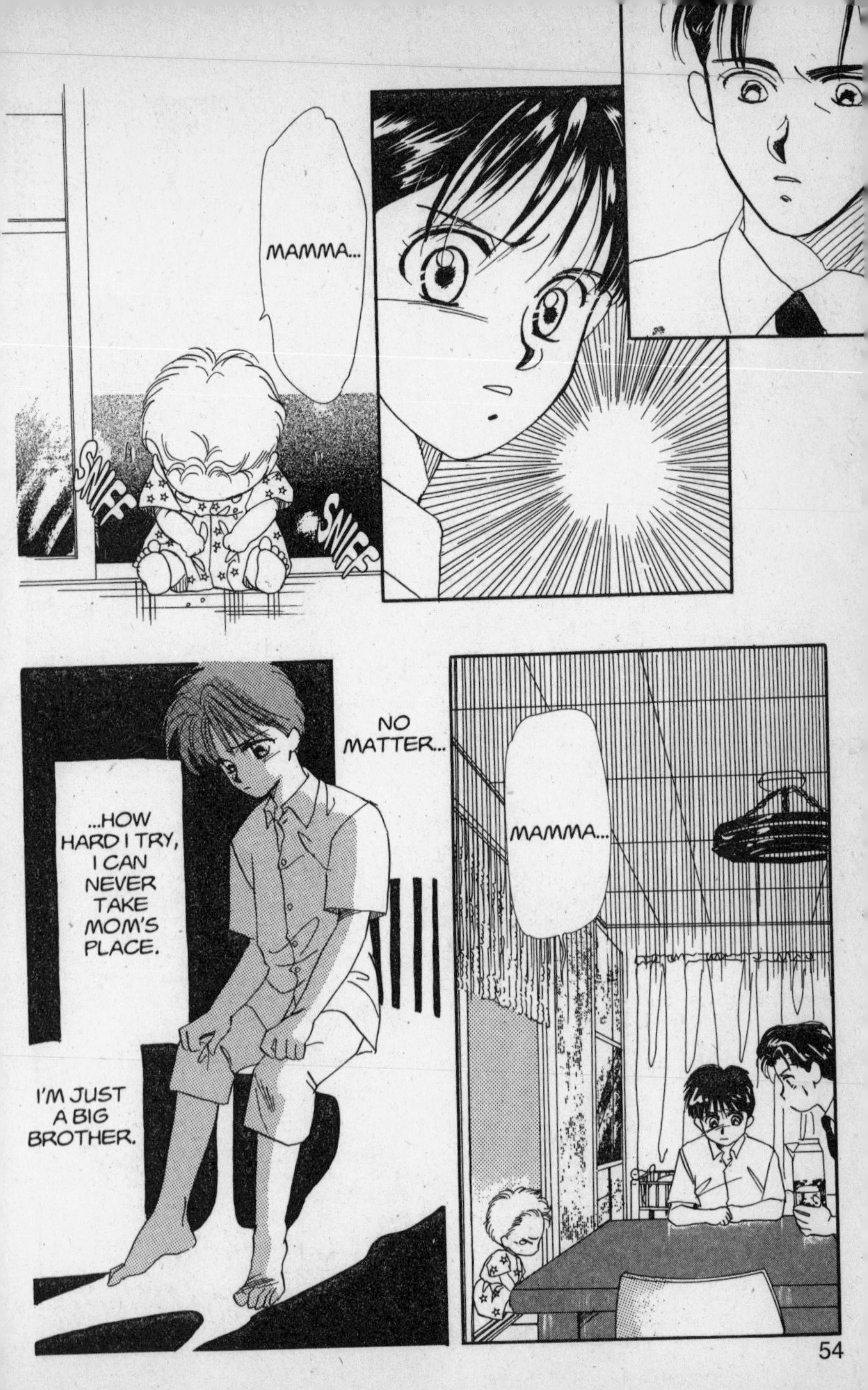
MAMMA...
SNIFF
SNIFF
MAMMA...
NO MATTER...
...HOW HARD I TRY, I CAN NEVER TAKE MOM'S PLACE.
I'M JUST A BIG BROTHER.

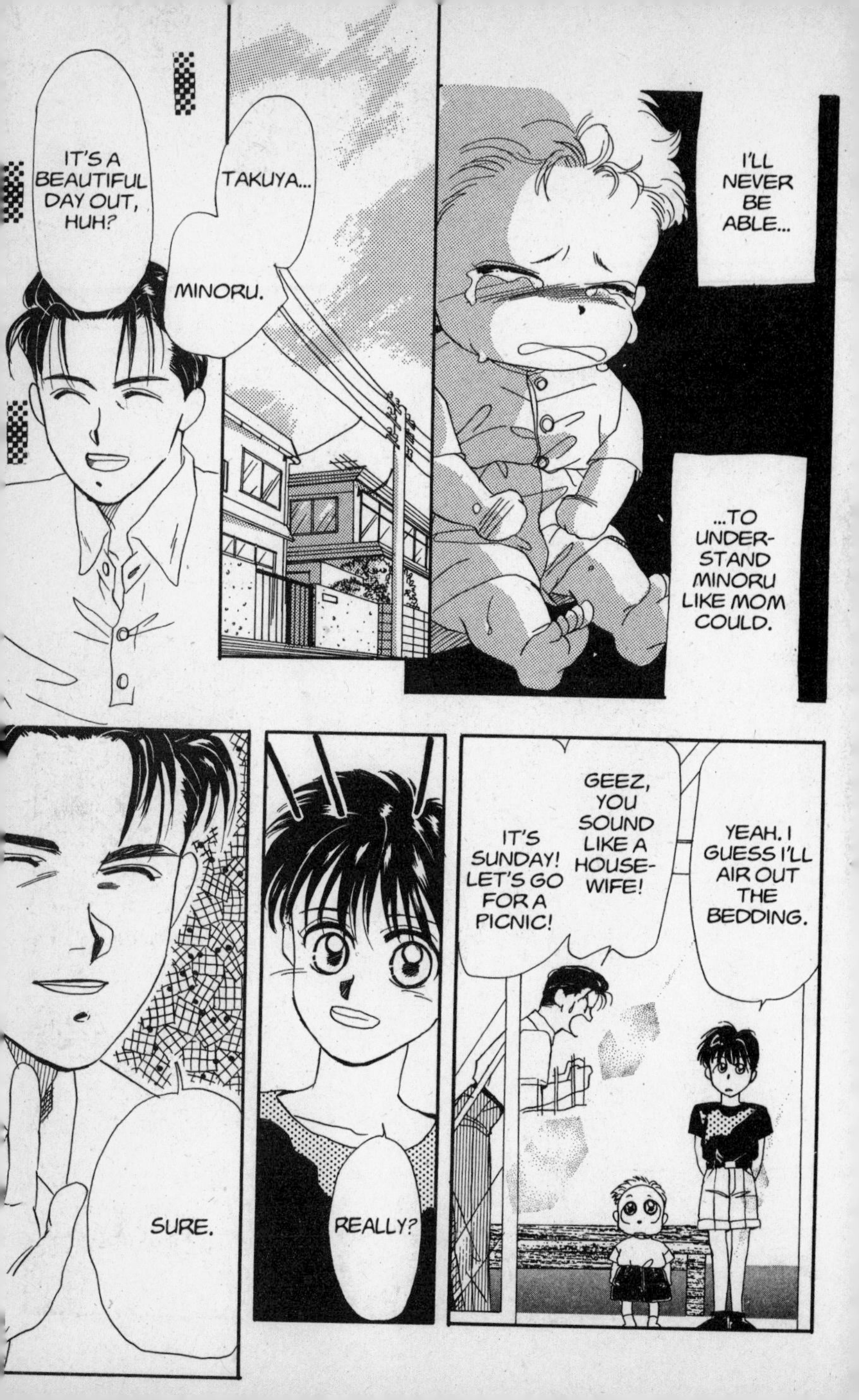
I'LL NEVER BE ABLE...
...TO UNDER-STAND MINORU LIKE MOM COULD.
TAKUYA...
MINORU.
IT'S A BEAUTIFUL DAY OUT, HUH?
YEAH. I GUESS I'LL AIR OUT THE BEDDING.
GEEZ, YOU SOUND LIKE A HOUSE-WIFE!
IT'S SUNDAY! LET'S GO FOR A PICNIC!
REALLY?
SURE.

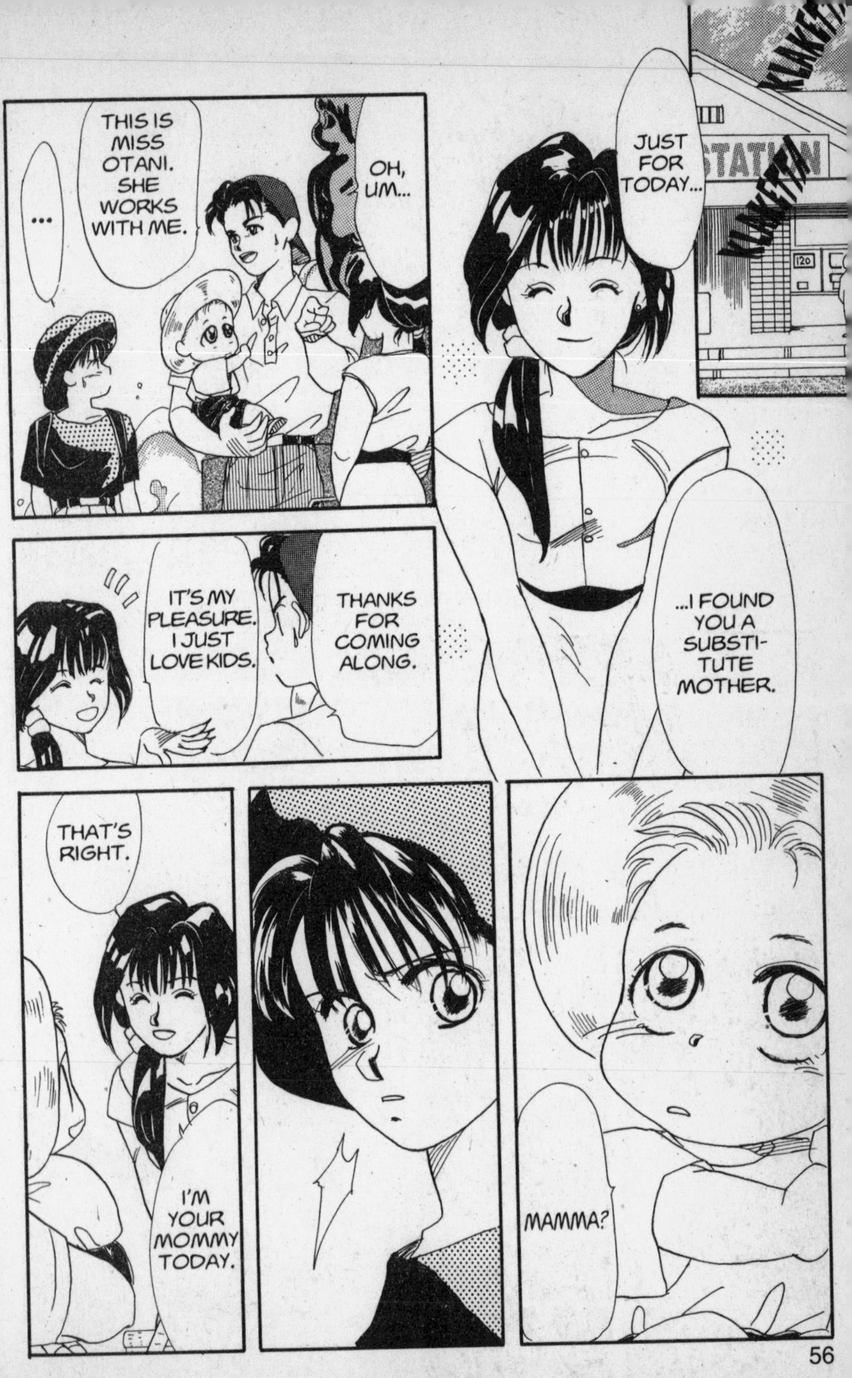
KLAKETTA
STATION
KLAKETTA
JUST FOR TODAY...
...I FOUND YOU A SUBSTITUTE MOTHER.
OH, UM...
THIS IS MISS OTANI. SHE WORKS WITH ME.
...
THANKS FOR COMING ALONG.
IT'S MY PLEASURE. I JUST LOVE KIDS.
MAMMA?
THAT'S RIGHT.
I'M YOUR MOMMY TODAY.

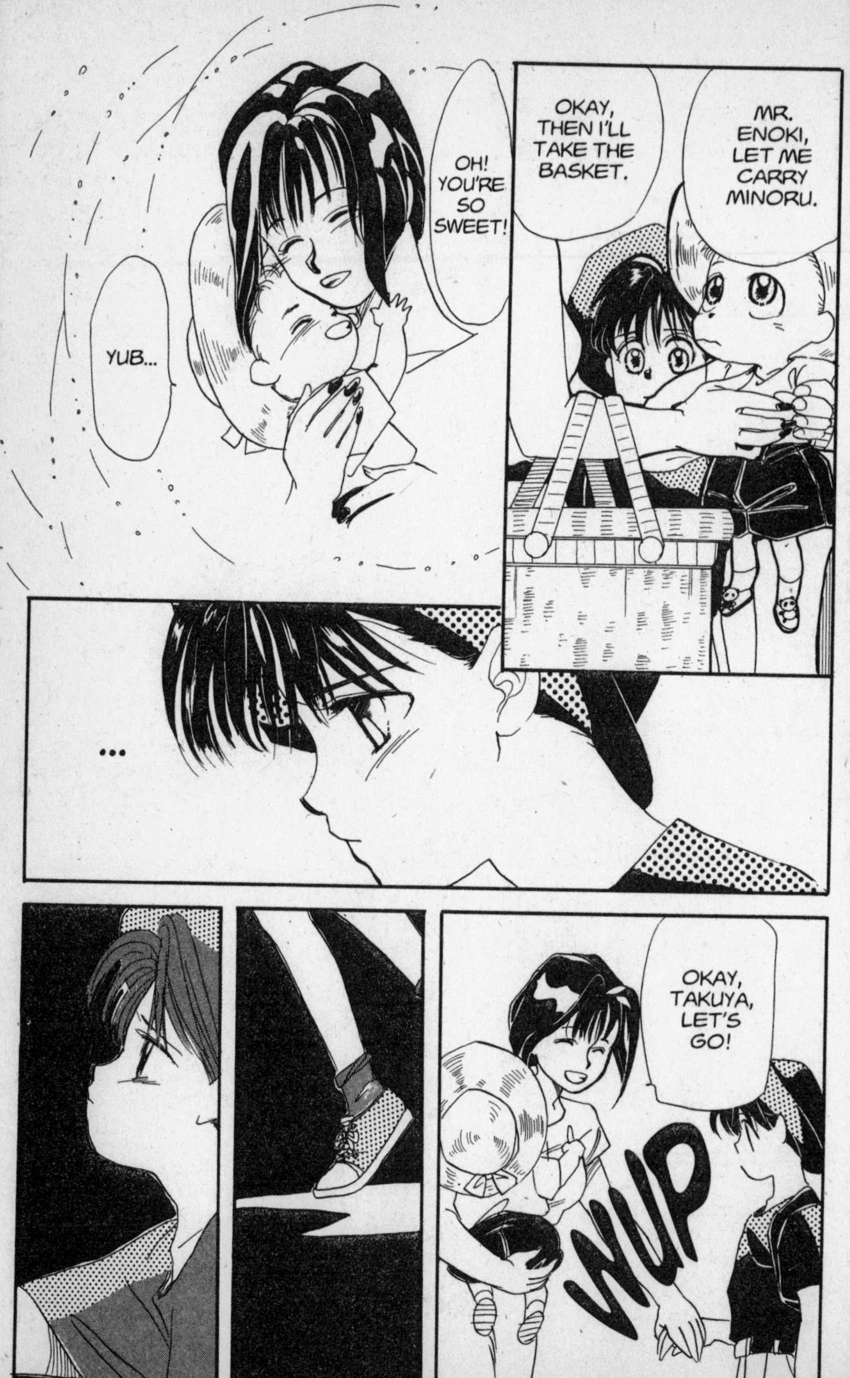
MR. ENOKI, LET ME CARRY MINORU.
OKAY, THEN I'LL TAKE THE BASKET.
OH! YOU'RE SO SWEET!
YUB...
...
OKAY, TAKUYA, LET'S GO!
WHUP

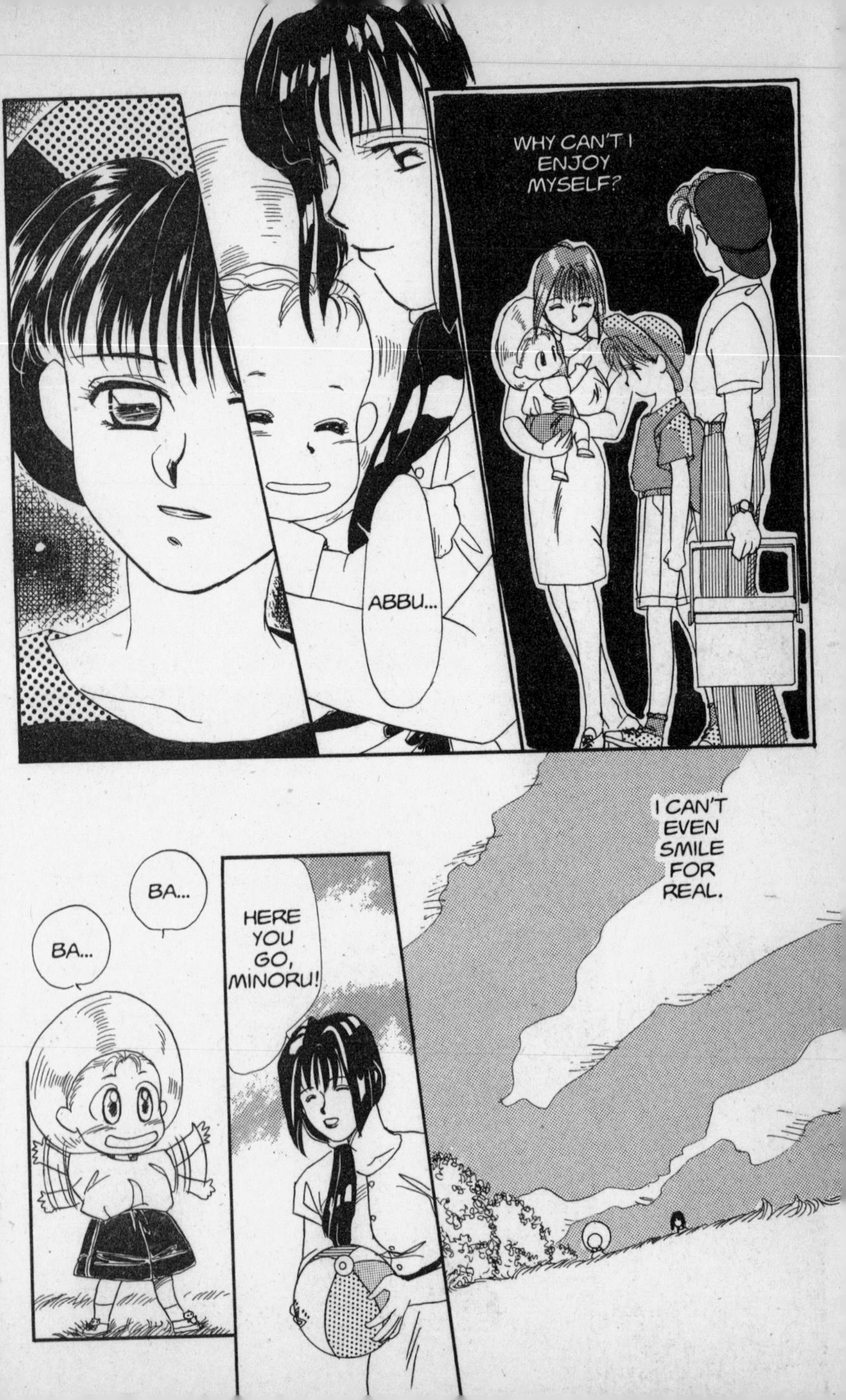
WHY CAN'T I ENJOY MYSELF?
ABBU...
I CAN'T EVEN SMILE FOR REAL.
HERE YOU GO, MINORU!
BA...
BA...

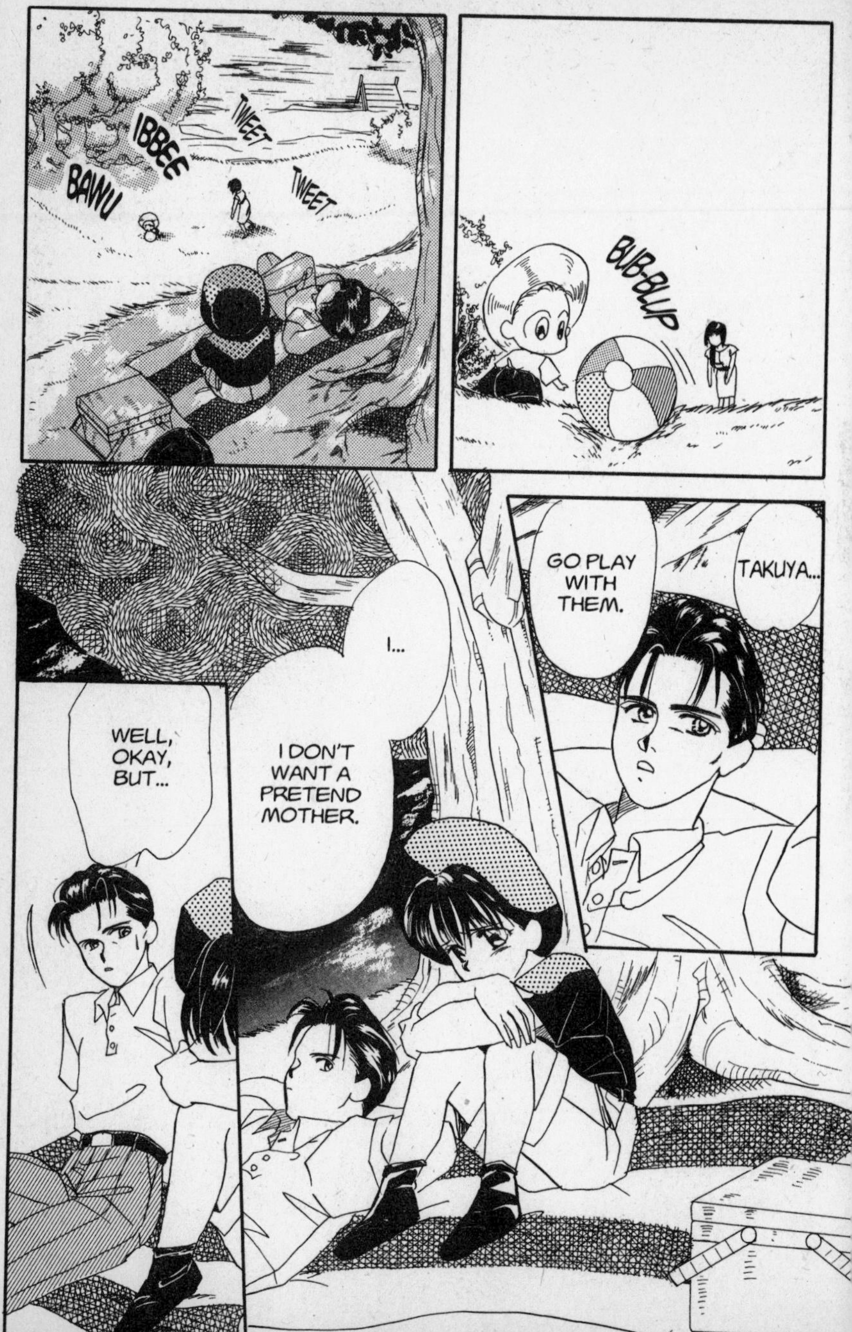
BUB-BLUP
TWEET
IBBEE
TWEET
BAWU
TAKUYA...
GO PLAY WITH THEM.
I...
I DON'T WANT A PRETEND MOTHER.
WELL, OKAY, BUT...

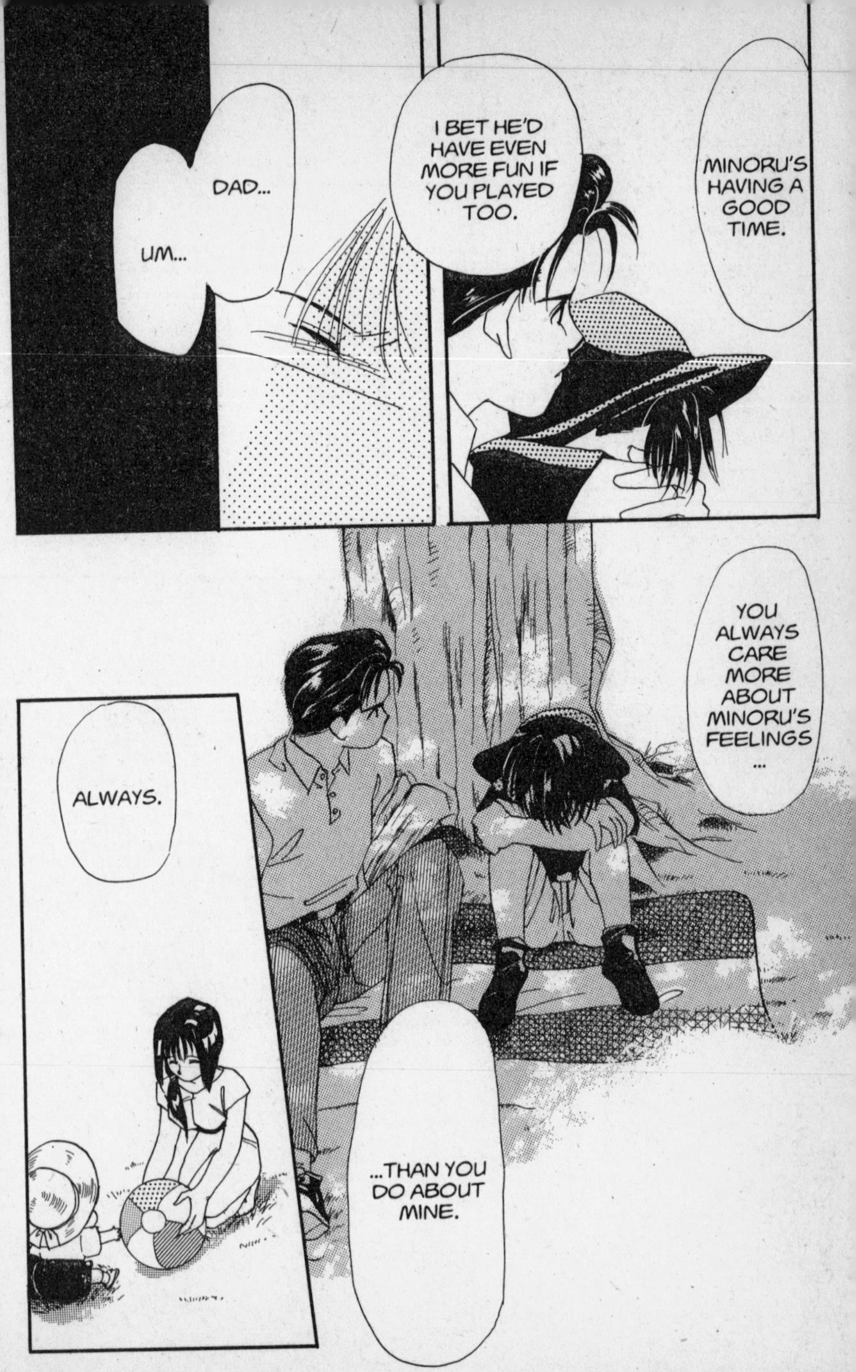
MINORU'S HAVING A GOOD TIME.
I BET HE'D HAVE EVEN MORE FUN IF YOU PLAYED TOO.
DAD...
UM...
YOU ALWAYS CARE MORE ABOUT MINORU'S FEELINGS ...
...THAN YOU DO ABOUT MINE.
ALWAYS.

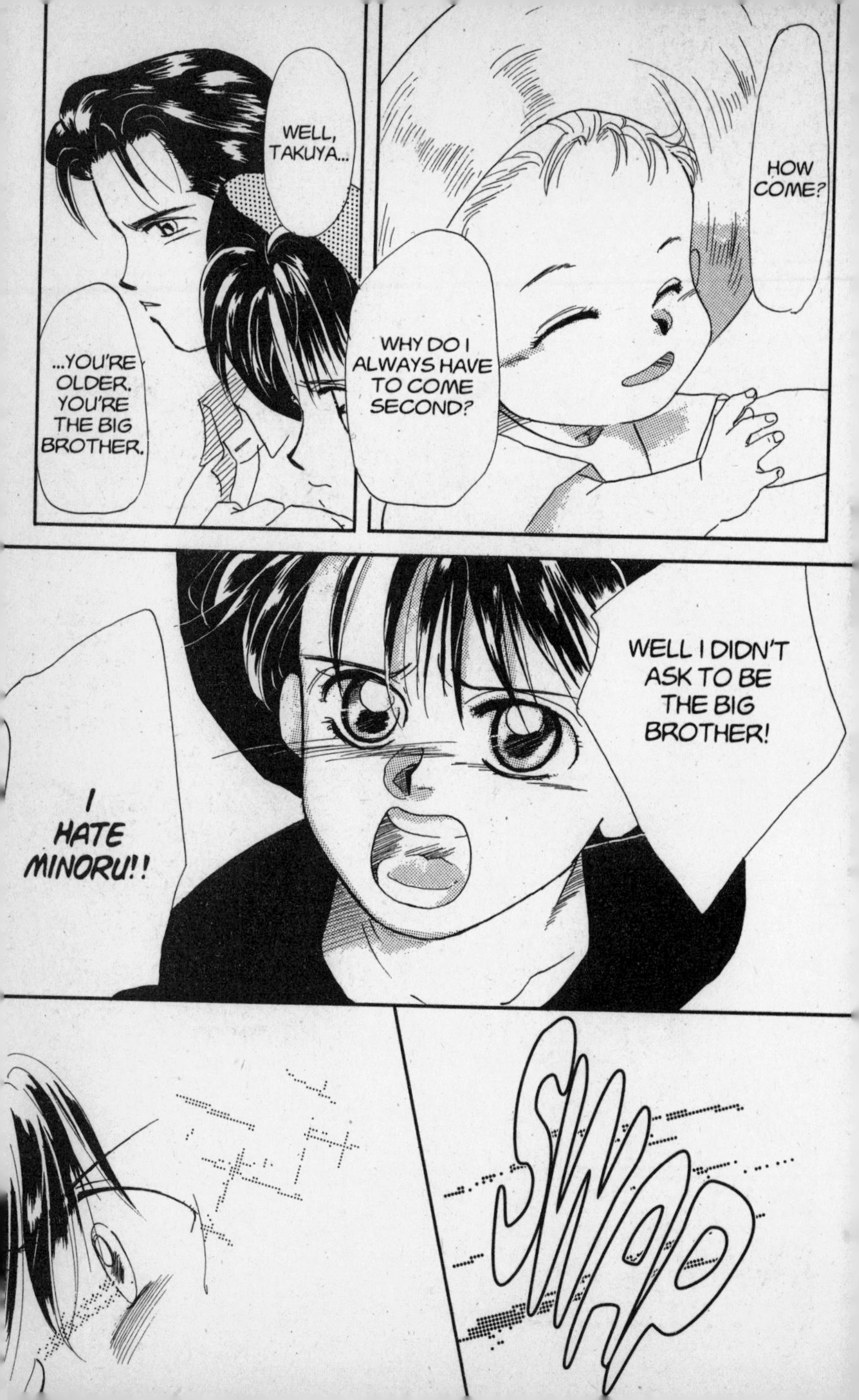
HOW COME?
WHY DO I ALWAYS HAVE TO COME SECOND?
WELL, TAKUYA...
...YOU'RE OLDER. YOU'RE THE BIG BROTHER.
WELL I DIDN'T ASK TO BE THE BIG BROTHER!
I HATE MINORU!!

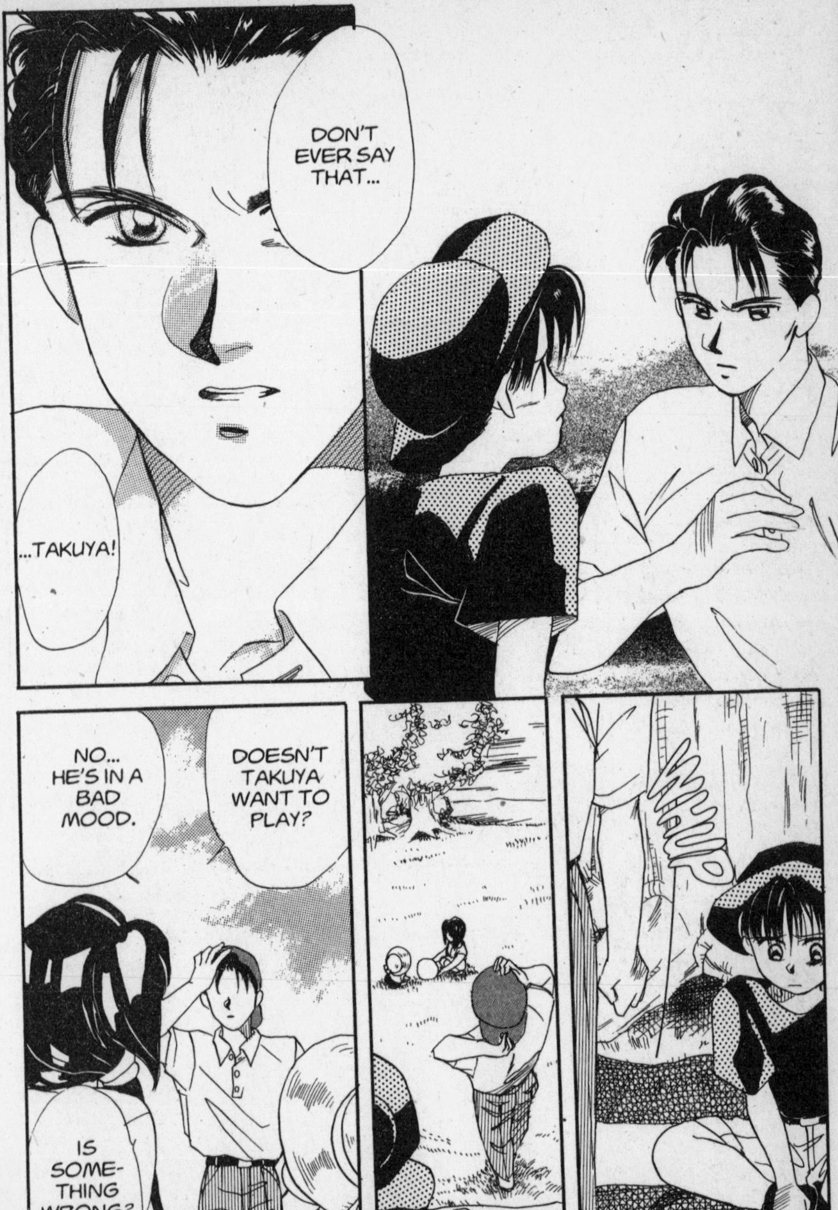
DON'T EVER SAY THAT...
...TAKUYA!
WHAP
DOESN'T TAKUYA WANT TO PLAY?
NO... HE'S IN A BAD MOOD.
IS SOME-THING WRONG?

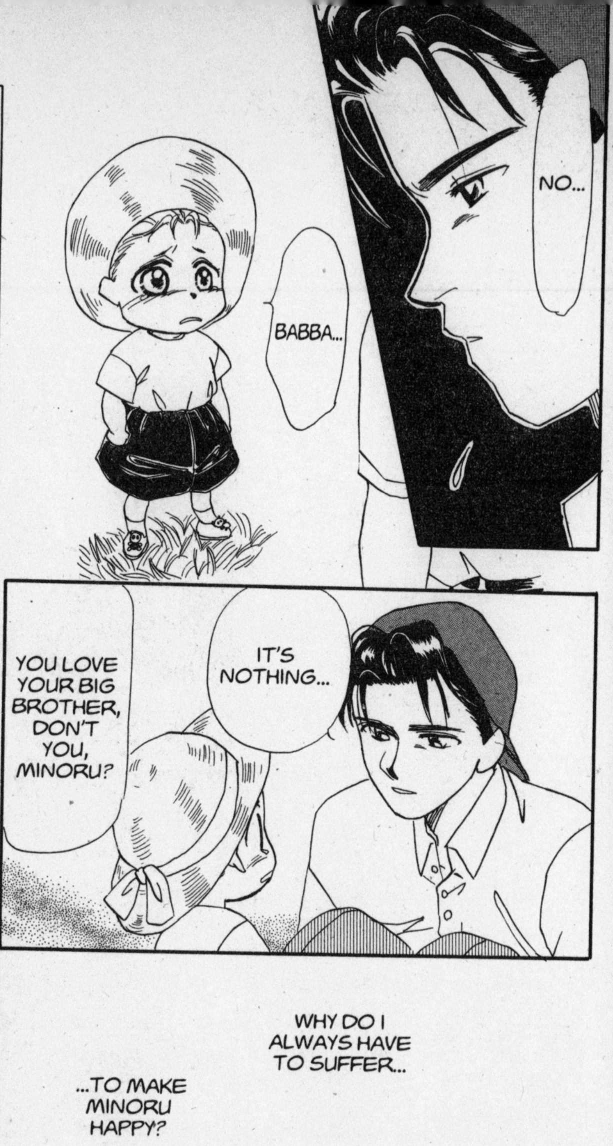
NO...
BABBA...
IT'S NOTHING...
YOU LOVE YOUR BIG BROTHER, DON'T YOU, MINORU?
WHY DO I ALWAYS HAVE TO SUFFER...
...TO MAKE MINORU HAPPY?

AUTHOR'S NOTE 3

About four years ago (it is now 1992), in the animated series Pro Golfer Monkey, there was a handsome character named Kyoshiro Nagare. Do you remember him? I fell in love with him. (I even taped all the shows.) The supporting characters were good-looking too, in a strange way. (Like Benibachi...) Anyway, Nagare had heart trouble, so he would stumble a lot when he was golfing. There was a preview scene where Nagare was in bed, writhing in pain, but to me it always looked like he was in ecstasy.

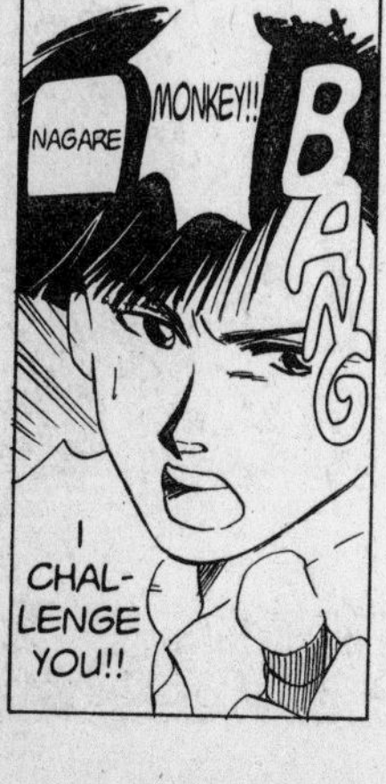
BANG
MONKEY!!
NAGARE
I CHALLENGE YOU!!

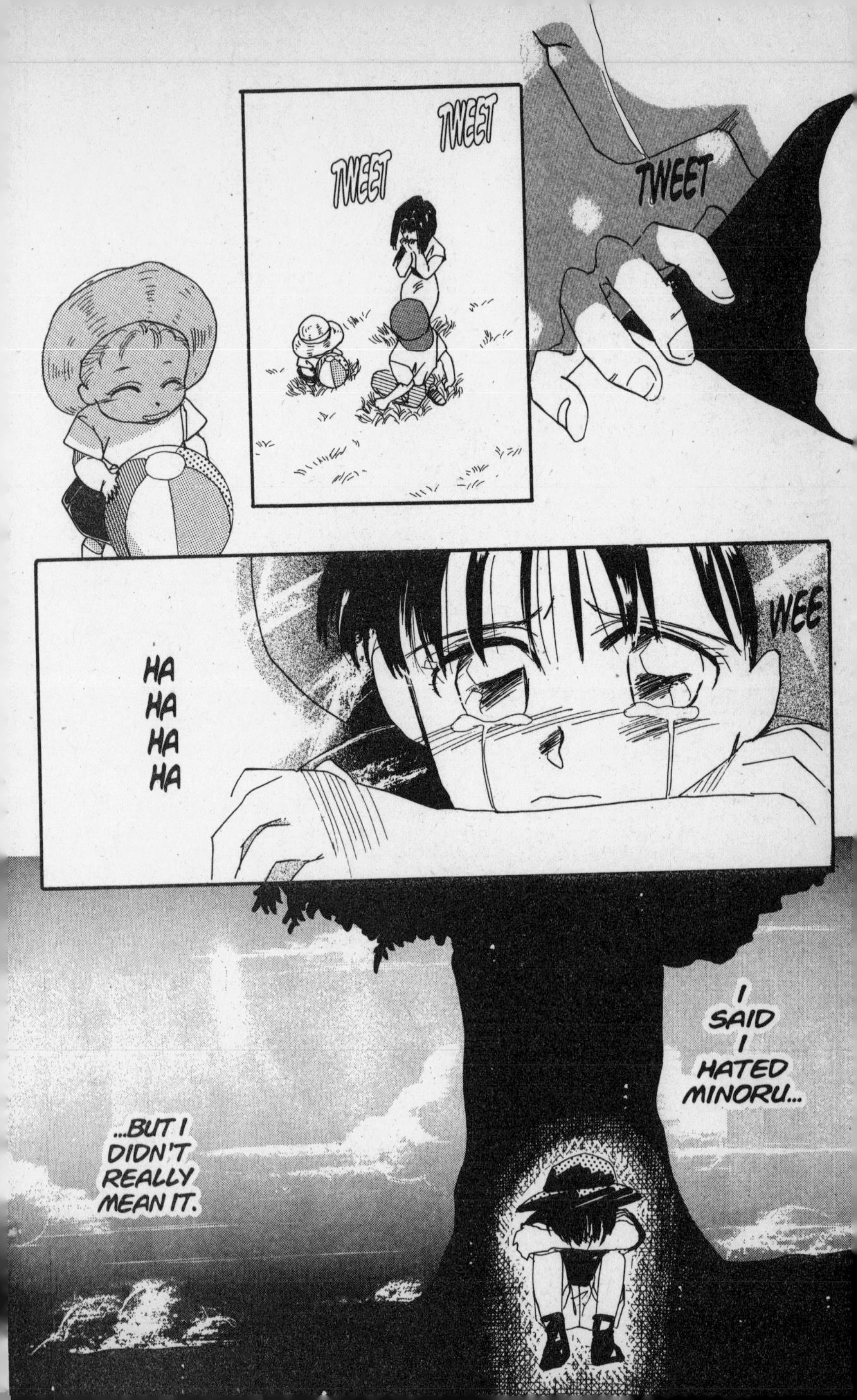
TWEET
TWEET
TWEET
WEE
HA HA HA HA
I SAID I HATED MINORU...
...BUT I DIDN'T REALLY MEAN IT.

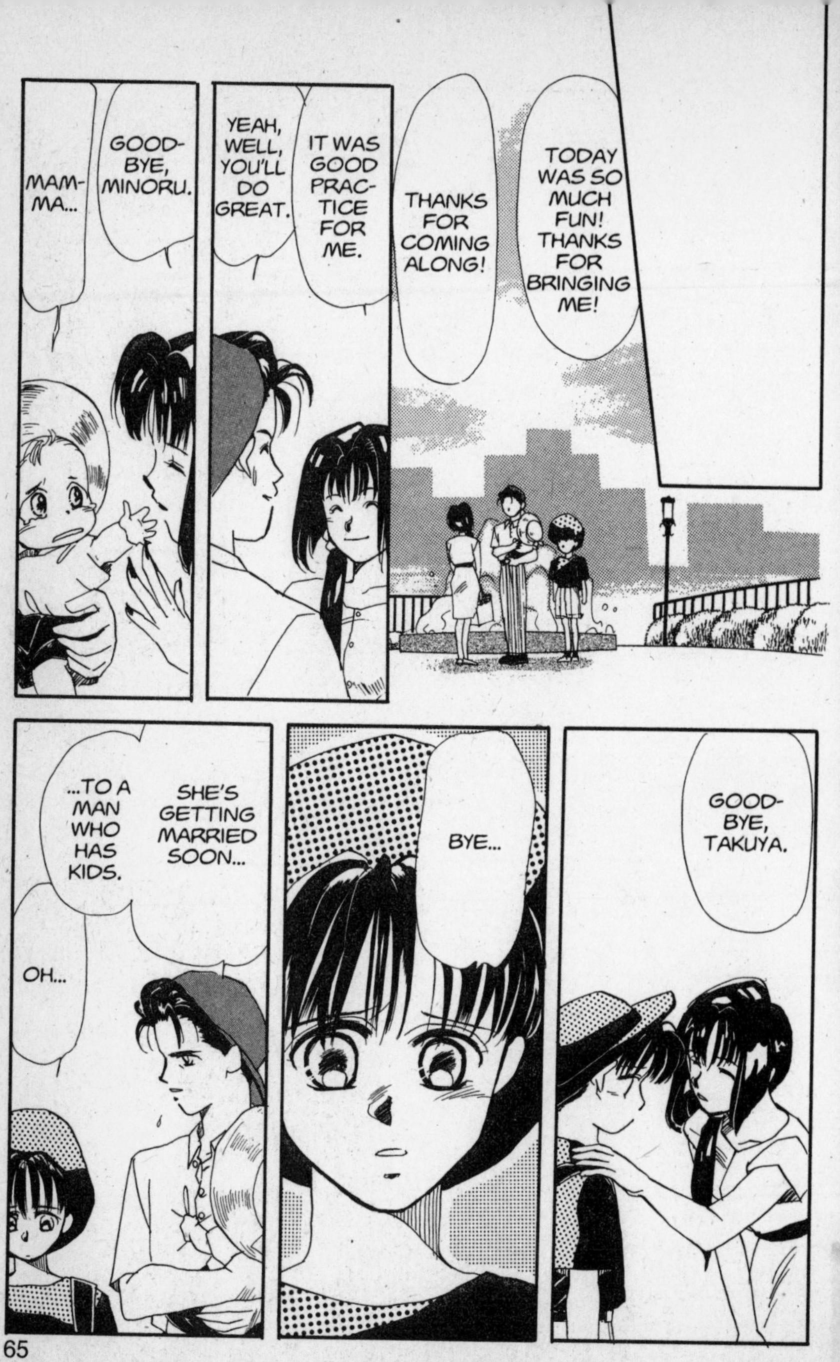
TODAY WAS SO MUCH FUN! THANKS FOR BRINGING ME!
THANKS FOR COMING ALONG!
IT WAS GOOD PRAC-TICE FOR ME.
YEAH, WELL, YOU'LL DO GREAT.
GOOD-BYE, MINORU.
MAM-MA...
GOOD-BYE, TAKUYA.
BYE...
SHE'S GETTING MARRIED SOON...
...TO A MAN WHO HAS KIDS.
OH...

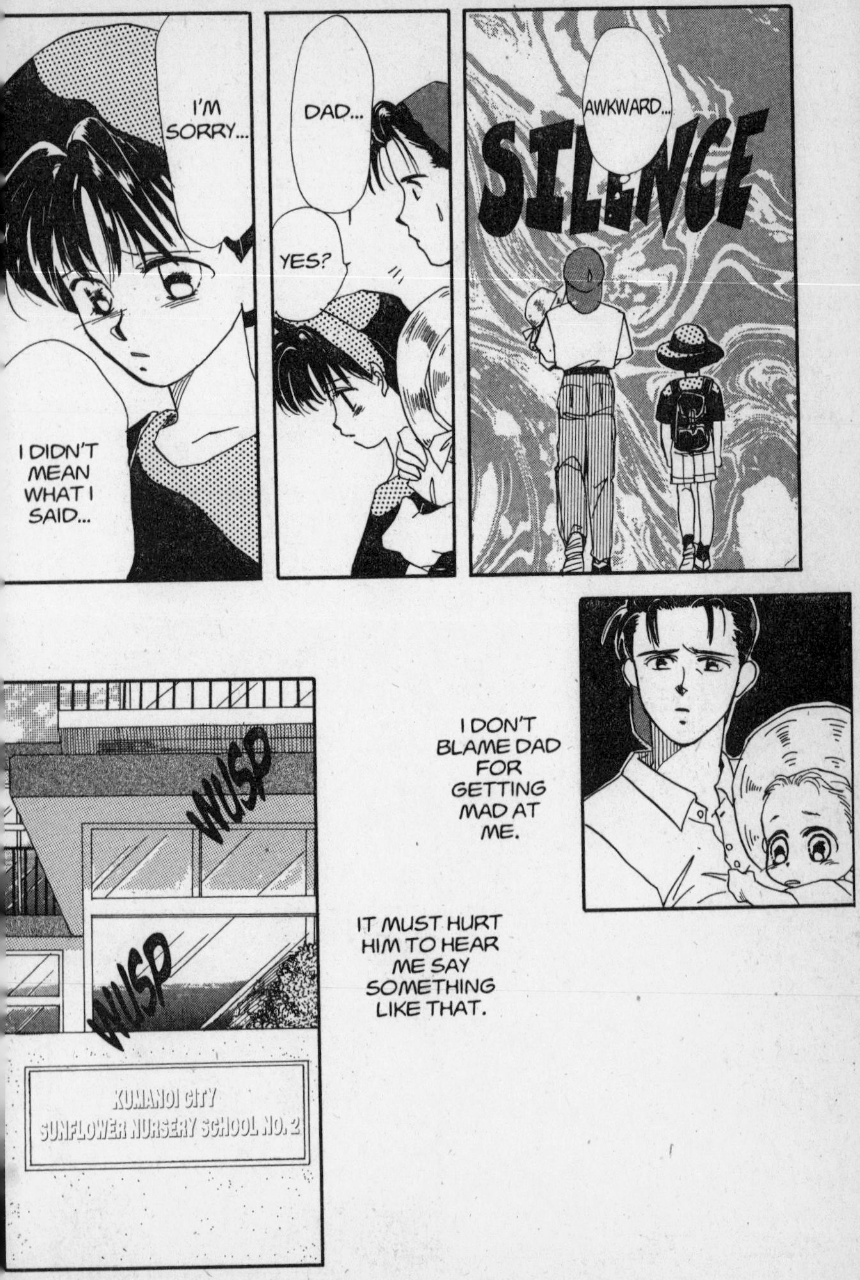
AWKWARD...
SILENCE
DAD...
YES?
I'M SORRY...
I DIDN'T MEAN WHAT I SAID...
I DON'T BLAME DAD FOR GETTING MAD AT ME.
IT MUST HURT HIM TO HEAR ME SAY SOMETHING LIKE THAT.
WUSP
WUSP
KUMANOI CITY
SUNFLOWER NURSERY SCHOOL NO. 2

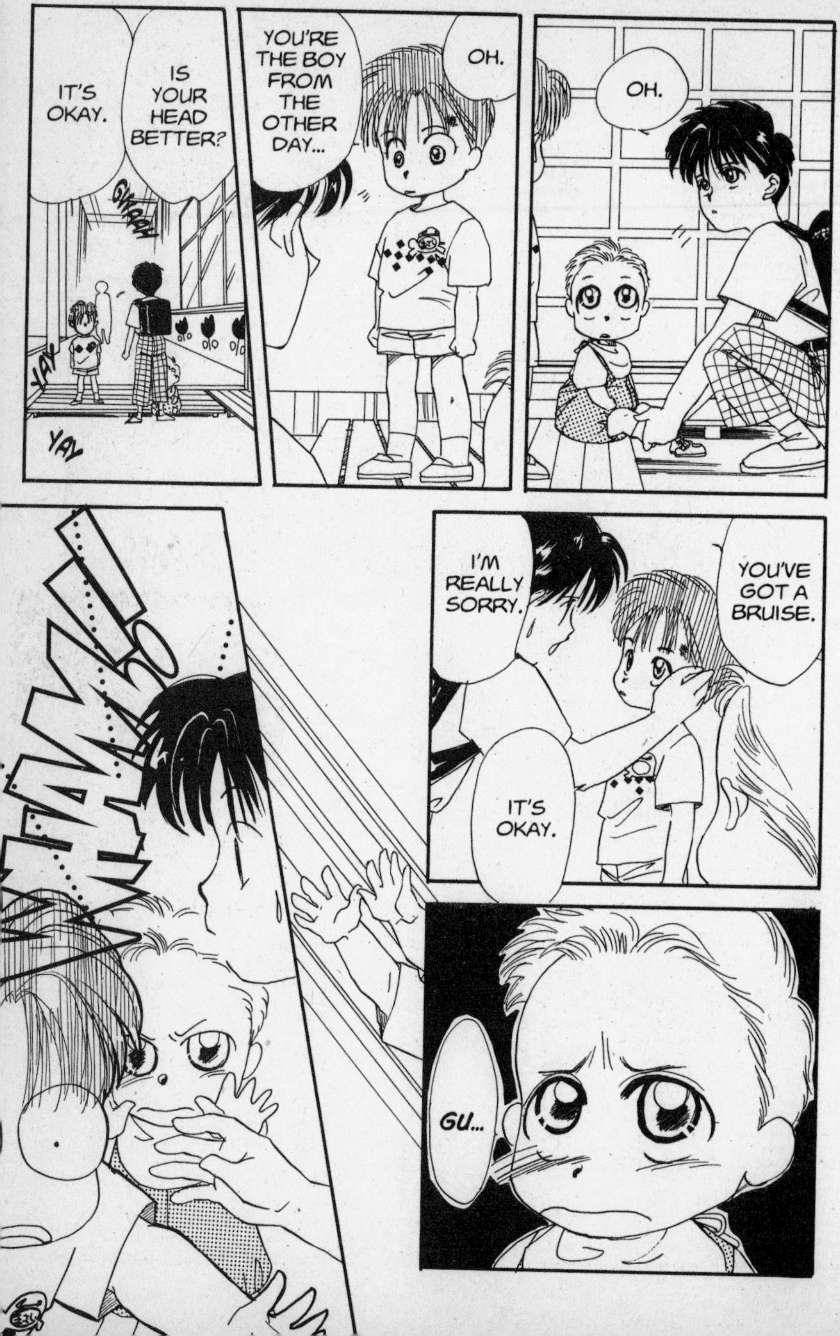
OH.
OH.
YOU'RE THE BOY FROM THE OTHER DAY...
IS YOUR HEAD BETTER?
IT'S OKAY.
YAY
YAY
YOU'VE GOT A BRUISE.
I'M REALLY SORRY.
IT'S OKAY.
GU...

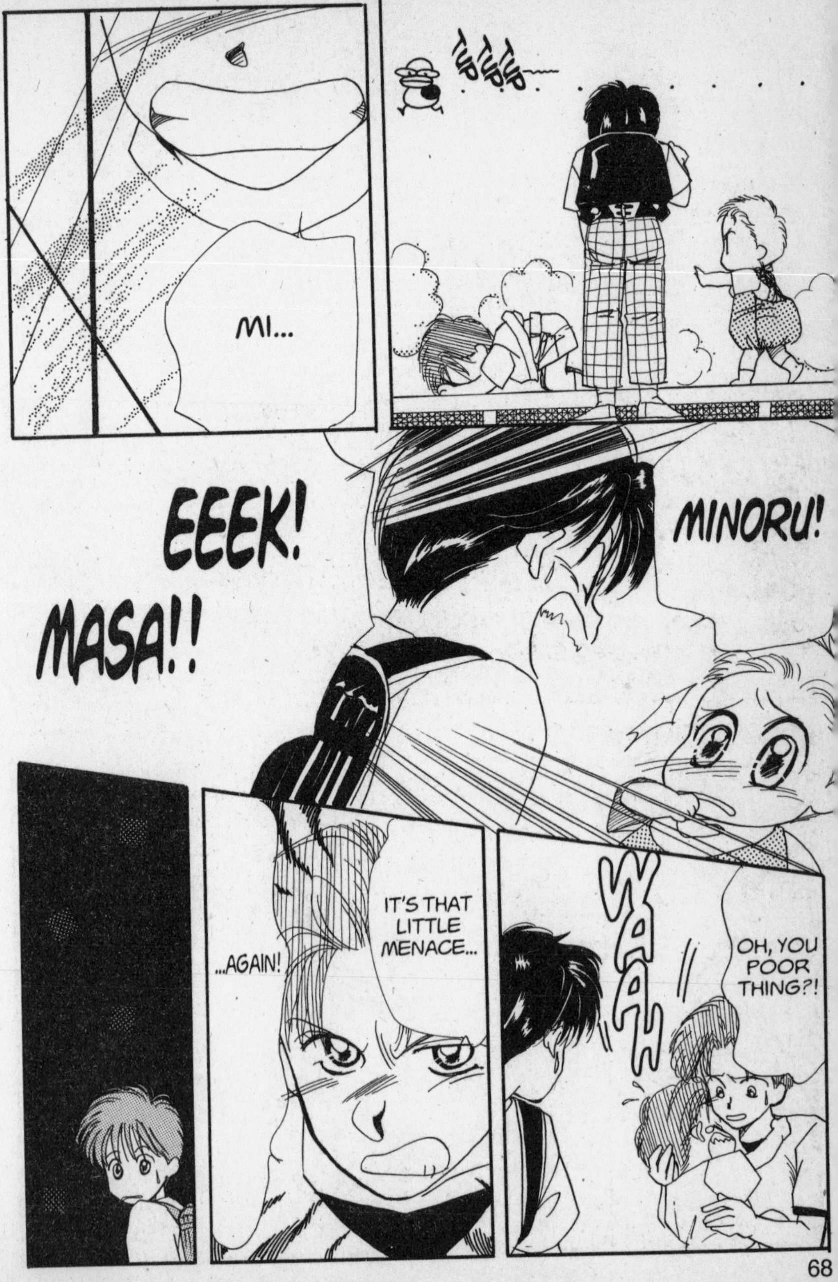
TUP TUP TUP
MI...
MINORU!
EEEK!
MASA!!
WAAH
OH, YOU POOR THING?!
IT'S THAT LITTLE MENACE...
...AGAIN!

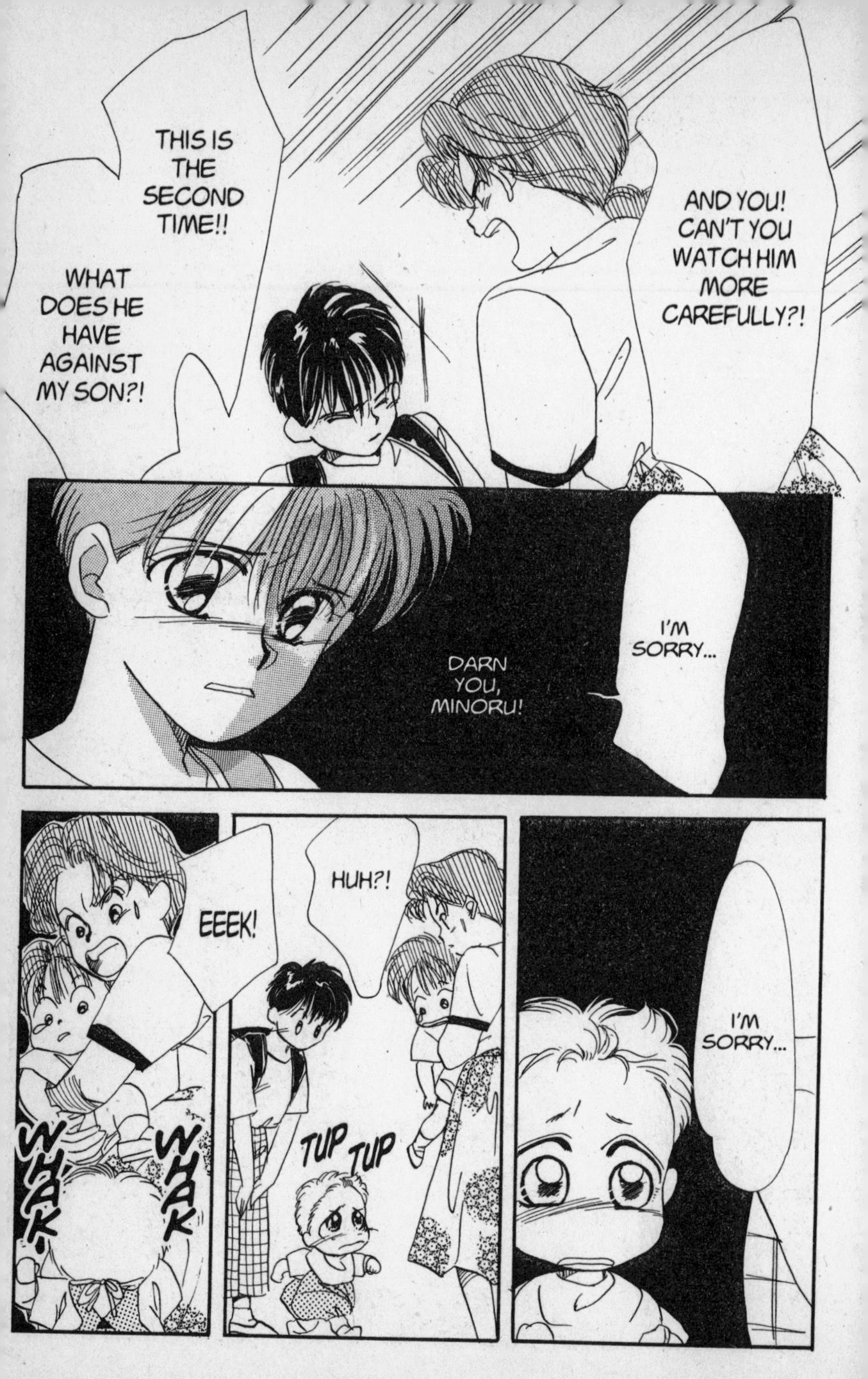
THIS IS THE SECOND TIME!!
WHAT DOES HE HAVE AGAINST MY SON?!
AND YOU! CAN'T YOU WATCH HIM MORE CAREFULLY?!
I'M SORRY...
DARN YOU, MINORU!
I'M SORRY...
HUH?!
TUP TUP
EEEK!
WHAK
WHAK

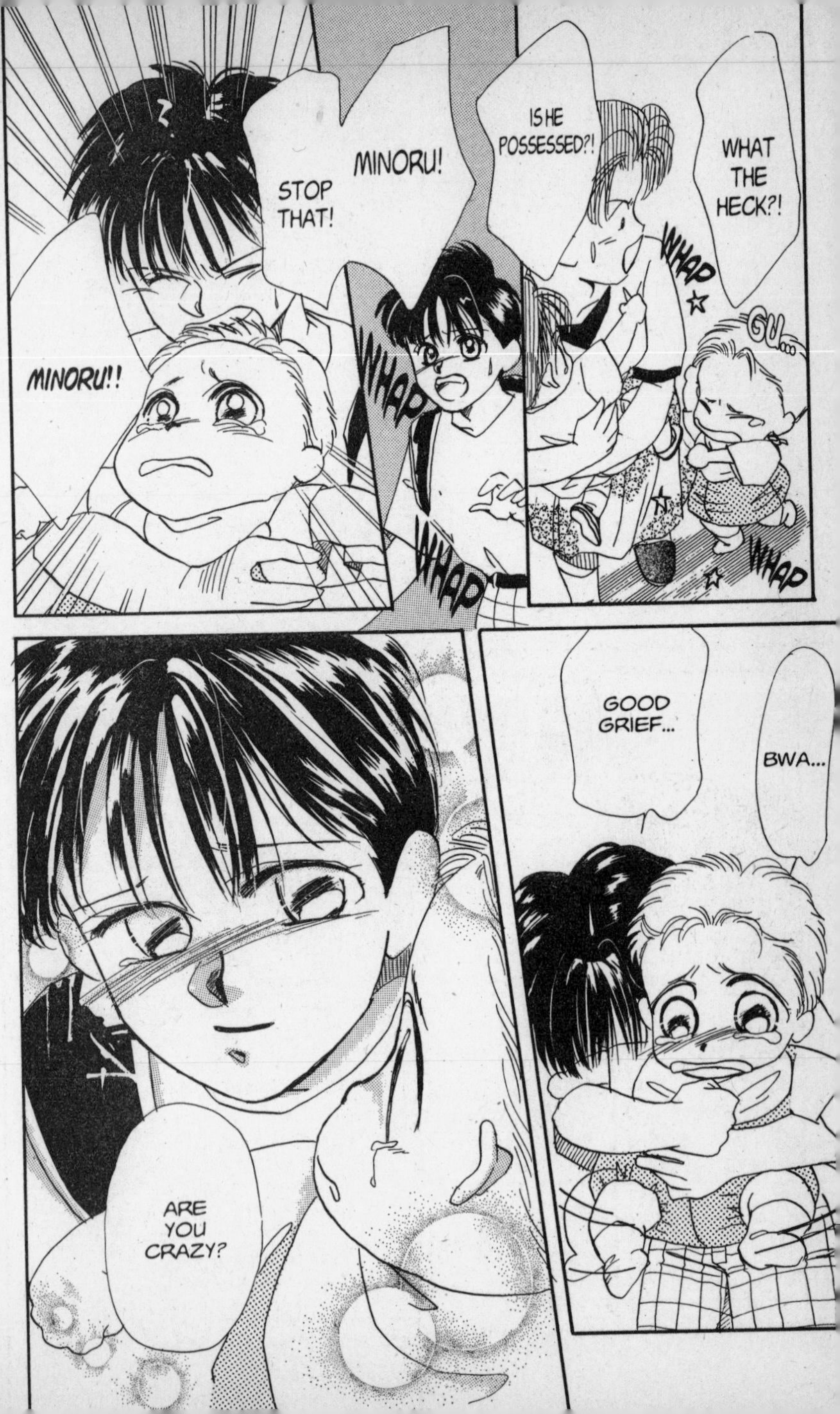
WHAT THE HECK?!
IS HE POSSESSED?!
WHAP
GU...
WHAP
MINORU! STOP THAT!
WHAP
WHAP
MINORU!!
BWA...
GOOD GRIEF...
ARE YOU CRAZY?

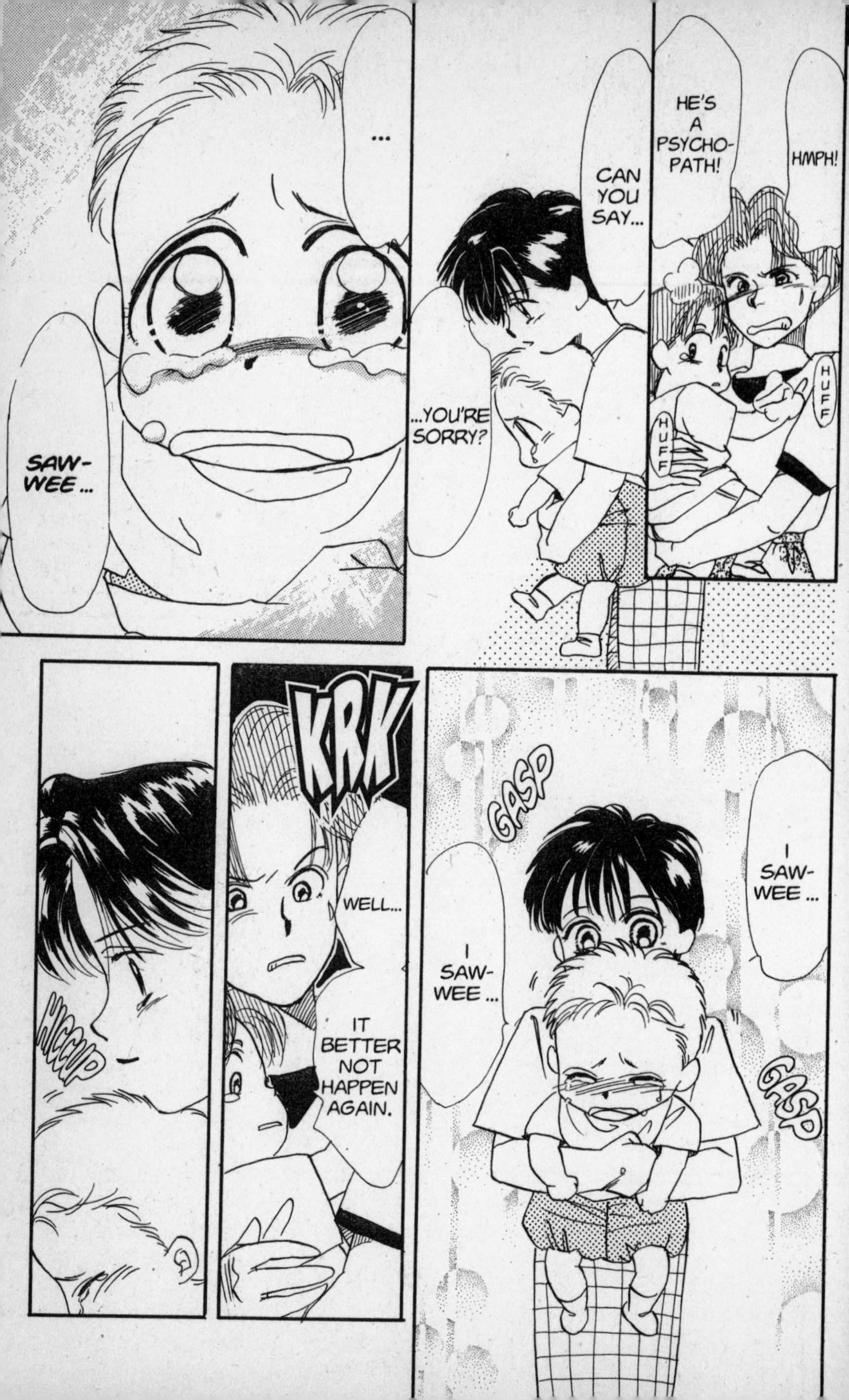
HMPH!
HE'S A PSYCHO-PATH!
HUFF
HUFF
CAN YOU SAY...
...YOU'RE SORRY?
...
SAW-WEE...
I SAW-WEE...
GASP
GASP
I SAW-WEE...
KRK
WELL...
IT BETTER NOT HAPPEN AGAIN.
HICCUP

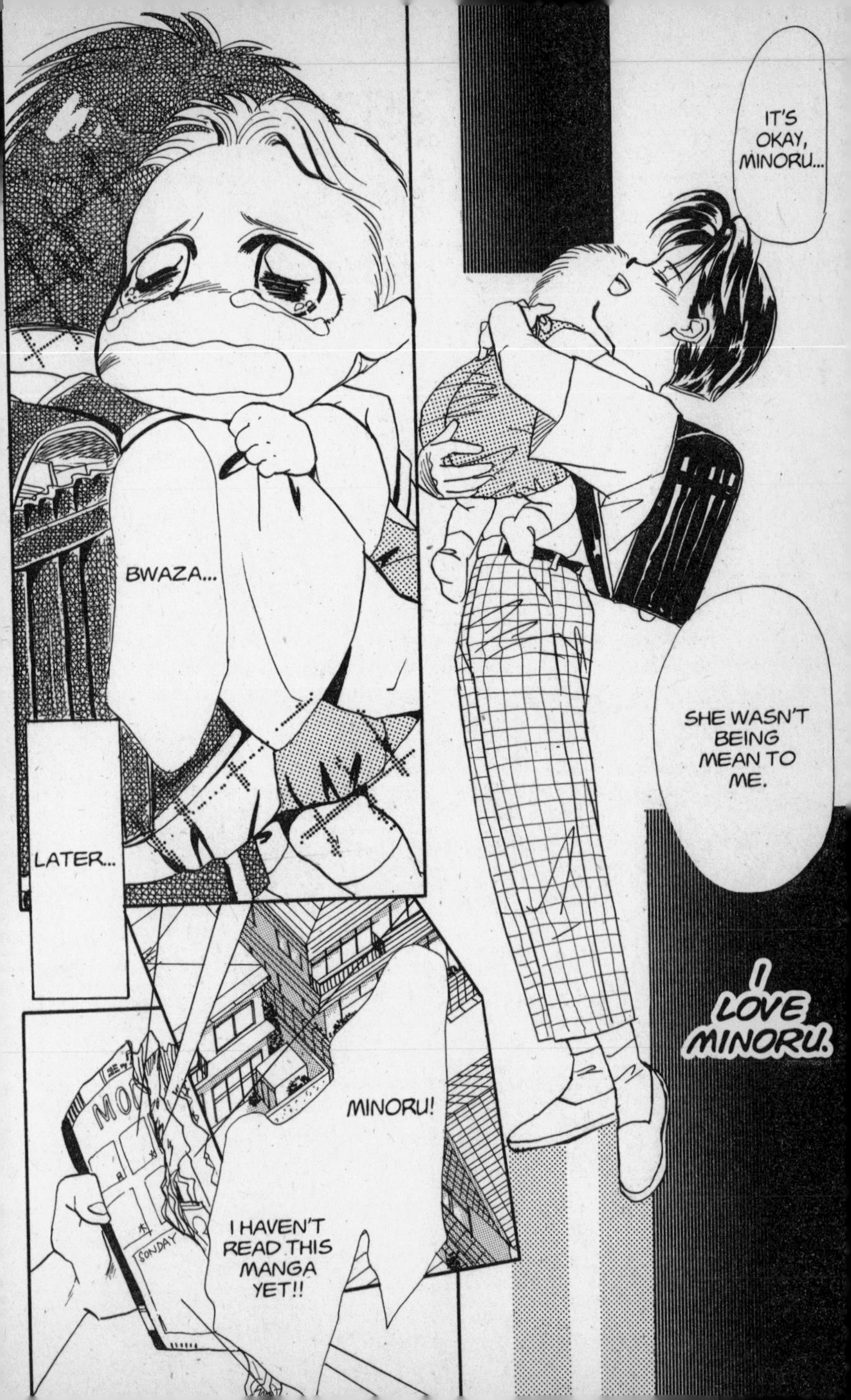
IT'S OKAY, MINORU...
SHE WASN'T BEING MEAN TO ME.
I LOVE MINORU.
BWAZA...
LATER...
MINORU!
I HAVEN'T READ THIS MANGA YET!!

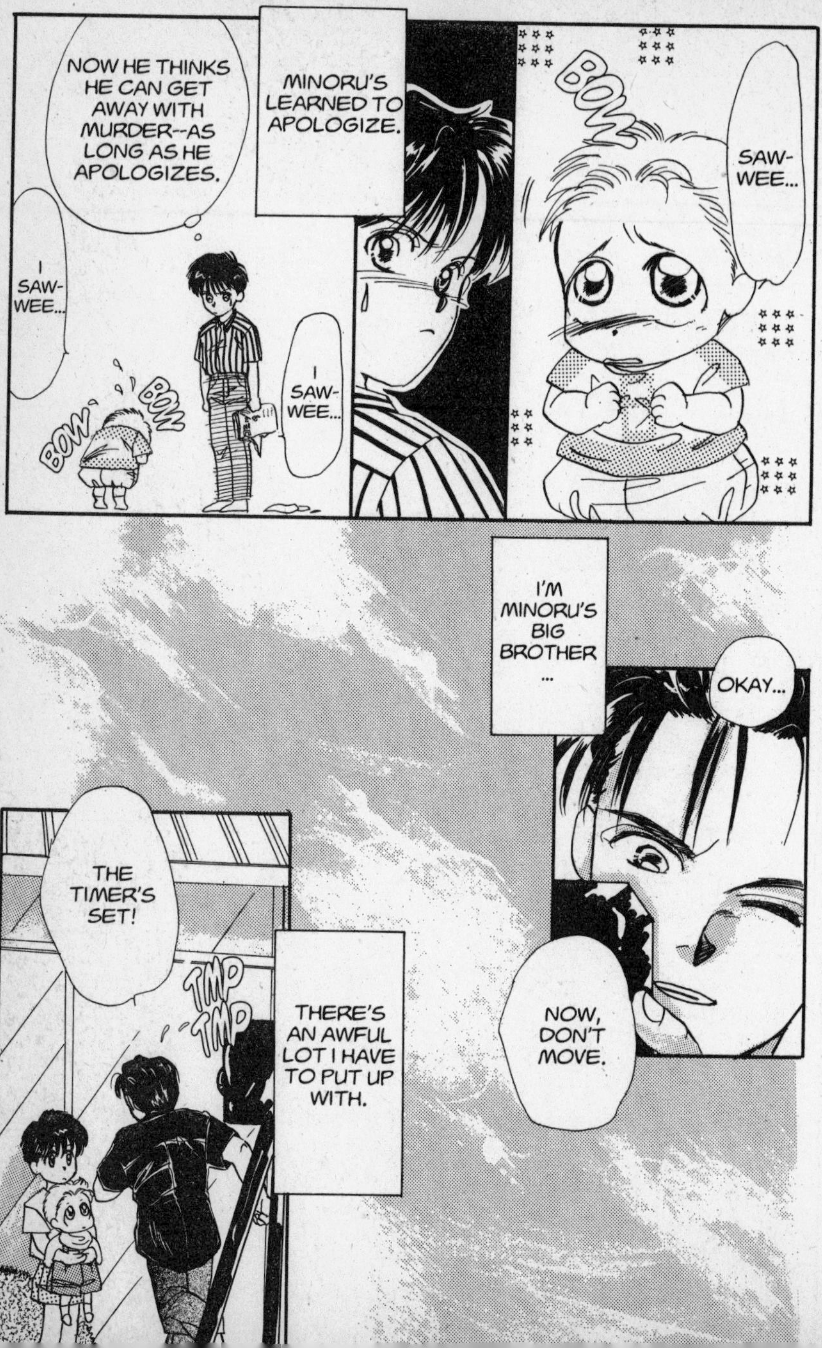
BOW
SAW-WEE...
MINORU'S LEARNED TO APOLOGIZE.
NOW HE THINKS HE CAN GET AWAY WITH MURDER--AS LONG AS HE APOLOGIZES.
I SAW-WEE...
BOW
BOW
I SAW-WEE...
I'M MINORU'S BIG BROTHER ...
OKAY...
NOW, DON'T MOVE.
THERE'S AN AWFUL LOT I HAVE TO PUT UP WITH.
THE TIMER'S SET!
TMP TMP

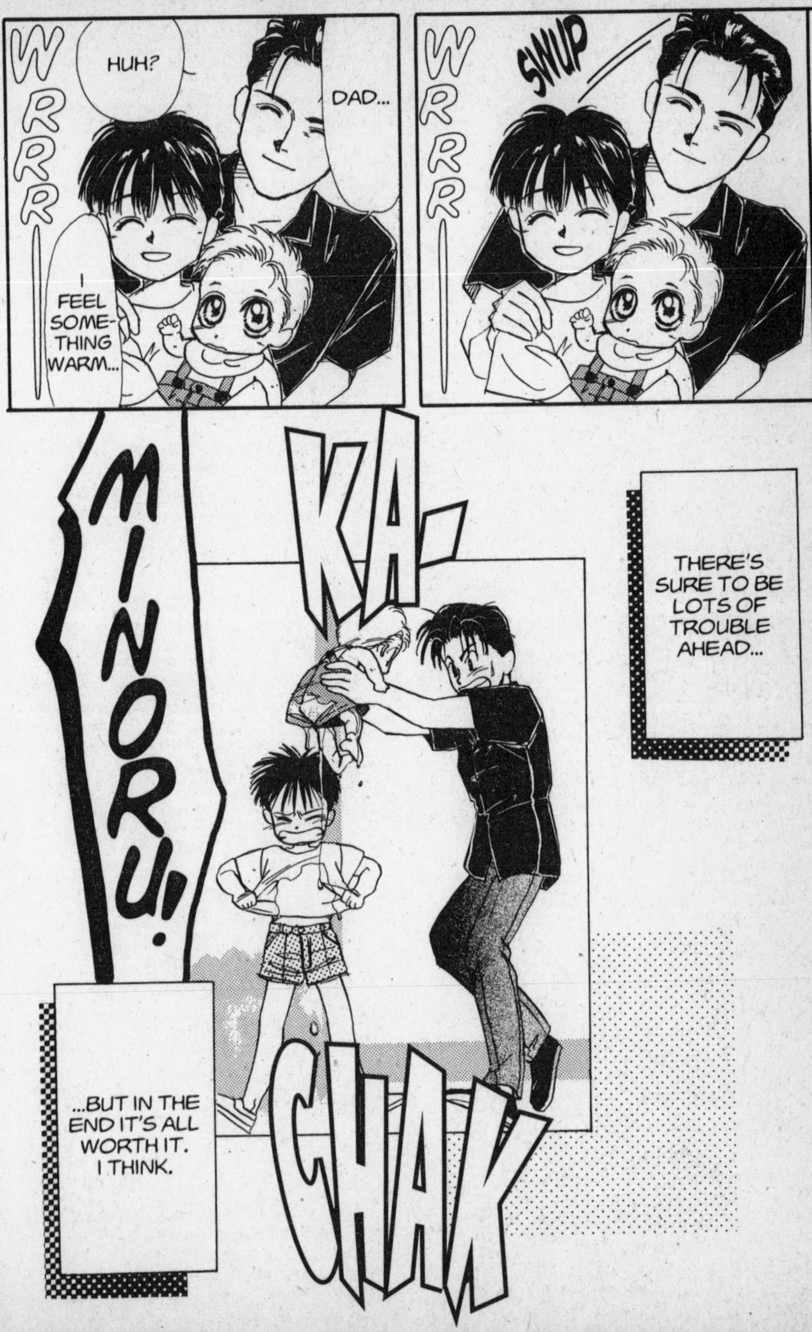
SWUP
WRRR
DAD...
HUH?
WRRR
I FEEL SOMETHING WARM...
THERE'S SURE TO BE LOTS OF TROUBLE AHEAD...
KA-
MINORU!!
CHAK
...BUT IN THE END IT'S ALL WORTH IT. I THINK.

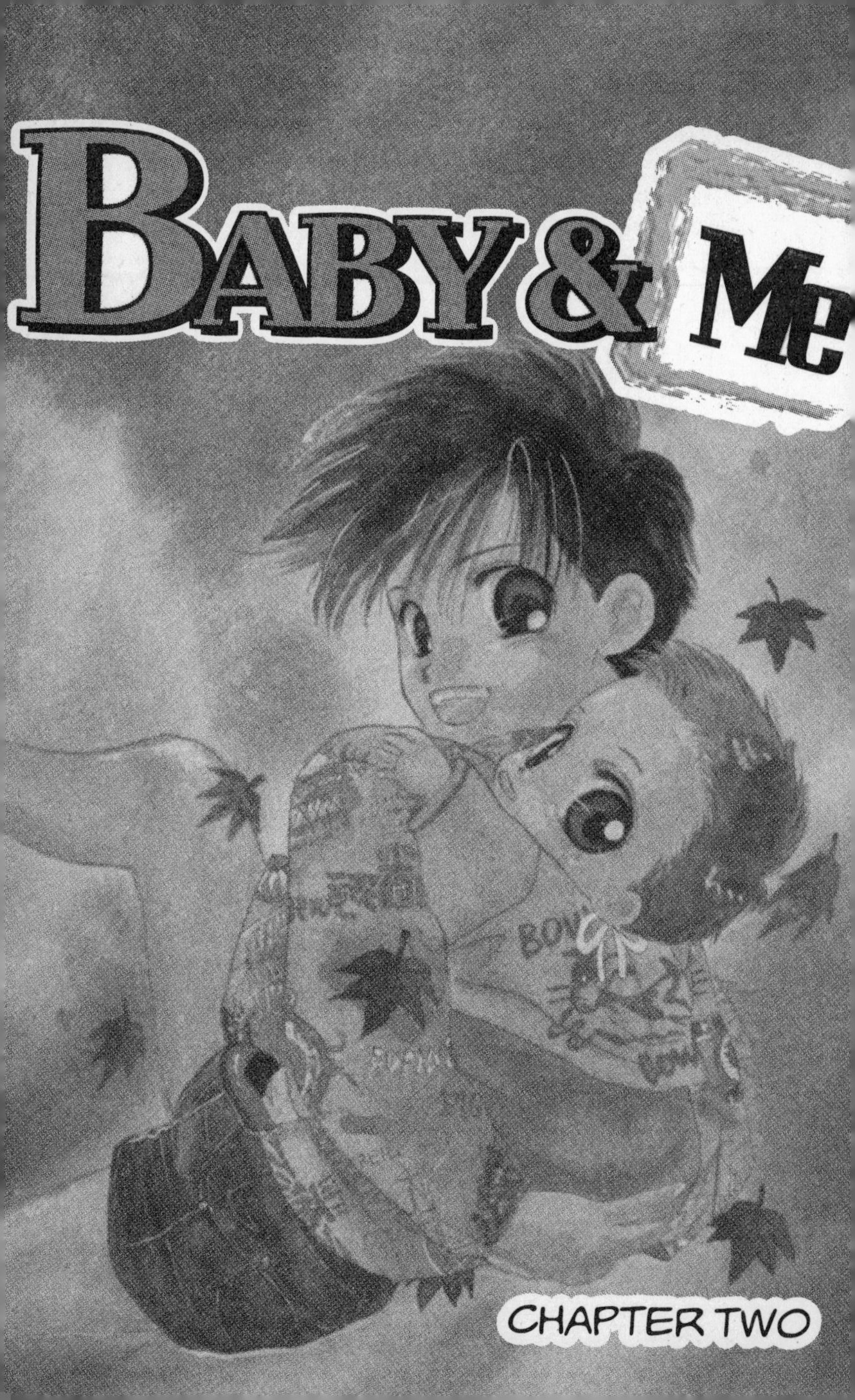
BABY & ME
CHAPTER TWO

Although they are protected animals, the goat antelopes damage forests by eating buds of recently planted cy-

Union trai

Farm laborers lea

A nationwide farm union is scheduled t free courses to its next fiscal year to assist the el the success of s mental training

The Central U cultural Coope the move beca number of its me having problems their farming op

Workers

By ANGELA JEFFS
There was a reason ranging to meet Am pro wrestler Madusa, w real name is Debor Hard Rock Cafe in Ro an image of her loc combat with King hanging off the side building could be a good

But by turning up in whi silk, black leather, the big est of high heels, and a fu amount of gold dangling from her wrists and neck, she soon frustrated that bright idea.

conventional mold. A friend introduced her to "a wild-looking 50-year-old stunt-man." Initially she thought he was "a real sleaze ball." He kept staring, asking if she liked her job, and whether she would rather be in the mov-ies.

"I thou
on to m
wrestl'
which
kno
fas'

s
the '
and th
her c

he was coming
n he suggested
profession in
get myself
ve forward
)h, he means
what a jerk!'
ter I was in a
of the Ameri-
, Association."
ar of touring, of-
in her car, and
it in order to
it, disturbed at
trol from AWA
of objectives in

for a
ut to
n the
offer

stler's
A real
., the
nour;

er
bers
them
loving
experi-
ams.
of Agri-
made
growing
ers are
andling
rations

onth,
throw i
phone r.
from Jap.
"It's e
dream," s
honor. Bac
sport was

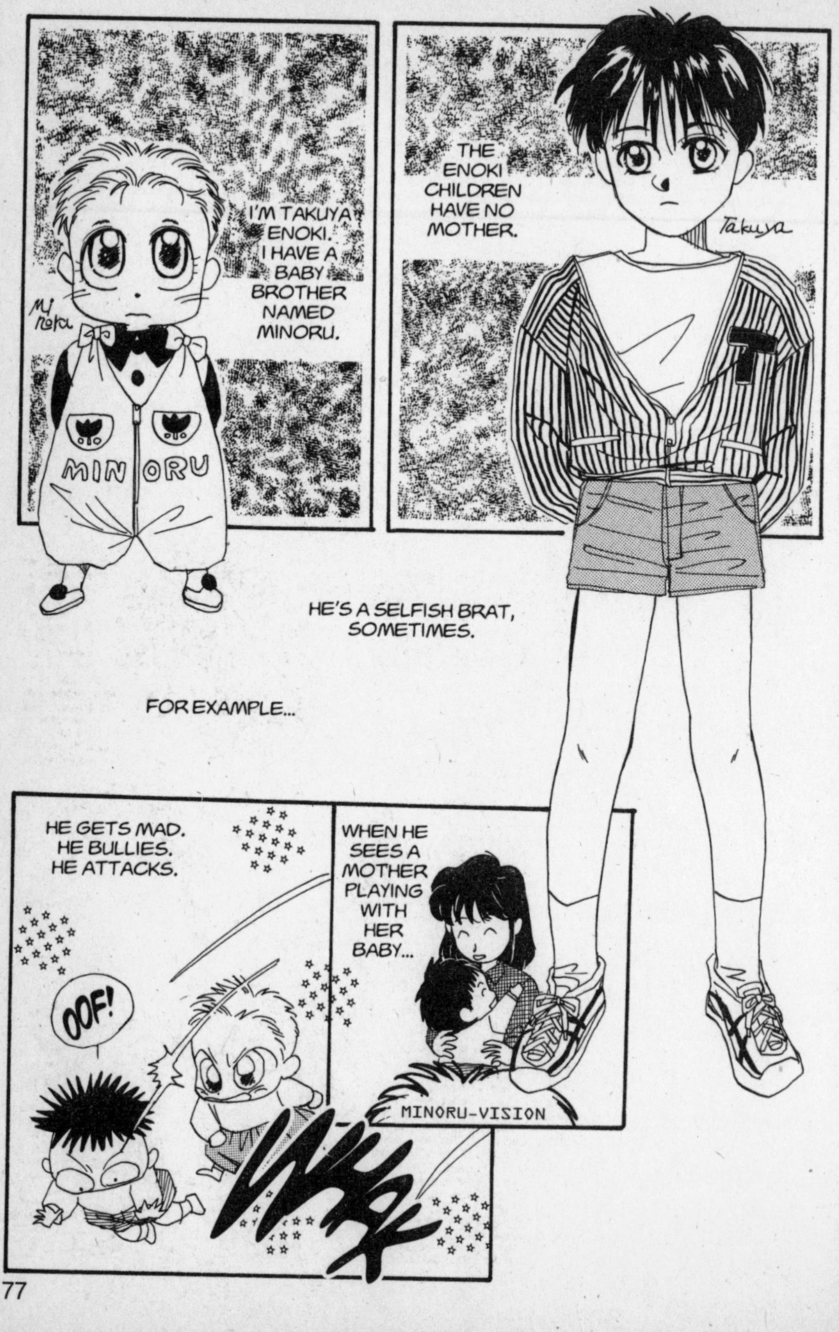
THE ENOKI CHILDREN HAVE NO MOTHER.
Takuya
I'M TAKUYA ENOKI. I HAVE A BABY BROTHER NAMED MINORU.
Minoru
MIN ORU
HE'S A SELFISH BRAT, SOMETIMES.
FOR EXAMPLE...
WHEN HE SEES A MOTHER PLAYING WITH HER BABY...
MINORU-VISION
HE GETS MAD. HE BULLIES. HE ATTACKS.
OOF!
WHAK

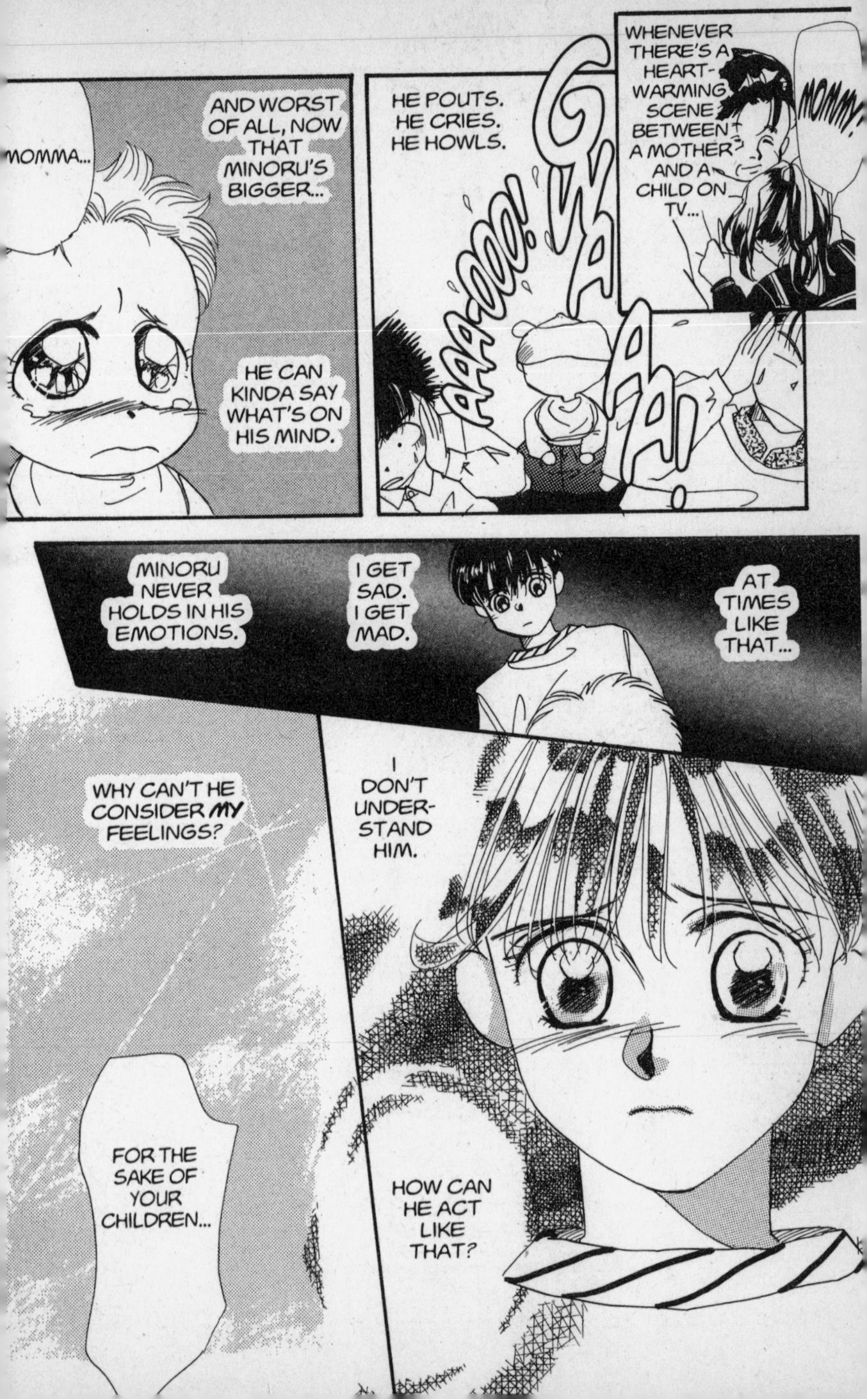
WHENEVER THERE'S A HEART-WARMING SCENE BETWEEN A MOTHER AND A CHILD ON TV...
MOMMY!
HE POUTS. HE CRIES. HE HOWLS.
GYAAA!
AAA-OOO!
AND WORST OF ALL, NOW THAT MINORU'S BIGGER...
MOMMA...
HE CAN KINDA SAY WHAT'S ON HIS MIND.
AT TIMES LIKE THAT...
I GET SAD. I GET MAD.
MINORU NEVER HOLDS IN HIS EMOTIONS.
I DON'T UNDER-STAND HIM.
HOW CAN HE ACT LIKE THAT?
WHY CAN'T HE CONSIDER *MY* FEELINGS?
FOR THE SAKE OF YOUR CHILDREN...

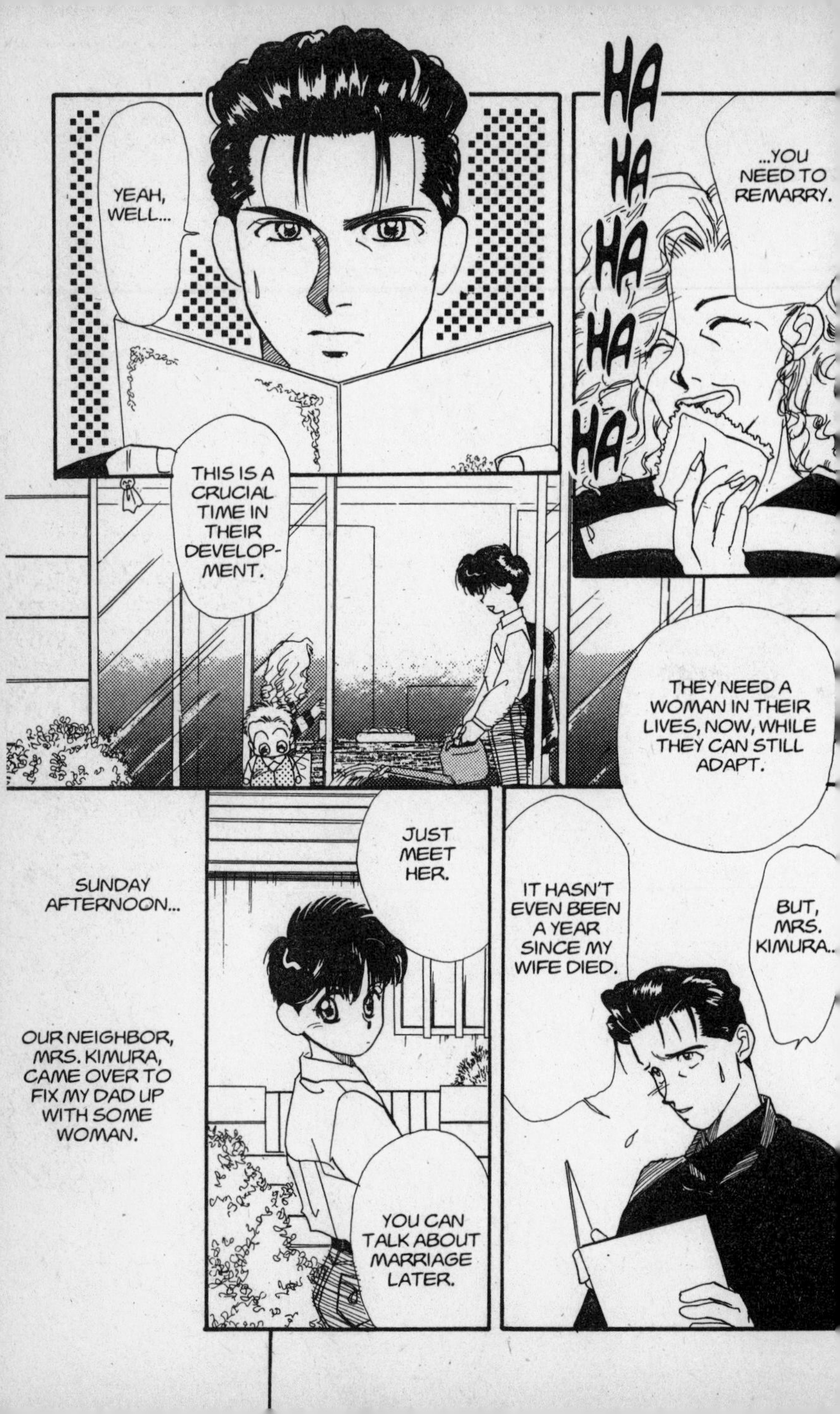
HA HA HA HA HA HA
...YOU NEED TO REMARRY.
YEAH, WELL...
THEY NEED A WOMAN IN THEIR LIVES, NOW, WHILE THEY CAN STILL ADAPT.
THIS IS A CRUCIAL TIME IN THEIR DEVELOPMENT.
BUT, MRS. KIMURA..
IT HASN'T EVEN BEEN A YEAR SINCE MY WIFE DIED.
JUST MEET HER.
YOU CAN TALK ABOUT MARRIAGE LATER.
SUNDAY AFTERNOON...
OUR NEIGHBOR, MRS. KIMURA, CAME OVER TO FIX MY DAD UP WITH SOME WOMAN.

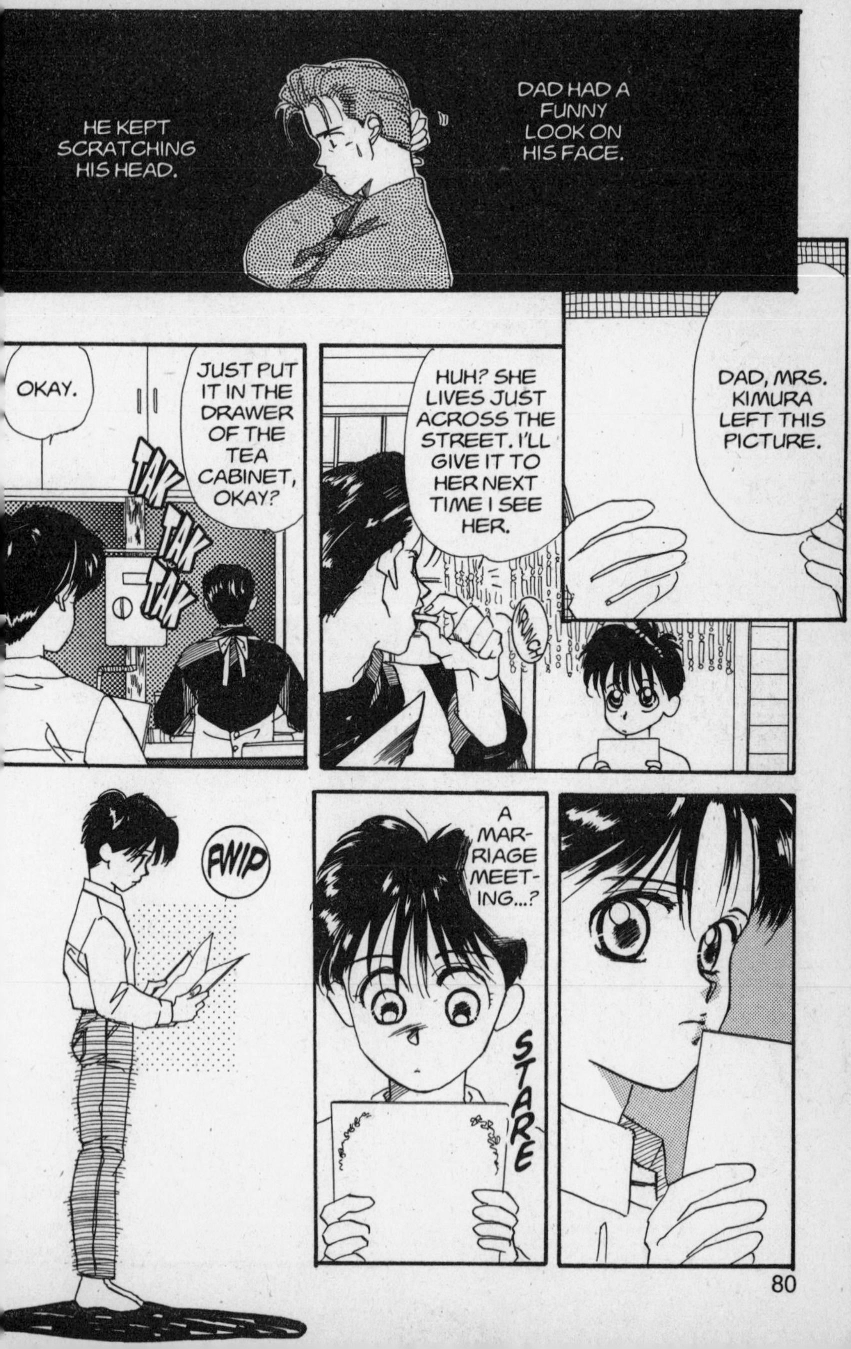
DAD HAD A FUNNY LOOK ON HIS FACE.
HE KEPT SCRATCHING HIS HEAD.
DAD, MRS. KIMURA LEFT THIS PICTURE.
HUH? SHE LIVES JUST ACROSS THE STREET. I'LL GIVE IT TO HER NEXT TIME I SEE HER.
CRUNCH
JUST PUT IT IN THE DRAWER OF THE TEA CABINET, OKAY?
TAK TAK TAK
OKAY.
A MAR-RIAGE MEET-ING...?
STARE
FWIP

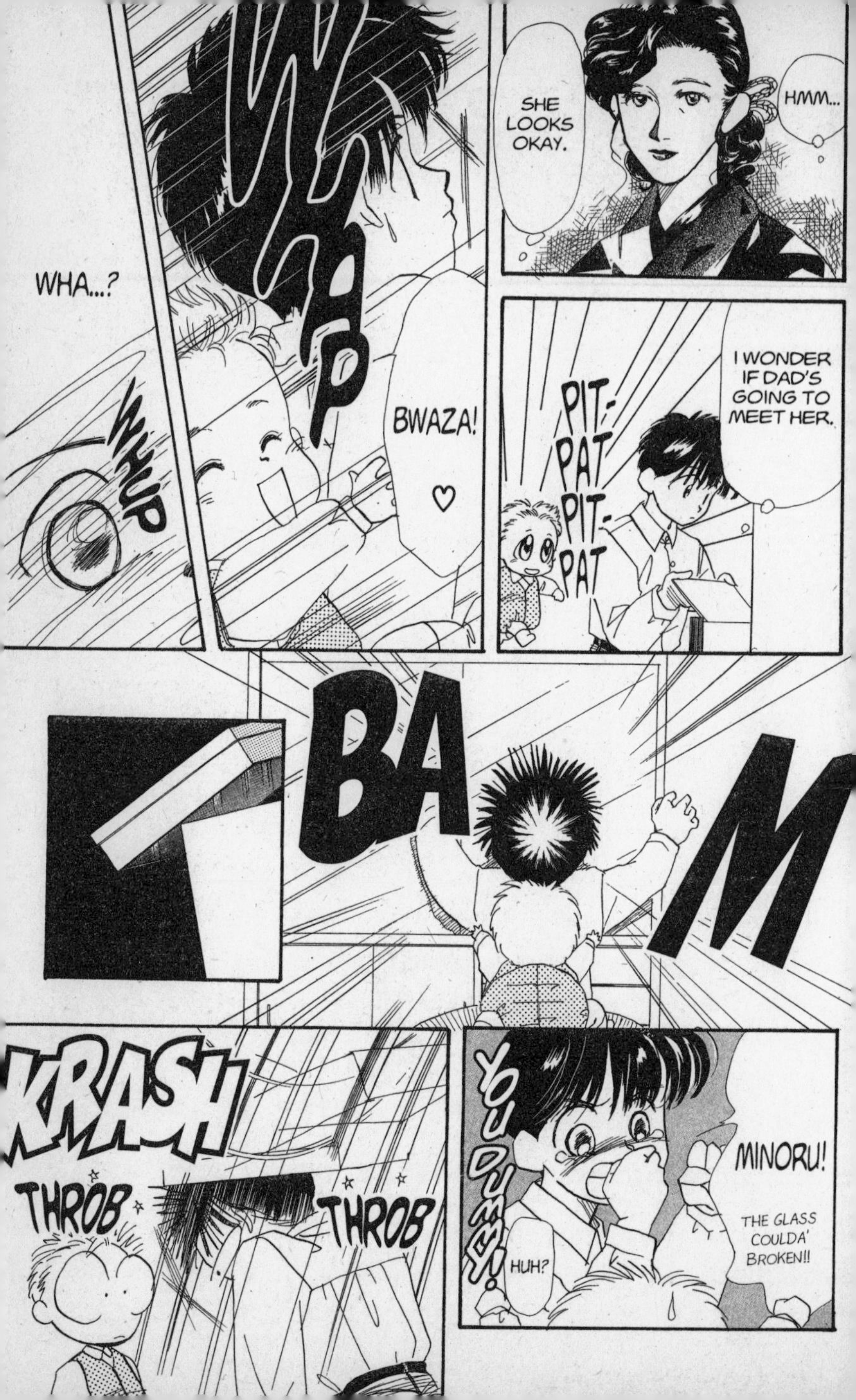
HMM...
SHE LOOKS OKAY.
I WONDER IF DAD'S GOING TO MEET HER.
PIT-PAT PIT-PAT
BWAZA!
♥
WHAP
WHUP
WHA...?
BAM
MINORU!
THE GLASS COULDA' BROKEN!!
YOU DUMMY!
HUH?
KRASH
THROB
THROB

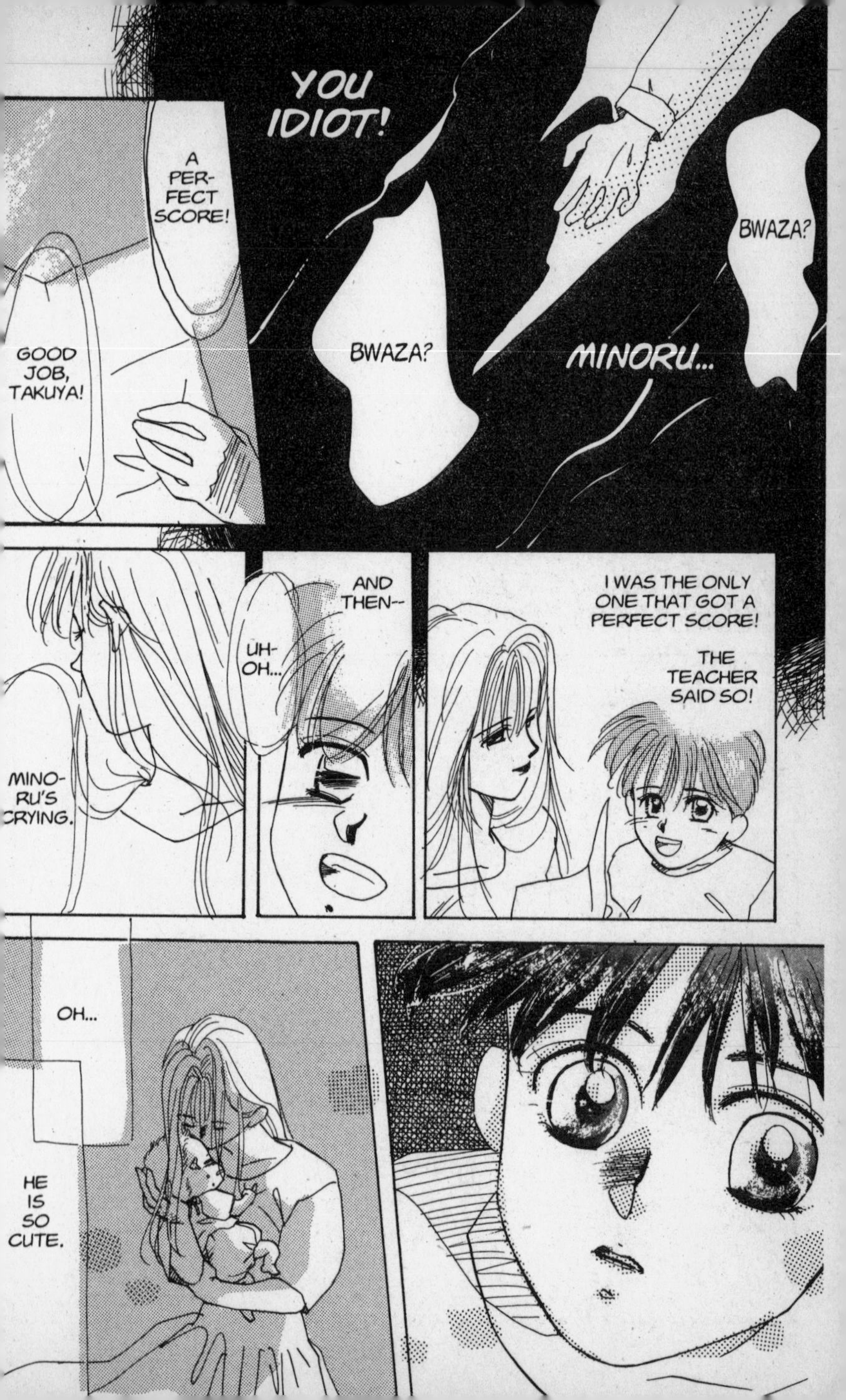
YOU IDIOT!
BWAZA?
MINORU...
BWAZA?
A PERFECT SCORE!
GOOD JOB, TAKUYA!
I WAS THE ONLY ONE THAT GOT A PERFECT SCORE!
THE TEACHER SAID SO!
AND THEN--
UH-OH...
MINORU'S CRYING.
OH...
HE IS SO CUTE.

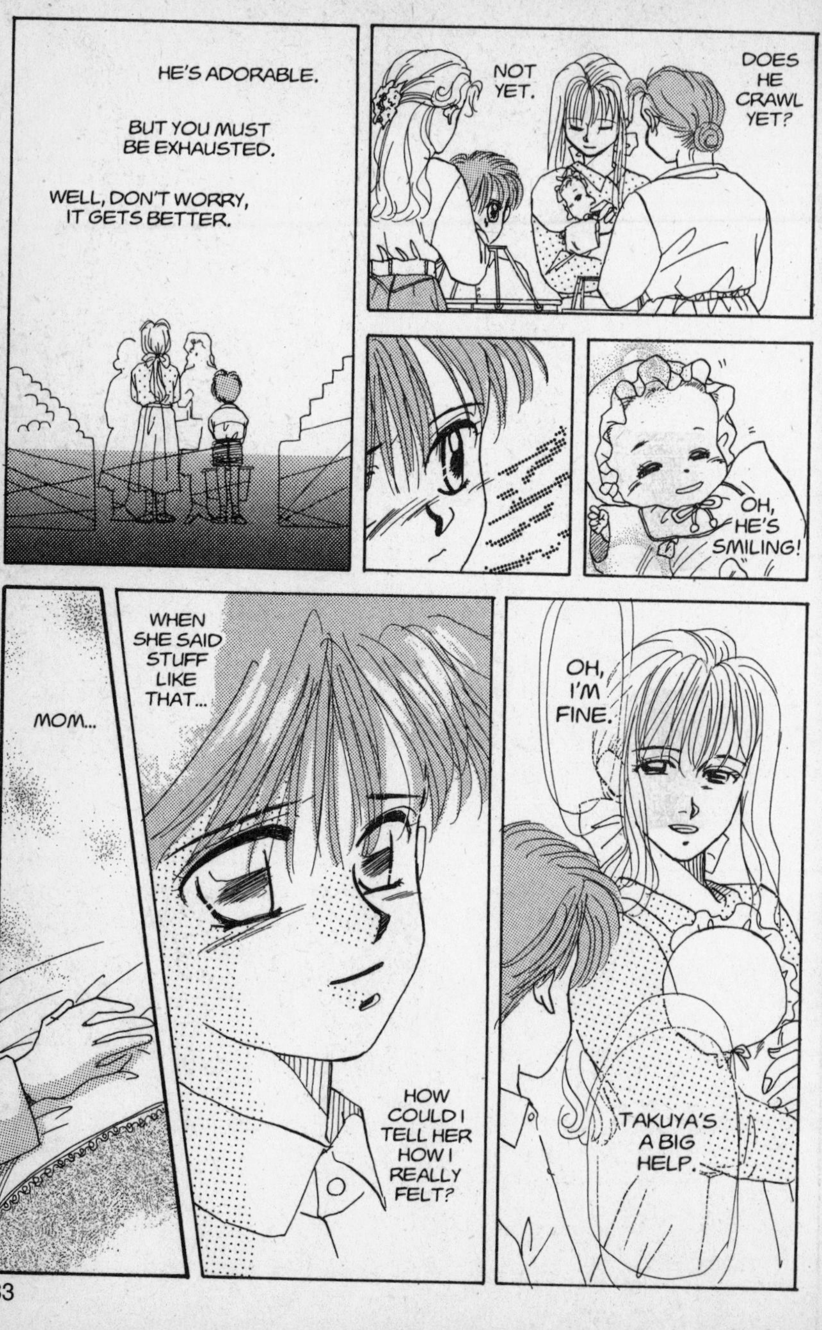
DOES HE CRAWL YET?
NOT YET.
OH, HE'S SMILING!
HE'S ADORABLE.
BUT YOU MUST BE EXHAUSTED.
WELL, DON'T WORRY, IT GETS BETTER.
OH, I'M FINE.
TAKUYA'S A BIG HELP.
WHEN SHE SAID STUFF LIKE THAT...
HOW COULD I TELL HER HOW I REALLY FELT?
MOM...

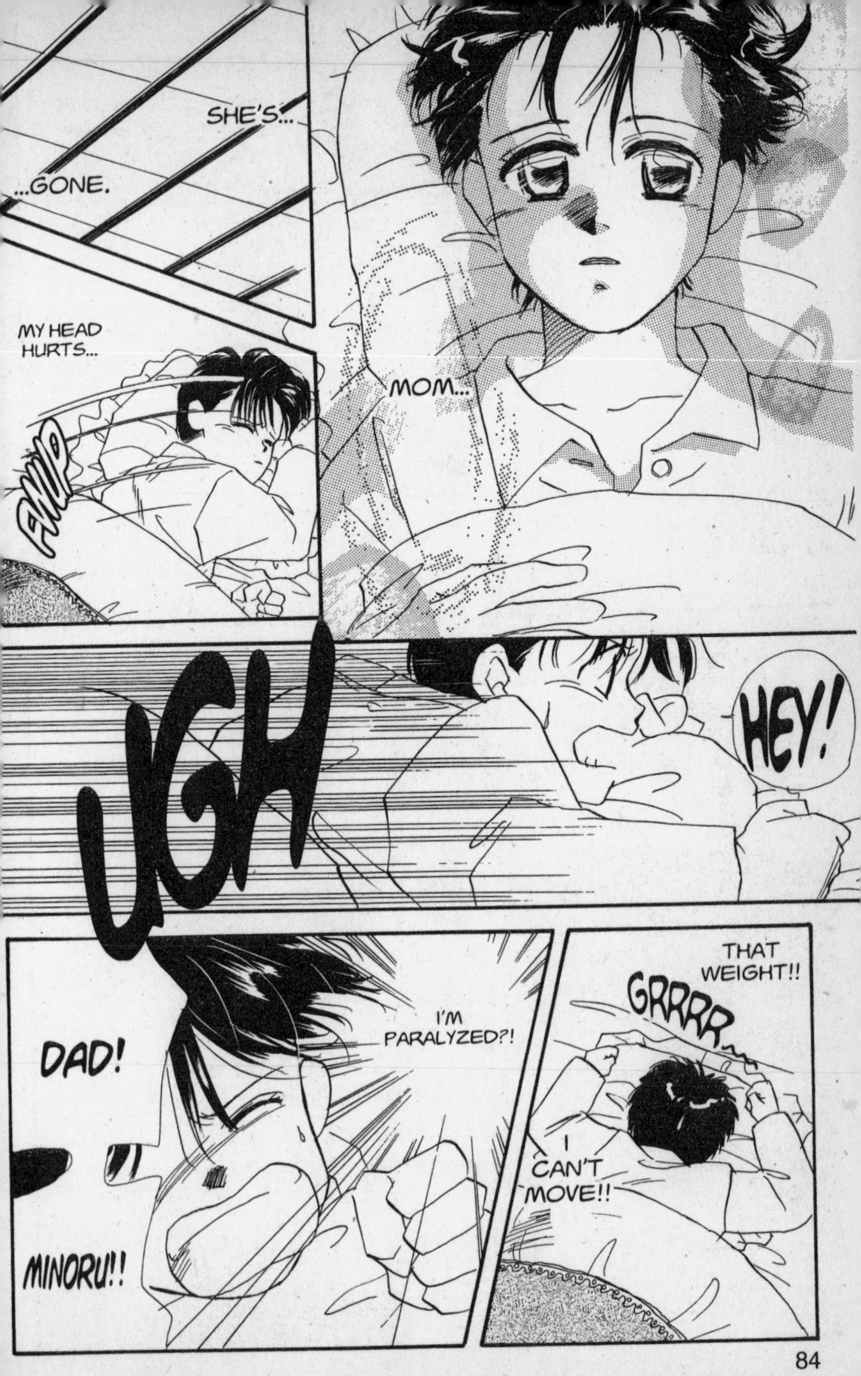
MOM...
SHE'S...
...GONE.
MY HEAD HURTS...
FWUP
HEY!
UGH
THAT WEIGHT!!
GRRRR
I CAN'T MOVE!!
I'M PARALYZED?!
DAD!
MINORU!!

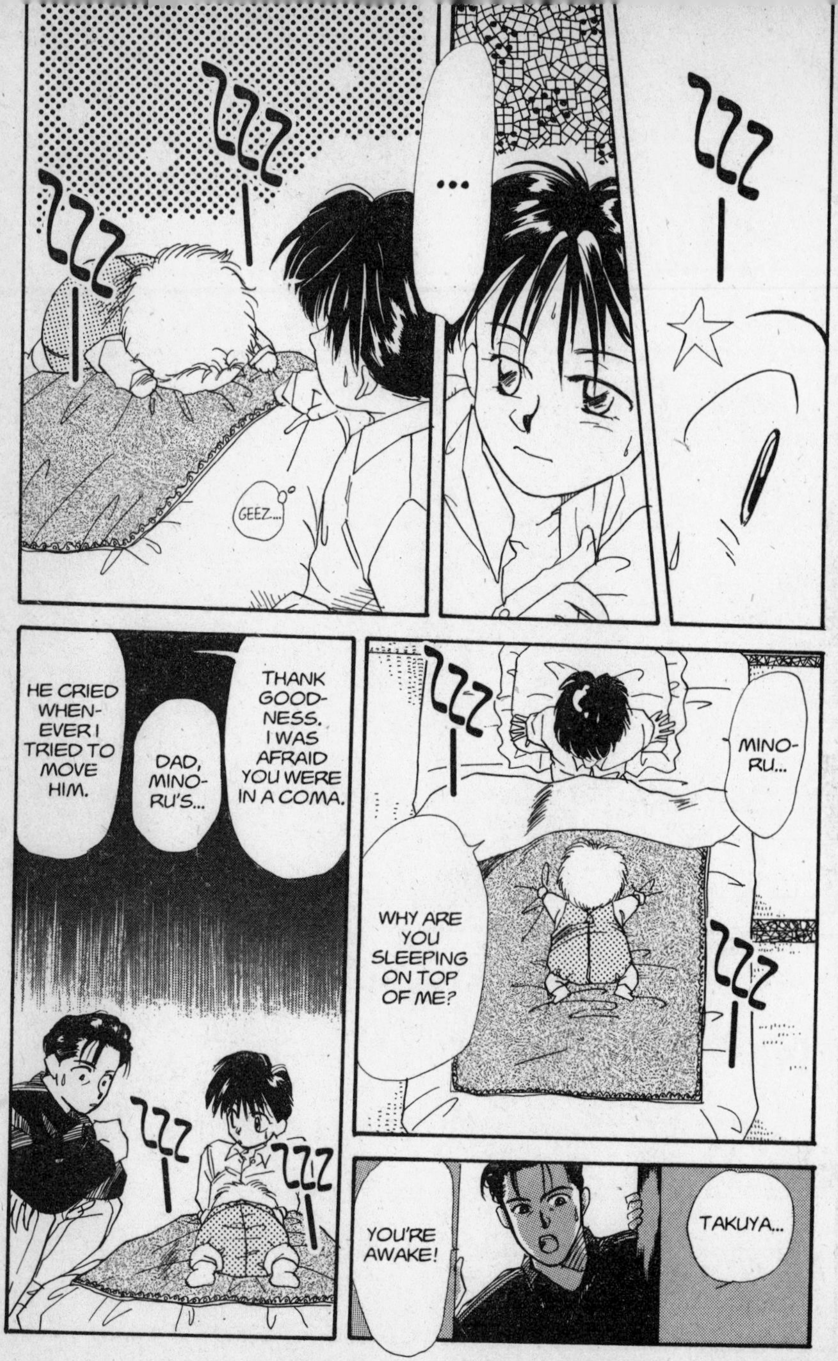
ZZZ
...
ZZZ
ZZZ
GEEZ...
MINO-RU...
WHY ARE YOU SLEEPING ON TOP OF ME?
ZZZ
ZZZ
TAKUYA...
YOU'RE AWAKE!
THANK GOOD-NESS. I WAS AFRAID YOU WERE IN A COMA.
DAD, MINO-RU'S...
HE CRIED WHEN-EVER I TRIED TO MOVE HIM.
ZZZ
ZZZ

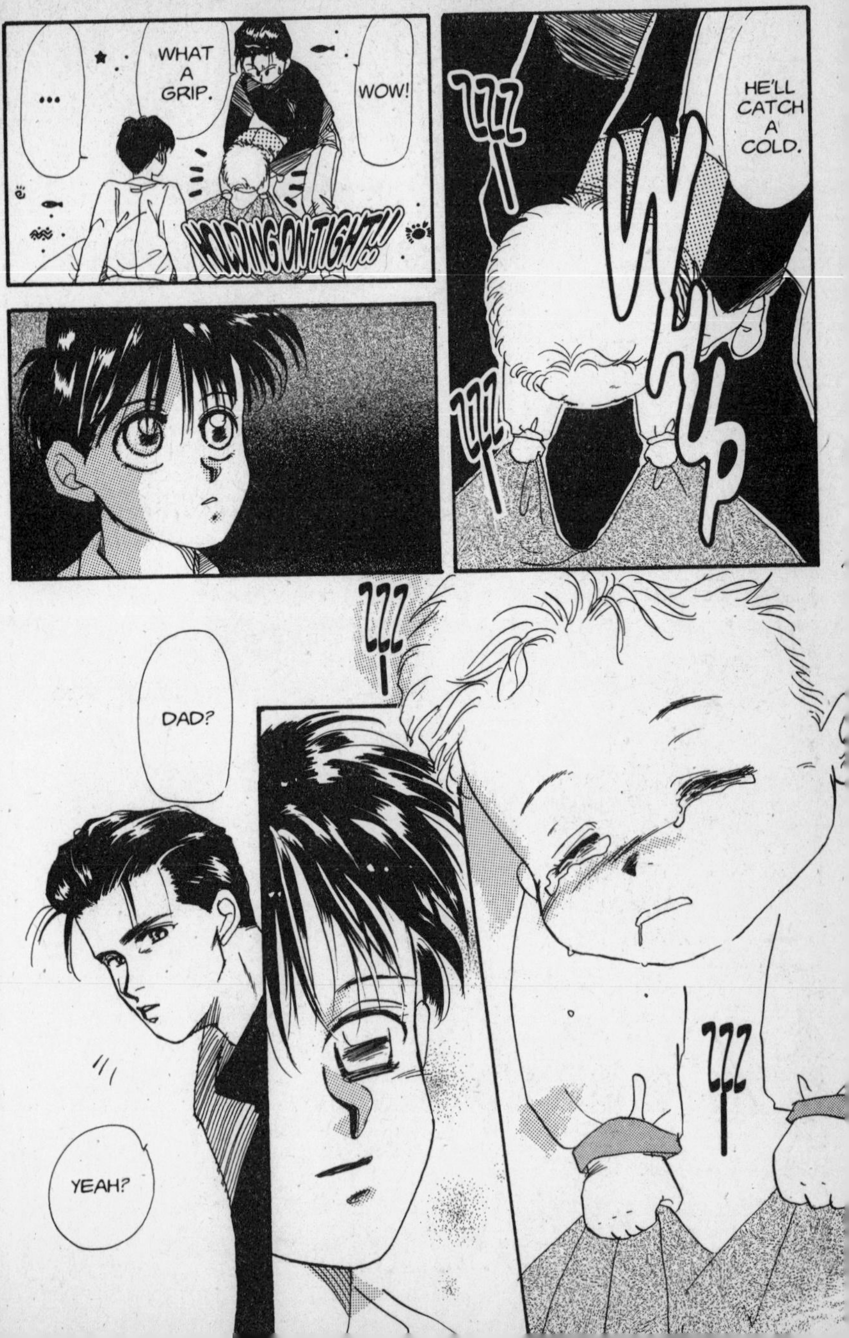
ZZZ
HE'LL CATCH A COLD.
WHIP
ZZZ
WOW!
WHAT A GRIP.
...
HOLDING ON TIGHT!!
ZZZ
DAD?
ZZZ
YEAH?

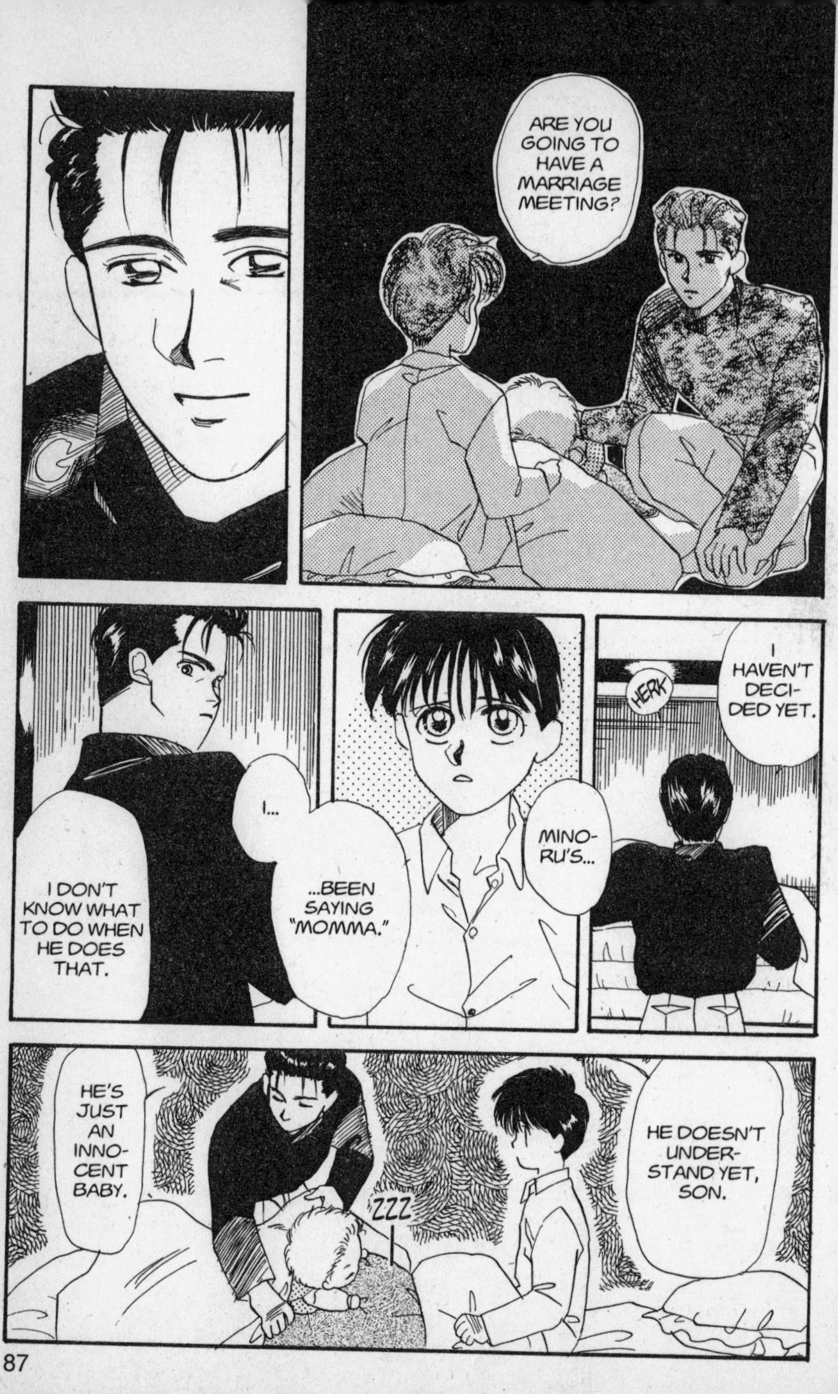
ARE YOU GOING TO HAVE A MARRIAGE MEETING?
HERK
I HAVEN'T DECIDED YET.
MINO-RU'S...
...BEEN SAYING "MOMMA."
I...
I DON'T KNOW WHAT TO DO WHEN HE DOES THAT.
HE DOESN'T UNDER-STAND YET, SON.
ZZZ
HE'S JUST AN INNO-CENT BABY.

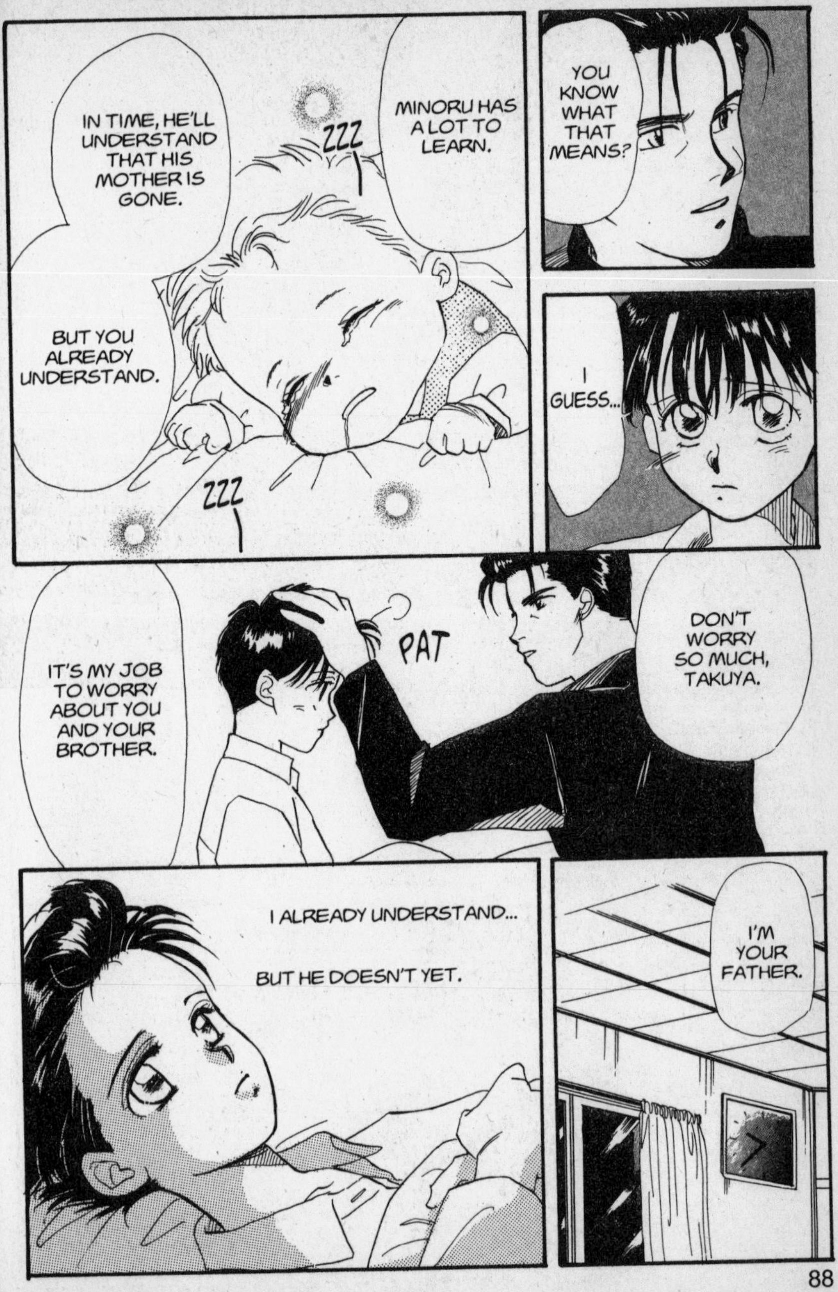
YOU KNOW WHAT THAT MEANS?
I GUESS...
MINORU HAS A LOT TO LEARN.
ZZZ
IN TIME, HE'LL UNDERSTAND THAT HIS MOTHER IS GONE.
BUT YOU ALREADY UNDERSTAND.
ZZZ
DON'T WORRY SO MUCH, TAKUYA.
PAT
IT'S MY JOB TO WORRY ABOUT YOU AND YOUR BROTHER.
I'M YOUR FATHER.
I ALREADY UNDERSTAND...
BUT HE DOESN'T YET.

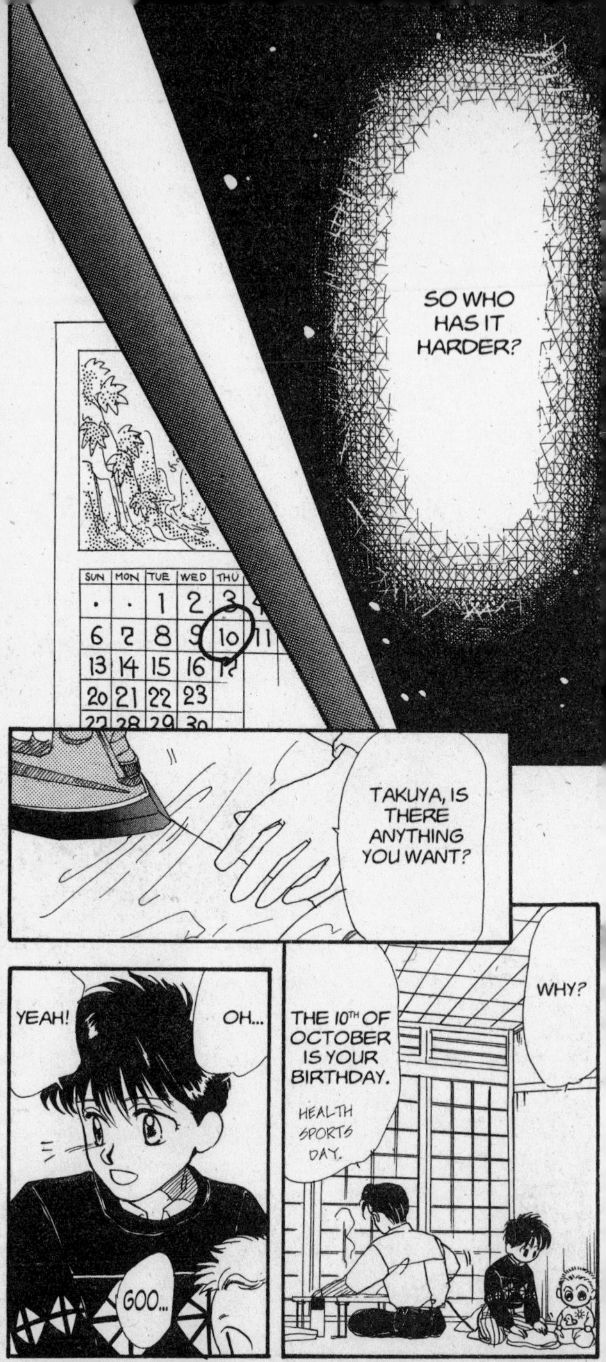
SO WHO HAS IT HARDER?
TAKUYA, IS THERE ANYTHING YOU WANT?
WHY?
THE 10TH OF OCTOBER IS YOUR BIRTHDAY.
HEALTH SPORTS DAY.
OH...
YEAH!
GOO...

AUTHOR'S NOTE 4

YOSHIZO THE RABBIT

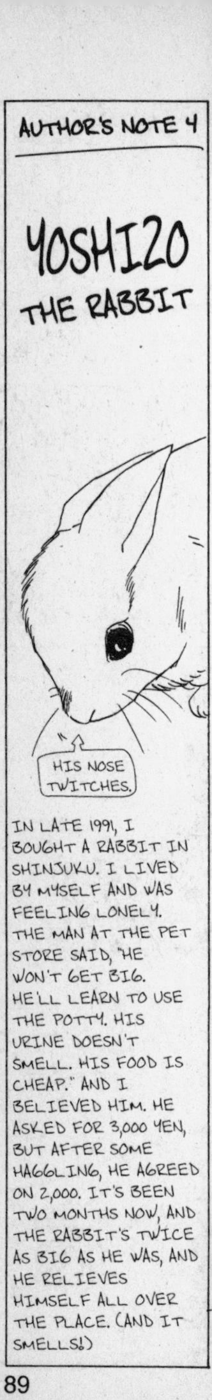
HIS NOSE TWITCHES.

IN LATE 1991, I BOUGHT A RABBIT IN SHINJUKU. I LIVED BY MYSELF AND WAS FEELING LONELY. THE MAN AT THE PET STORE SAID, "HE WON'T GET BIG. HE'LL LEARN TO USE THE POTTY. HIS URINE DOESN'T SMELL. HIS FOOD IS CHEAP." AND I BELIEVED HIM. HE ASKED FOR 3,000 YEN, BUT AFTER SOME HAGGLING, HE AGREED ON 2,000. IT'S BEEN TWO MONTHS NOW, AND THE RABBIT'S TWICE AS BIG AS HE WAS, AND HE RELIEVES HIMSELF ALL OVER THE PLACE. (AND IT SMELLS!)

*IN JAPAN, OCTOBER 10TH IS OFFICIAL "HEALTH SPORTS DAY."

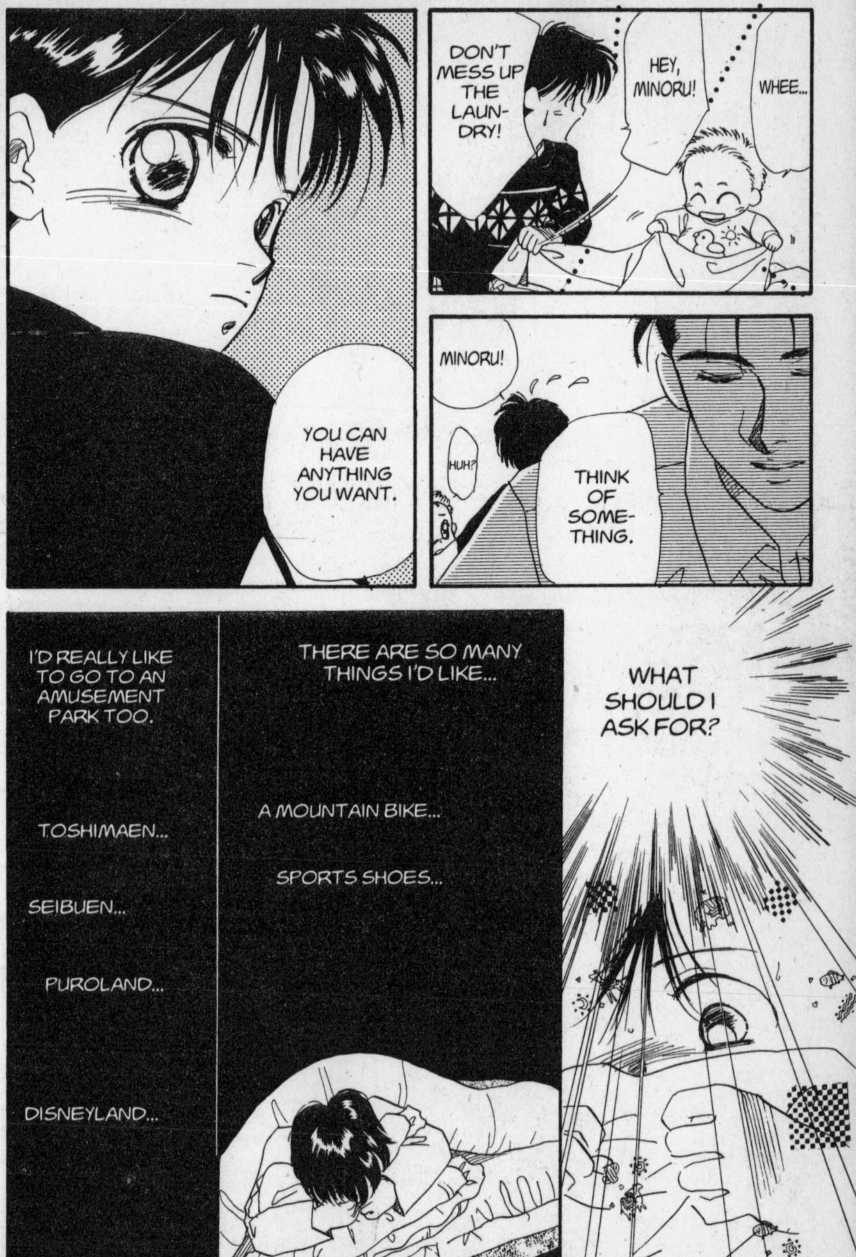
WHEE...
HEY, MINORU!
DON'T MESS UP THE LAUNDRY!
MINORU!
THINK OF SOMETHING.
HUH?
YOU CAN HAVE ANYTHING YOU WANT.
WHAT SHOULD I ASK FOR?
THERE ARE SO MANY THINGS I'D LIKE...
A MOUNTAIN BIKE...
SPORTS SHOES...
I'D REALLY LIKE TO GO TO AN AMUSEMENT PARK TOO.
TOSHIMAEN...
SEIBUEN...
PUROLAND...
DISNEYLAND...

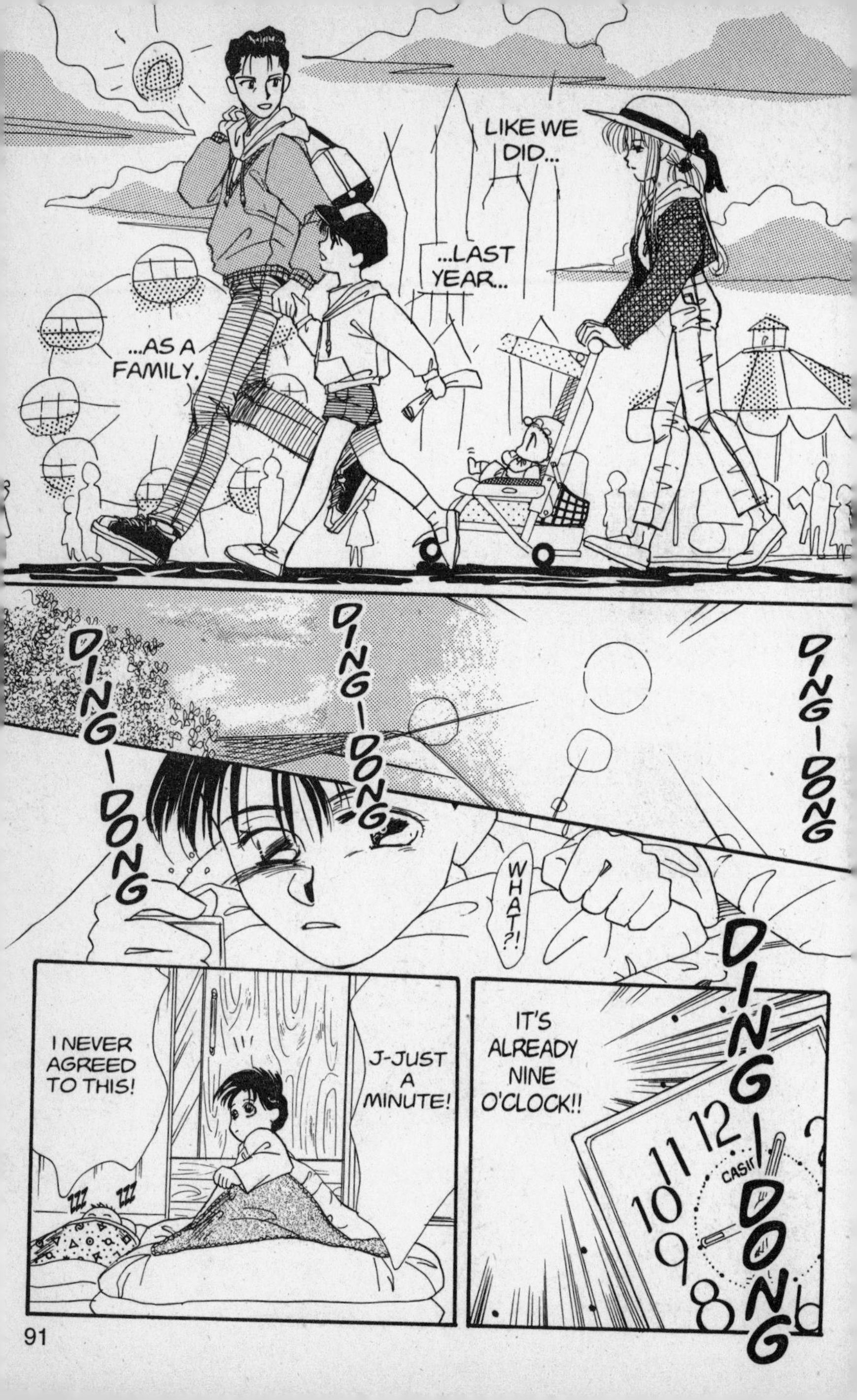
LIKE WE DID...
...LAST YEAR...
...AS A FAMILY.
DING-DONG
DING-DONG
DING-DONG
WHAT?!
DING-DONG
IT'S ALREADY NINE O'CLOCK!!
J-JUST A MINUTE!
I NEVER AGREED TO THIS!
ZZZ
ZZZ

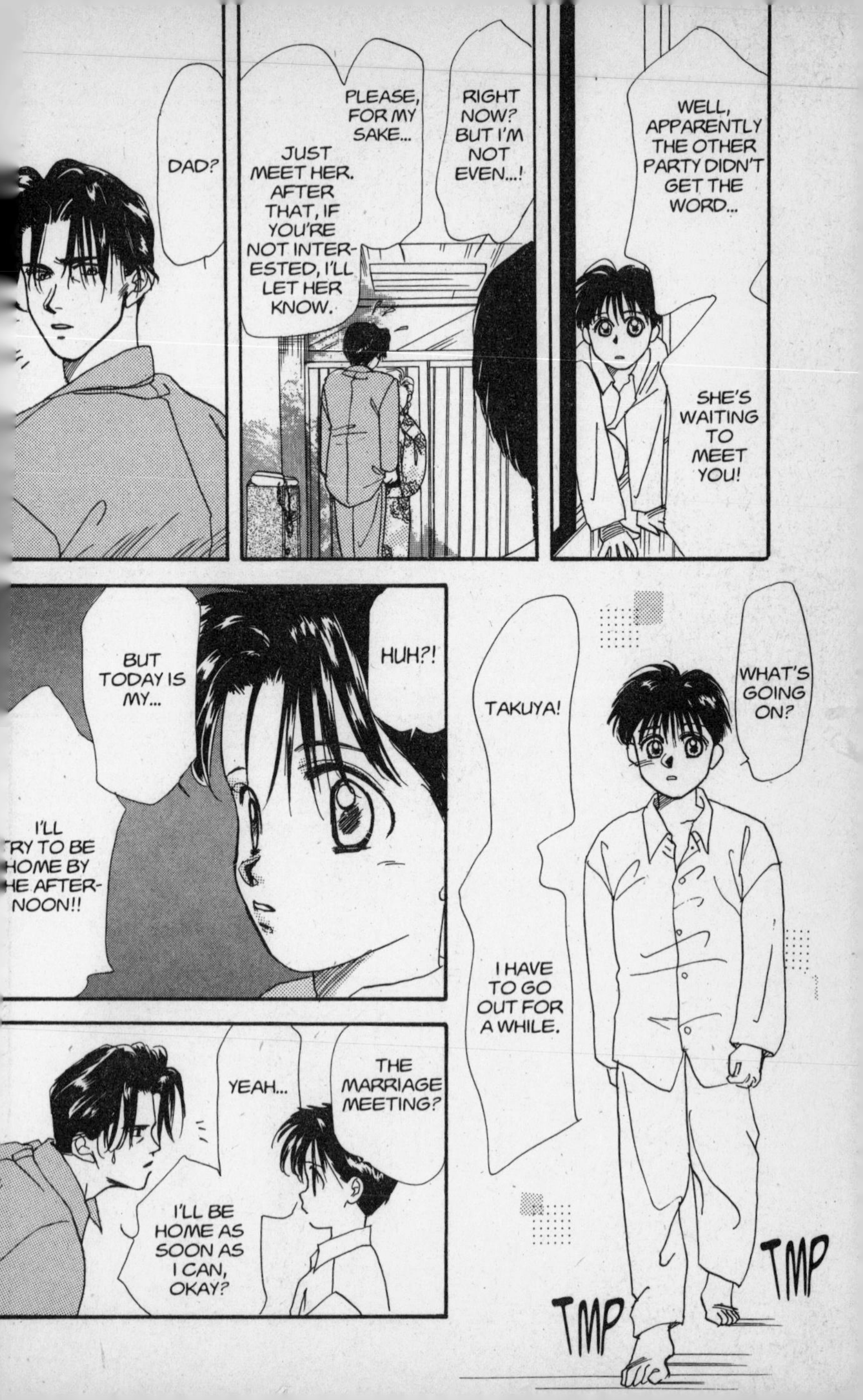
WELL, APPARENTLY THE OTHER PARTY DIDN'T GET THE WORD...
SHE'S WAITING TO MEET YOU!
RIGHT NOW? BUT I'M NOT EVEN...!
PLEASE, FOR MY SAKE...
JUST MEET HER. AFTER THAT, IF YOU'RE NOT INTER-ESTED, I'LL LET HER KNOW.
DAD?
WHAT'S GOING ON?
TAKUYA!
I HAVE TO GO OUT FOR A WHILE.
TMP
TMP
HUH?!
BUT TODAY IS MY...
I'LL RY TO BE HOME BY HE AFTER-NOON!!
THE MARRIAGE MEETING?
YEAH...
I'LL BE HOME AS SOON AS I CAN, OKAY?

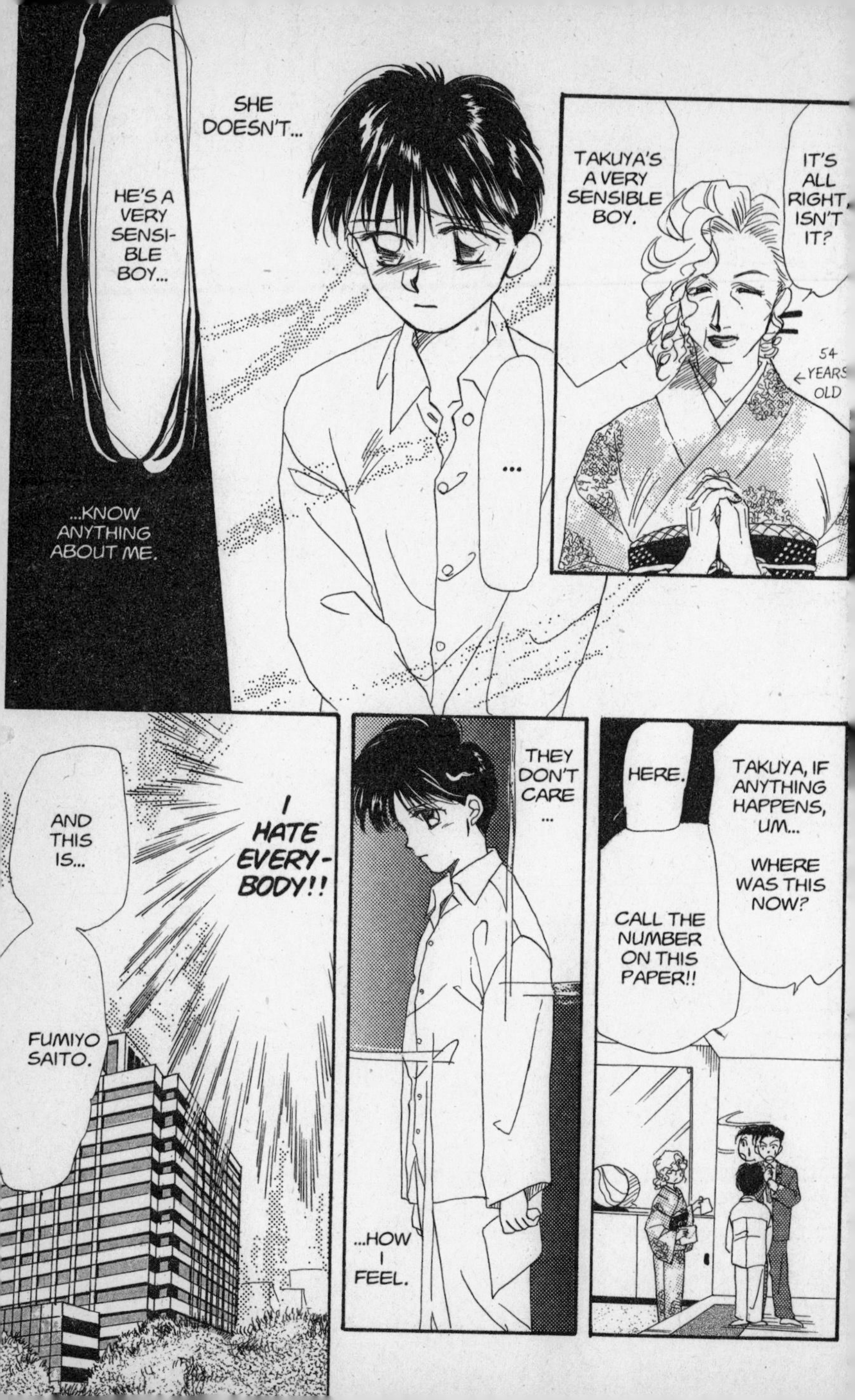
IT'S ALL RIGHT, ISN'T IT?
TAKUYA'S A VERY SENSIBLE BOY.
54 YEARS OLD
SHE DOESN'T...
HE'S A VERY SENSI-BLE BOY...
...
...KNOW ANYTHING ABOUT ME.
TAKUYA, IF ANYTHING HAPPENS, UM...
WHERE WAS THIS NOW?
HERE.
CALL THE NUMBER ON THIS PAPER!!
THEY DON'T CARE ...
...HOW I FEEL.
I HATE EVERY-BODY!!
AND THIS IS...
FUMIYO SAITO.

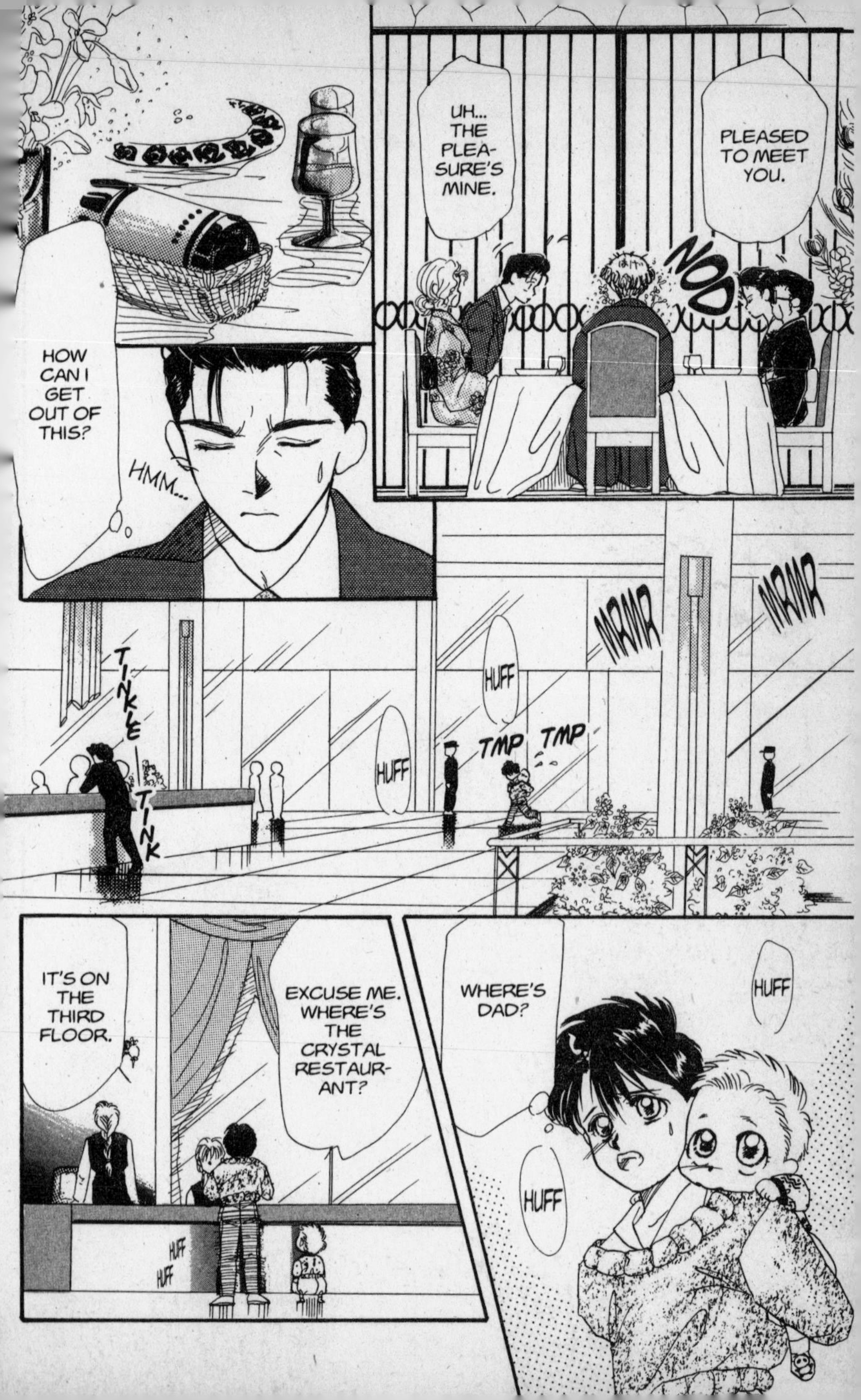
PLEASED TO MEET YOU.
NOD
UH... THE PLEASURE'S MINE.
HOW CAN I GET OUT OF THIS?
HMM...
MRMR
MRMR
HUFF
TMP TMP
HUFF
TINKLE
TINK
HUFF
WHERE'S DAD?
HUFF
EXCUSE ME. WHERE'S THE CRYSTAL RESTAURANT?
IT'S ON THE THIRD FLOOR.
HUFF
HUFF

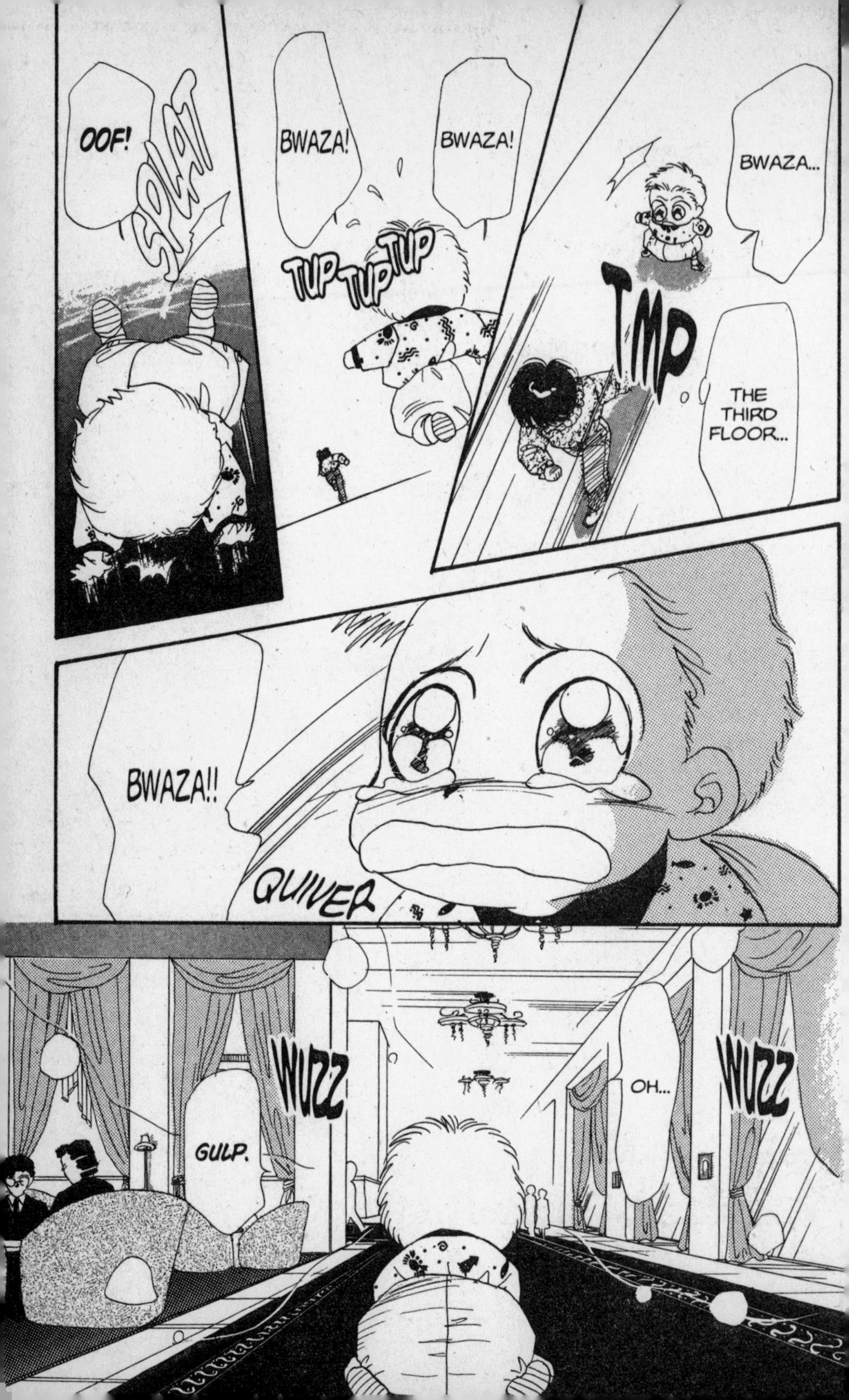
BWAZA...
TMP
THE THIRD FLOOR...
BWAZA!
BWAZA!
TUP TUP TUP
OOF!
SPLAT
BWAZA!!
QUIVER
WUZZ
OH...
WUZZ
GULP.

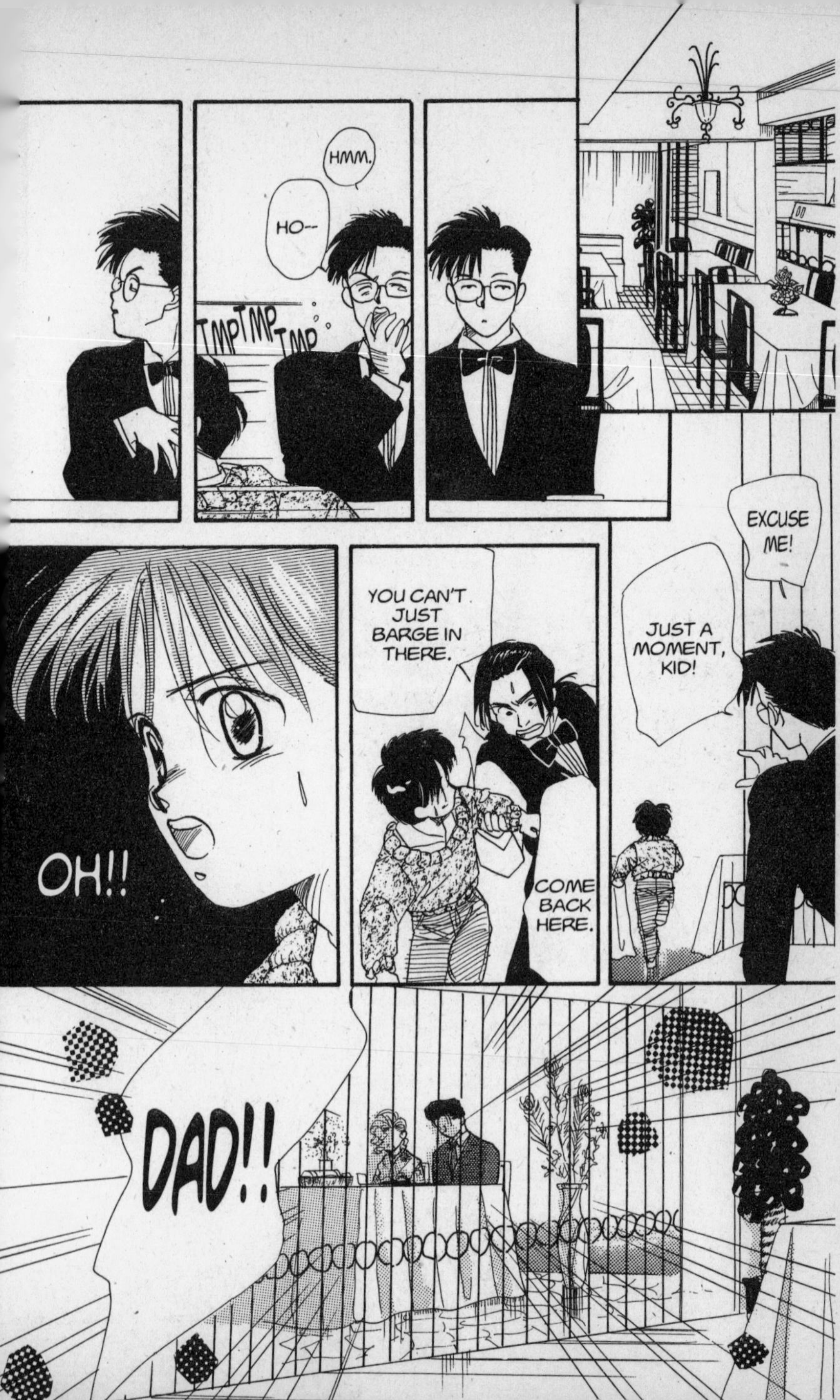
HMM.
HO--
TMPTMPTMP
EXCUSE ME!
JUST A MOMENT, KID!
YOU CAN'T JUST BARGE IN THERE.
COME BACK HERE.
OH!!
DAD!!

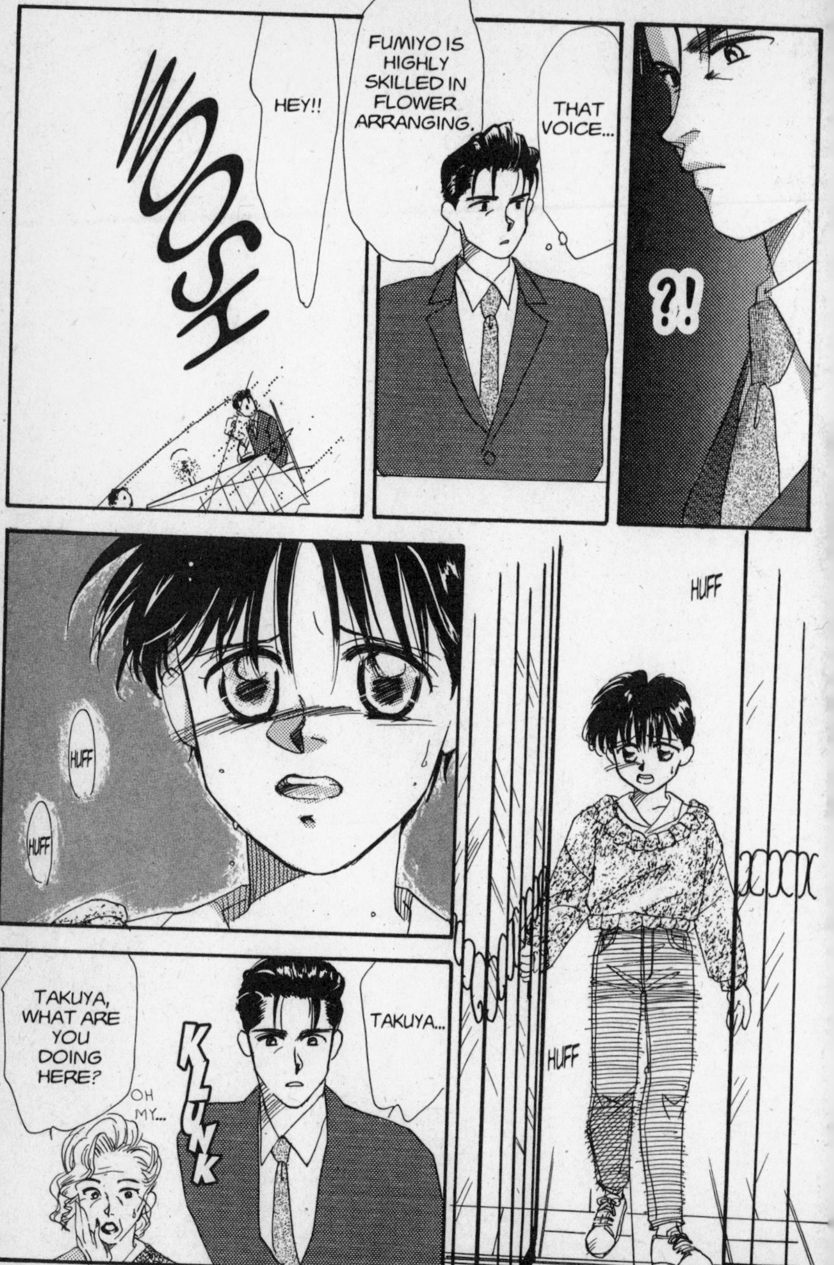
?!
FUMIYO IS HIGHLY SKILLED IN FLOWER ARRANGING.
THAT VOICE...
HEY!!
WOOSH
HUFF
HUFF
HUFF
HUFF
TAKUYA...
KLUNK
TAKUYA, WHAT ARE YOU DOING HERE?
OH MY...

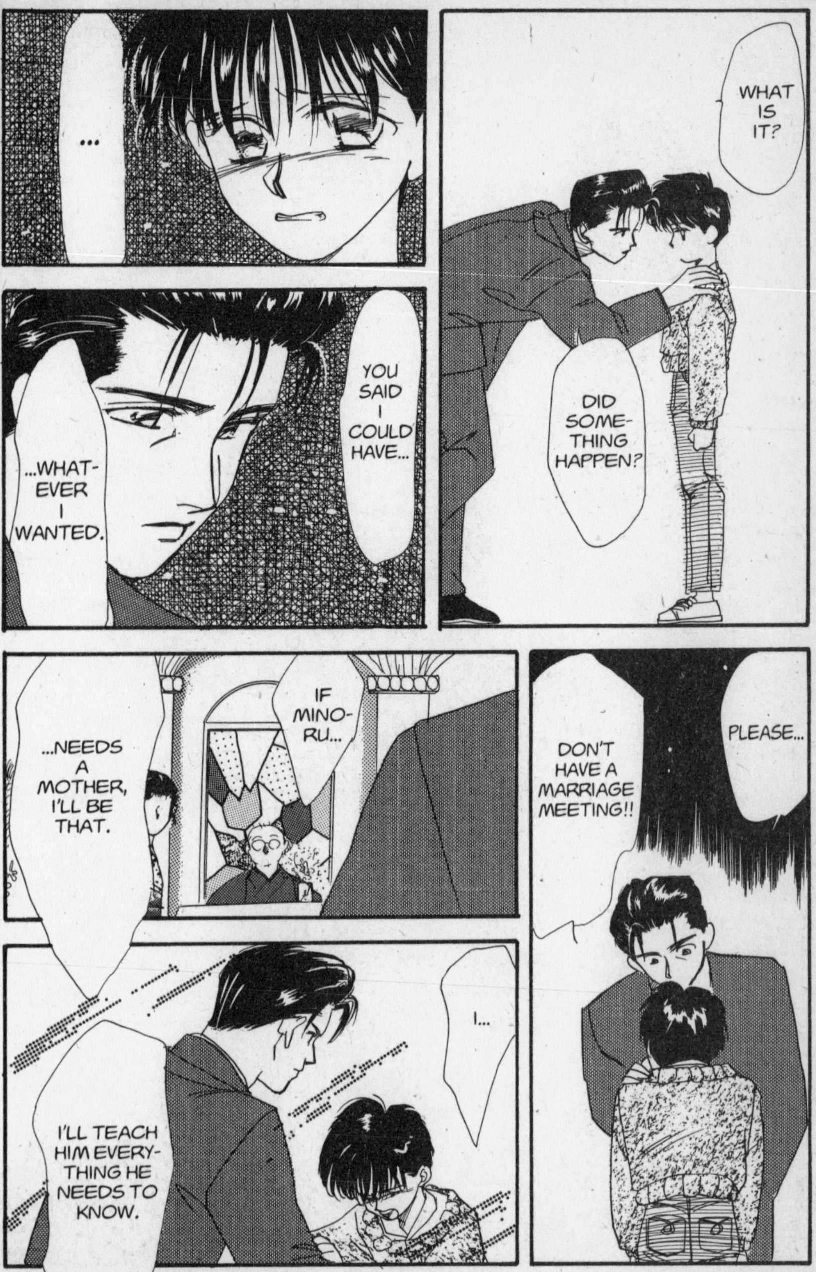
WHAT IS IT?
DID SOMETHING HAPPEN?
...
YOU SAID I COULD HAVE...
...WHATEVER I WANTED.
PLEASE...
DON'T HAVE A MARRIAGE MEETING!!
IF MINORU...
...NEEDS A MOTHER, I'LL BE THAT.
I...
I'LL TEACH HIM EVERYTHING HE NEEDS TO KNOW.

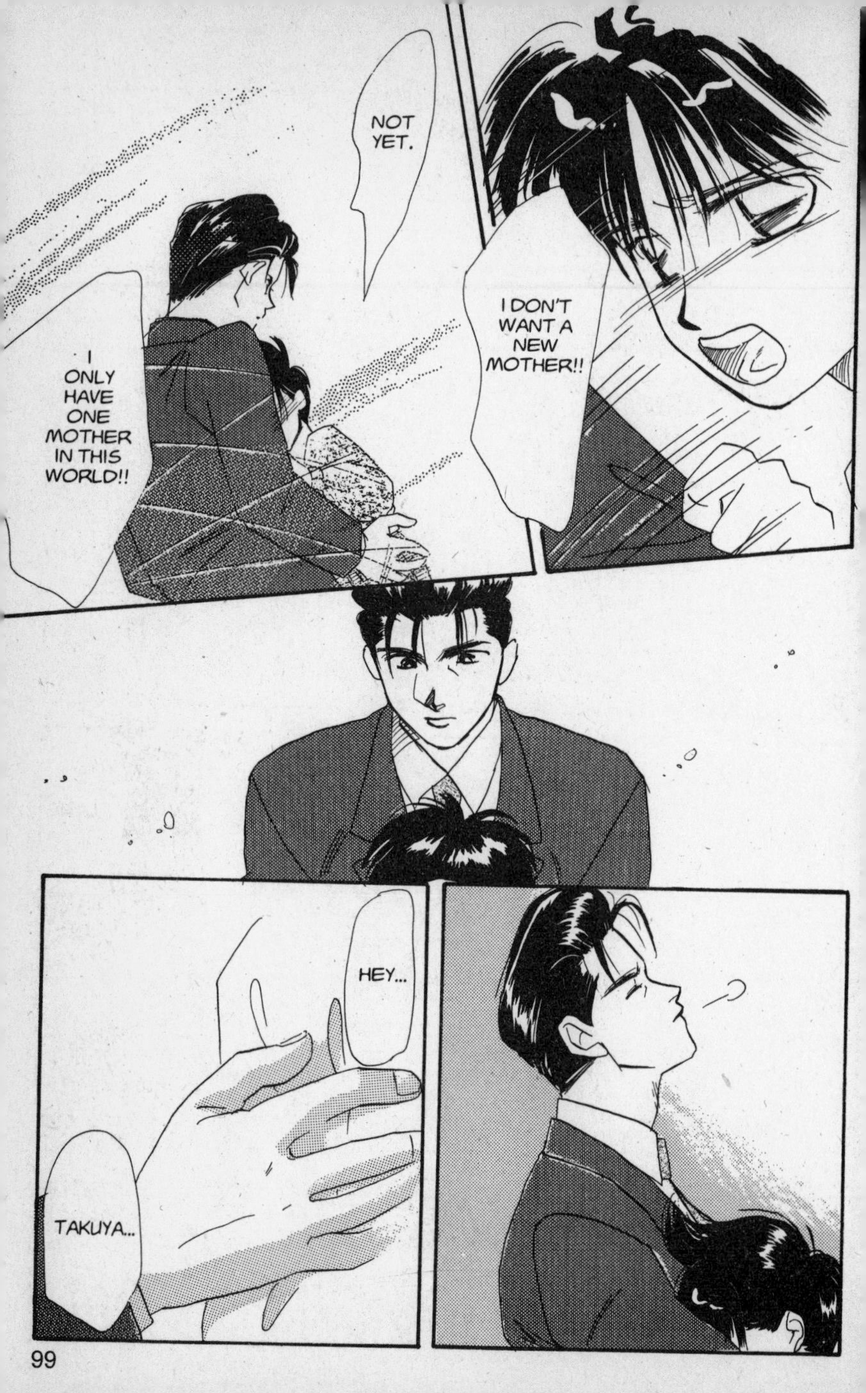

I DON'T WANT A NEW MOTHER!!
NOT YET.
I ONLY HAVE ONE MOTHER IN THIS WORLD!!
HEY...
TAKUYA...

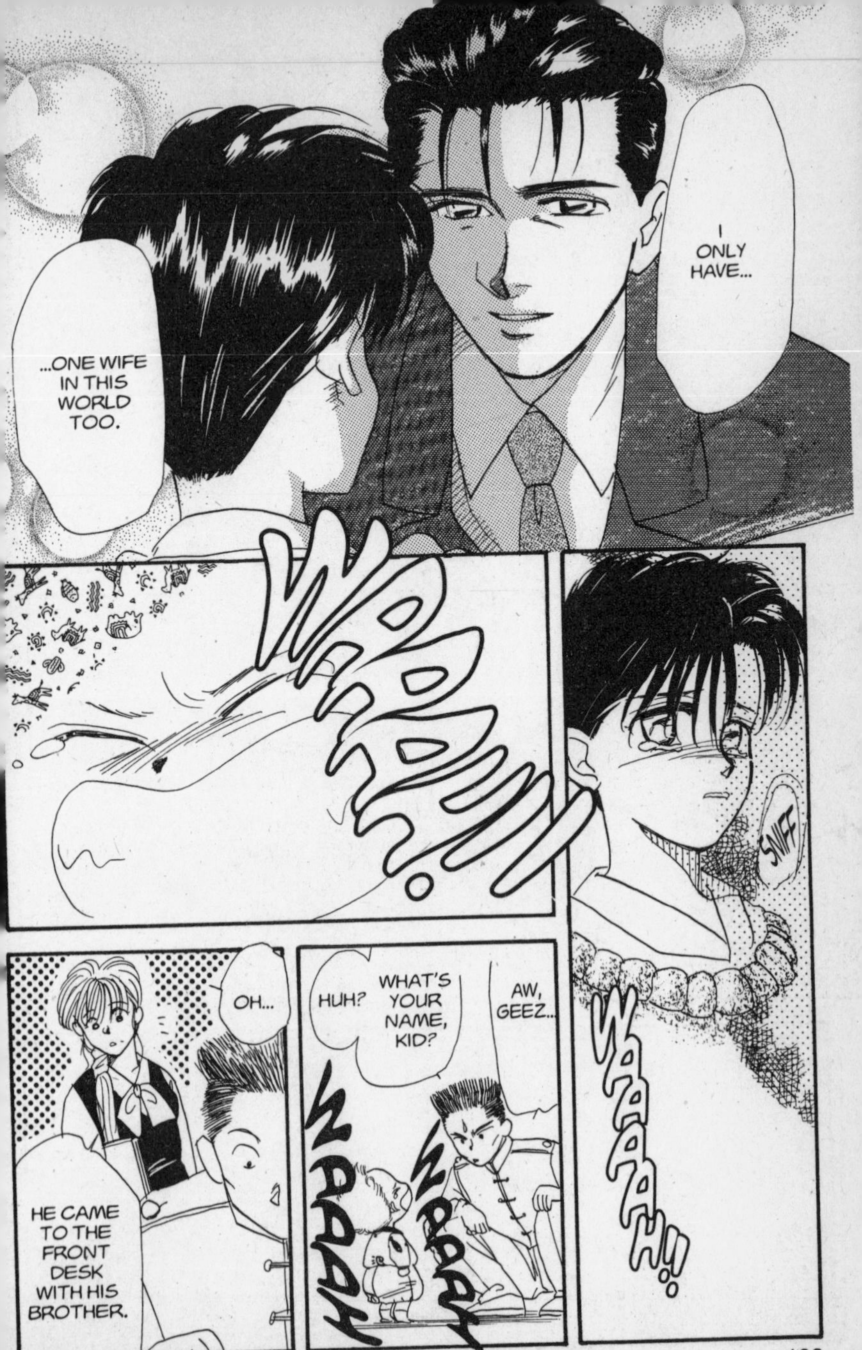

I ONLY HAVE...
...ONE WIFE IN THIS WORLD TOO.
SNIFF
WAAAAH!!
WAAAAAH!
AW, GEEZ...
WHAT'S YOUR NAME, KID?
HUH?
WAAAH
WAAAH
OH...
HE CAME TO THE FRONT DESK WITH HIS BROTHER.

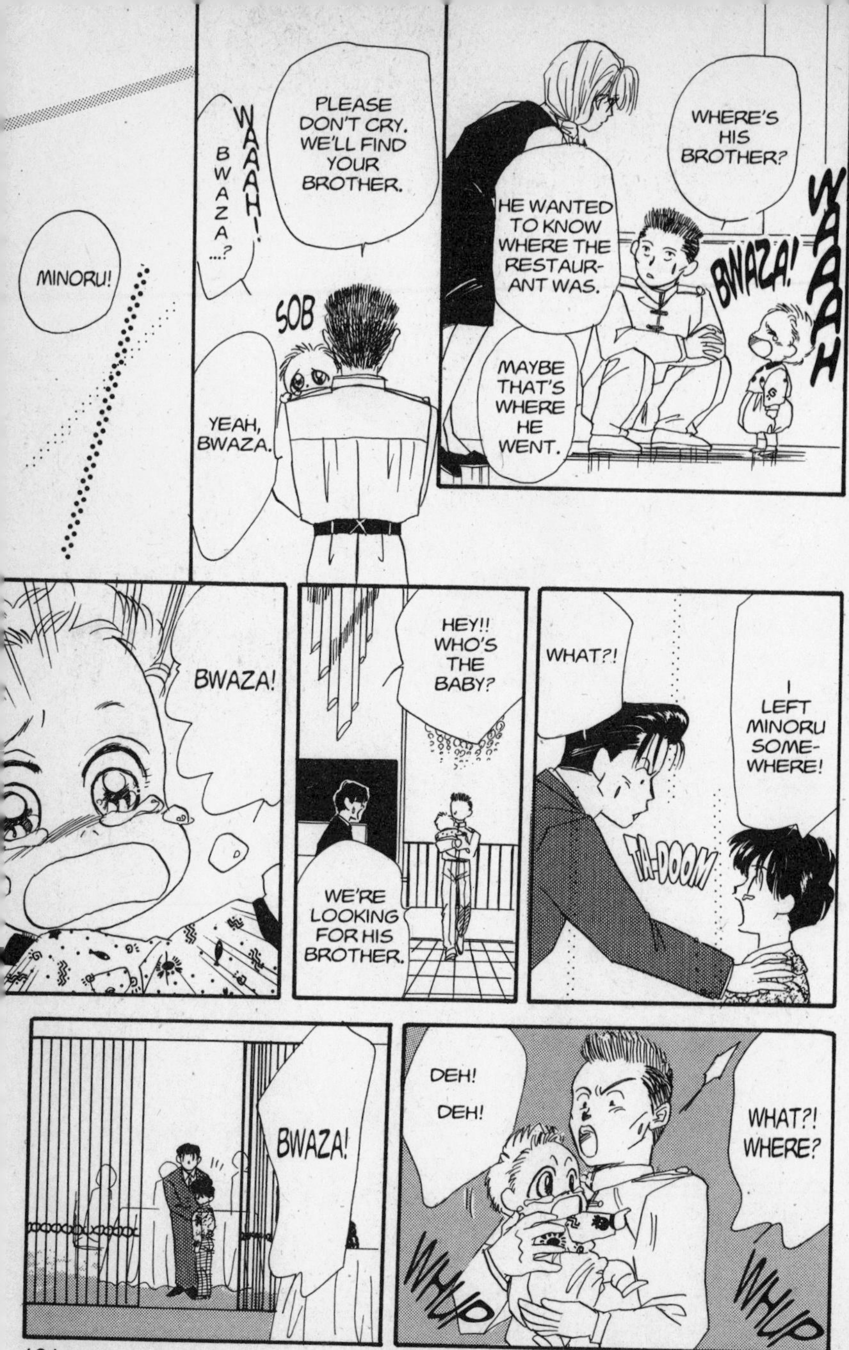
WHERE'S HIS BROTHER?
WAAAAH
BWAZA!
HE WANTED TO KNOW WHERE THE RESTAURANT WAS.
MAYBE THAT'S WHERE HE WENT.
PLEASE DON'T CRY. WE'LL FIND YOUR BROTHER.
WAAAH!
BWAZA...?
SOB
YEAH, BWAZA.
MINORU!
I LEFT MINORU SOMEWHERE!
WHAT?!
TA-DOOM
HEY!! WHO'S THE BABY?
WE'RE LOOKING FOR HIS BROTHER.
BWAZA!
WHAT?! WHERE?
DEH!
DEH!
WHUP
WHUP
BWAZA!

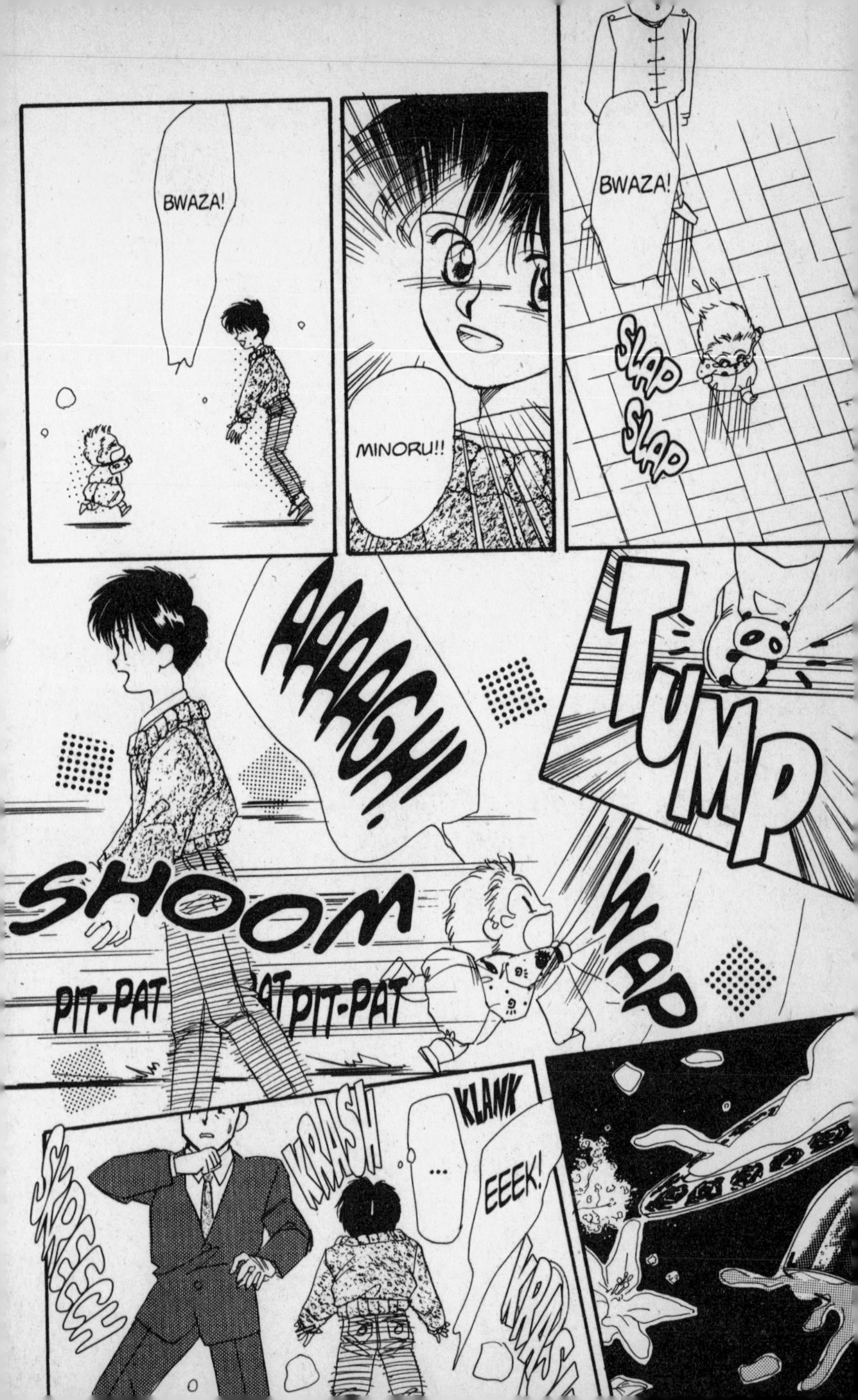
BWAZA!
SLAP SLAP
MINORU!!
BWAZA!
TUMP
AAAGH!!
WAP
SHOOM
PIT-PAT
PIT-PAT
KLANK
...
EEEK!
KRASH
KRASH

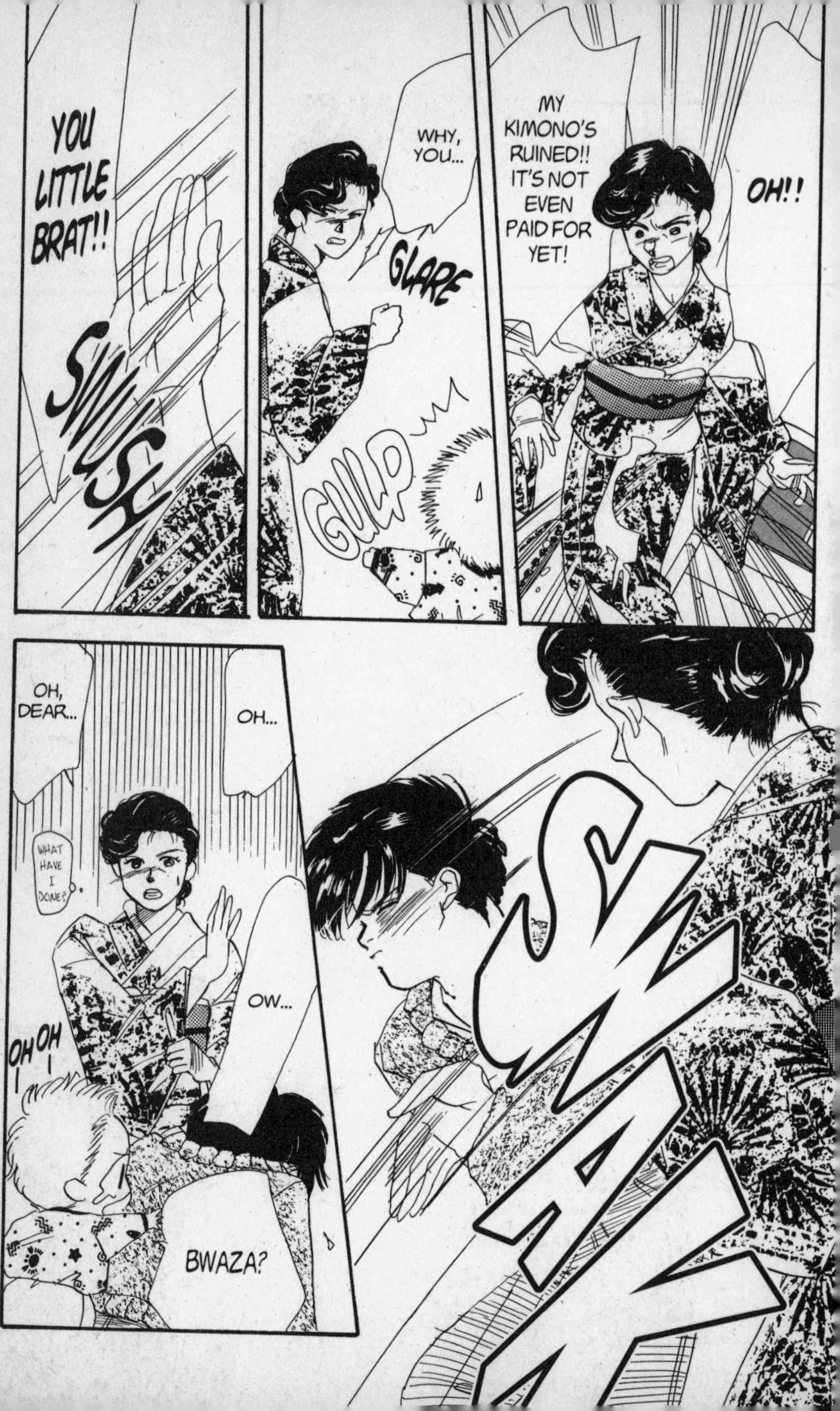
OH!!
MY KIMONO'S RUINED!! IT'S NOT EVEN PAID FOR YET!
WHY, YOU...
GLARE
GULP
YOU LITTLE BRAT!!
SWUSH
OH...
OH, DEAR...
WHAT HAVE I DONE?
OW...
OH OH
BWAZA?

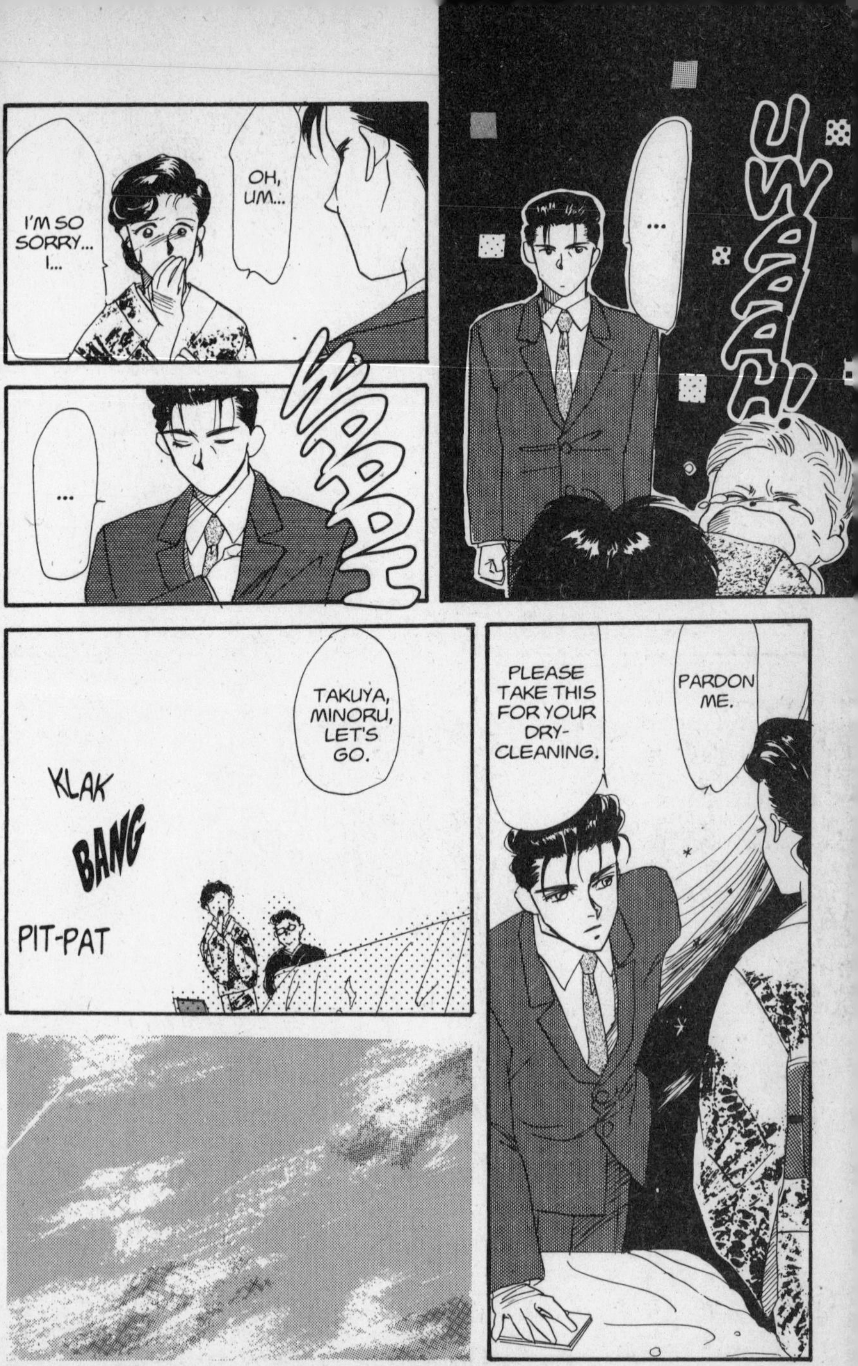
...
UWAAAH!
OH, UM...
I'M SO SORRY... I...
WAAAI
...
PARDON ME.
PLEASE TAKE THIS FOR YOUR DRY-CLEANING.
TAKUYA, MINORU, LET'S GO.
KLAK
BANG
PIT-PAT

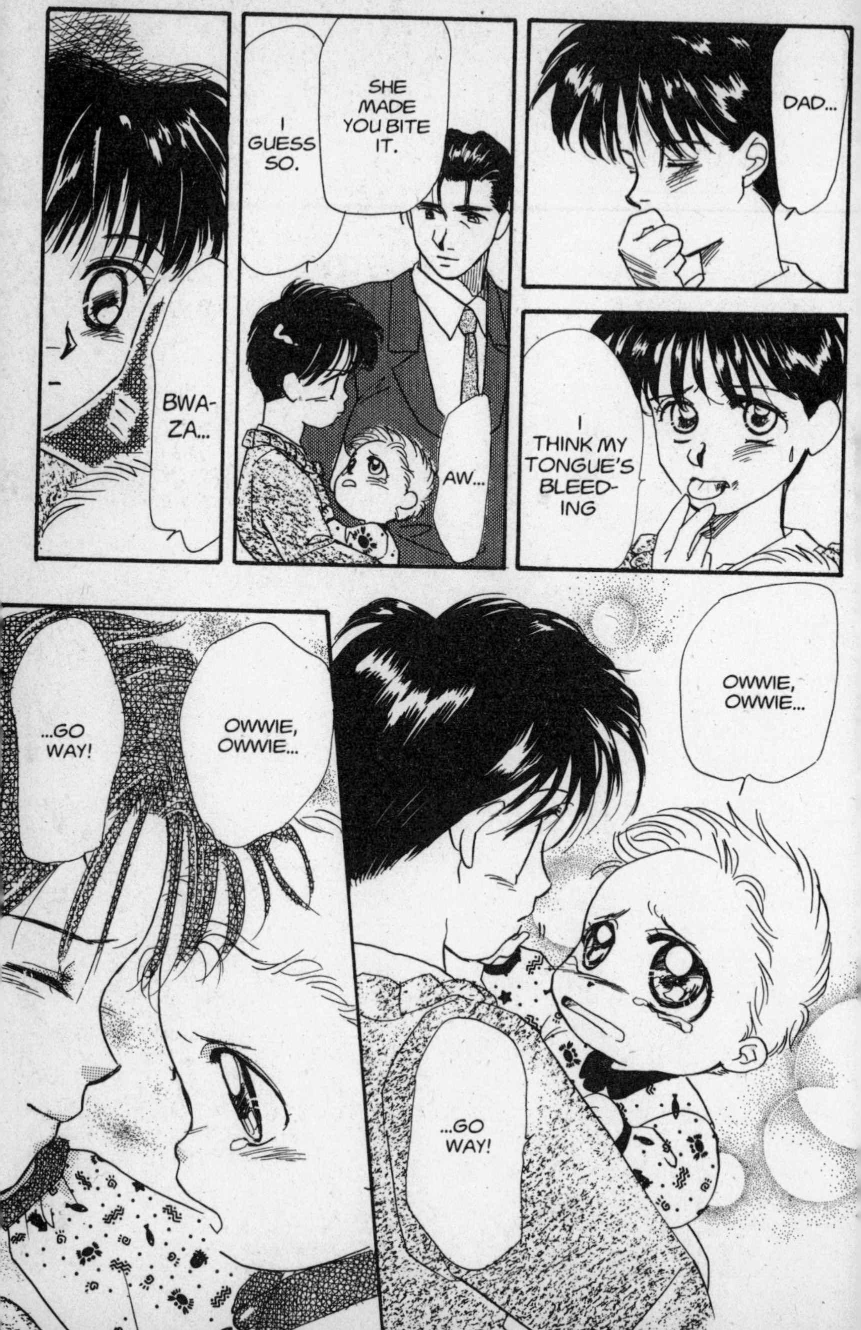
DAD...
I THINK MY TONGUE'S BLEED-ING
SHE MADE YOU BITE IT.
I GUESS SO.
AW...
BWA-ZA...
OWWIE, OWWIE...
...GO WAY!
OWWIE, OWWIE...
...GO WAY!

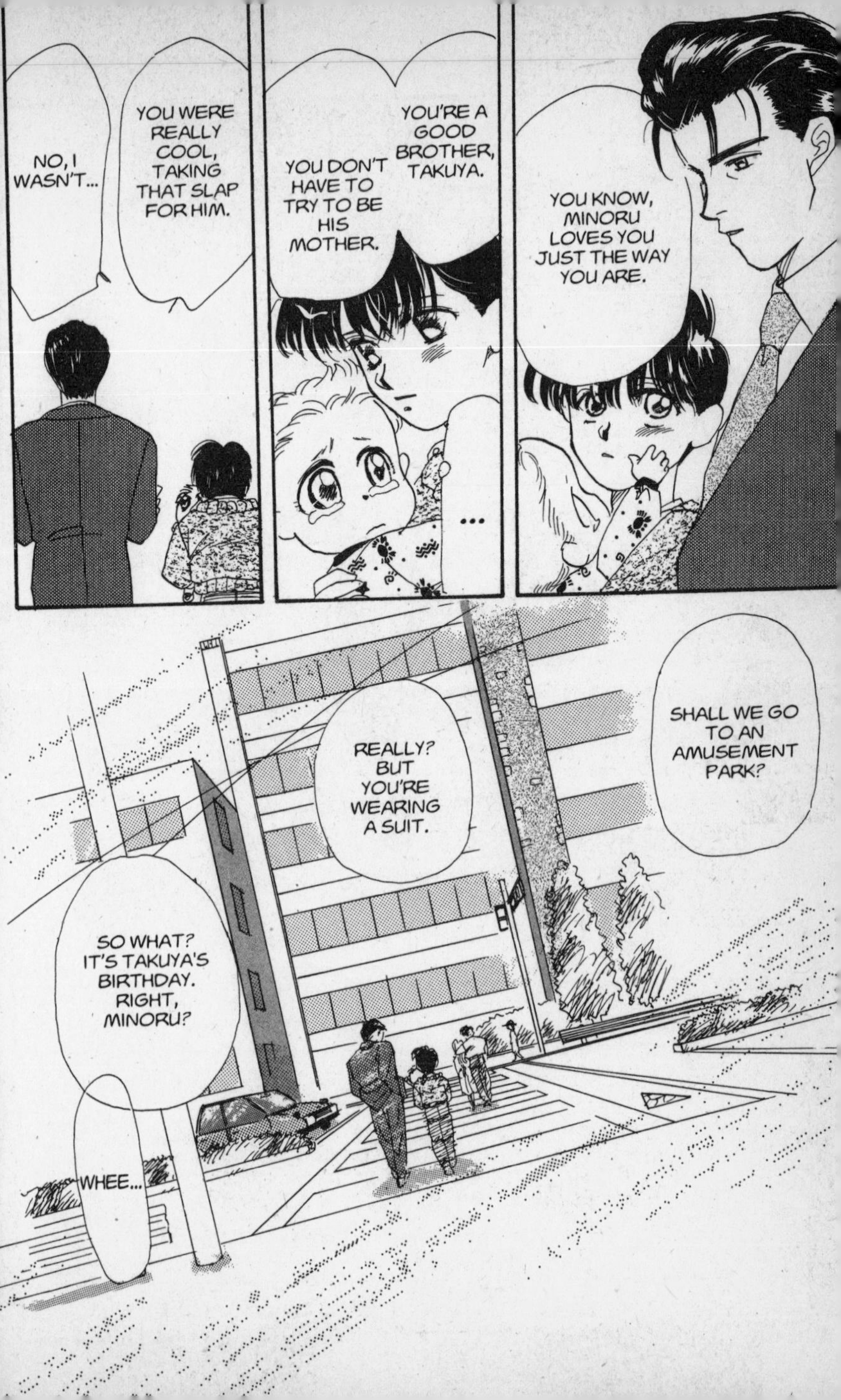
YOU KNOW, MINORU LOVES YOU JUST THE WAY YOU ARE.
YOU'RE A GOOD BROTHER, TAKUYA.
YOU DON'T HAVE TO TRY TO BE HIS MOTHER.
...
YOU WERE REALLY COOL, TAKING THAT SLAP FOR HIM.
NO, I WASN'T...
SHALL WE GO TO AN AMUSEMENT PARK?
REALLY? BUT YOU'RE WEARING A SUIT.
SO WHAT? IT'S TAKUYA'S BIRTHDAY. RIGHT, MINORU?
WHEE...

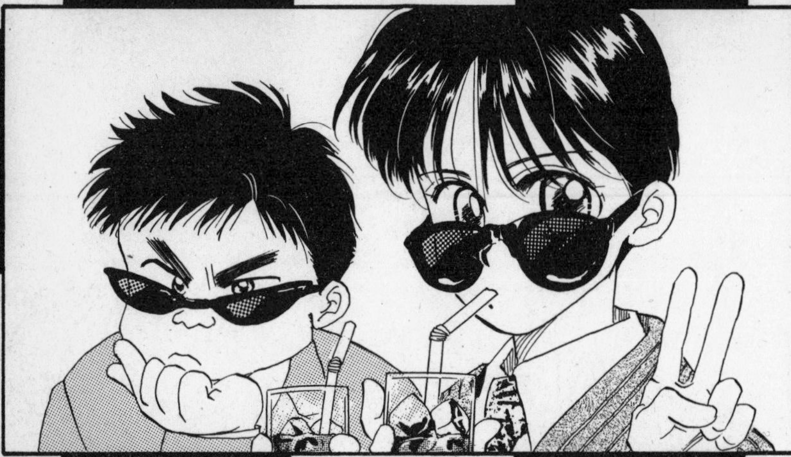

BABY & ME

CHAPTER THREE

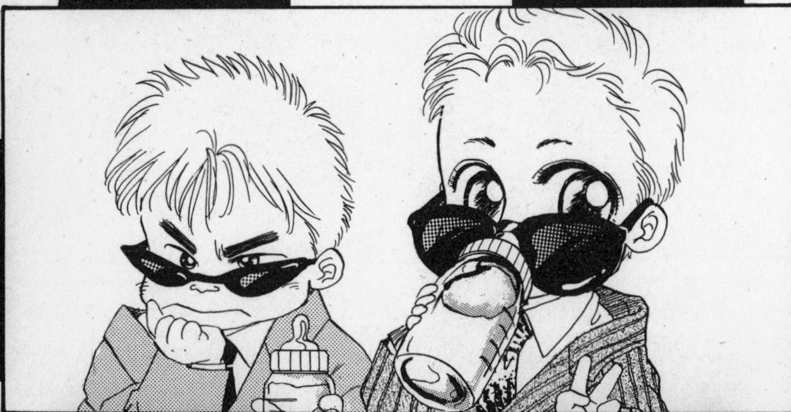

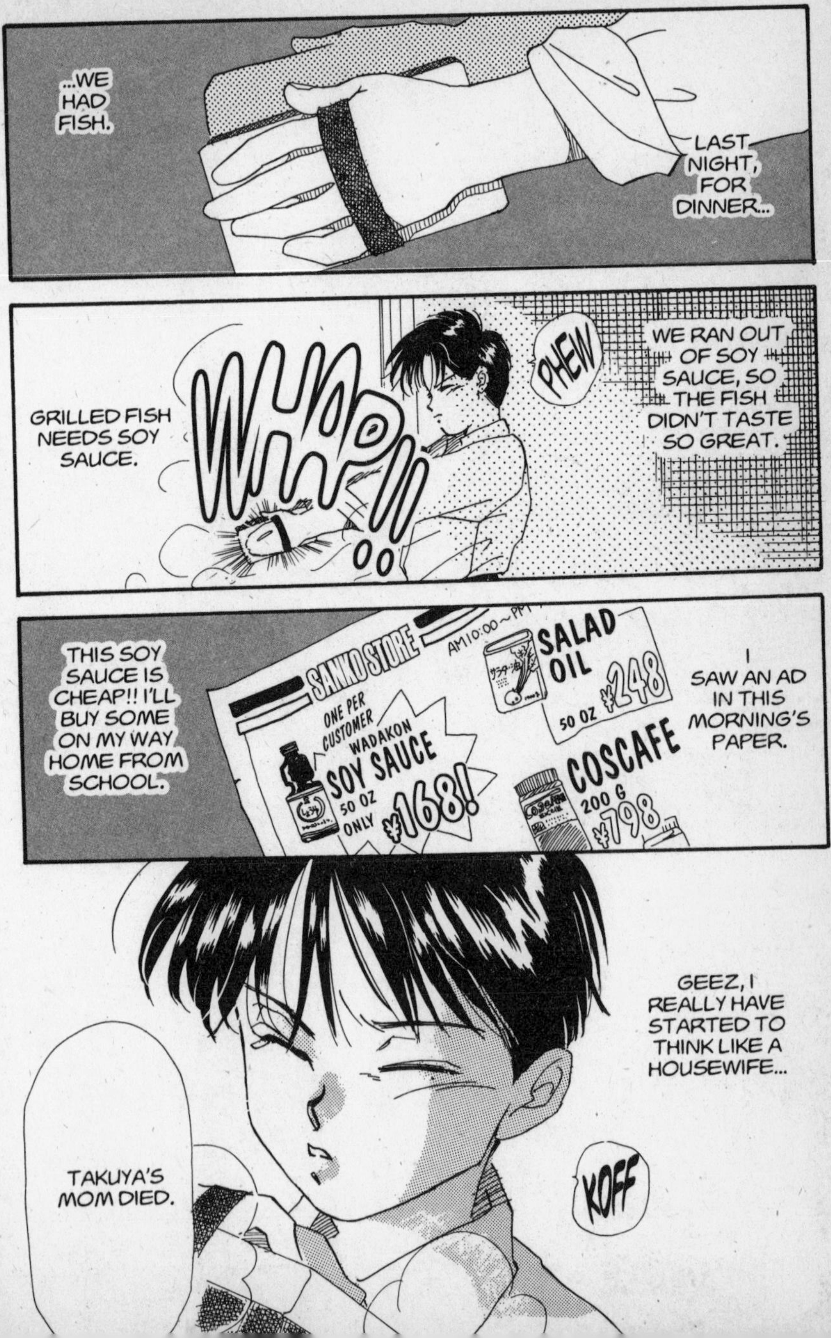
LAST NIGHT, FOR DINNER...
...WE HAD FISH.
WE RAN OUT OF SOY SAUCE, SO THE FISH DIDN'T TASTE SO GREAT.
PHEW
WHAP!!
GRILLED FISH NEEDS SOY SAUCE.
I SAW AN AD IN THIS MORNING'S PAPER.
SANKO STORE
AM10:00~PM
SALAD OIL
50 OZ ¥248
ONE PER CUSTOMER
WADAKON SOY SAUCE
50 OZ ONLY ¥168!
COSCAFE
200 G ¥798
THIS SOY SAUCE IS CHEAP!! I'LL BUY SOME ON MY WAY HOME FROM SCHOOL.
GEEZ, I REALLY HAVE STARTED TO THINK LIKE A HOUSEWIFE...
KOFF
TAKUYA'S MOM DIED.

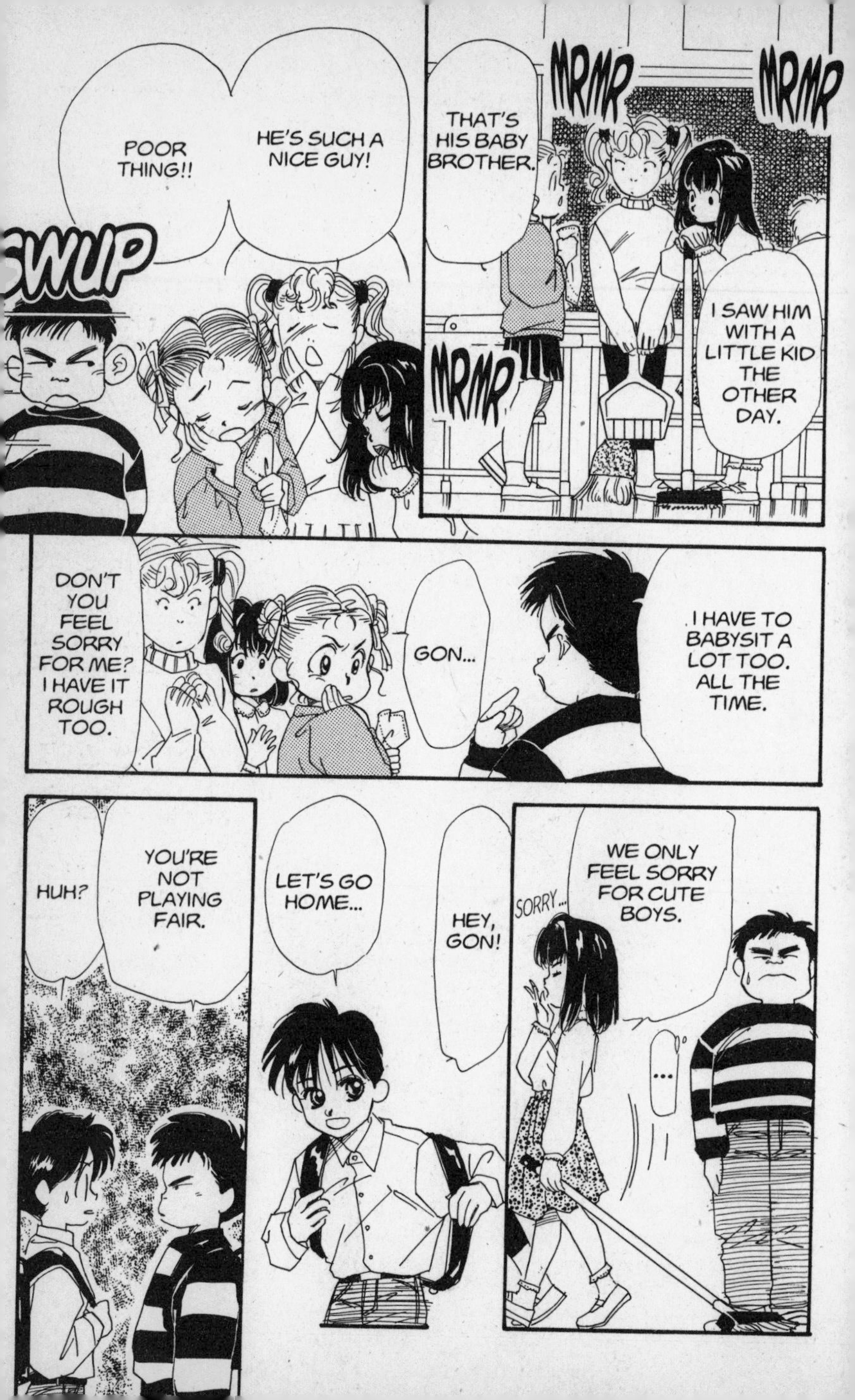
MRMR
MRMR
THAT'S HIS BABY BROTHER.
I SAW HIM WITH A LITTLE KID THE OTHER DAY.
MRMR
HE'S SUCH A NICE GUY!
POOR THING!!
SWUP
I HAVE TO BABYSIT A LOT TOO. ALL THE TIME.
GON...
DON'T YOU FEEL SORRY FOR ME? I HAVE IT ROUGH TOO.
WE ONLY FEEL SORRY FOR CUTE BOYS.
SORRY...
...
HEY, GON!
LET'S GO HOME...
YOU'RE NOT PLAYING FAIR.
HUH?

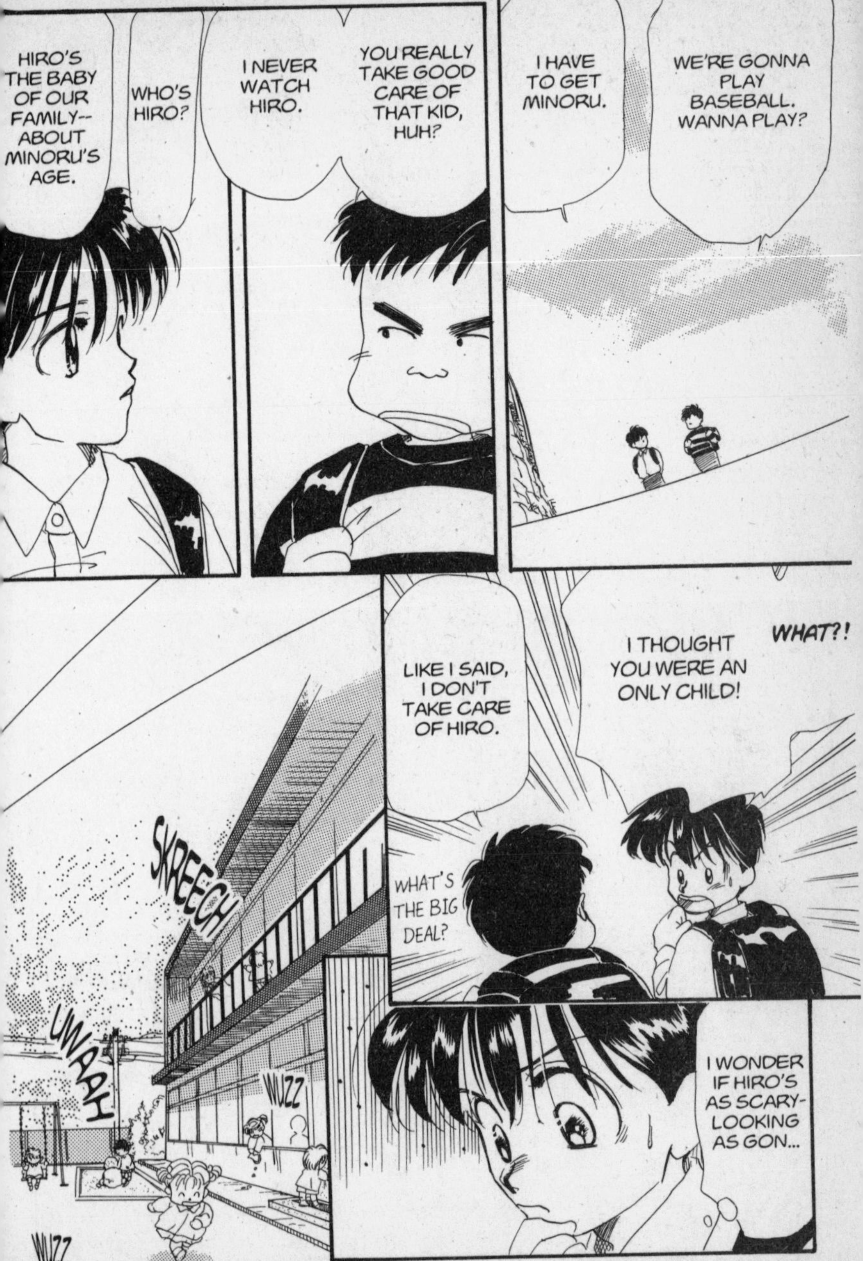
WE'RE GONNA PLAY BASEBALL. WANNA PLAY?
I HAVE TO GET MINORU.
YOU REALLY TAKE GOOD CARE OF THAT KID, HUH?
I NEVER WATCH HIRO.
WHO'S HIRO?
HIRO'S THE BABY OF OUR FAMILY-- ABOUT MINORU'S AGE.
WHAT?!
I THOUGHT YOU WERE AN ONLY CHILD!
LIKE I SAID, I DON'T TAKE CARE OF HIRO.
WHAT'S THE BIG DEAL?
I WONDER IF HIRO'S AS SCARY-LOOKING AS GON...
SKREECH
UWAAH
WUZZ
WUZZ

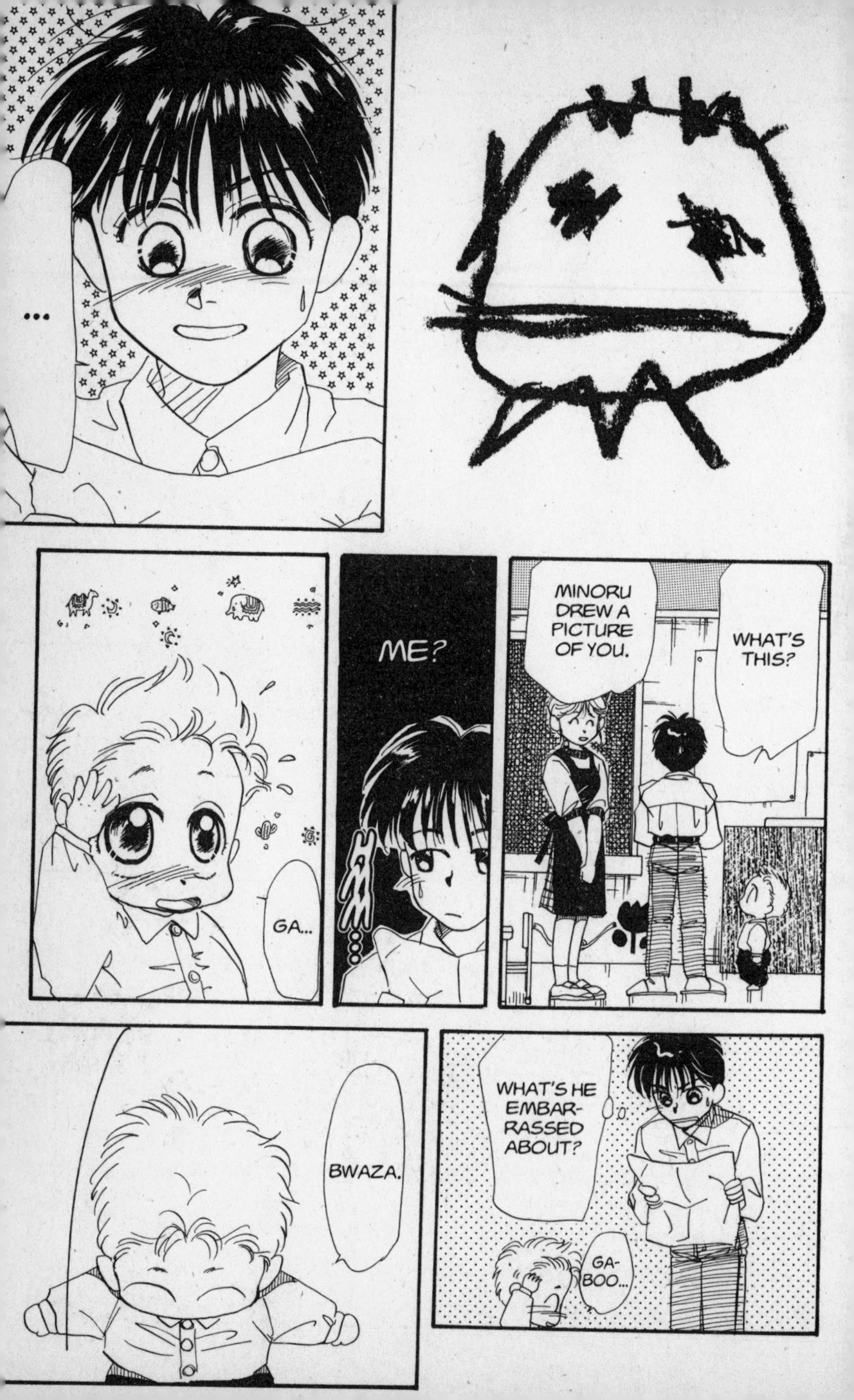
...
WHAT'S THIS?
MINORU DREW A PICTURE OF YOU.
ME?
GA...
WHAT'S HE EMBARRASSED ABOUT?
GA-BOO...
BWAZA.

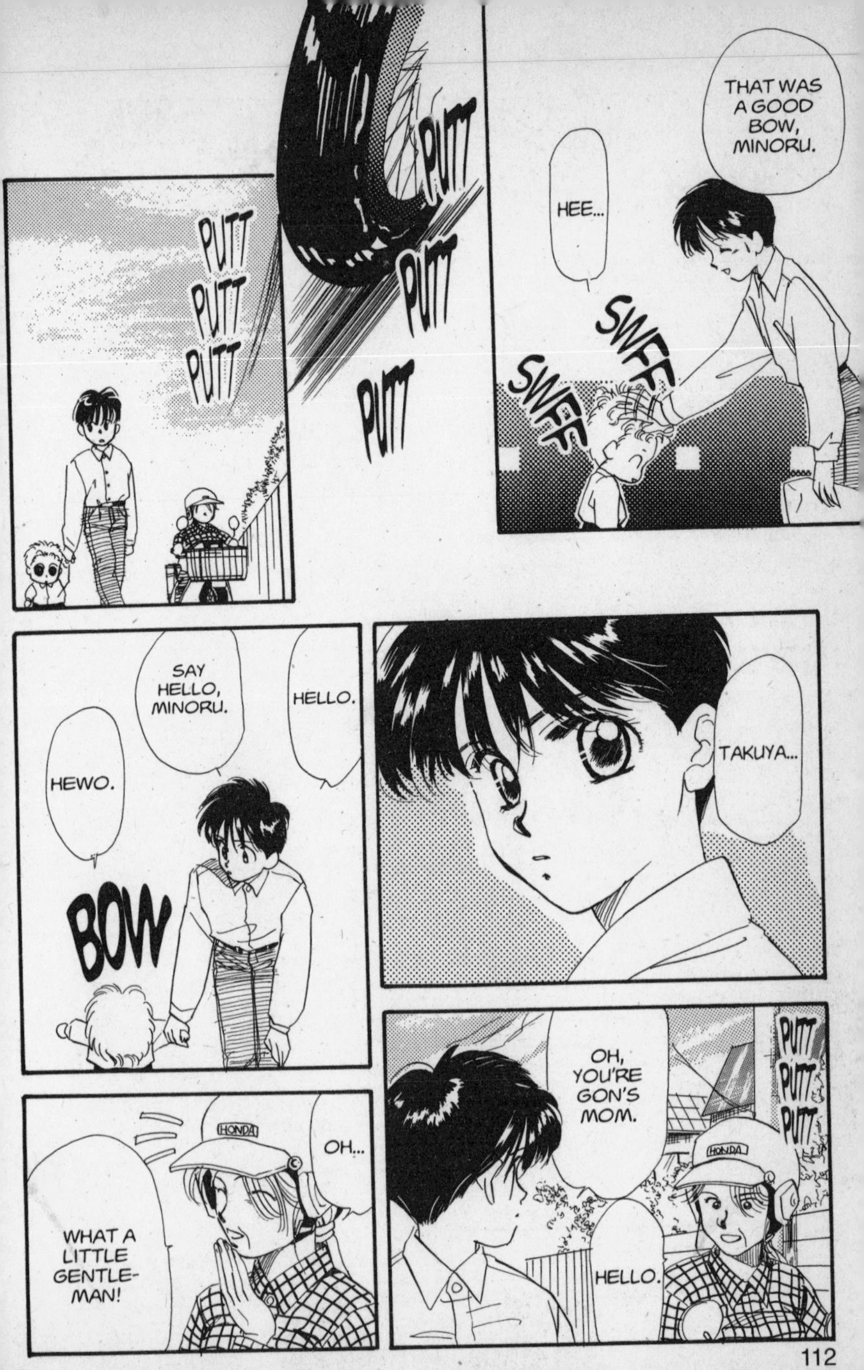
THAT WAS A GOOD BOW, MINORU.
HEE...
SWFF
SWFF
PUTT
PUTT
PUTT
PUTT
PUTT
PUTT
TAKUYA...
HELLO.
SAY HELLO, MINORU.
HEWO.
BOW
PUTT
PUTT
PUTT
OH, YOU'RE GON'S MOM.
HELLO.
OH...
WHAT A LITTLE GENTLE-MAN!

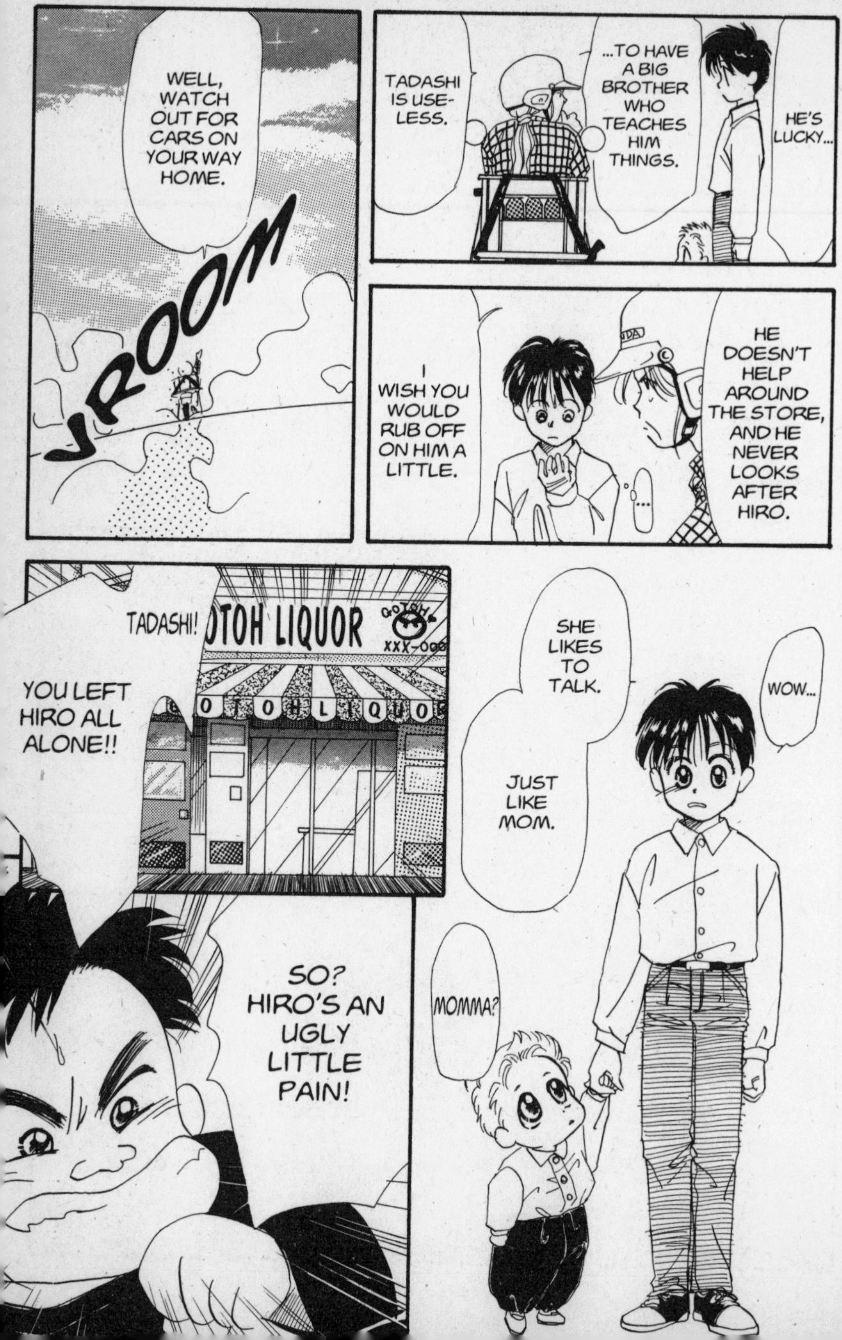
HE'S LUCKY...
...TO HAVE A BIG BROTHER WHO TEACHES HIM THINGS.
TADASHI IS USE-LESS.
HE DOESN'T HELP AROUND THE STORE, AND HE NEVER LOOKS AFTER HIRO.
I WISH YOU WOULD RUB OFF ON HIM A LITTLE.
...
WELL, WATCH OUT FOR CARS ON YOUR WAY HOME.
VROOM
WOW...
SHE LIKES TO TALK.
JUST LIKE MOM.
MOMMA?
OTOH LIQUOR
TADASHI!
YOU LEFT HIRO ALL ALONE!!
SO? HIRO'S AN UGLY LITTLE PAIN!

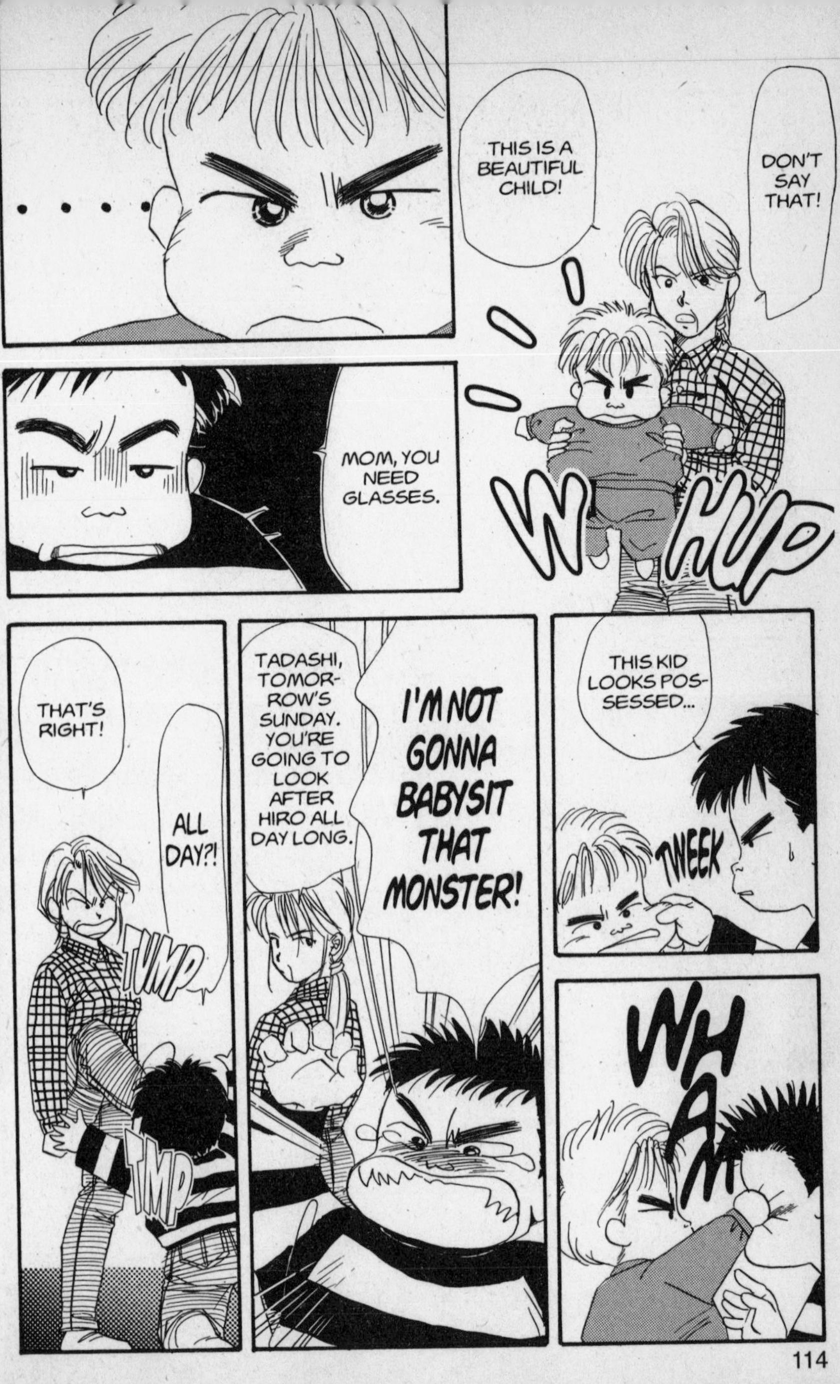
DON'T SAY THAT!
THIS IS A BEAUTIFUL CHILD!
WHUP
. . . . .
MOM, YOU NEED GLASSES.
THIS KID LOOKS POS-SESSED...
TWEEK
WHAM
I'M NOT GONNA BABYSIT THAT MONSTER!
TADASHI, TOMOR-ROW'S SUNDAY. YOU'RE GOING TO LOOK AFTER HIRO ALL DAY LONG.
ALL DAY?!
THAT'S RIGHT!
TUMP
TMP

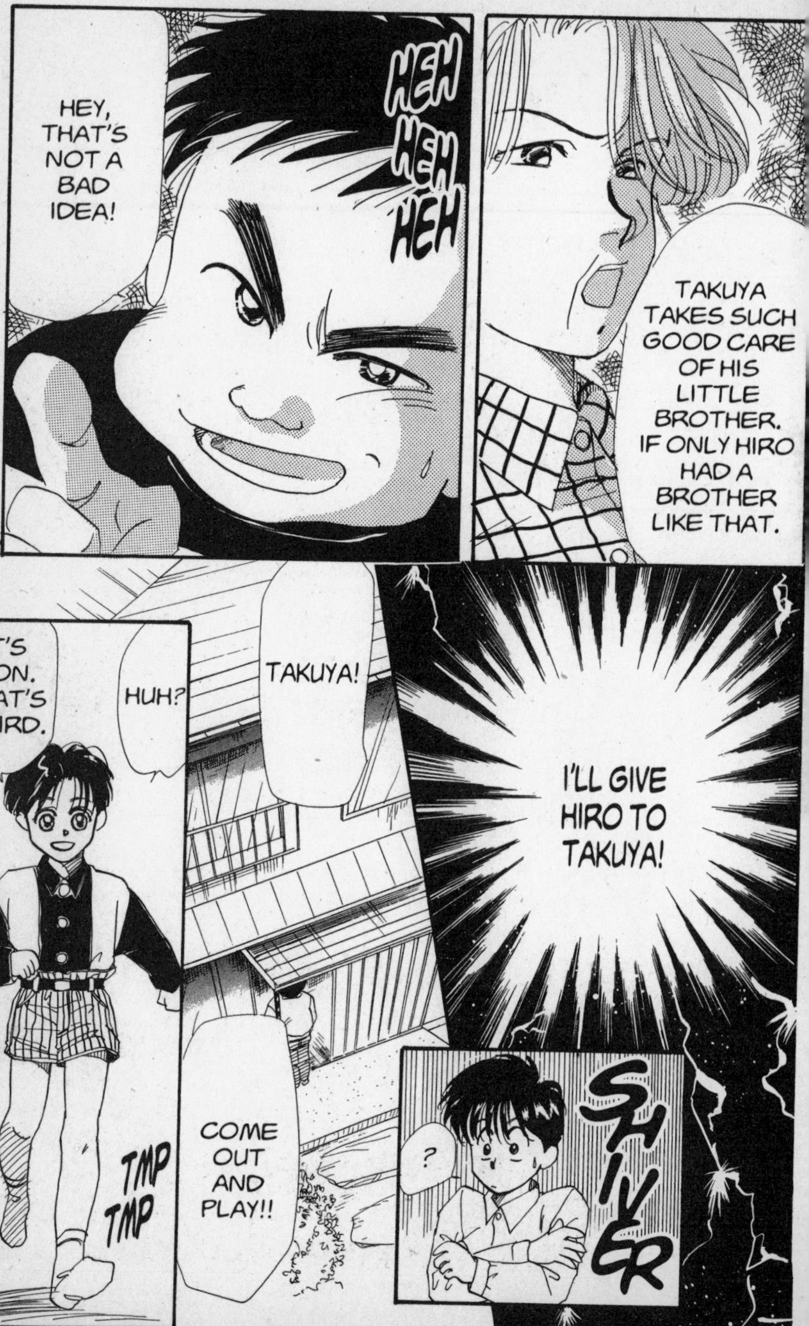
TAKUYA TAKES SUCH GOOD CARE OF HIS LITTLE BROTHER. IF ONLY HIRO HAD A BROTHER LIKE THAT.
HEH HEH HEH
HEY, THAT'S NOT A BAD IDEA!
I'LL GIVE HIRO TO TAKUYA!
SHIVER
?
TAKUYA!
COME OUT AND PLAY!!
HUH?
IT'S GON. THAT'S WEIRD.
TMP TMP

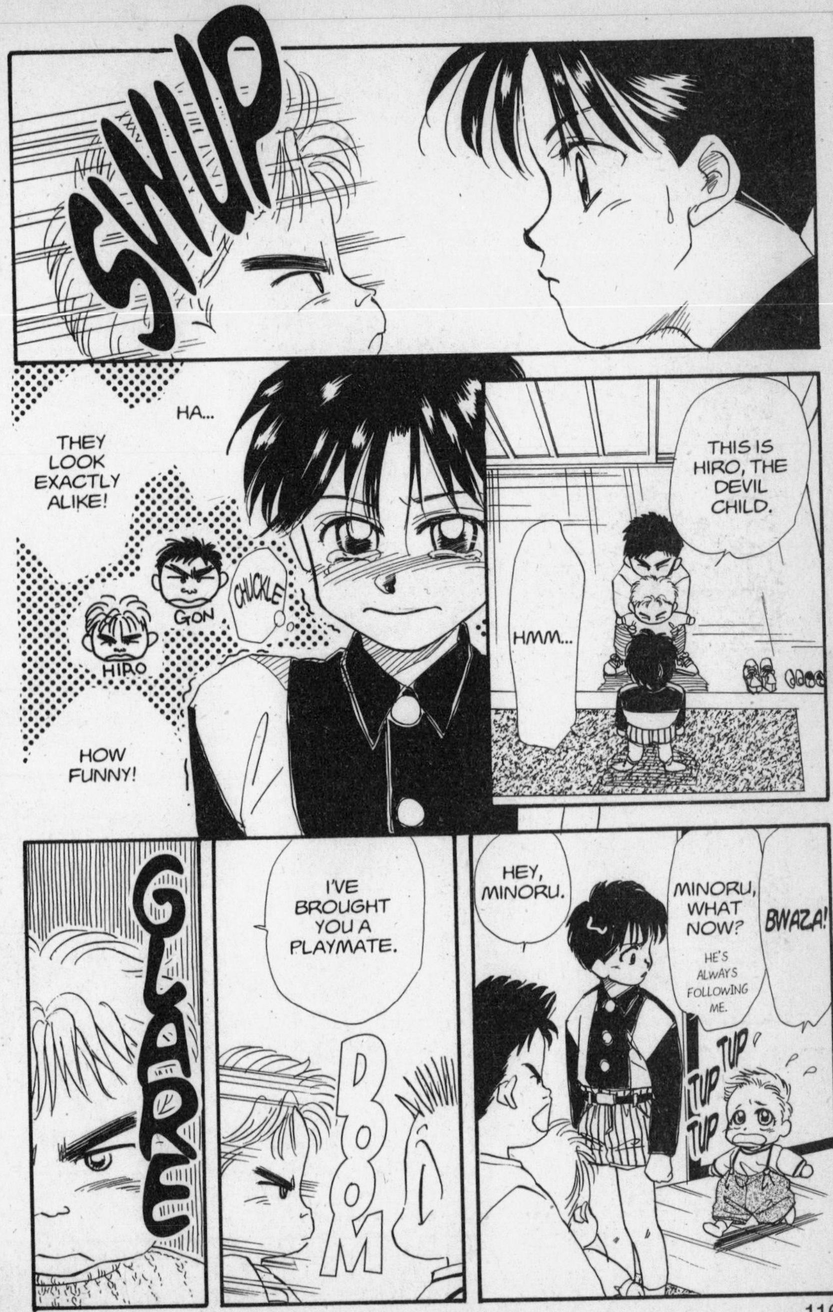
SWIP
THIS IS HIRO, THE DEVIL CHILD.
HMM...
HA...
THEY LOOK EXACTLY ALIKE!
GON
HIRO
CHUCKLE
HOW FUNNY!
BWAZA!
MINORU, WHAT NOW?
HE'S ALWAYS FOLLOWING ME.
HEY, MINORU.
TUP TUP TUP TUP
I'VE BROUGHT YOU A PLAYMATE.
DOOM
GLARE

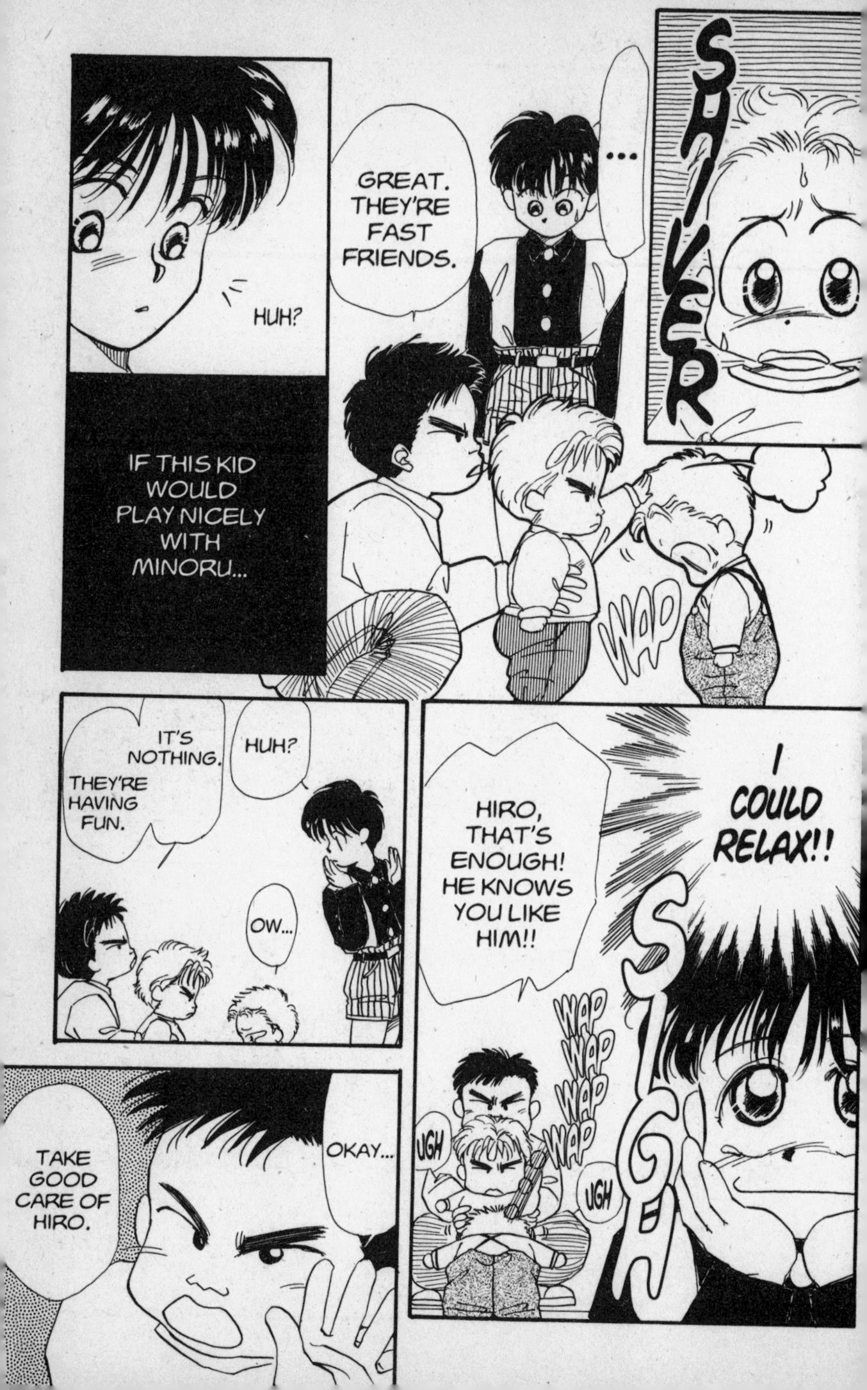
SHIVER
...
GREAT. THEY'RE FAST FRIENDS.
WAP
HUH?
IF THIS KID WOULD PLAY NICELY WITH MINORU...
I COULD RELAX!!
SIGH
HIRO, THAT'S ENOUGH! HE KNOWS YOU LIKE HIM!!
WAP WAP WAP WAP
UGH
UGH
HUH?
IT'S NOTHING.
THEY'RE HAVING FUN.
OW...
OKAY...
TAKE GOOD CARE OF HIRO.

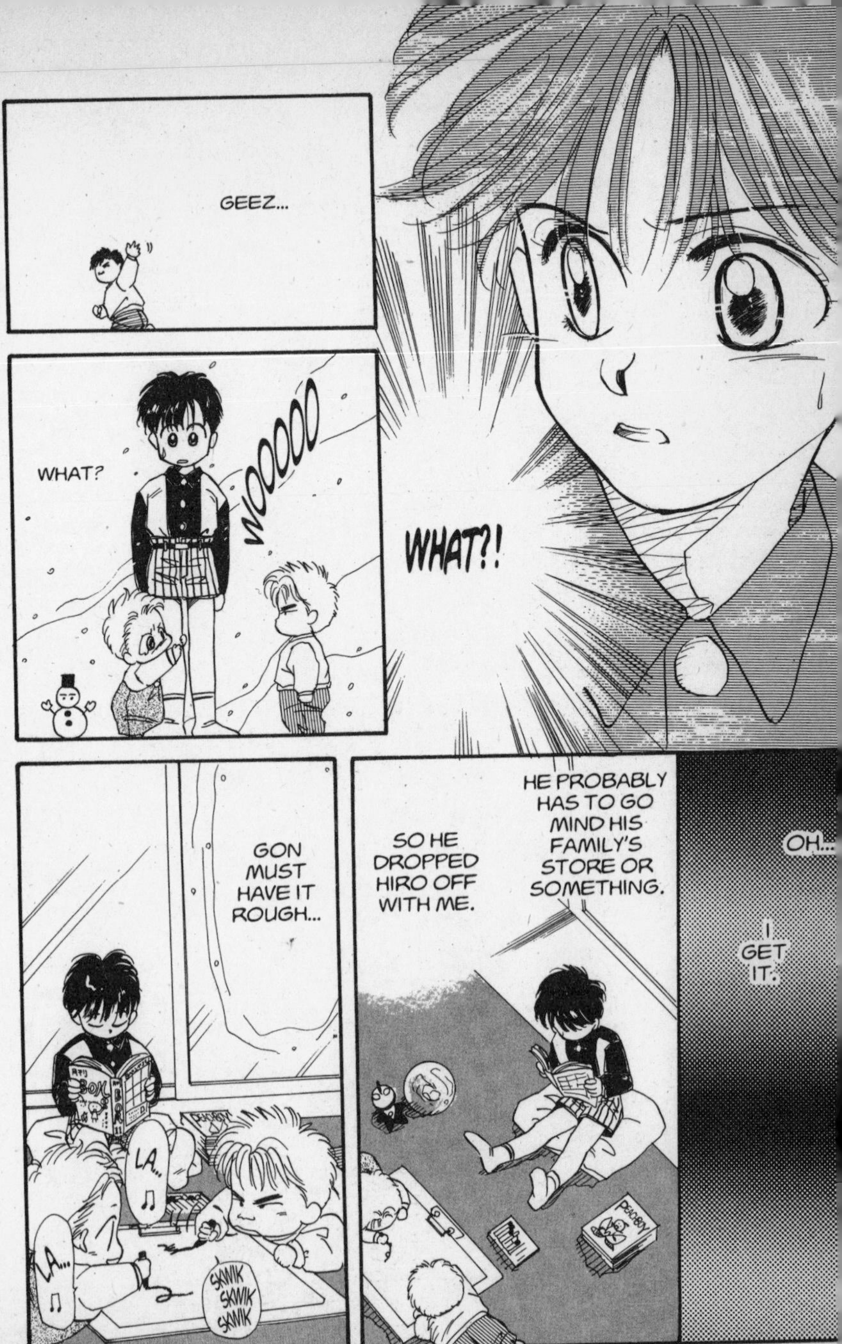
WHAT?!
GEEZ...
WOOOOO
WHAT?
OH...
I GET IT.
HE PROBABLY HAS TO GO MIND HIS FAMILY'S STORE OR SOMETHING.
SO HE DROPPED HIRO OFF WITH ME.
GON MUST HAVE IT ROUGH...
LA...
LA...
SKWIK SKWIK SKWIK

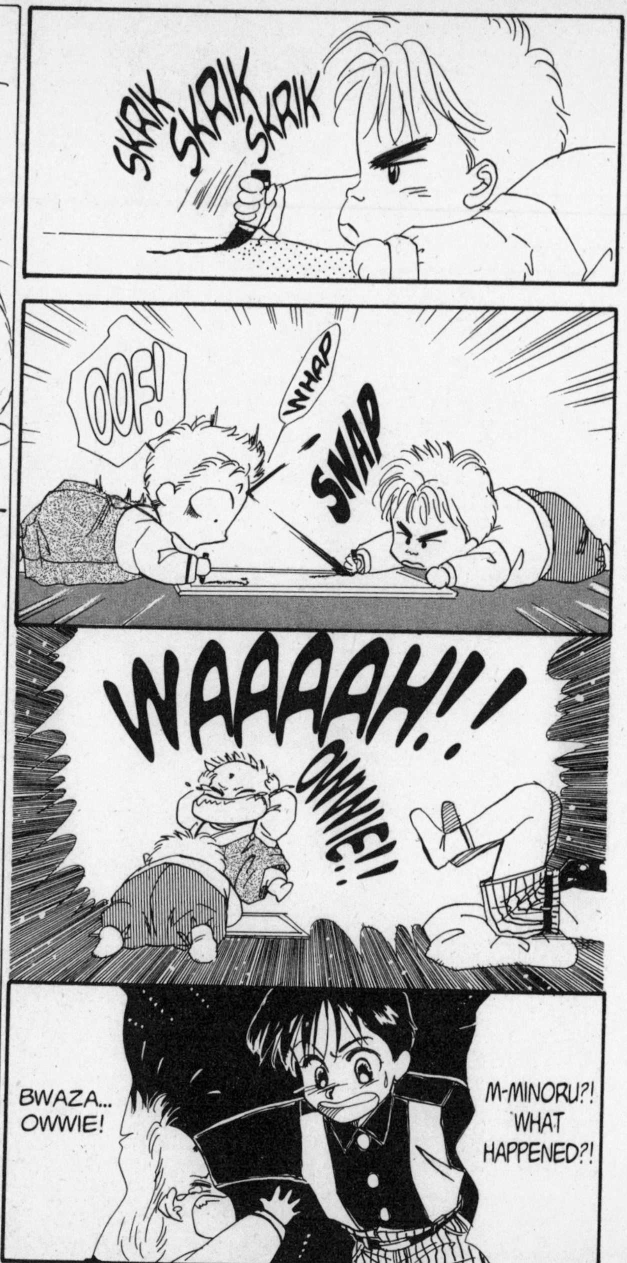
SKRIK SKRIK SKRIK
SNAP
WHAP
OOF!
WAAAAH!!!
OWWIE!!
M-MINORU?! WHAT HAPPENED?!
BWAZA... OWWIE!

AUTHOR'S NOTE 5

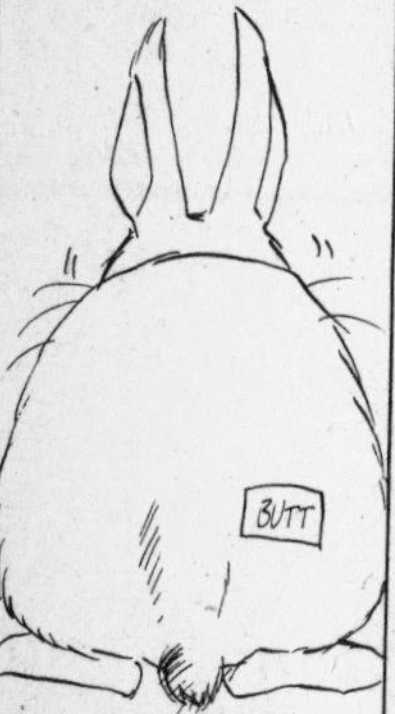
BUTT

YOSHIZO THE RABBIT PART 2

THE LITTLE GROUP OF RABBITS THAT WERE BEING SOLD UNDER THE COLD MID-WINTER SKY HUDDLED TOGETHER IN A BOX. I WAS FORCED TO BUY THE ONLY ONE THAT WAS HOPPING AROUND. HE WAS A LITTLE BIGGER THAN THE REST, AND LOOKED A BIT GRUBBY. AT THE TIME I THOUGHT THE LIVELIER THE RABBIT THE BETTER, BUT HE NIBBLED HOLES IN MY JEANS AND CHEWED UP MY BOOKS. I GOT MAD AND PUT HIM IN AN ORANGE BOX, BUT BY THE NEXT MORNING HE HAD CHEWED HIS WAY OUT THROUGH THE SIDE AND RUN AWAY.

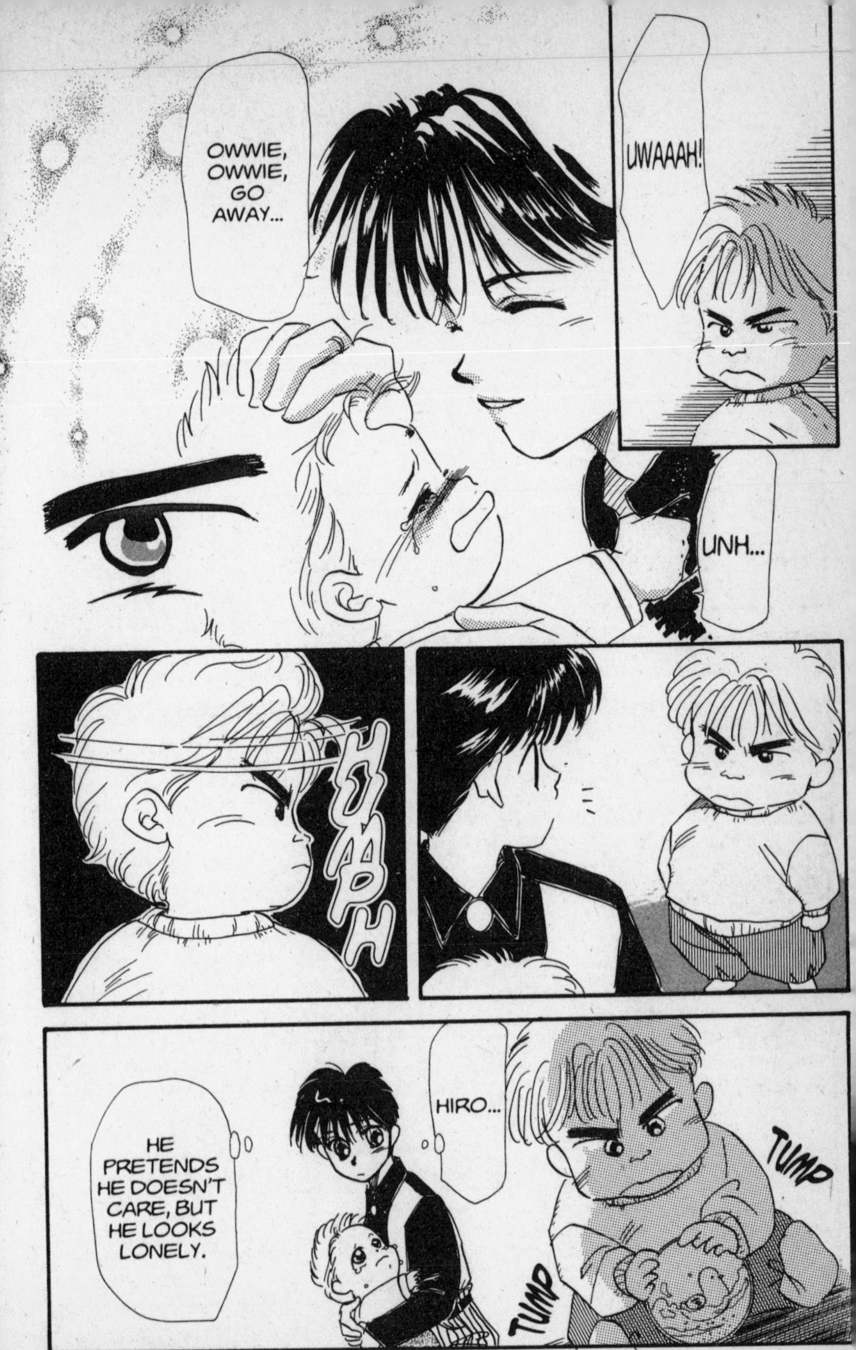
UWAAAH!
OWWIE, OWWIE, GO AWAY...
UNH...
HUMPH
TUMP
HIRO...
HE PRETENDS HE DOESN'T CARE, BUT HE LOOKS LONELY.
TUMP

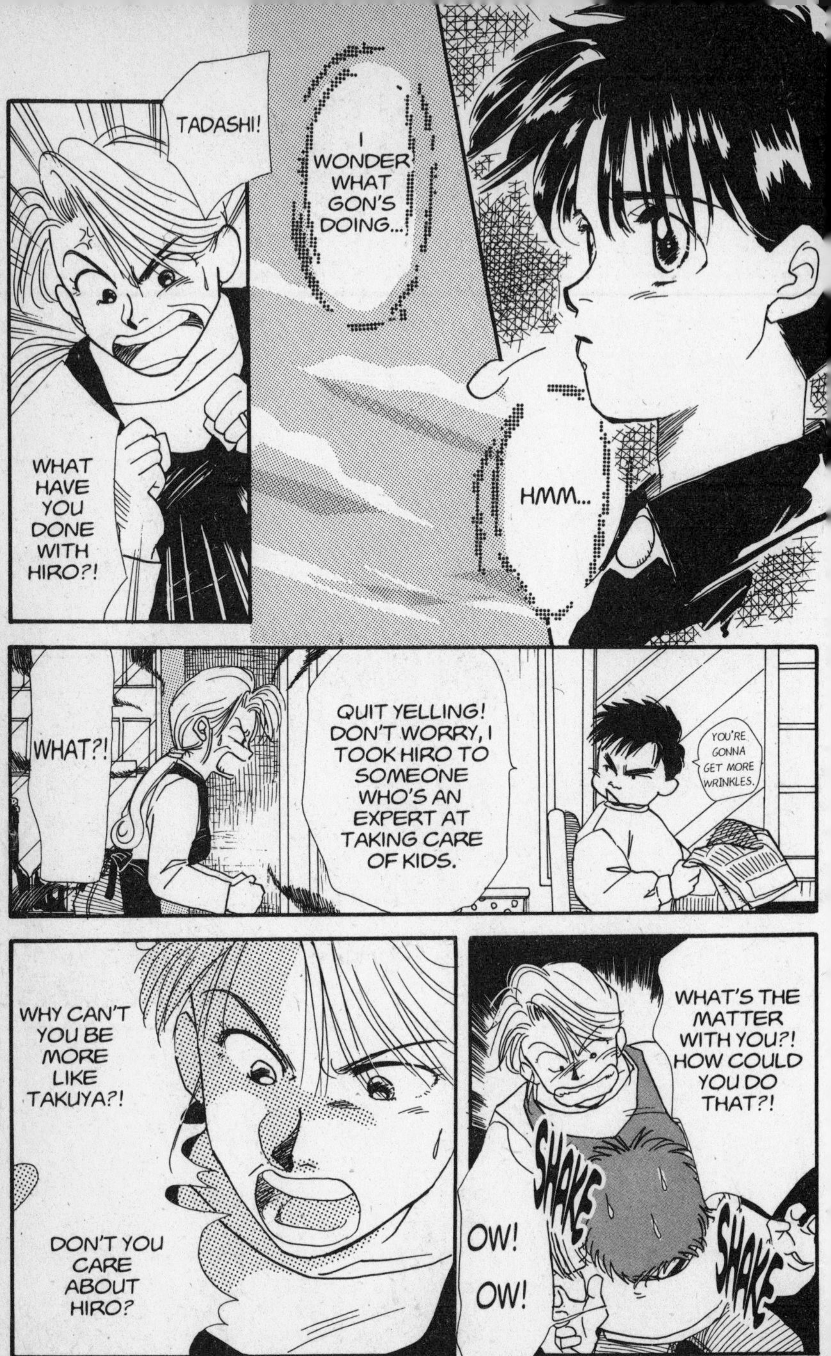
I WONDER WHAT GON'S DOING...
HMM...
TADASHI!
WHAT HAVE YOU DONE WITH HIRO?!
QUIT YELLING! DON'T WORRY, I TOOK HIRO TO SOMEONE WHO'S AN EXPERT AT TAKING CARE OF KIDS.
YOU'RE GONNA GET MORE WRINKLES.
WHAT?!
WHAT'S THE MATTER WITH YOU?! HOW COULD YOU DO THAT?!
SHAKE
SHAKE
OW!
OW!
WHY CAN'T YOU BE MORE LIKE TAKUYA?!
DON'T YOU CARE ABOUT HIRO?

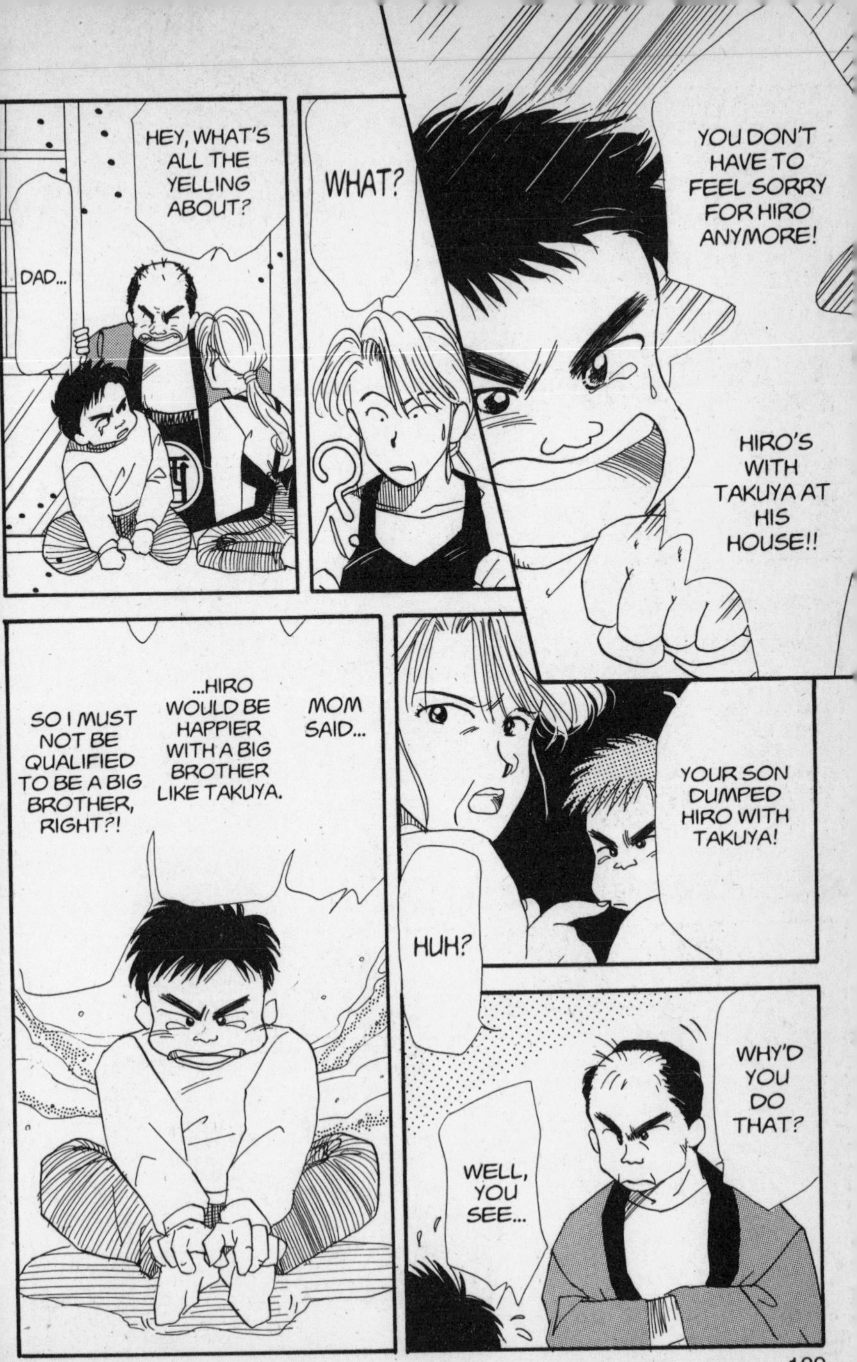
YOU DON'T HAVE TO FEEL SORRY FOR HIRO ANYMORE!
HIRO'S WITH TAKUYA AT HIS HOUSE!!
WHAT?
HEY, WHAT'S ALL THE YELLING ABOUT?
DAD...
YOUR SON DUMPED HIRO WITH TAKUYA!
HUH?
WHY'D YOU DO THAT?
WELL, YOU SEE...
MOM SAID...
...HIRO WOULD BE HAPPIER WITH A BIG BROTHER LIKE TAKUYA.
SO I MUST NOT BE QUALIFIED TO BE A BIG BROTHER, RIGHT?!

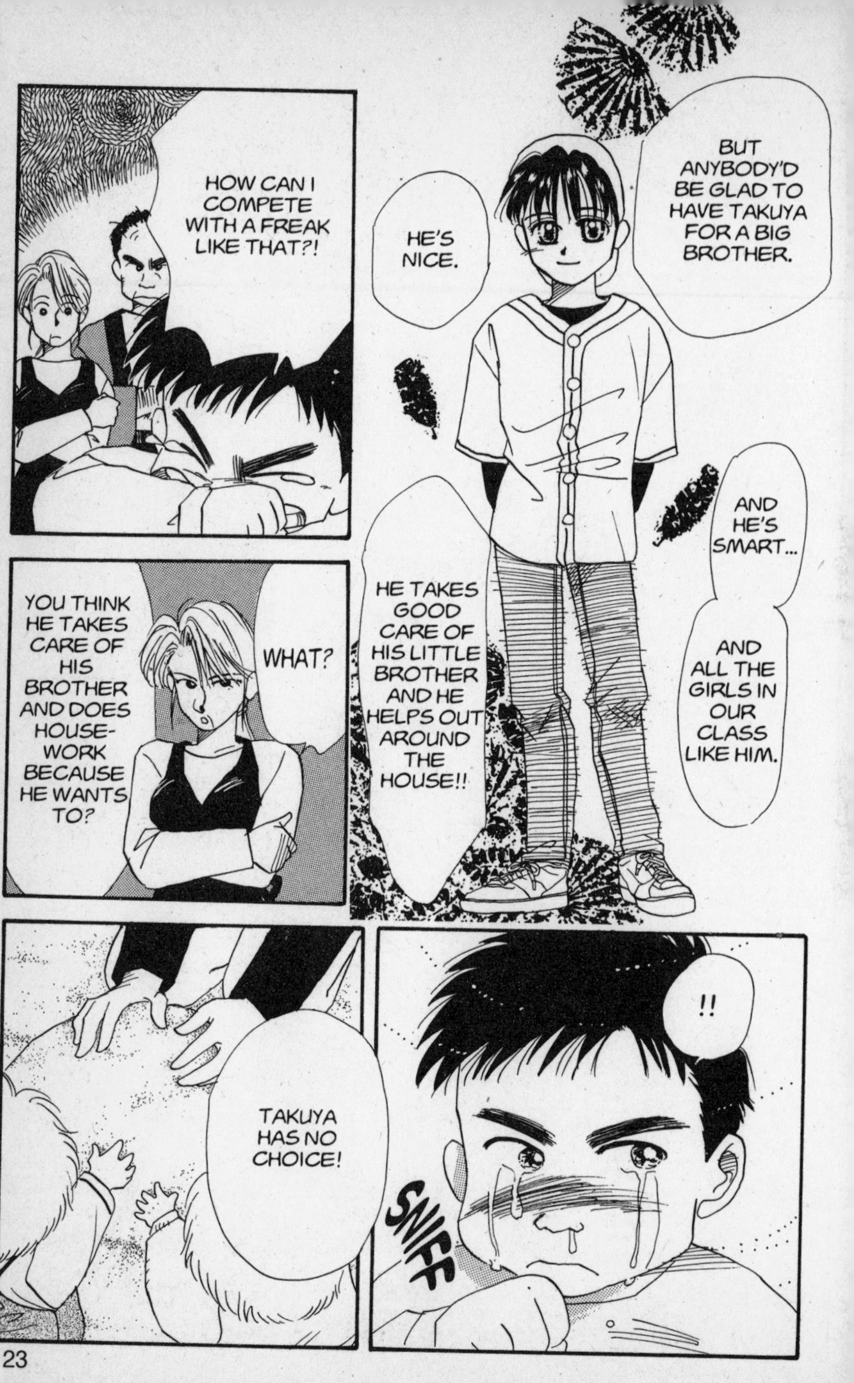
BUT ANYBODY'D BE GLAD TO HAVE TAKUYA FOR A BIG BROTHER.
HE'S NICE.
AND HE'S SMART...
AND ALL THE GIRLS IN OUR CLASS LIKE HIM.
HE TAKES GOOD CARE OF HIS LITTLE BROTHER AND HE HELPS OUT AROUND THE HOUSE!!
HOW CAN I COMPETE WITH A FREAK LIKE THAT?!
WHAT?
YOU THINK HE TAKES CARE OF HIS BROTHER AND DOES HOUSE-WORK BECAUSE HE WANTS TO?
!!
SNIFF
TAKUYA HAS NO CHOICE!

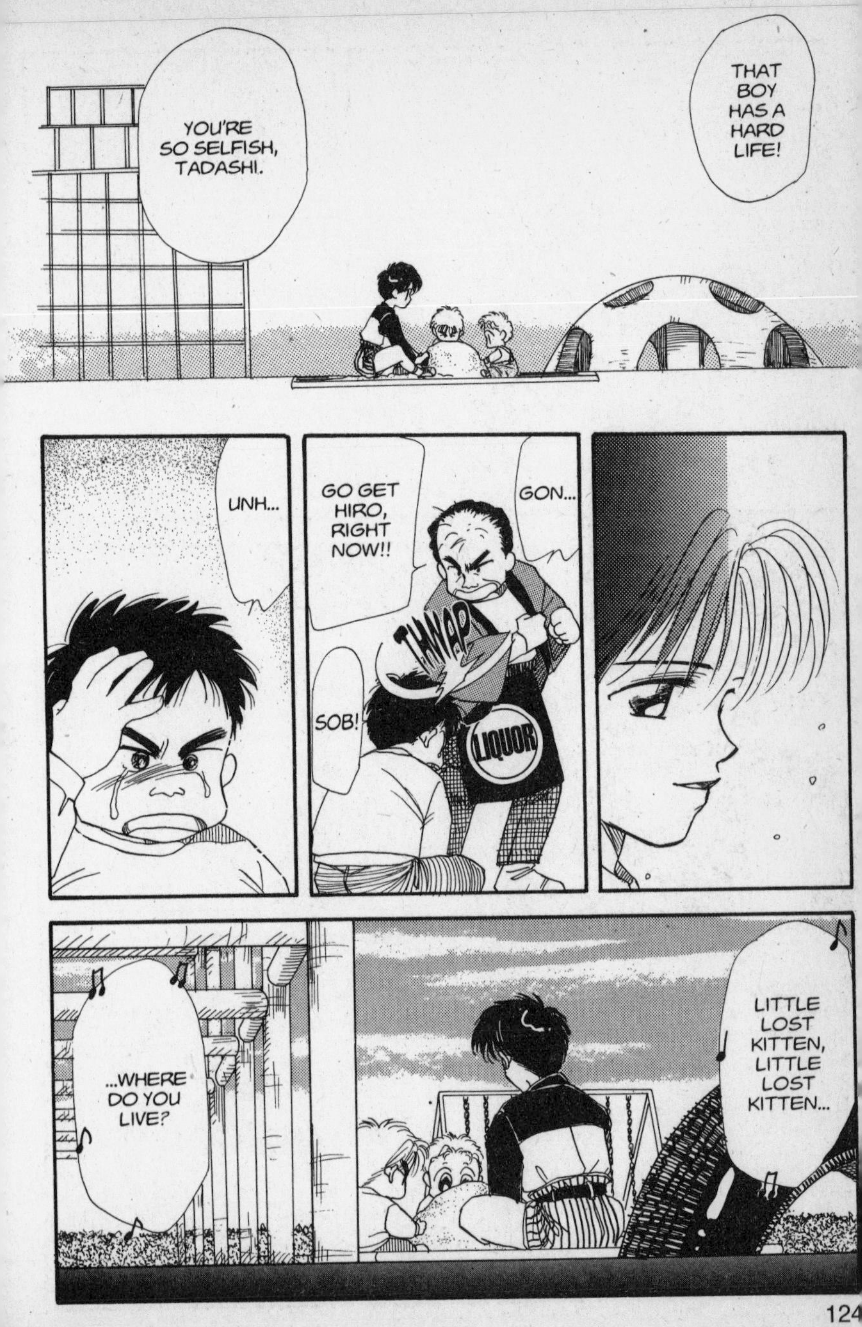
THAT BOY HAS A HARD LIFE!
YOU'RE SO SELFISH, TADASHI.
GON...
GO GET HIRO, RIGHT NOW!!
THWAP
LIQUOR
SOB!
UNH...
LITTLE LOST KITTEN, LITTLE LOST KITTEN...
...WHERE DO YOU LIVE?

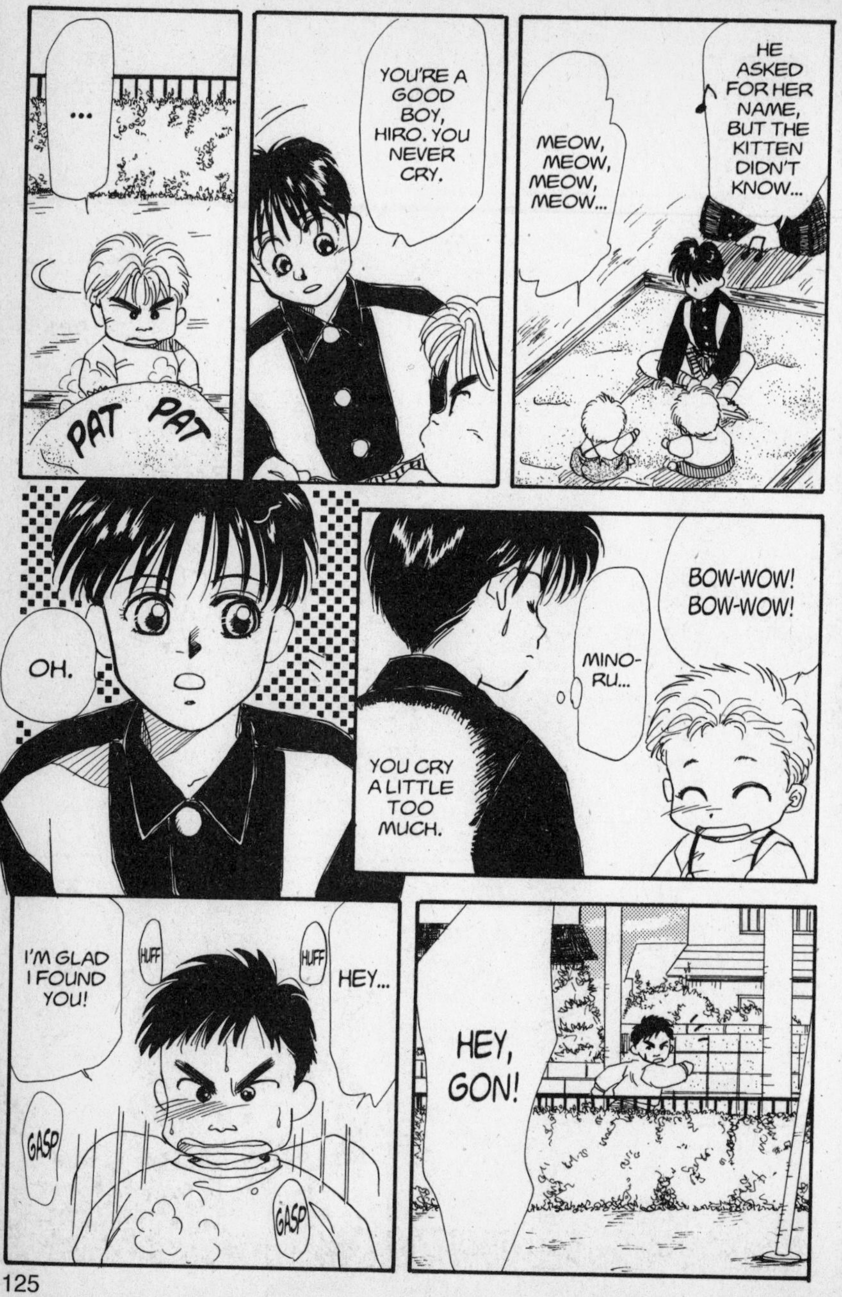
HE ASKED FOR HER NAME, BUT THE KITTEN DIDN'T KNOW...
MEOW, MEOW, MEOW, MEOW...
YOU'RE A GOOD BOY, HIRO. YOU NEVER CRY.
...
PAT PAT
BOW-WOW! BOW-WOW!
MINO-RU...
YOU CRY A LITTLE TOO MUCH.
OH.
HEY, GON!
HEY...
HUFF
HUFF
I'M GLAD I FOUND YOU!
GASP
GASP

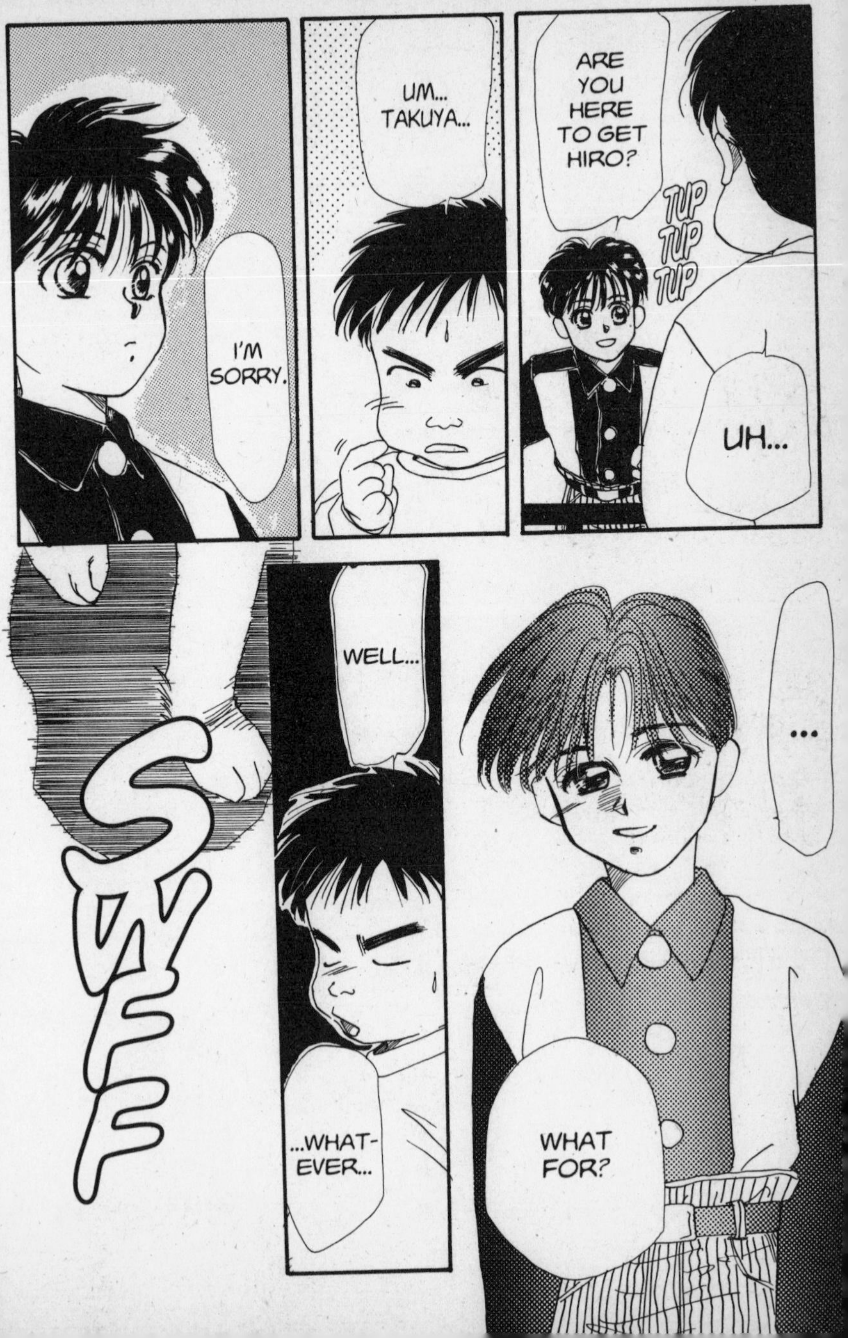
ARE YOU HERE TO GET HIRO?
TUP TUP TUP
UH...
UM... TAKUYA...
I'M SORRY.
...
WHAT FOR?
WELL...
...WHAT-EVER...
SWFF

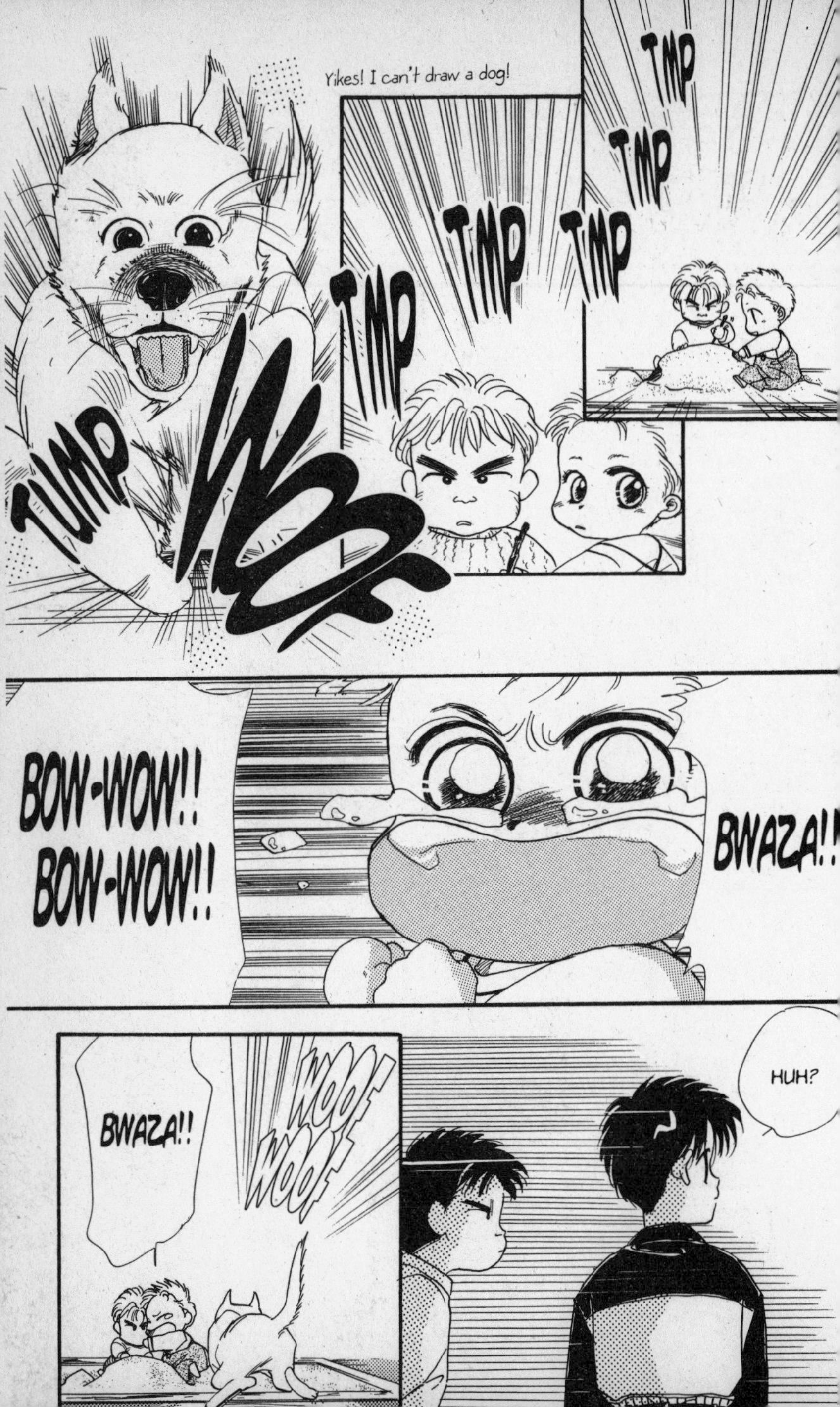
TMP
TMP
TMP
Yikes! I can't draw a dog!
TMP
TMP
TUMP
WOOF
BWAZA!!
BOW-WOW!!
BOW-WOW!!
HUH?
WOOF
WOOF
BWAZA!!

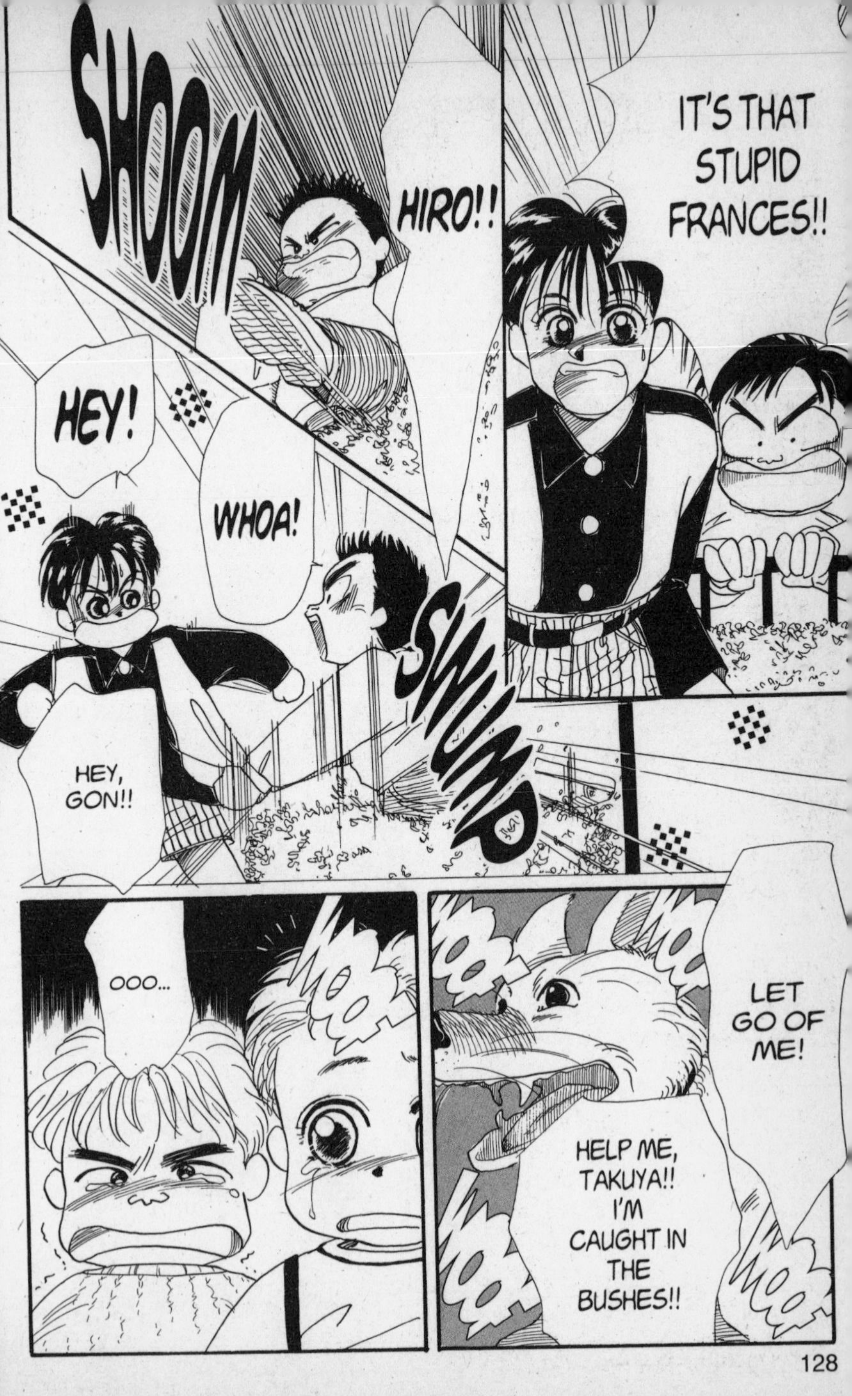
IT'S THAT STUPID FRANCES!!
HIRO!!
SHOOM
HEY!
WHOA!
SWUMP
HEY, GON!!
LET GO OF ME!
MOO
HELP ME, TAKUYA!! I'M CAUGHT IN THE BUSHES!!
MOO
OOO...
MOO

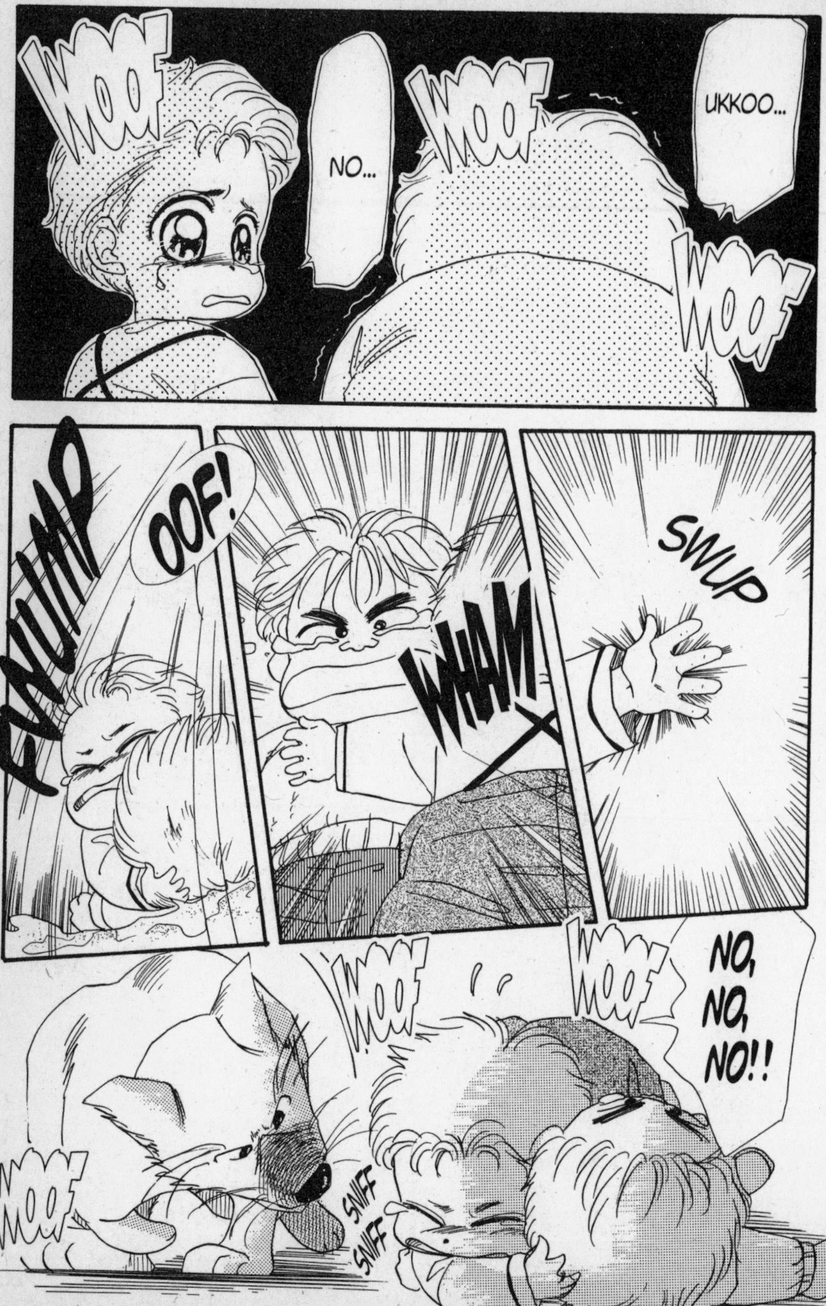
UKKOO...
WOOF
WOOF
NO...
WOOF
SWUP
WHAM
OOF!
FWUMP
NO, NO, NO!!
WOOF
WOOF
SNIFF SNIFF
WOOF

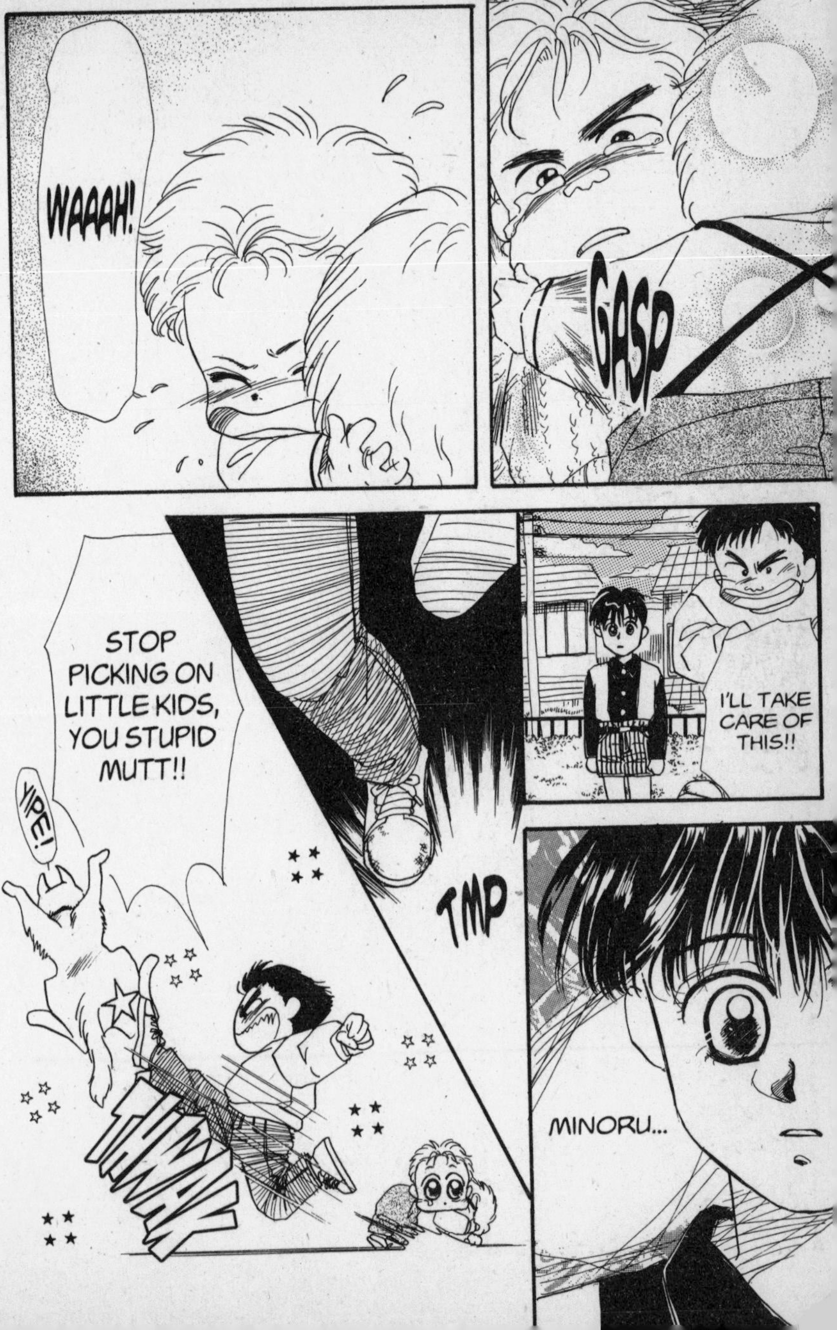
GASP
WAAAH!
I'LL TAKE CARE OF THIS!!
MINORU...
TMP
STOP PICKING ON LITTLE KIDS, YOU STUPID MUTT!!
YIPE!
THWAK

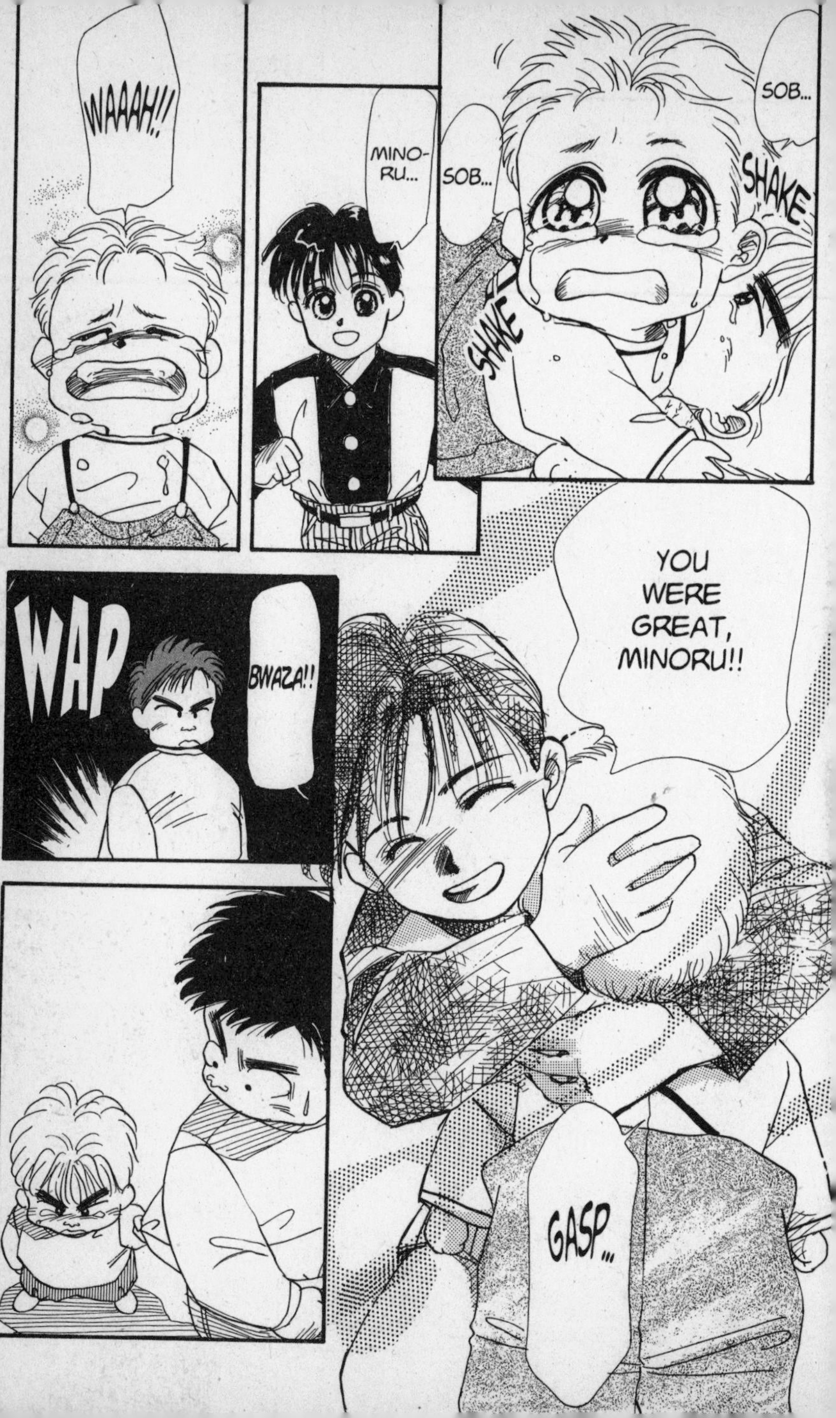
SOB...
SHAKE
SOB...
SHAKE
MINO-RU...
WAAAH!!
YOU WERE GREAT, MINORU!!
GASP...
BWAZA!!
WAP

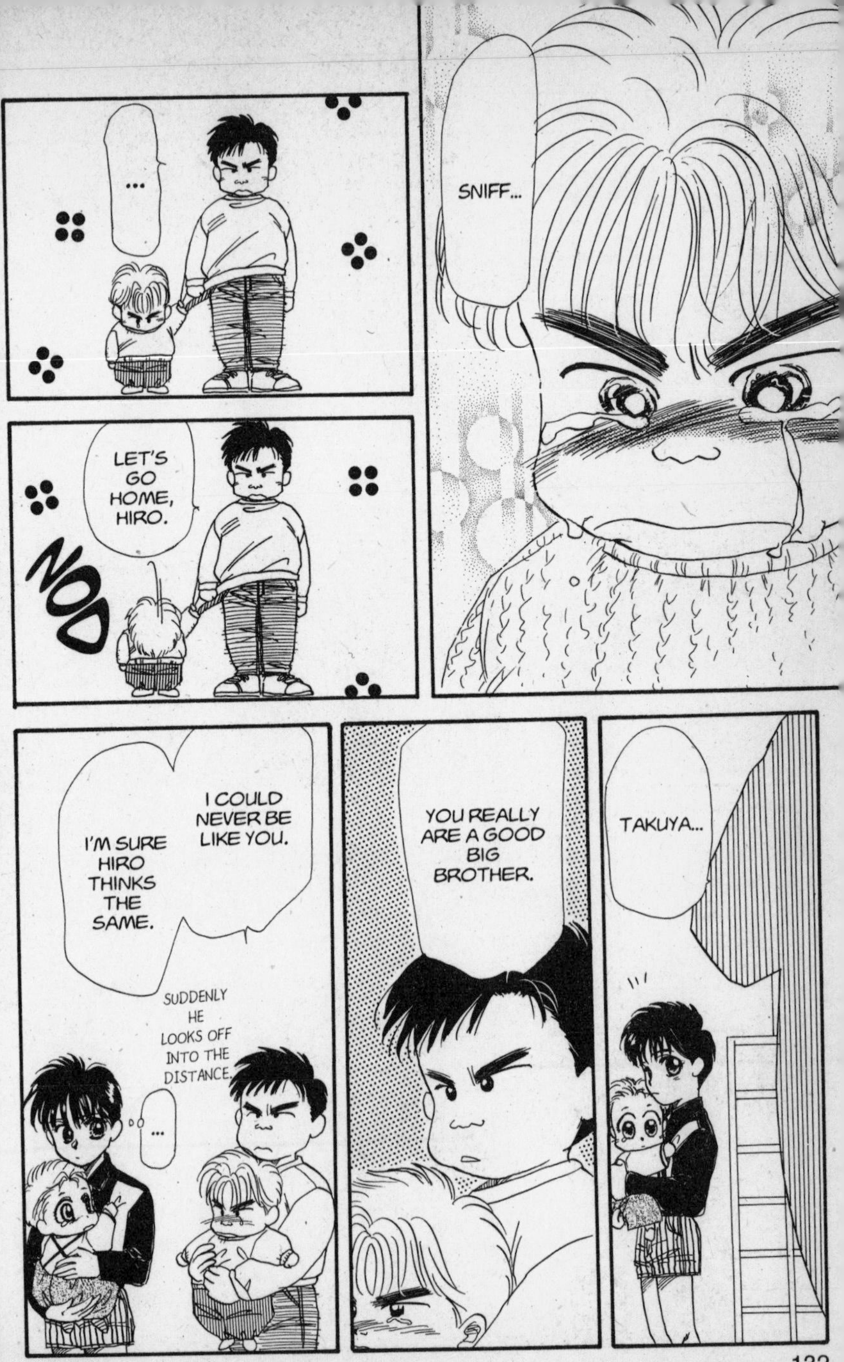
SNIFF...
...
LET'S GO HOME, HIRO.
NOD
TAKUYA...
YOU REALLY ARE A GOOD BIG BROTHER.
I COULD NEVER BE LIKE YOU.
I'M SURE HIRO THINKS THE SAME.
SUDDENLY HE LOOKS OFF INTO THE DISTANCE.
...

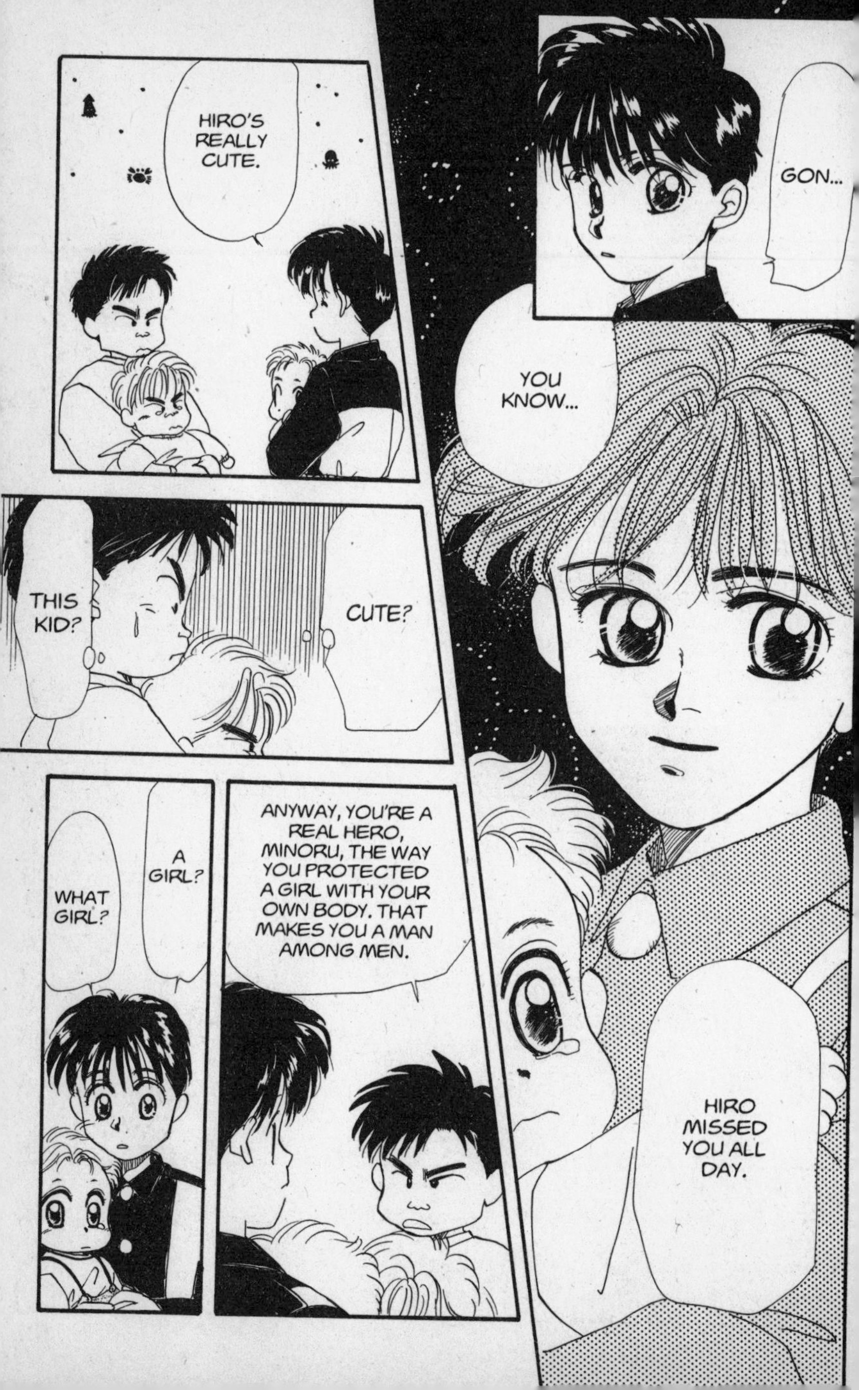
GON...
YOU KNOW...
HIRO MISSED YOU ALL DAY.
HIRO'S REALLY CUTE.
CUTE?
THIS KID?
ANYWAY, YOU'RE A REAL HERO, MINORU, THE WAY YOU PROTECTED A GIRL WITH YOUR OWN BODY. THAT MAKES YOU A MAN AMONG MEN.
A GIRL?
WHAT GIRL?

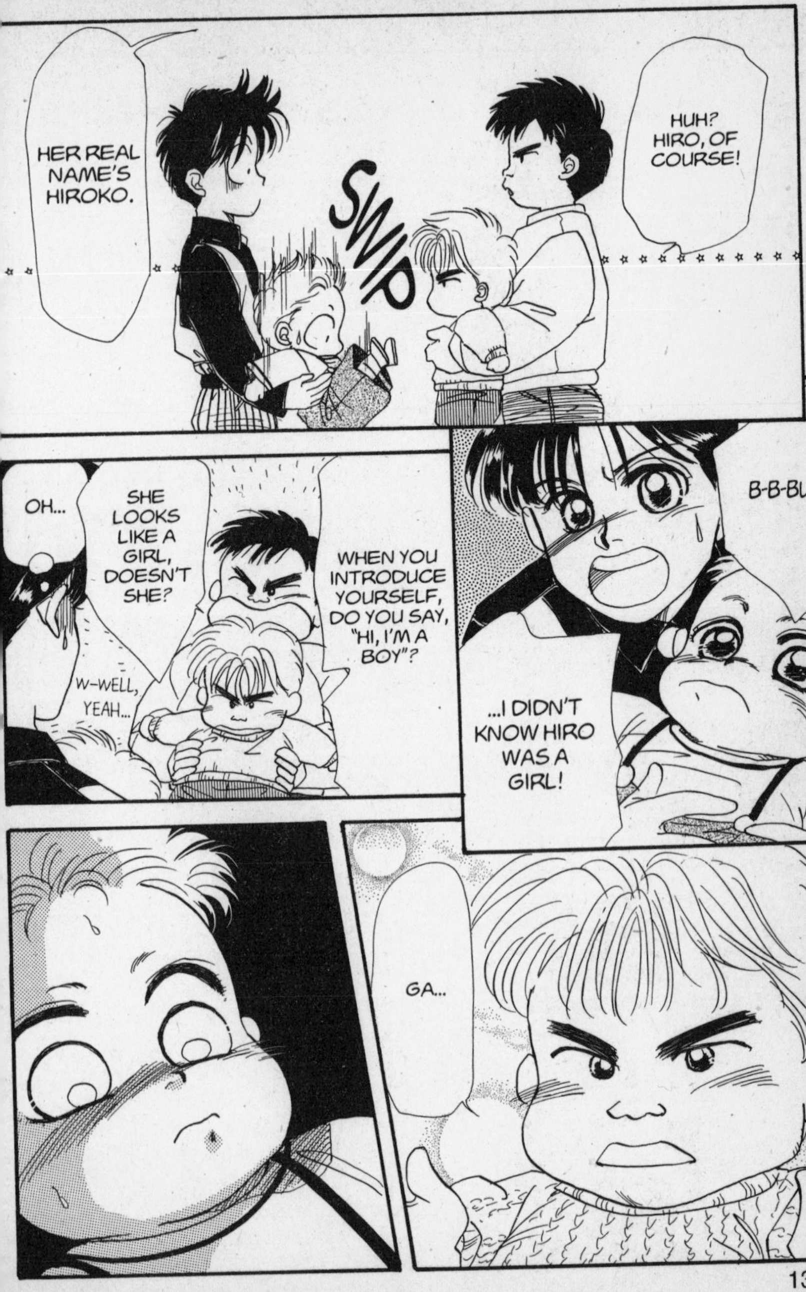
HUH? HIRO, OF COURSE!
SWIP
HER REAL NAME'S HIROKO.
B-B-BUT...
...I DIDN'T KNOW HIRO WAS A GIRL!
WHEN YOU INTRODUCE YOURSELF, DO YOU SAY, "HI, I'M A BOY"?
SHE LOOKS LIKE A GIRL, DOESN'T SHE?
OH...
W-WELL, YEAH...
GA...

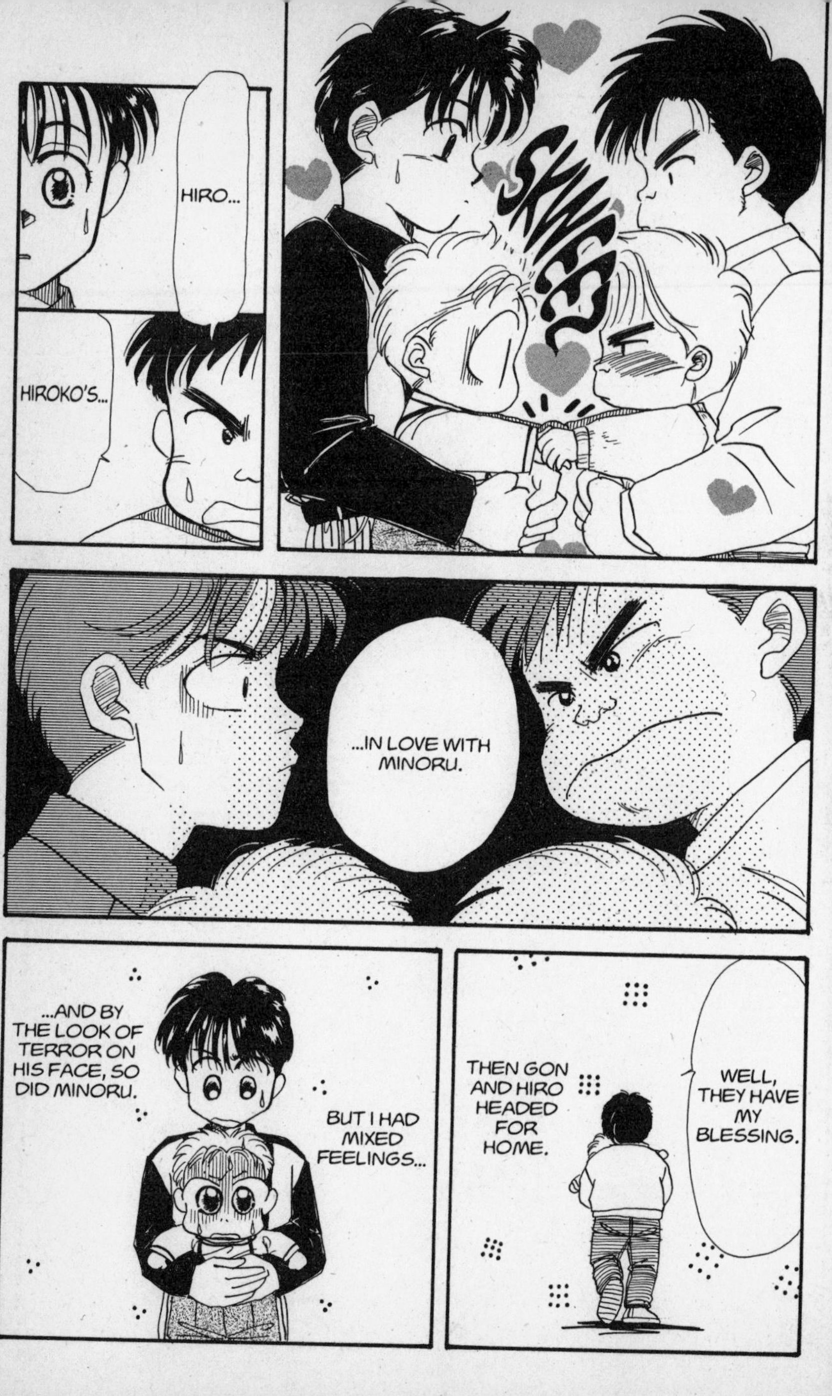
SKWEEZ
HIRO...
HIROKO'S...
...IN LOVE WITH MINORU.
WELL, THEY HAVE MY BLESSING.
THEN GON AND HIRO HEADED FOR HOME.
...AND BY THE LOOK OF TERROR ON HIS FACE, SO DID MINORU.
BUT I HAD MIXED FEELINGS...

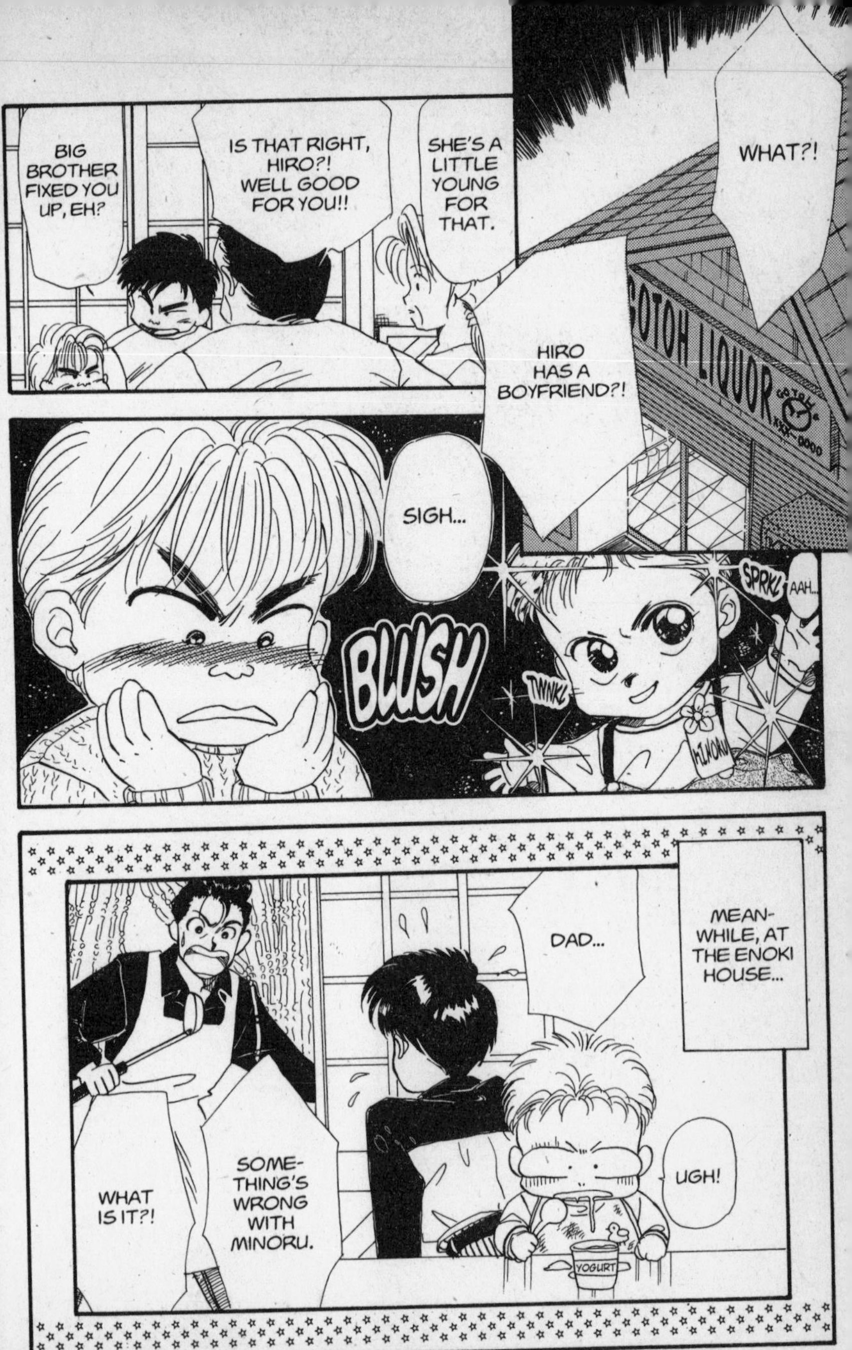
WHAT?!
HIRO HAS A BOYFRIEND?!
GOTOH LIQUOR
SHE'S A LITTLE YOUNG FOR THAT.
IS THAT RIGHT, HIRO?! WELL GOOD FOR YOU!!
BIG BROTHER FIXED YOU UP, EH?
SPRKL
AAH...
TWNKL
MINORU
SIGH...
BLUSH
MEAN-WHILE, AT THE ENOKI HOUSE...
DAD...
UGH!
YOGURT
SOME-THING'S WRONG WITH MINORU.
WHAT IS IT?!

CHAPTER 3/THE END

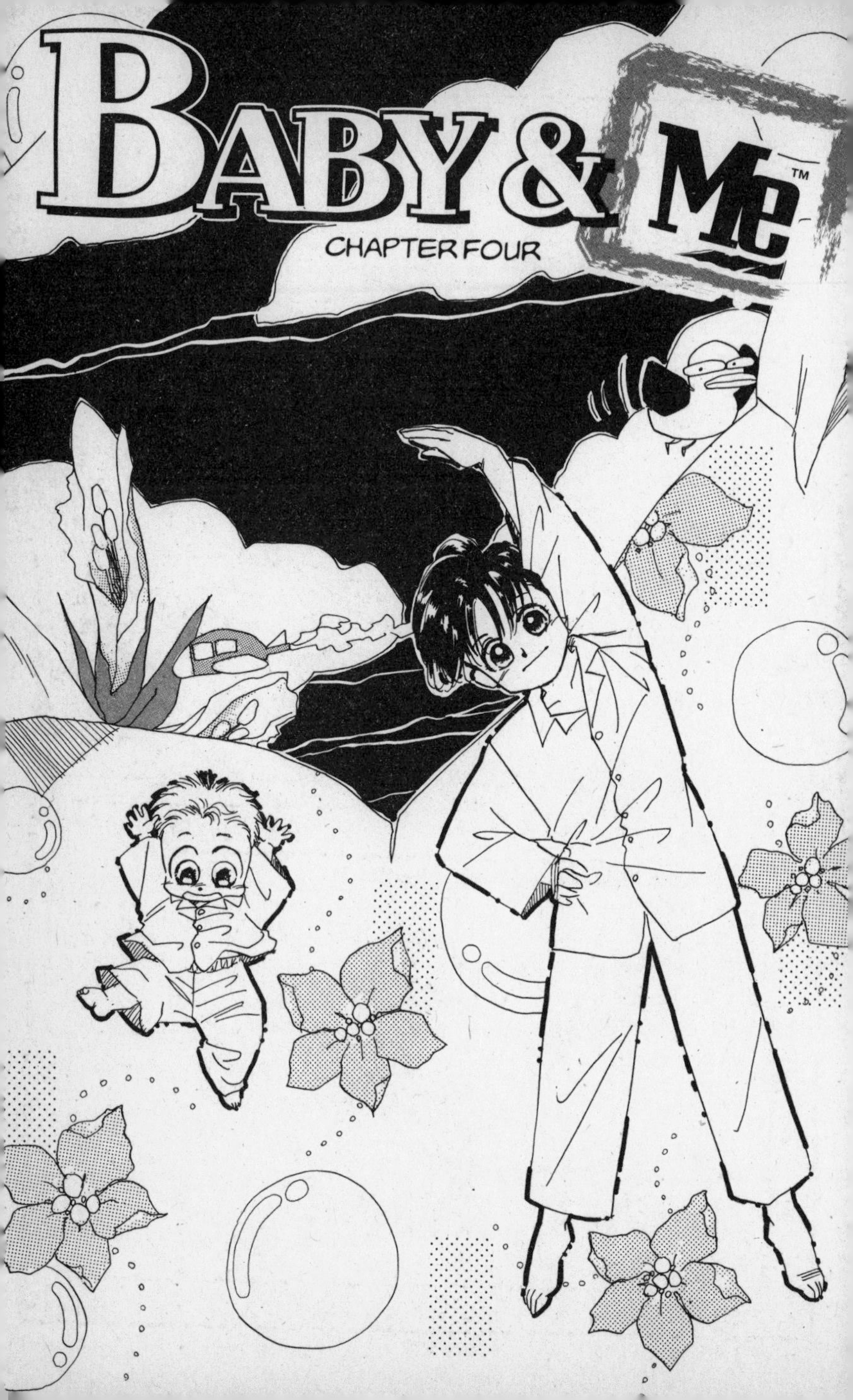
BABY & ME™
CHAPTER FOUR

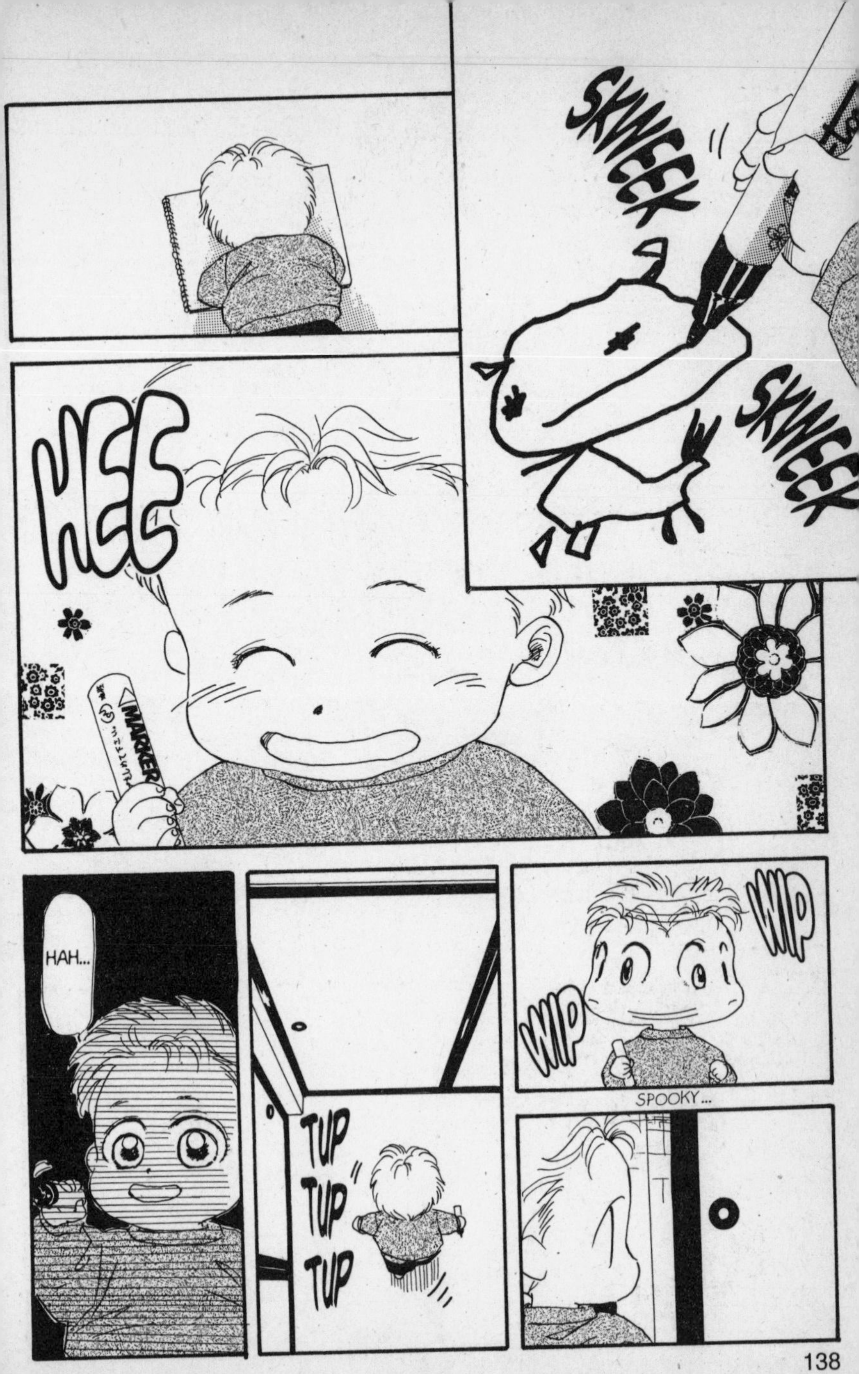
SKWEEK
SKWEEK
HEE
MARKER
WIP
WIP
SPOOKY...
TUP
TUP
TUP
TUP
HAH...

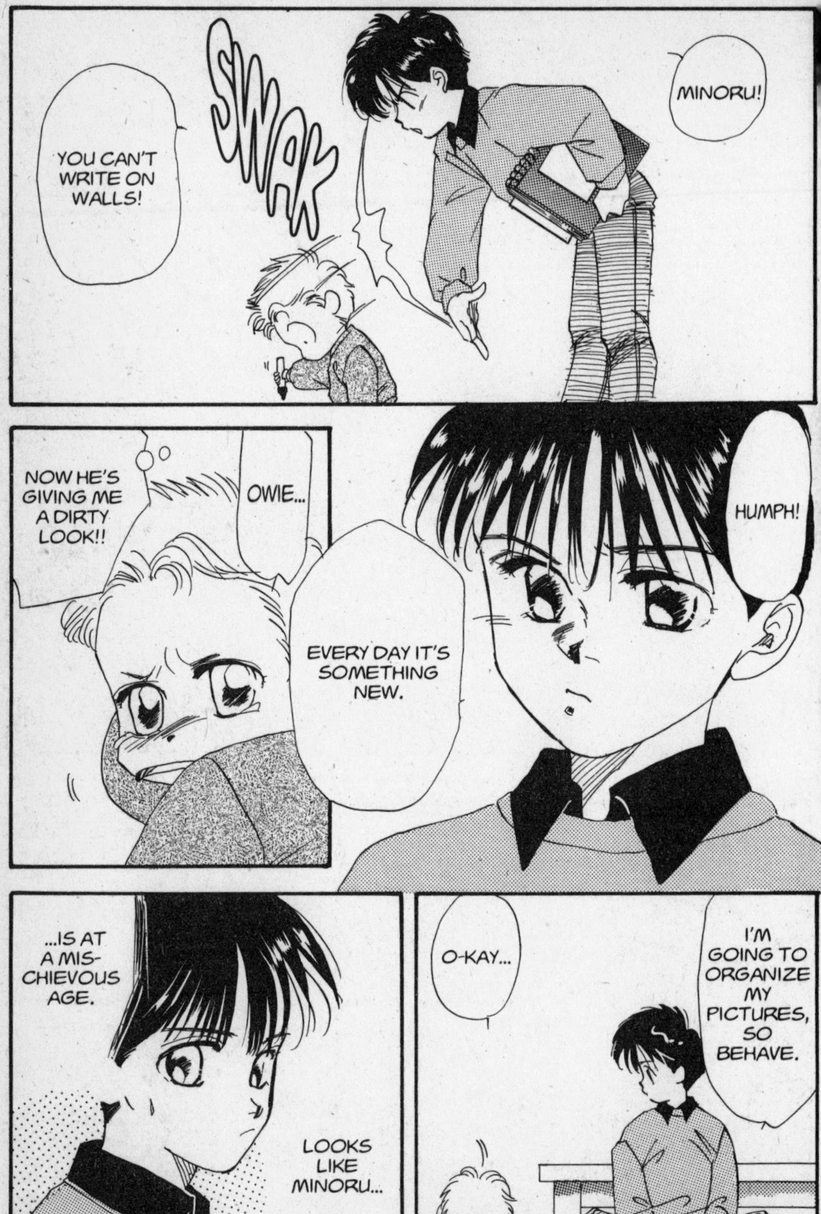
MINORU!
SWAK
YOU CAN'T WRITE ON WALLS!
HUMPH!
EVERY DAY IT'S SOMETHING NEW.
OWIE...
NOW HE'S GIVING ME A DIRTY LOOK!!
I'M GOING TO ORGANIZE MY PICTURES, SO BEHAVE.
O-KAY...
LOOKS LIKE MINORU...
...IS AT A MIS-CHIEVOUS AGE.

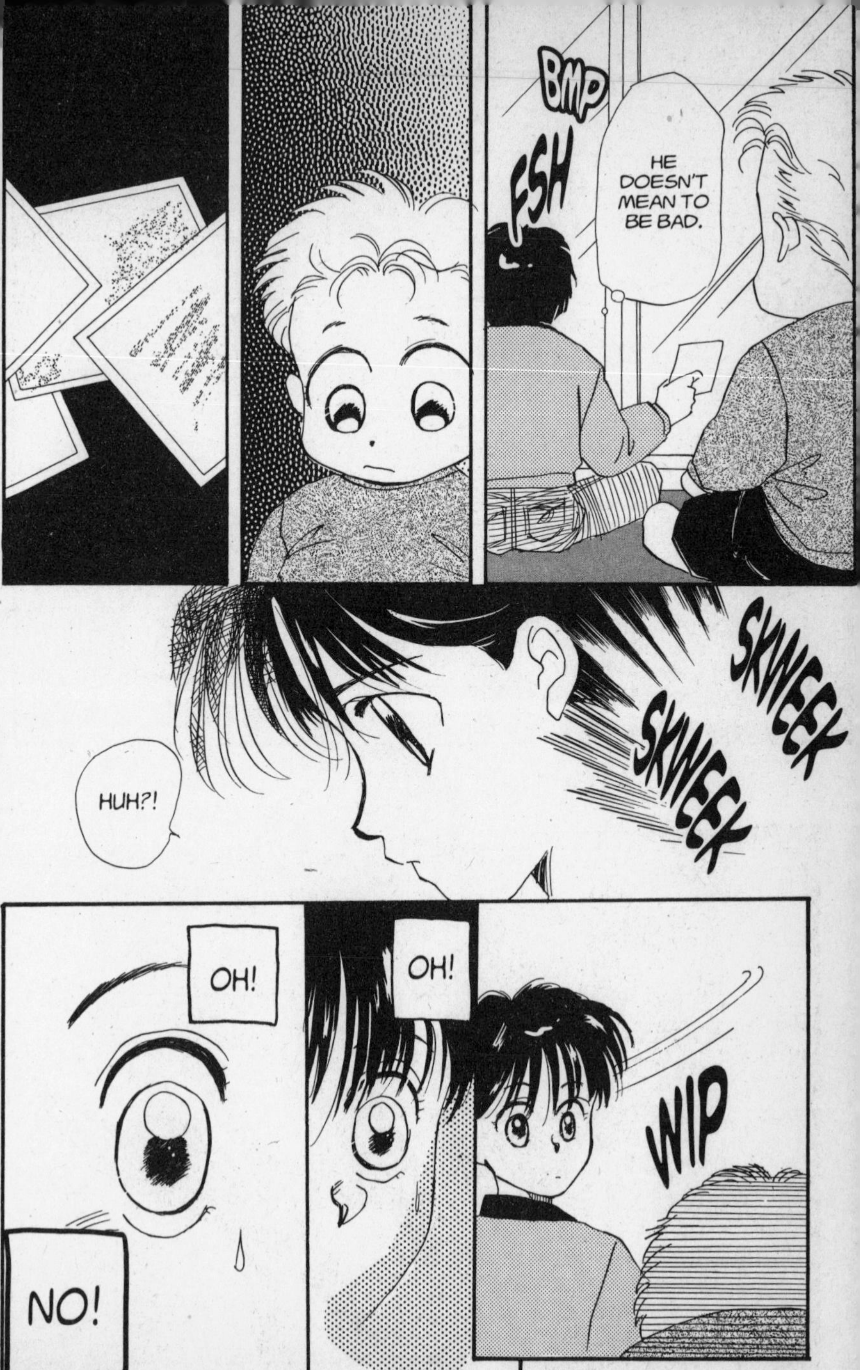
BMP
FSH
HE DOESN'T MEAN TO BE BAD.
SKWEEK
SKWEEK
HUH?!
OH!
WIP
OH!
NO!

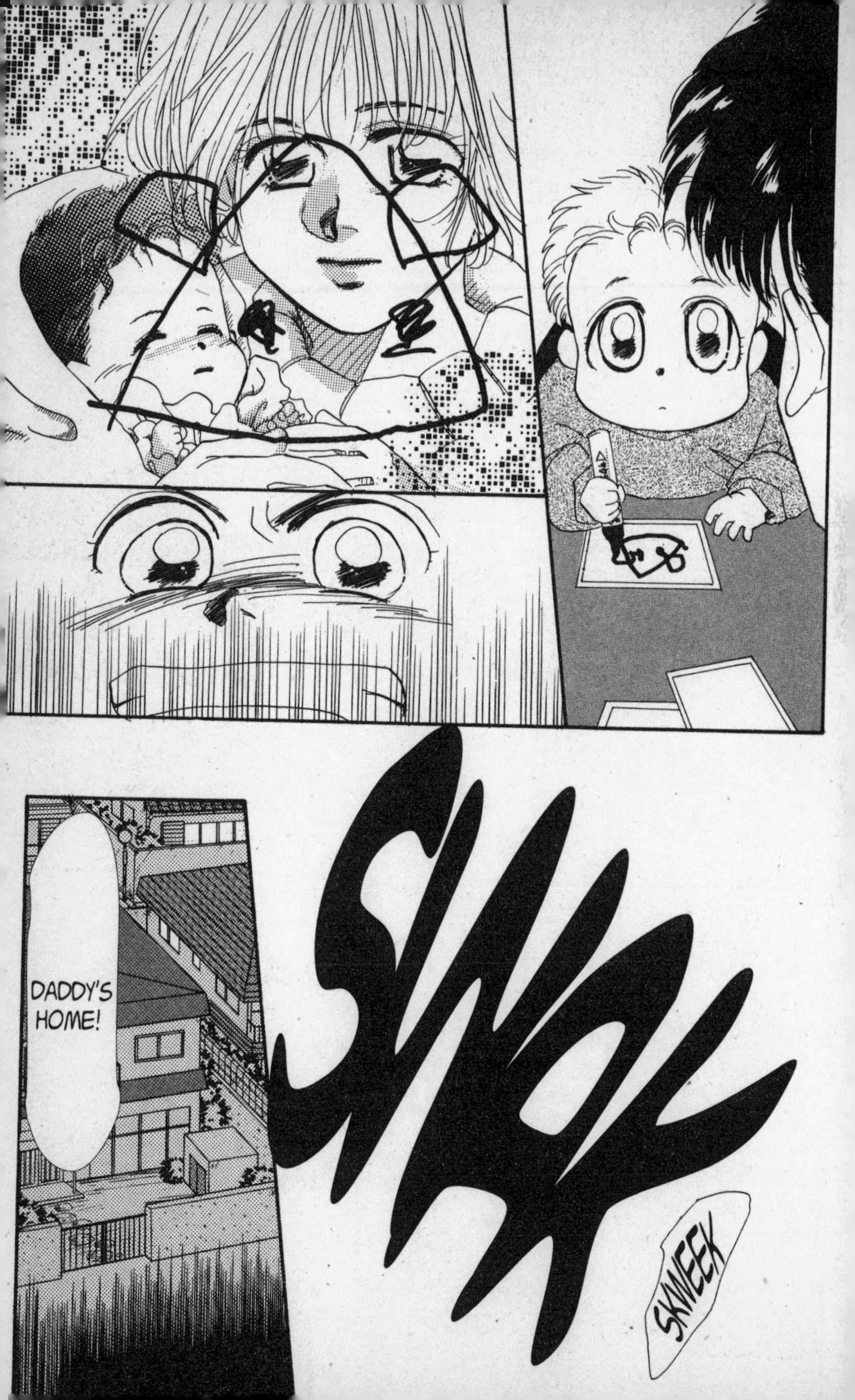
DADDY'S HOME!
SHA
SKWEEK

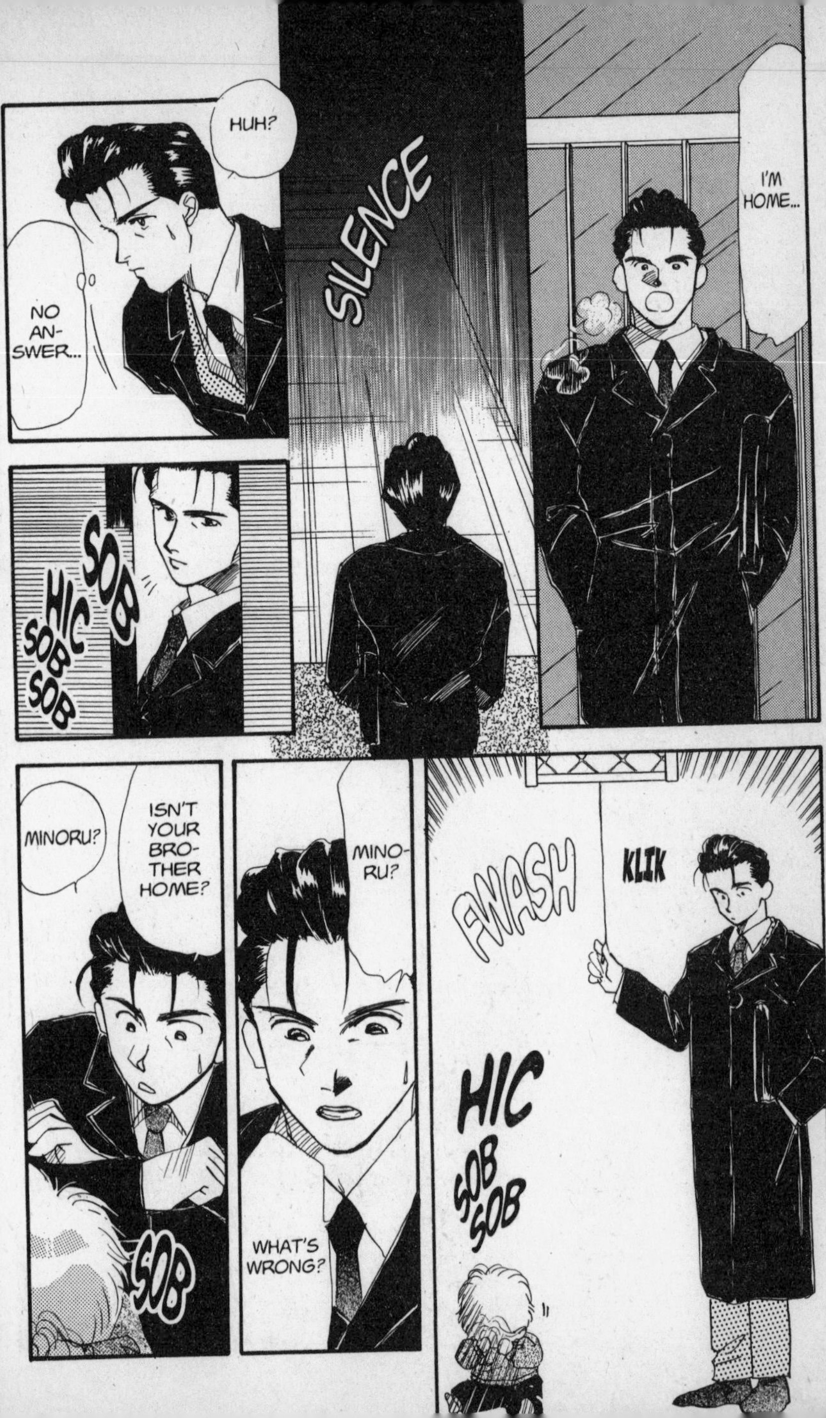
I'M HOME...
SILENCE
HUH?
NO ANSWER...
SOB HIC SOB SOB
KLIK
FWASH
HIC SOB SOB
MINORU?
WHAT'S WRONG?
ISN'T YOUR BROTHER HOME?
MINORU?
SOB

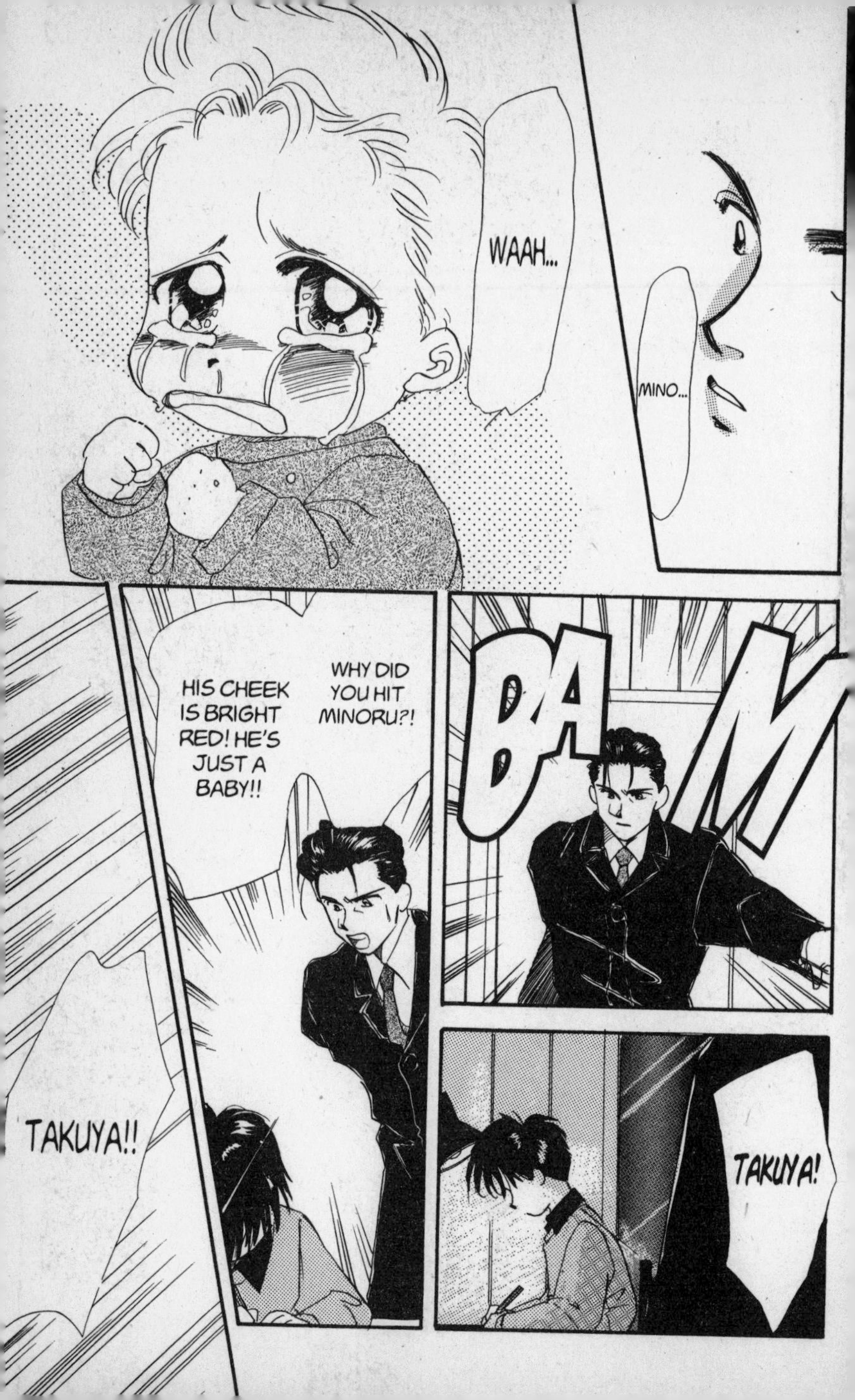
MINO...
WAAH...
BAM
TAKUYA!
WHY DID YOU HIT MINORU?!
HIS CHEEK IS BRIGHT RED! HE'S JUST A BABY!!
TAKUYA!!

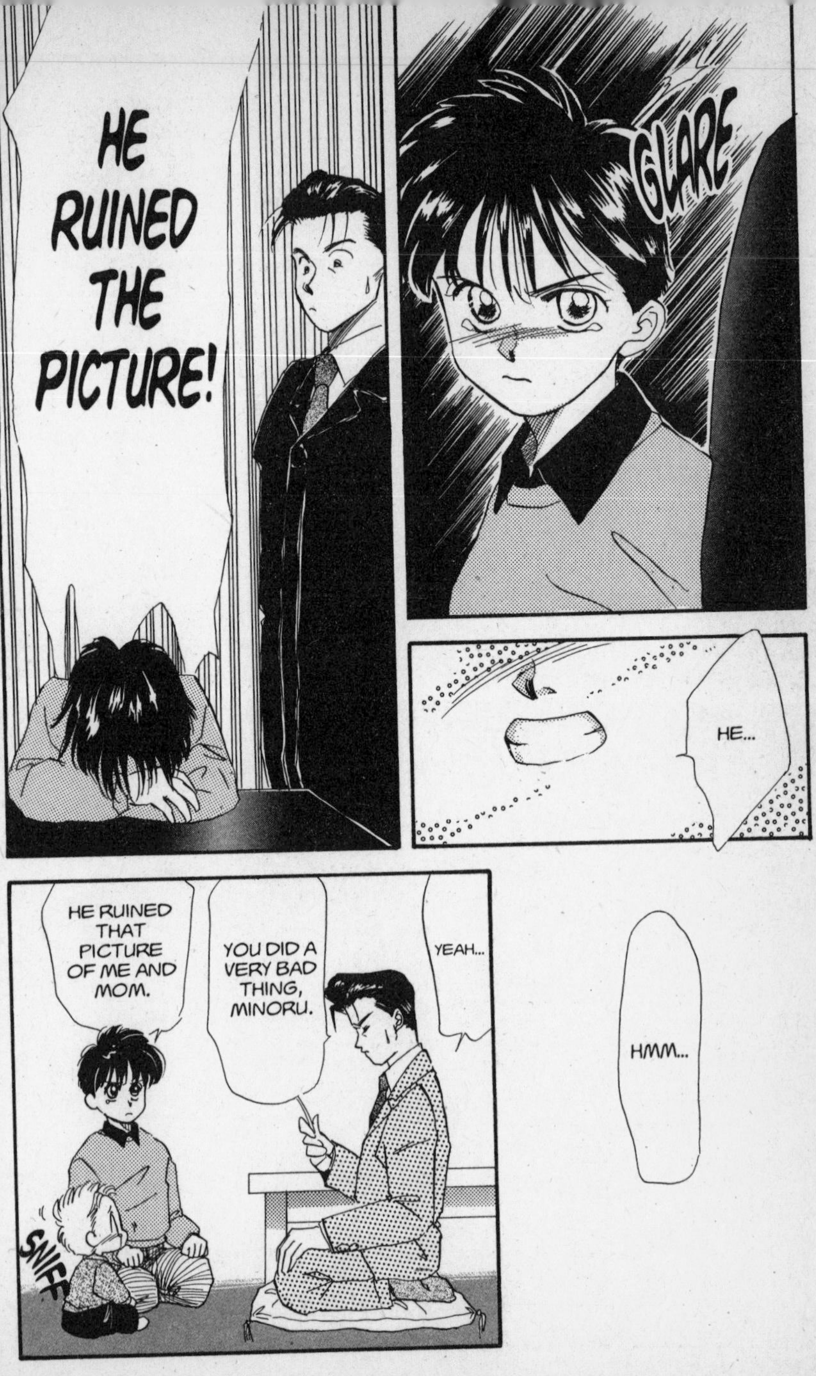
GLARE
HE...
HE RUINED THE PICTURE!
HMM...
YEAH...
YOU DID A VERY BAD THING, MINORU.
HE RUINED THAT PICTURE OF ME AND MOM.
SNIFF

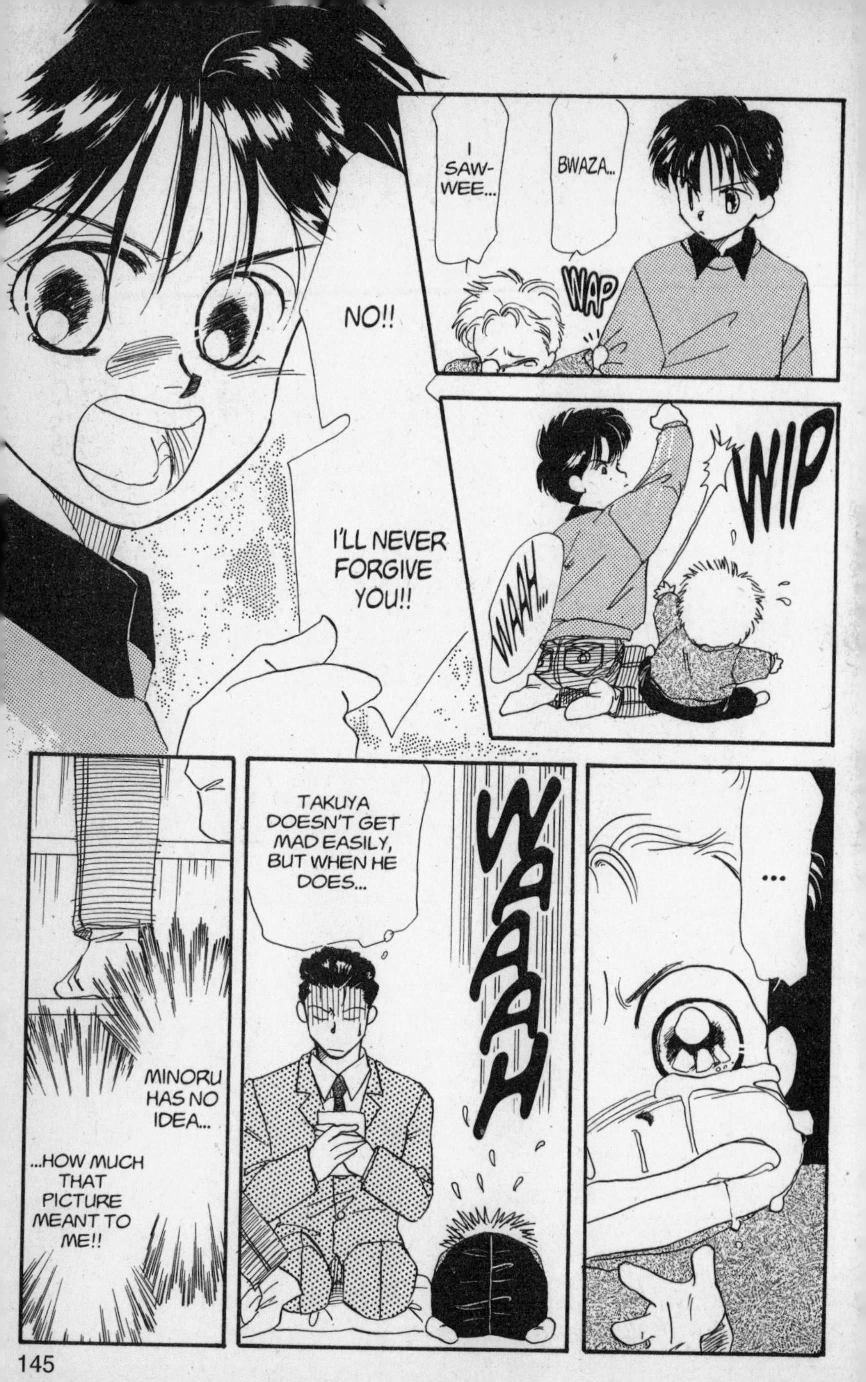
BWAZA...
I SAW-WEE...
WAP
WIP
WAAH
NO!!
I'LL NEVER FORGIVE YOU!!
...
WAAAAH
TAKUYA DOESN'T GET MAD EASILY, BUT WHEN HE DOES...
MINORU HAS NO IDEA...
...HOW MUCH THAT PICTURE MEANT TO ME!!

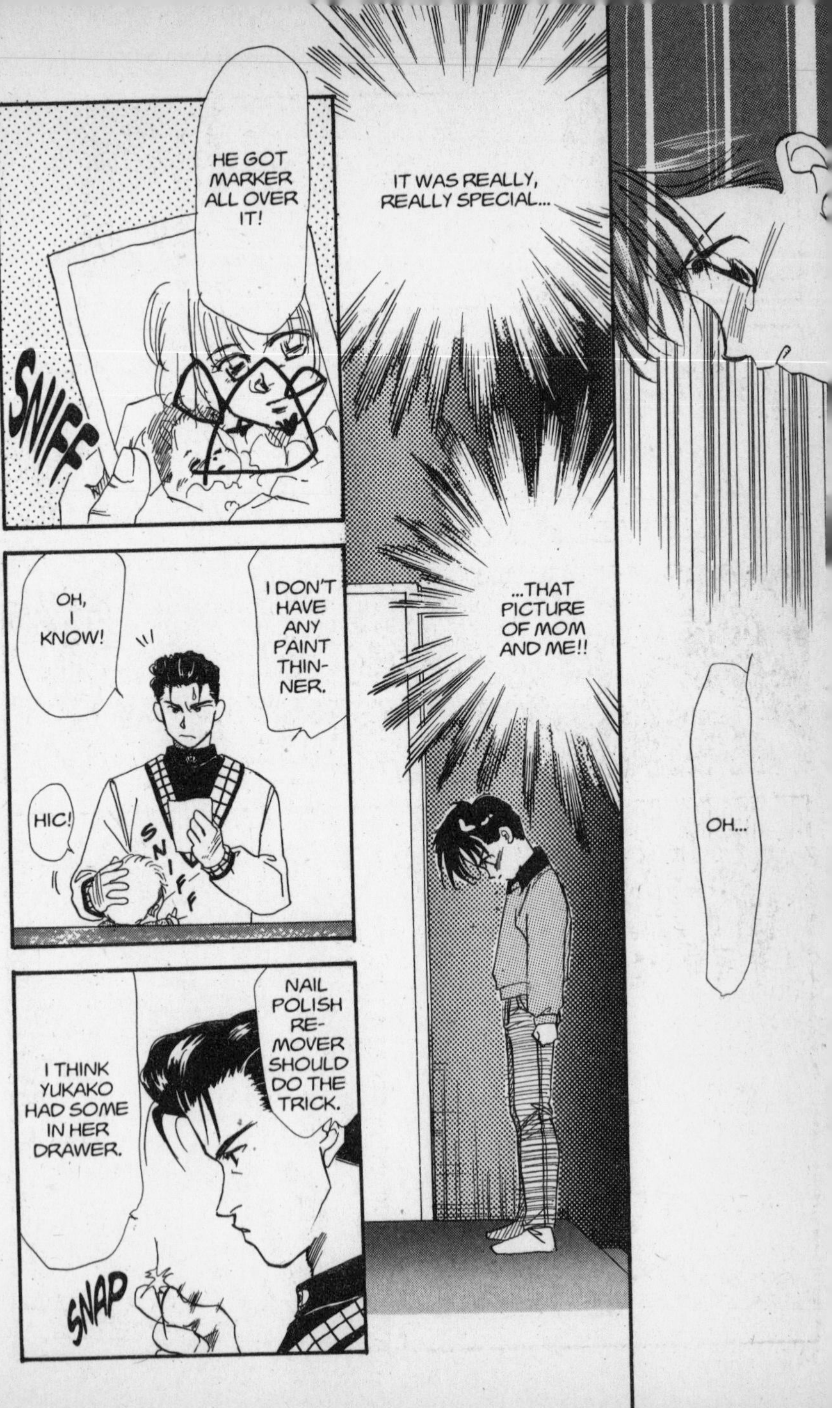
OH...
IT WAS REALLY, REALLY SPECIAL...
...THAT PICTURE OF MOM AND ME!!
HE GOT MARKER ALL OVER IT!
SNIFF
I DON'T HAVE ANY PAINT THIN-NER.
OH, I KNOW!
HIC!
SNIFF
NAIL POLISH RE-MOVER SHOULD DO THE TRICK.
I THINK YUKAKO HAD SOME IN HER DRAWER.
SNAP

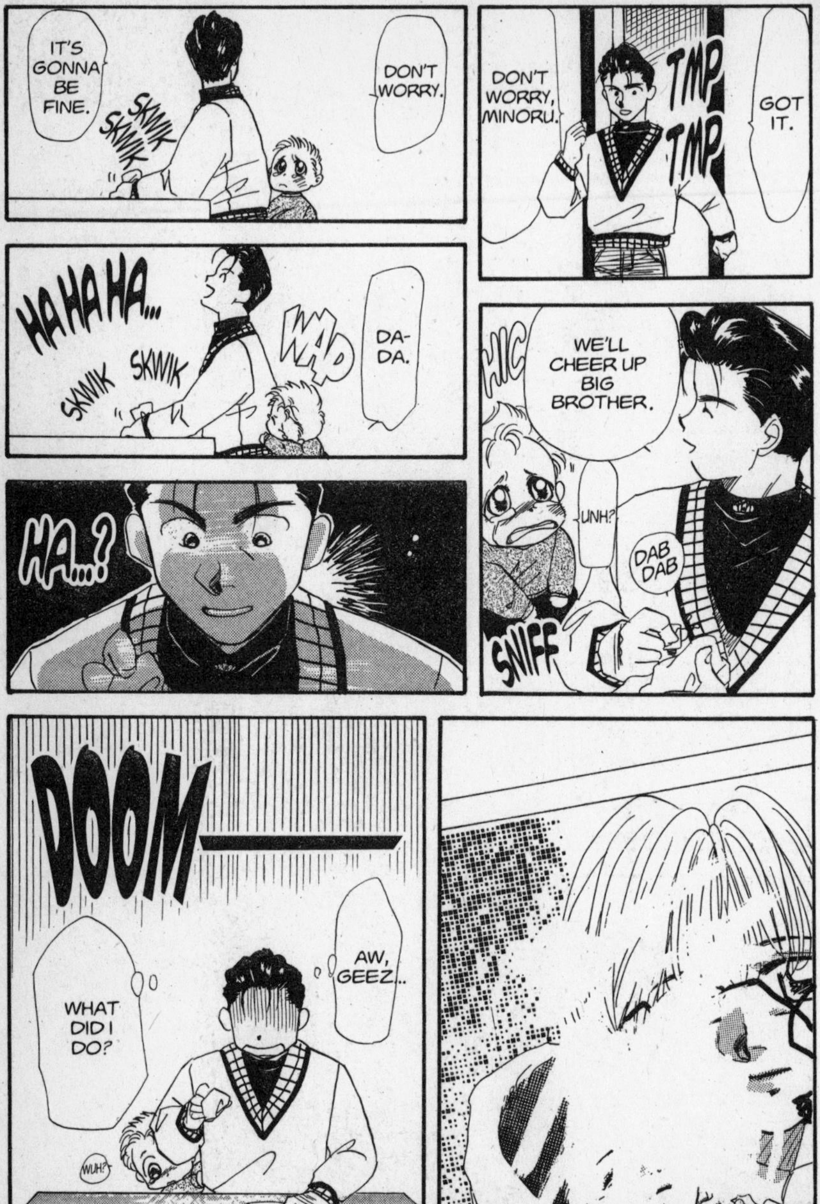
GOT IT.
TMP TMP
DON'T WORRY, MINORU.
DON'T WORRY.
IT'S GONNA BE FINE.
SKWIK SKWIK
WE'LL CHEER UP BIG BROTHER.
HIC
DAB DAB
UNH?
SNIFF
DA-DA.
WAP
HA HA HA...
SKWIK SKWIK
HA...?
DOOM
AW, GEEZ..
WHAT DID I DO?
WUH?

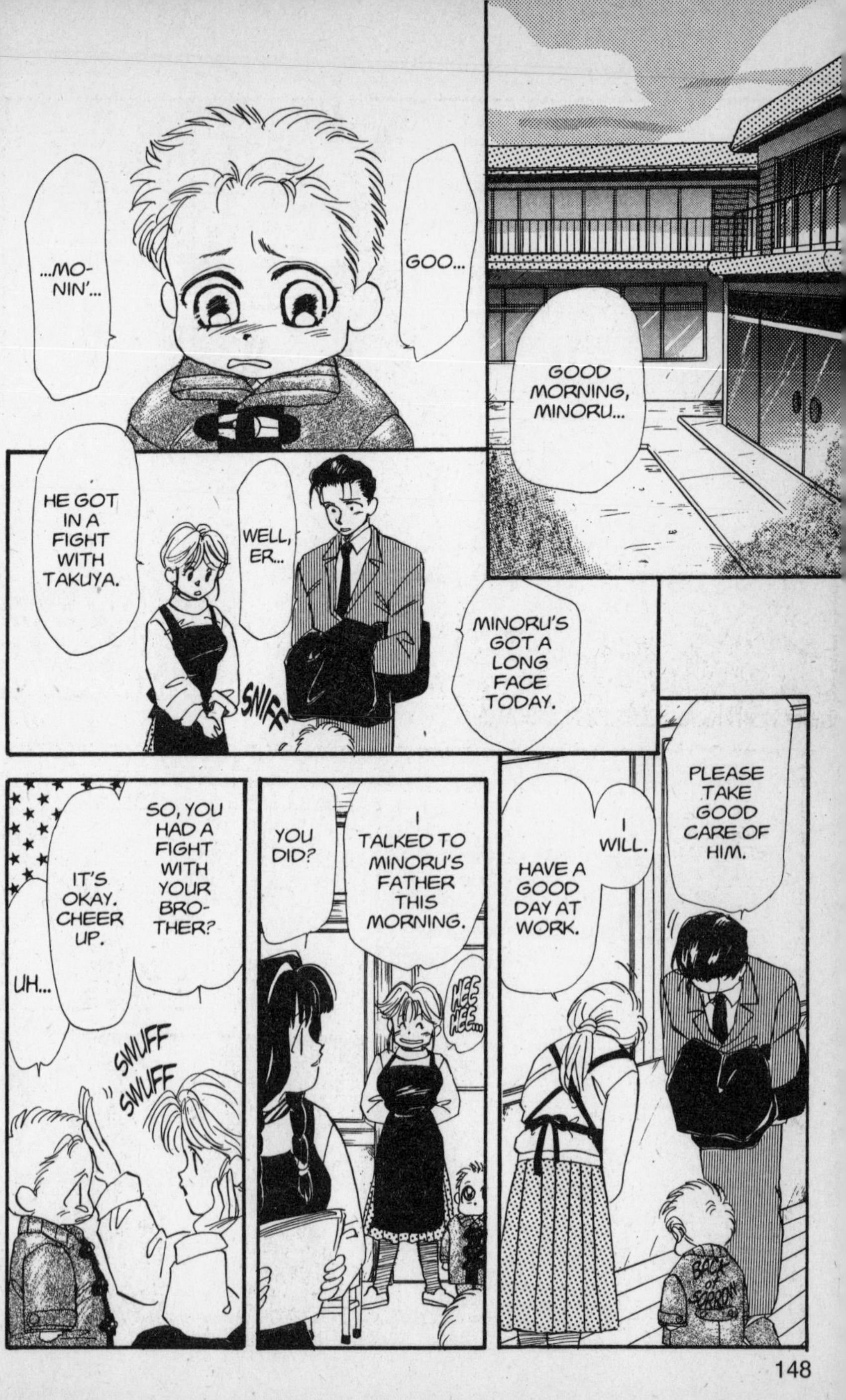
GOOD MORNING, MINORU...
GOO...
...MO-NIN'...
MINORU'S GOT A LONG FACE TODAY.
WELL, ER...
HE GOT IN A FIGHT WITH TAKUYA.
SNIFF
PLEASE TAKE GOOD CARE OF HIM.
I WILL.
HAVE A GOOD DAY AT WORK.
BACK OF SORROW
I TALKED TO MINORU'S FATHER THIS MORNING.
YOU DID?
HEE HEE...
SO, YOU HAD A FIGHT WITH YOUR BRO-THER?
IT'S OKAY. CHEER UP.
UH...
SWUFF SWUFF

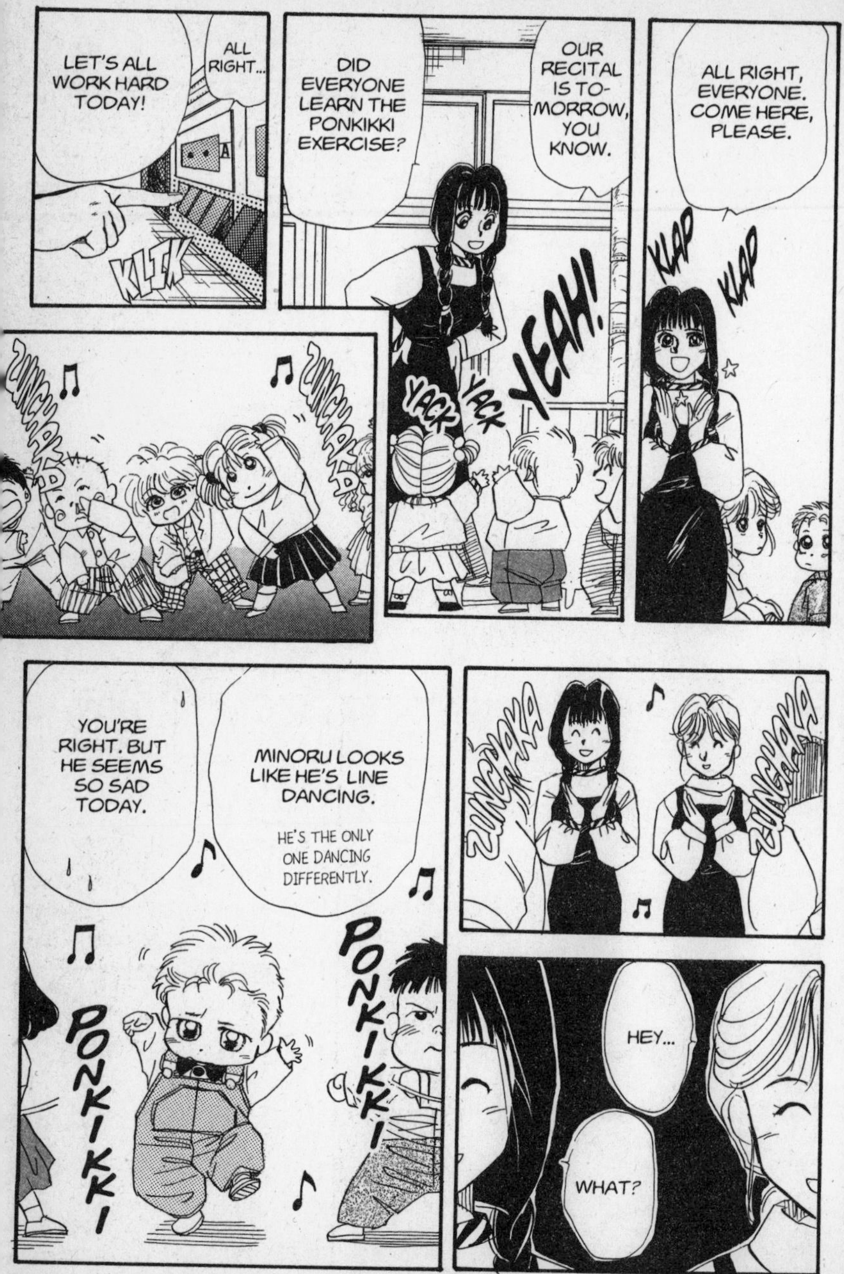
ALL RIGHT, EVERYONE. COME HERE, PLEASE.
KLAP
KLAP
OUR RECITAL IS TO-MORROW, YOU KNOW.
DID EVERYONE LEARN THE PONKIKKI EXERCISE?
YEAH!
YACK
YACK
ALL RIGHT...
LET'S ALL WORK HARD TODAY!
KLIK
ZUNCHAKAPO
ZUNCHAKAPO
ZUNCHAKA
ZUNCHAKA
HEY...
WHAT?
MINORU LOOKS LIKE HE'S LINE DANCING.
HE'S THE ONLY ONE DANCING DIFFERENTLY.
YOU'RE RIGHT. BUT HE SEEMS SO SAD TODAY.
PONKIKKI
PONKIKKI

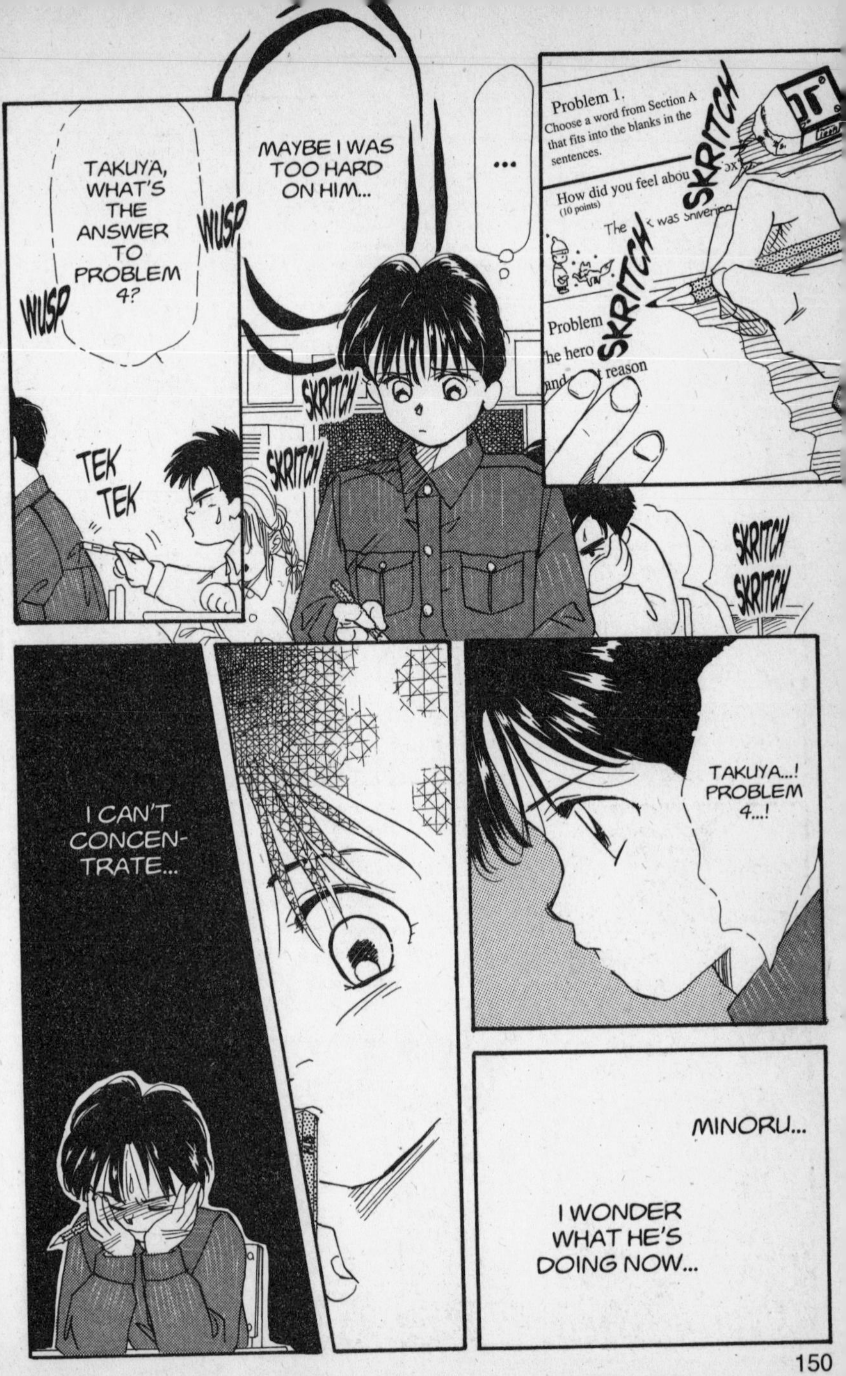
Problem 1.
Choose a word from Section A that fits into the blanks in the sentences.
How did you feel abou
(10 points)
The
was shivering
Problem
he hero
reason
SKRITCH
SKRITCH
SKRITCH
...
MAYBE I WAS TOO HARD ON HIM...
SKRITCH
SKRITCH
SKRITCH
SKRITCH
TAKUYA, WHAT'S THE ANSWER TO PROBLEM 4?
WUSP
WUSP
TEK
TEK
TAKUYA...! PROBLEM 4...!
MINORU...
I WONDER WHAT HE'S DOING NOW...
I CAN'T CONCENTRATE...

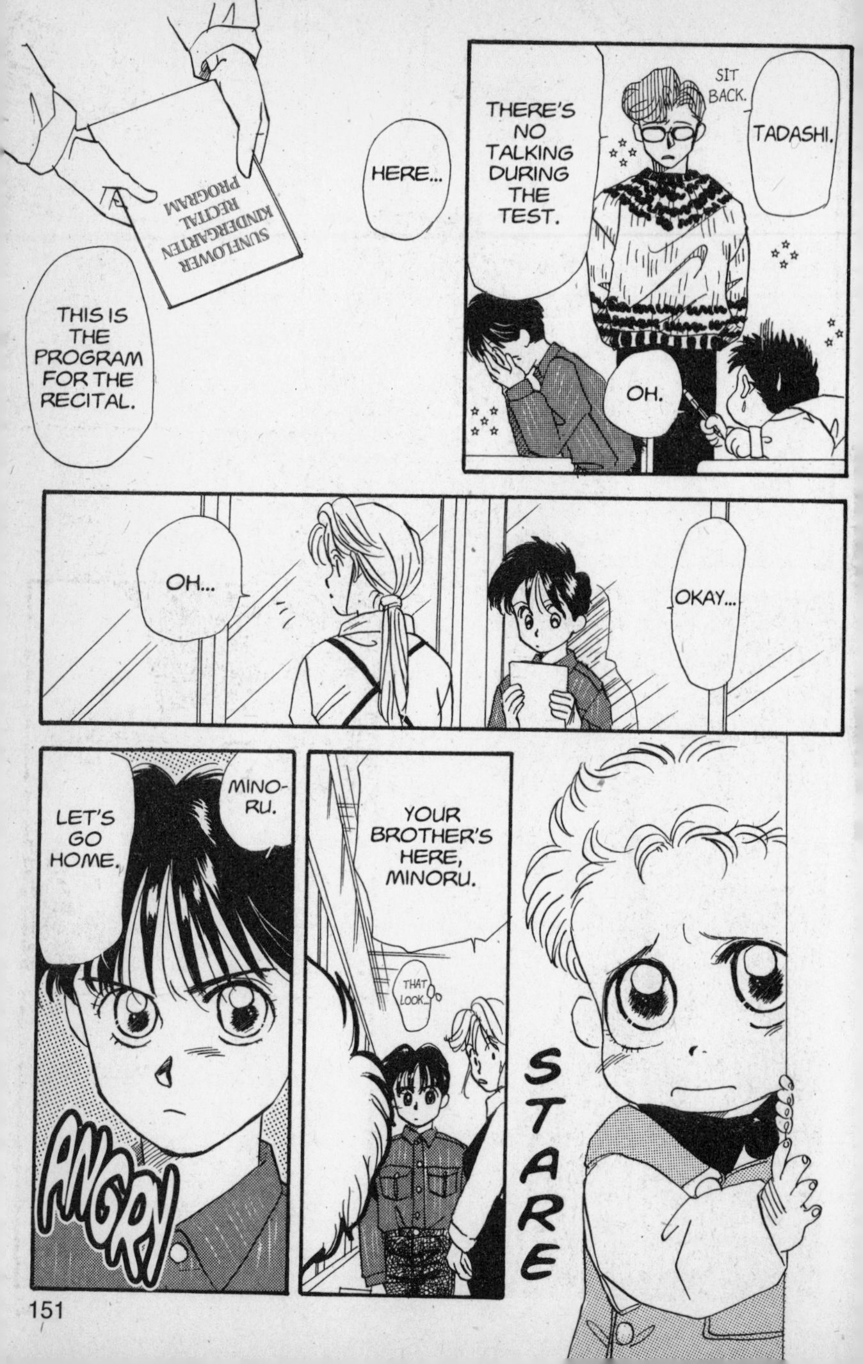
TADASHI.
SIT BACK.
THERE'S NO TALKING DURING THE TEST.
OH.
HERE...
SUNFLOWER KINDERGARTEN RECITAL PROGRAM
THIS IS THE PROGRAM FOR THE RECITAL.
OKAY...
OH...
STARE
YOUR BROTHER'S HERE, MINORU.
THAT LOOK...
MINO-RU.
LET'S GO HOME.
ANGRY

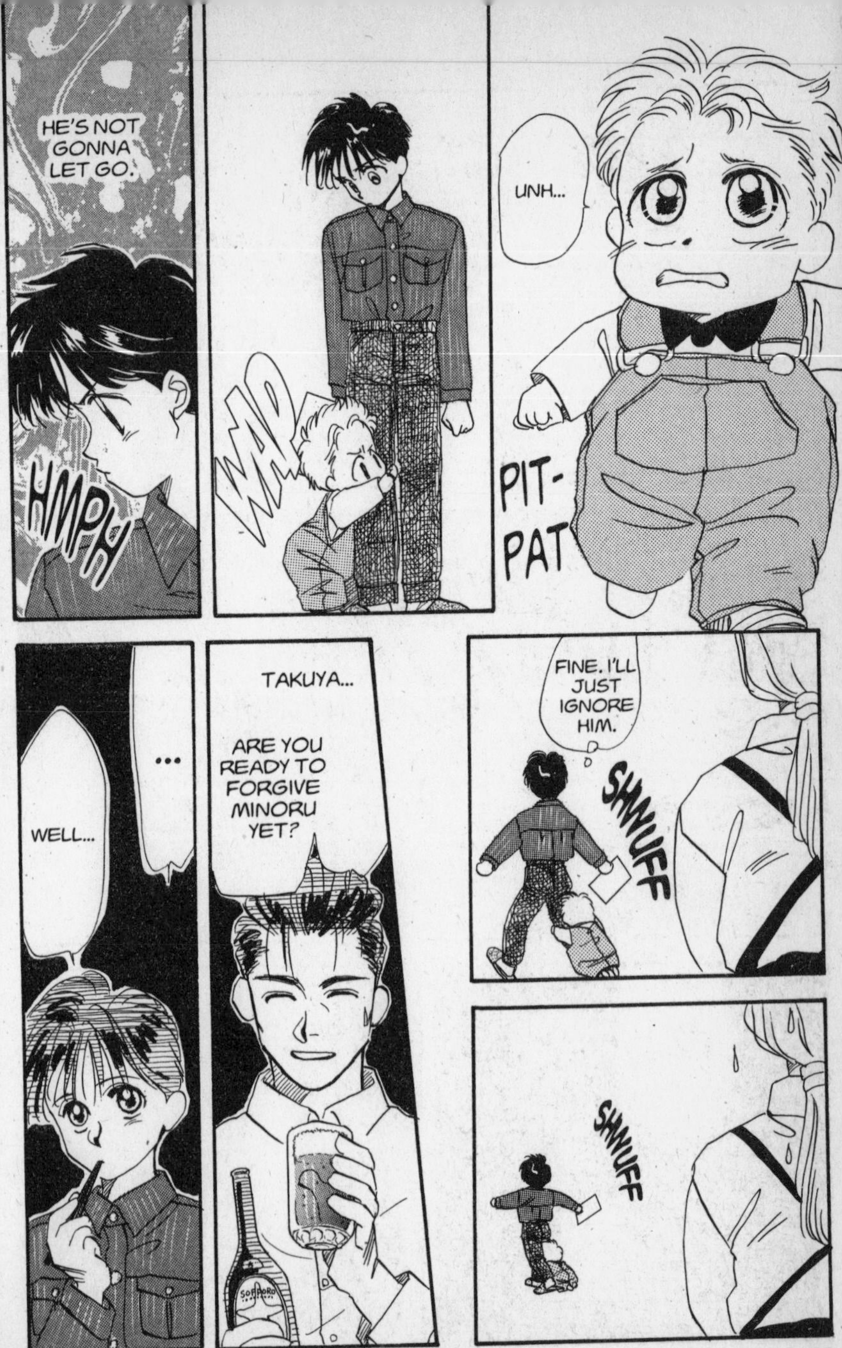
UNH...
PIT-PAT
WAP
HE'S NOT GONNA LET GO.
HMPH
FINE. I'LL JUST IGNORE HIM.
SHNUFF
SHNUFF
TAKUYA...
ARE YOU READY TO FORGIVE MINORU YET?
...
WELL...

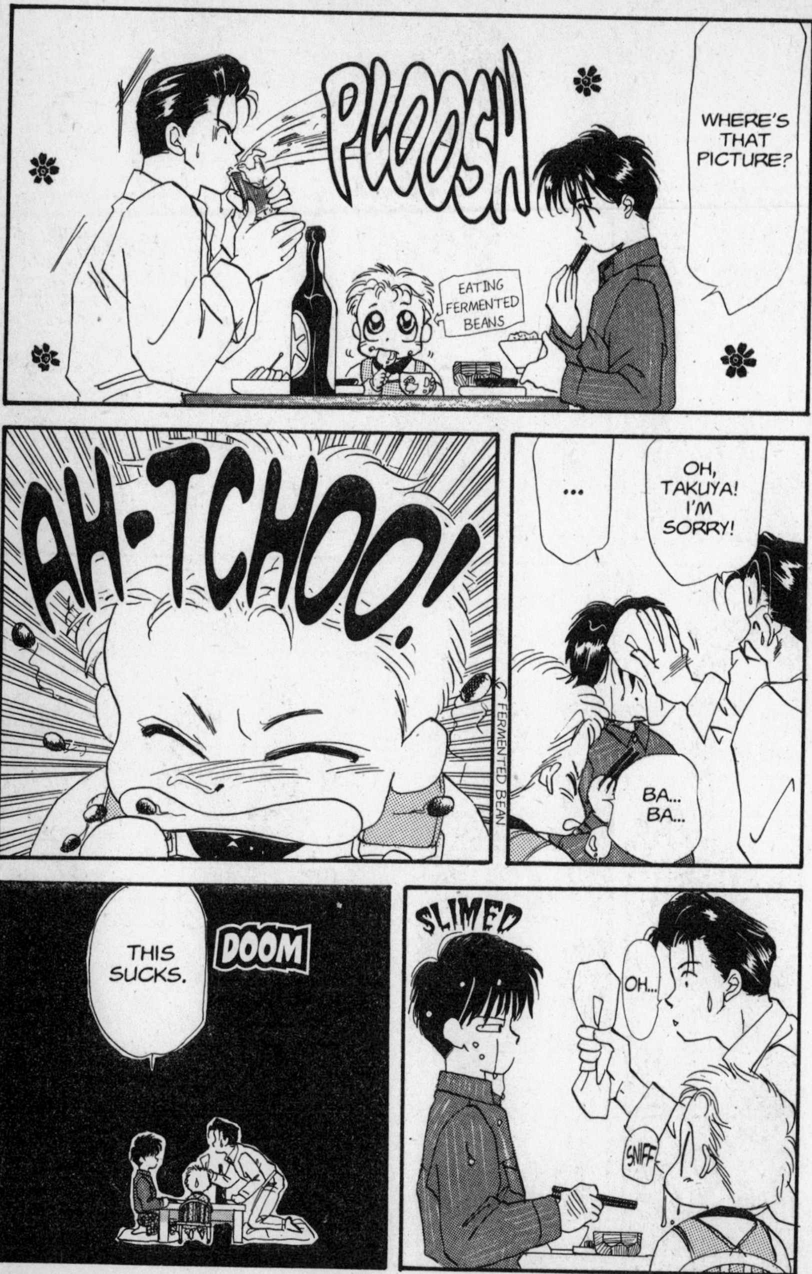
WHERE'S THAT PICTURE?
PLOOSH
EATING FERMENTED BEANS
OH, TAKUYA! I'M SORRY!
...
BA... BA...
AH-TCHOO!
FERMENTED BEAN
SLIMED
OH...
SNIFF
DOOM
THIS SUCKS.

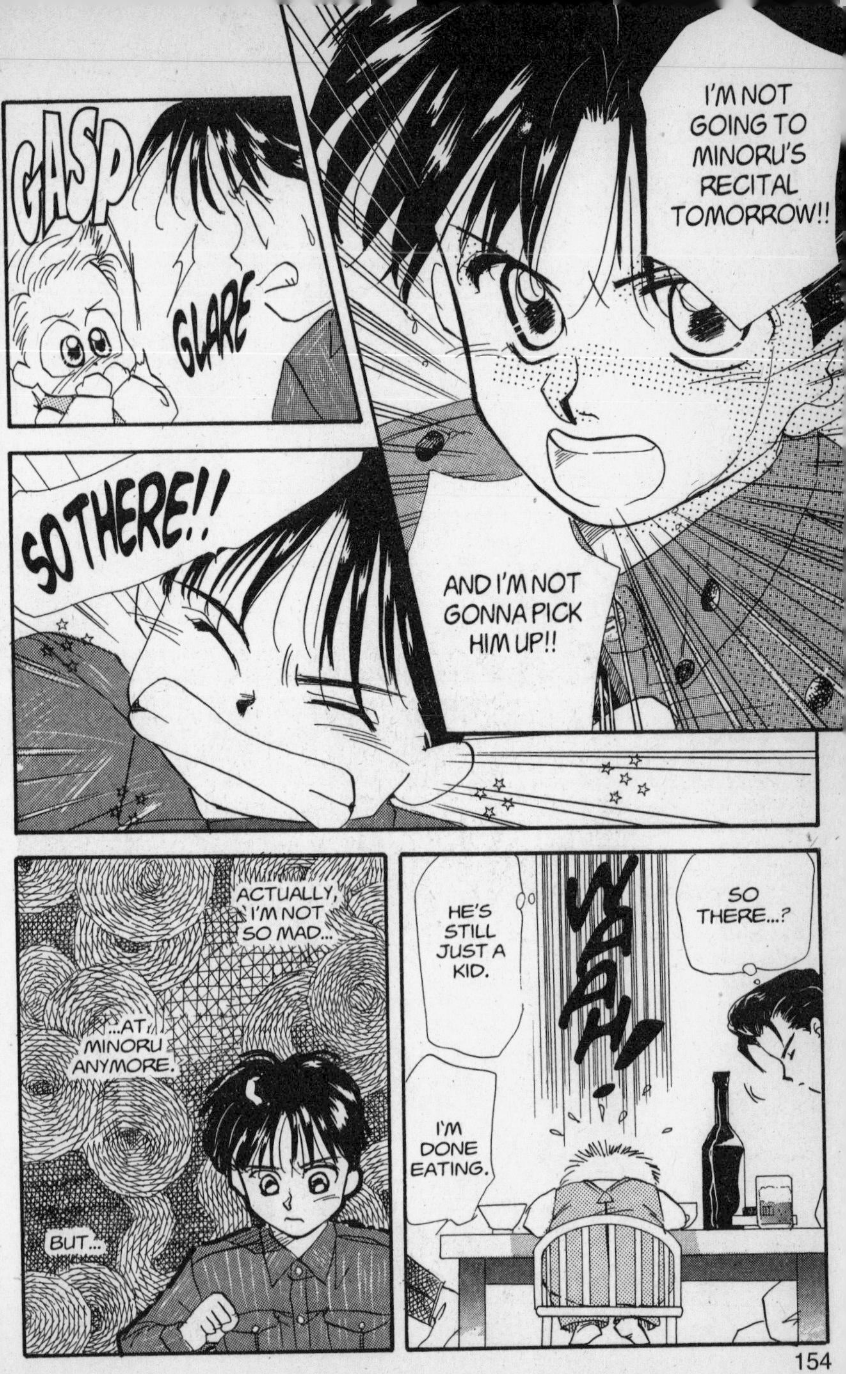
I'M NOT GOING TO MINORU'S RECITAL TOMORROW!!
AND I'M NOT GONNA PICK HIM UP!!
GASP
GLARE
SO THERE!!
SO THERE...?
HE'S STILL JUST A KID.
I'M DONE EATING.
ACTUALLY, I'M NOT SO MAD...
...AT MINORU ANYMORE.
BUT...

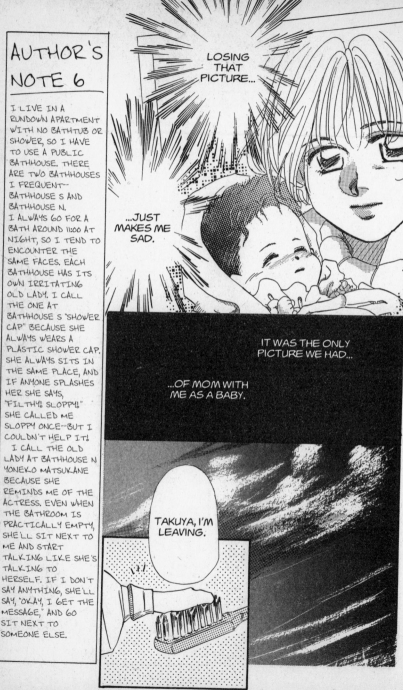

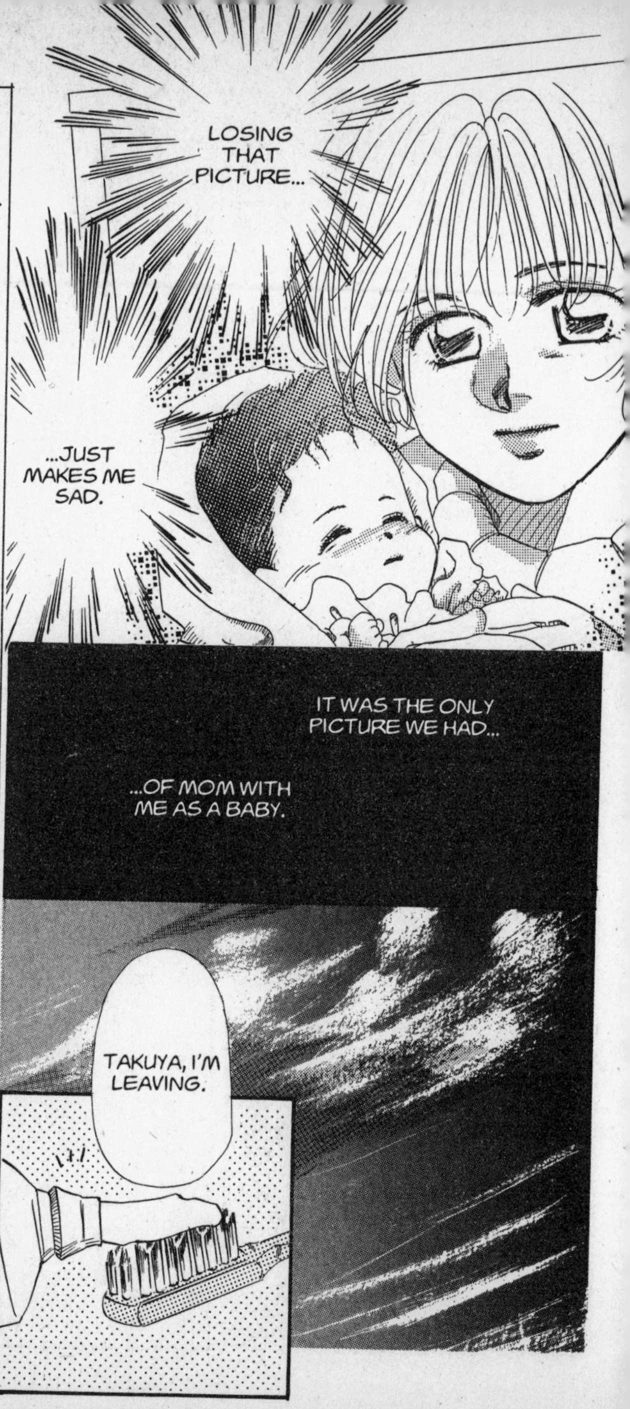
LOSING THAT PICTURE...
...JUST MAKES ME SAD.
IT WAS THE ONLY PICTURE WE HAD...
...OF MOM WITH ME AS A BABY.
TAKUYA, I'M LEAVING.

AUTHOR'S NOTE 6

I LIVE IN A RUNDOWN APARTMENT WITH NO BATHTUB OR SHOWER, SO I HAVE TO USE A PUBLIC BATHHOUSE. THERE ARE TWO BATHHOUSES I FREQUENT--BATHHOUSE S AND BATHHOUSE N. I ALWAYS GO FOR A BATH AROUND 11:00 AT NIGHT, SO I TEND TO ENCOUNTER THE SAME FACES. EACH BATHHOUSE HAS ITS OWN IRRITATING OLD LADY. I CALL THE ONE AT BATHHOUSE S "SHOWER CAP" BECAUSE SHE ALWAYS WEARS A PLASTIC SHOWER CAP. SHE ALWAYS SITS IN THE SAME PLACE, AND IF ANYONE SPLASHES HER SHE SAYS, "FILTHY! SLOPPY!" SHE CALLED ME SLOPPY ONCE--BUT I COULDN'T HELP IT!

I CALL THE OLD LADY AT BATHHOUSE N YONEKO MATSUKANE BECAUSE SHE REMINDS ME OF THE ACTRESS. EVEN WHEN THE BATHROOM IS PRACTICALLY EMPTY, SHE'LL SIT NEXT TO ME AND START TALKING LIKE SHE'S TALKING TO HERSELF. IF I DON'T SAY ANYTHING, SHE'LL SAY, "OKAY, I GET THE MESSAGE," AND GO SIT NEXT TO SOMEONE ELSE.

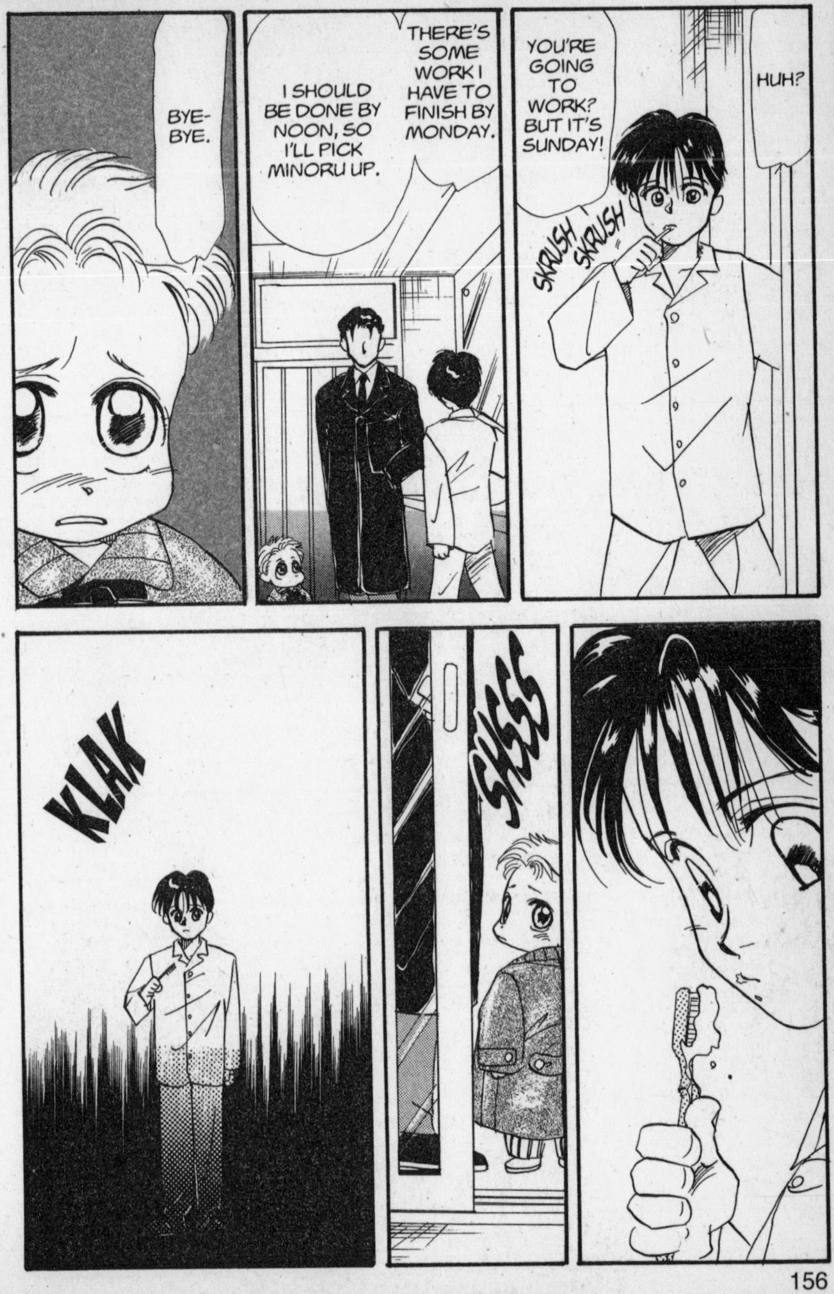
HUH?
YOU'RE GOING TO WORK? BUT IT'S SUNDAY!
SKRUSH SKRUSH
THERE'S SOME WORK I HAVE TO FINISH BY MONDAY.
I SHOULD BE DONE BY NOON, SO I'LL PICK MINORU UP.
BYE-BYE.
SHSSS
KLAK

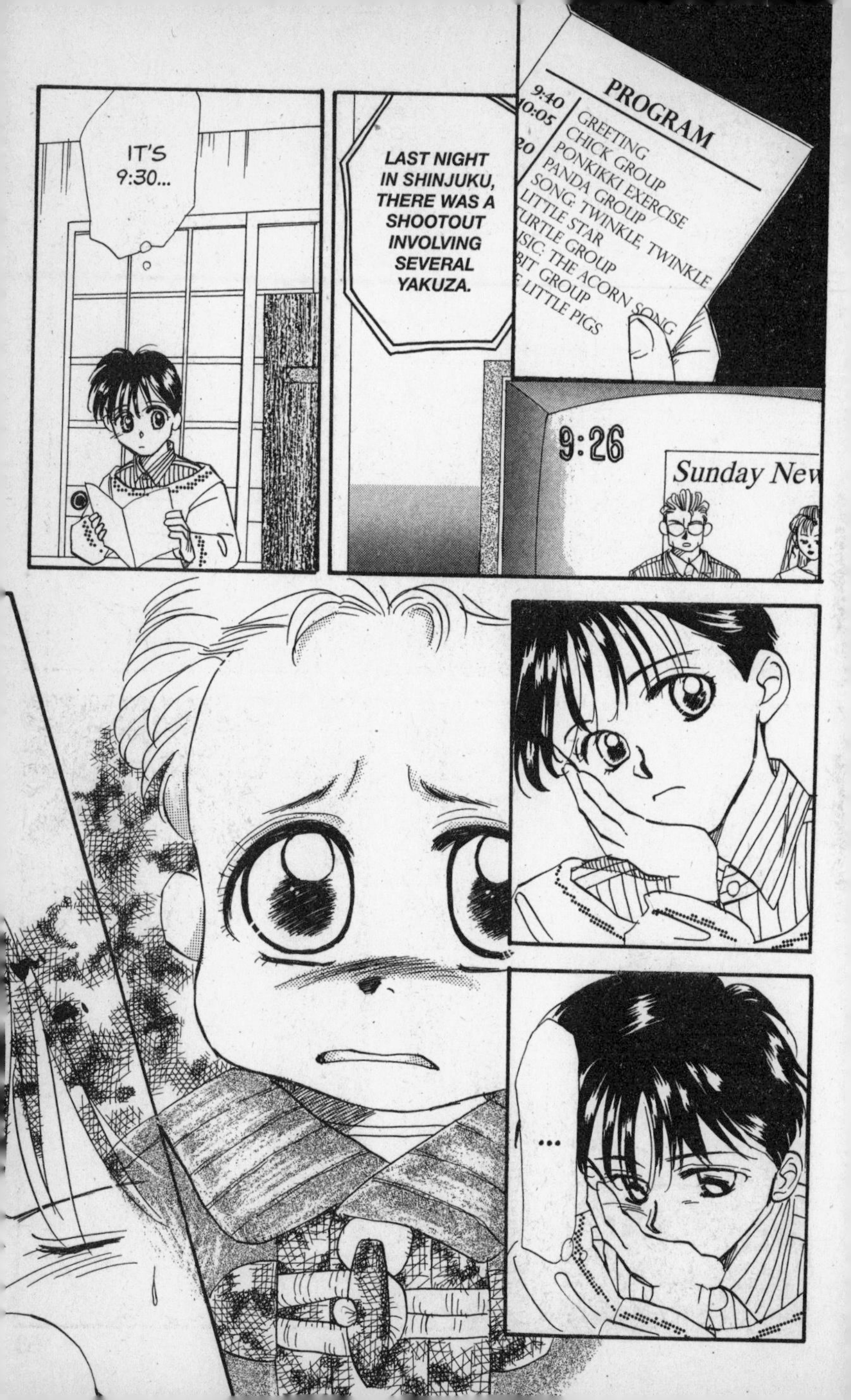

PROGRAM
9:40
10:05
20
GREETING
CHICK GROUP
PONKIKKI EXERCISE
PANDA GROUP
SONG: TWINKLE, TWINKLE
LITTLE STAR
TURTLE GROUP
SIC: THE ACORN SONG
BIT GROUP
E LITTLE PIGS
9:26
Sunday New
LAST NIGHT IN SHINJUKU, THERE WAS A SHOOTOUT INVOLVING SEVERAL YAKUZA.
IT'S 9:30...
...

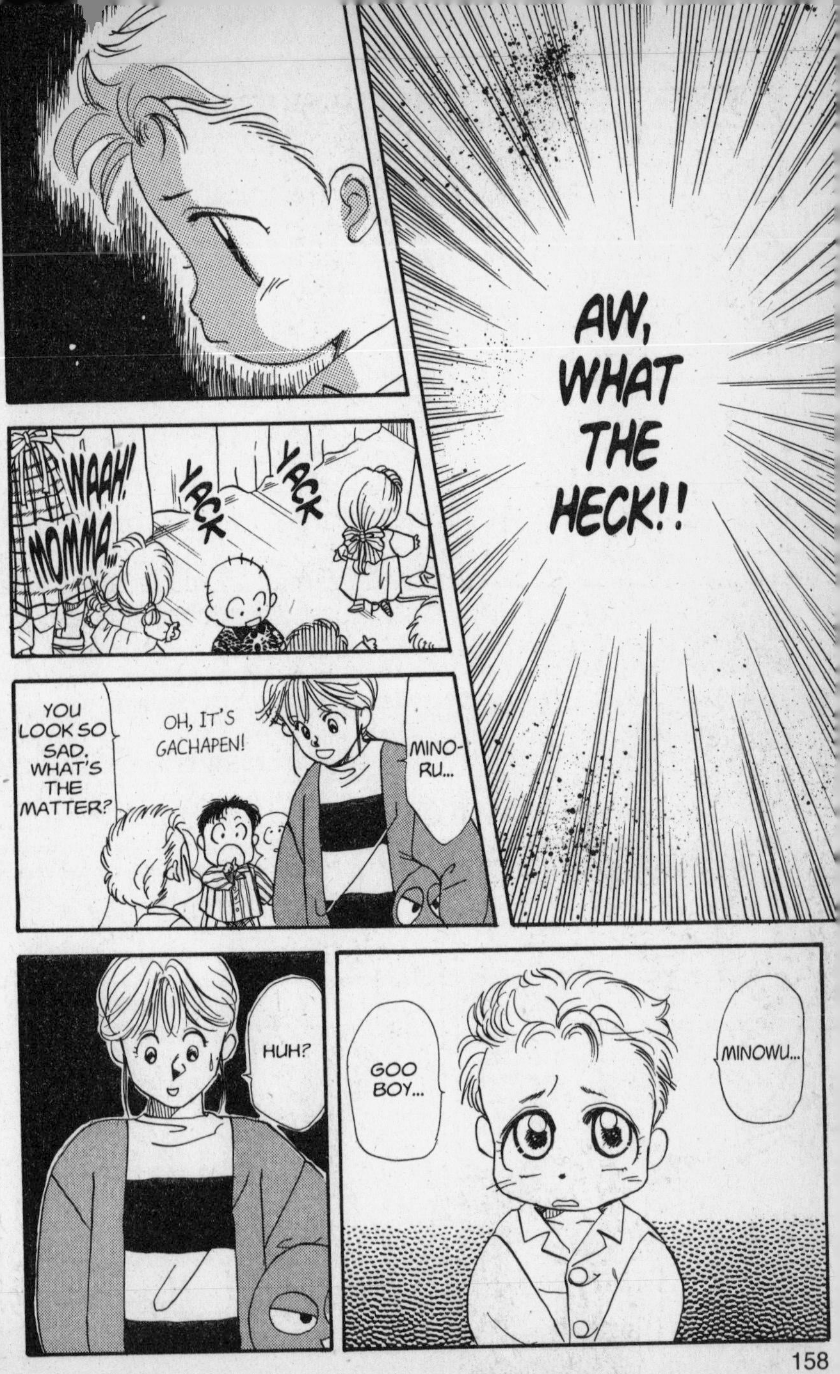
AW, WHAT THE HECK!!
YACK
YACK
WAAH! MOMMA...
MINO-RU...
OH, IT'S GACHAPEN!
YOU LOOK SO SAD. WHAT'S THE MATTER?
MINOWU...
GOO BOY...
HUH?

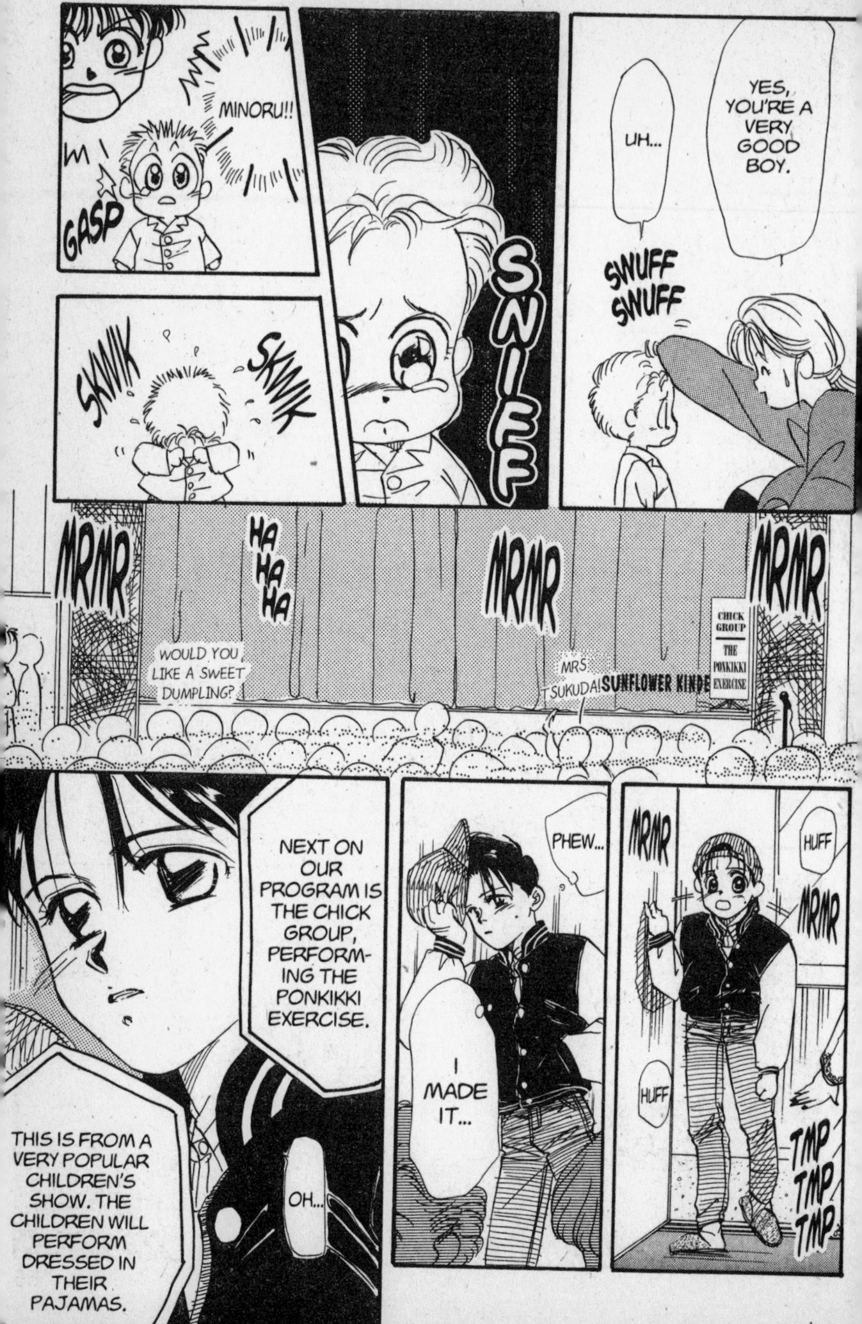
YES, YOU'RE A VERY GOOD BOY.
UH...
SNUFF SNUFF
SNIFF
MINORU!!
M
GASP
SKWIK
SKWIK
MRMR
CHICK GROUP
THE PONKIKKI EXERCISE
MRS. TSUKUDA!
SUNFLOWER KINDE
MRMR
HA HA HA HA
WOULD YOU LIKE A SWEET DUMPLING?
MRMR
HUFF
MRMR
MRMR
HUFF
TMP TMP TMP
PHEW...
I MADE IT...
NEXT ON OUR PROGRAM IS THE CHICK GROUP, PERFORMING THE PONKIKKI EXERCISE.
OH...
THIS IS FROM A VERY POPULAR CHILDREN'S SHOW. THE CHILDREN WILL PERFORM DRESSED IN THEIR PAJAMAS.

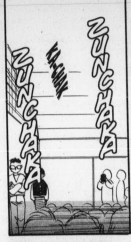

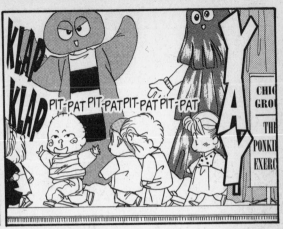

KLAP KLAP
PIT-PAT PIT-PAT PIT-PAT PIT-PAT
YAY
CHIC
GROU
THE
PONKI
EXERC
ZUNCHAKA
KA-CHAK
ZUNCHAKA
MR. SUN IS SMILING, SMILING! BUKU AND GACHAPEN, LET'S ALL PLAY!
UH-OH...
PONKIKKI
PONKIKKI
ART
R
MINORU'S NOT DANCING.
OH, DEAR...
MINORU?

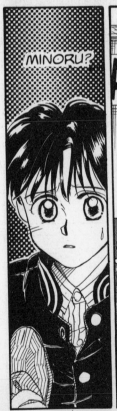

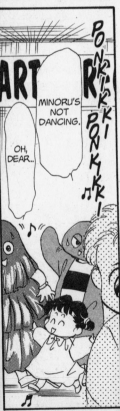

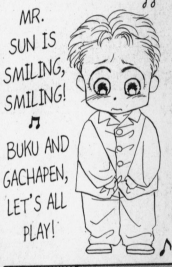

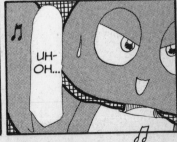

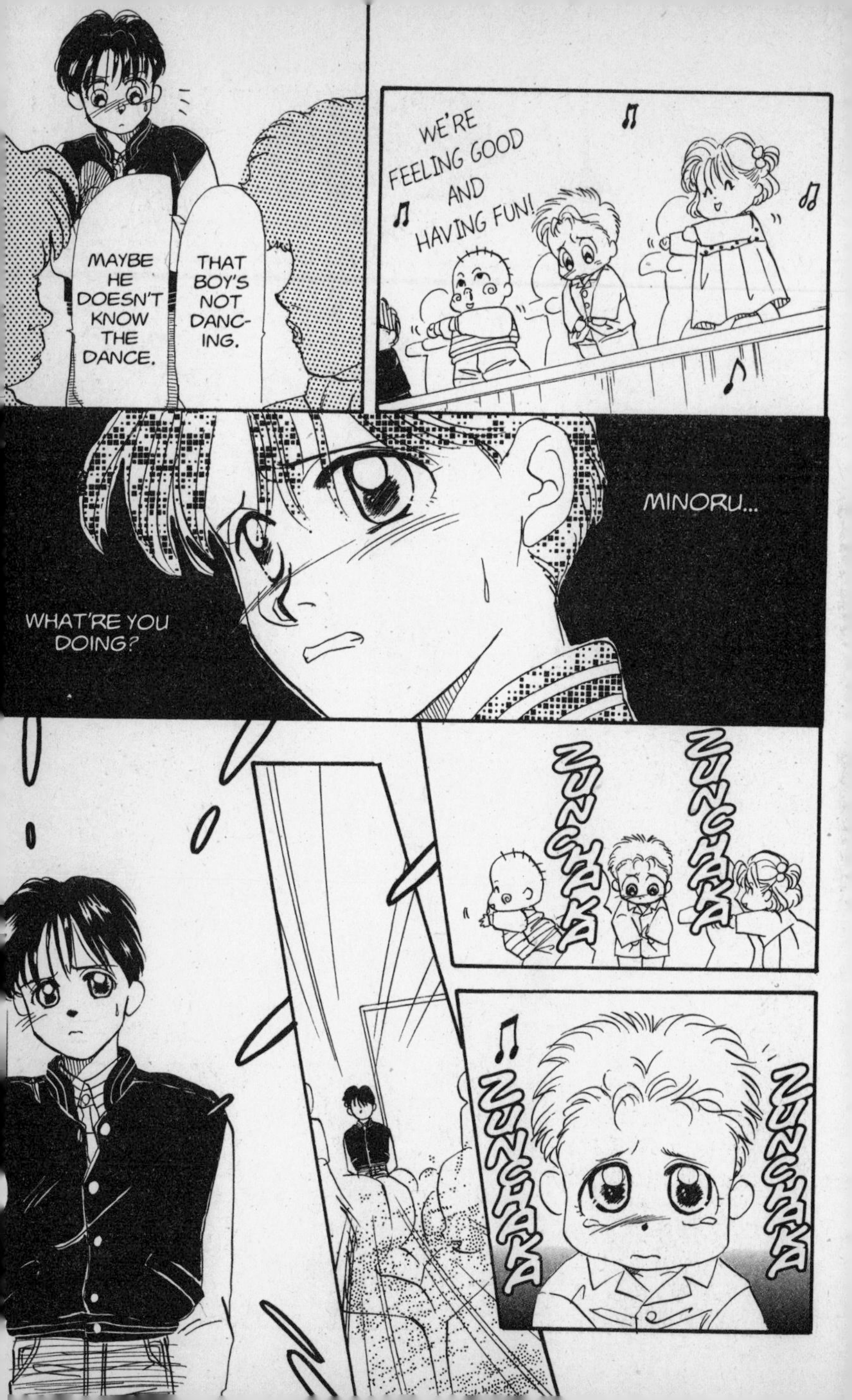
WE'RE FEELING GOOD AND HAVING FUN!
THAT BOY'S NOT DANCING.
MAYBE HE DOESN'T KNOW THE DANCE.
MINORU...
WHAT'RE YOU DOING?
ZUNCHAKA
ZUNCHAKA
ZUNCHAKA
ZUNCHAKA

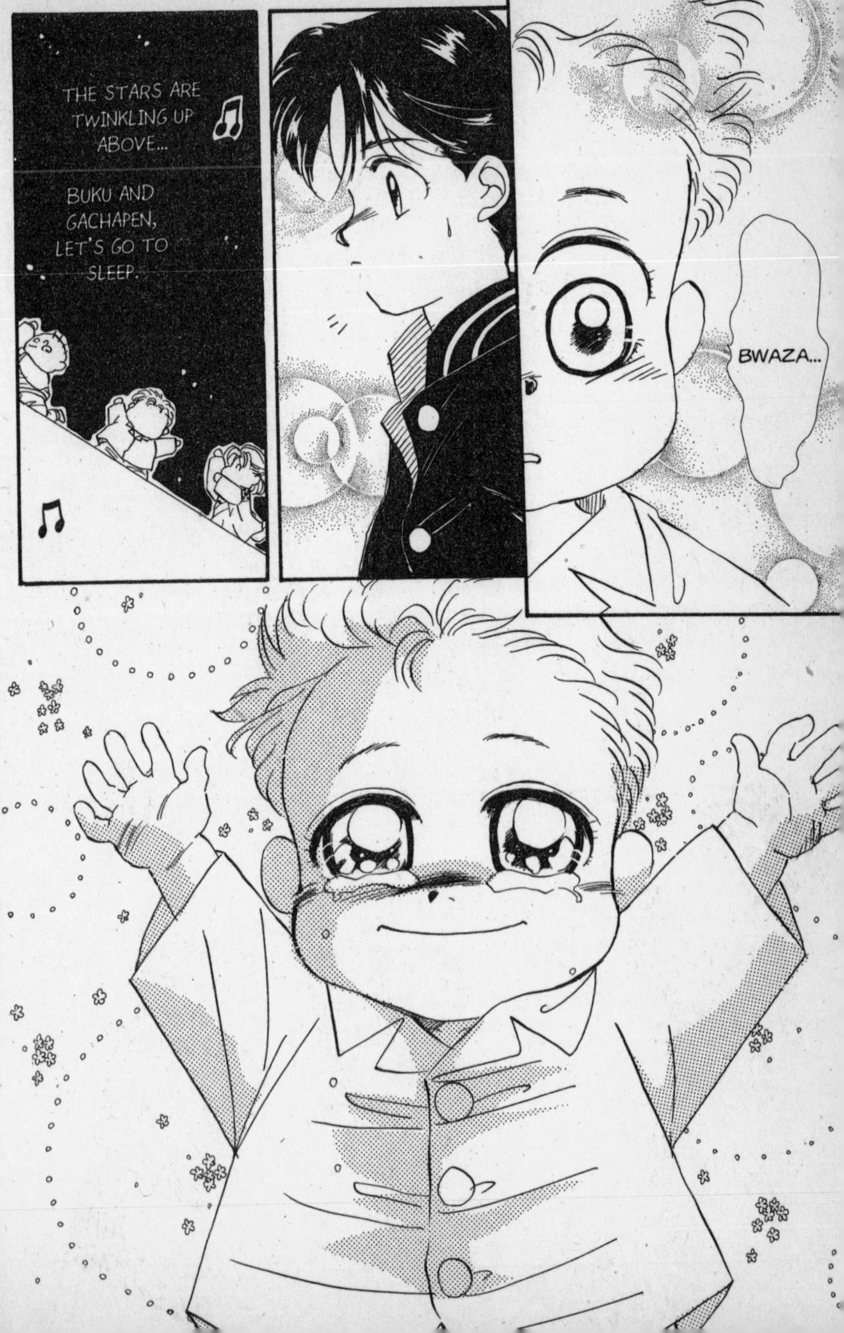
BWAZA...
THE STARS ARE TWINKLING UP ABOVE...
BUKU AND GACHAPEN, LET'S GO TO SLEEP.

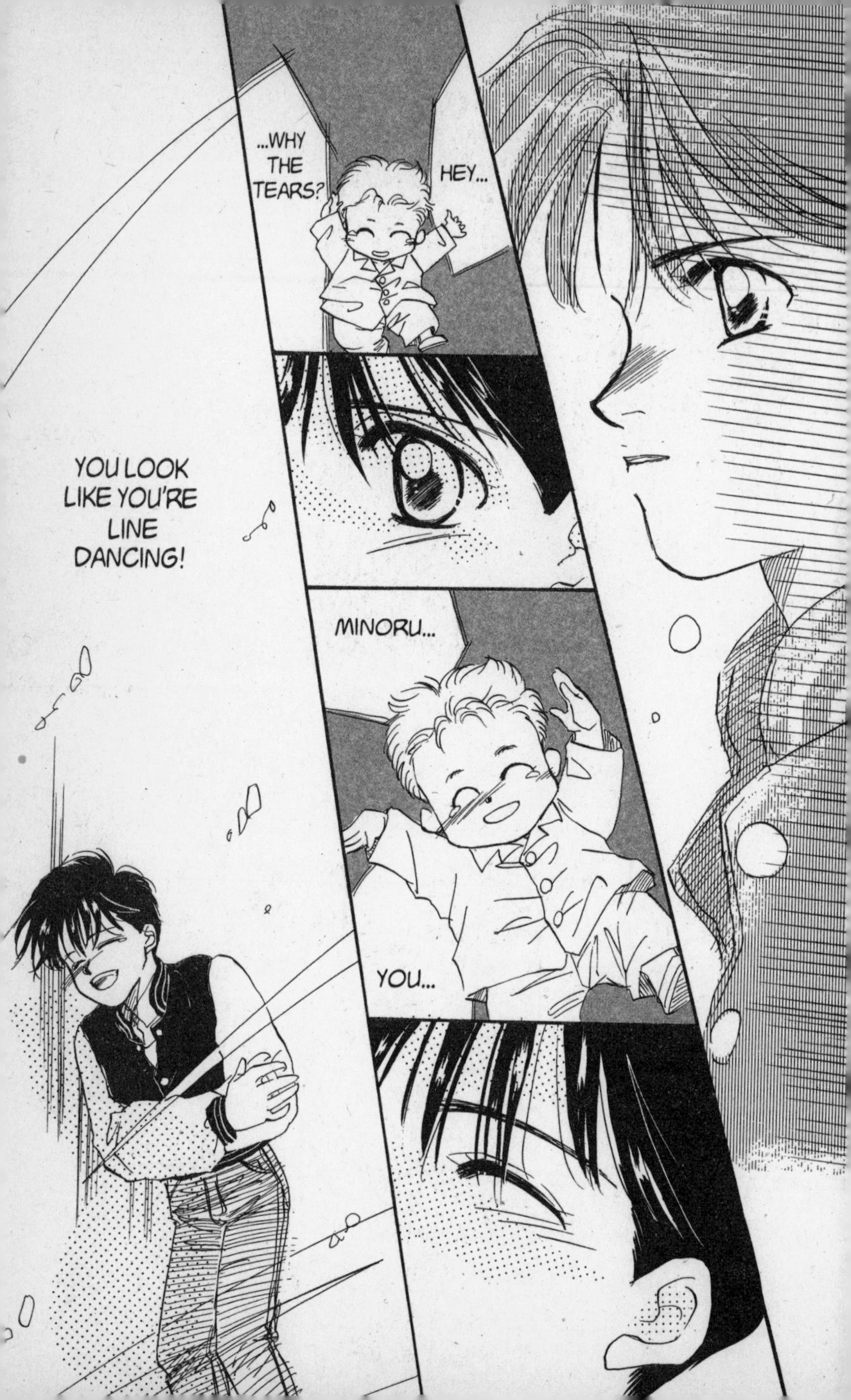
HEY...
...WHY THE TEARS?
MINORU...
YOU...
YOU LOOK LIKE YOU'RE LINE DANCING!

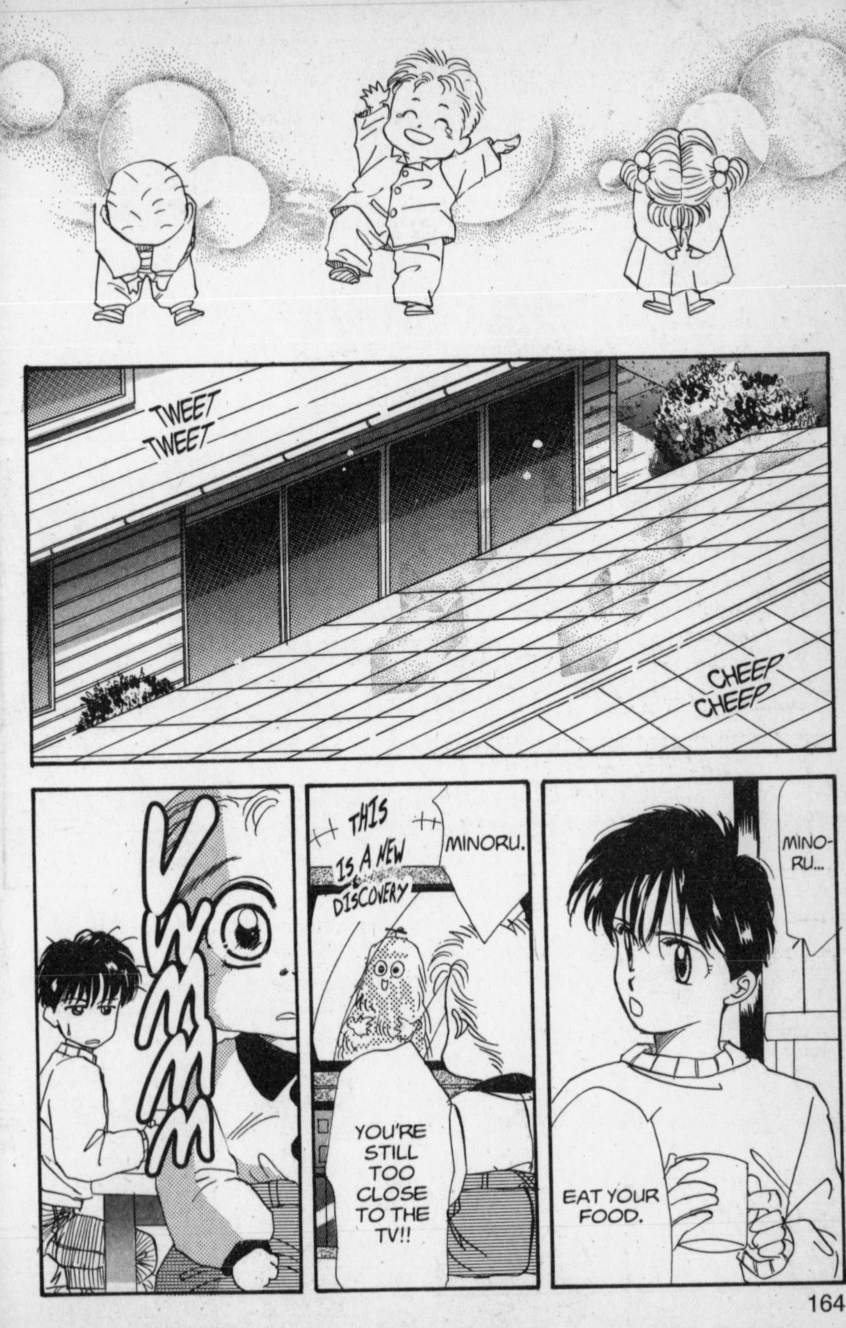
TWEET
TWEET
CHEEP
CHEEP
MINO-RU...
EAT YOUR FOOD.
MINORU.
THIS IS A NEW DISCOVERY
YOU'RE STILL TOO CLOSE TO THE TV!!

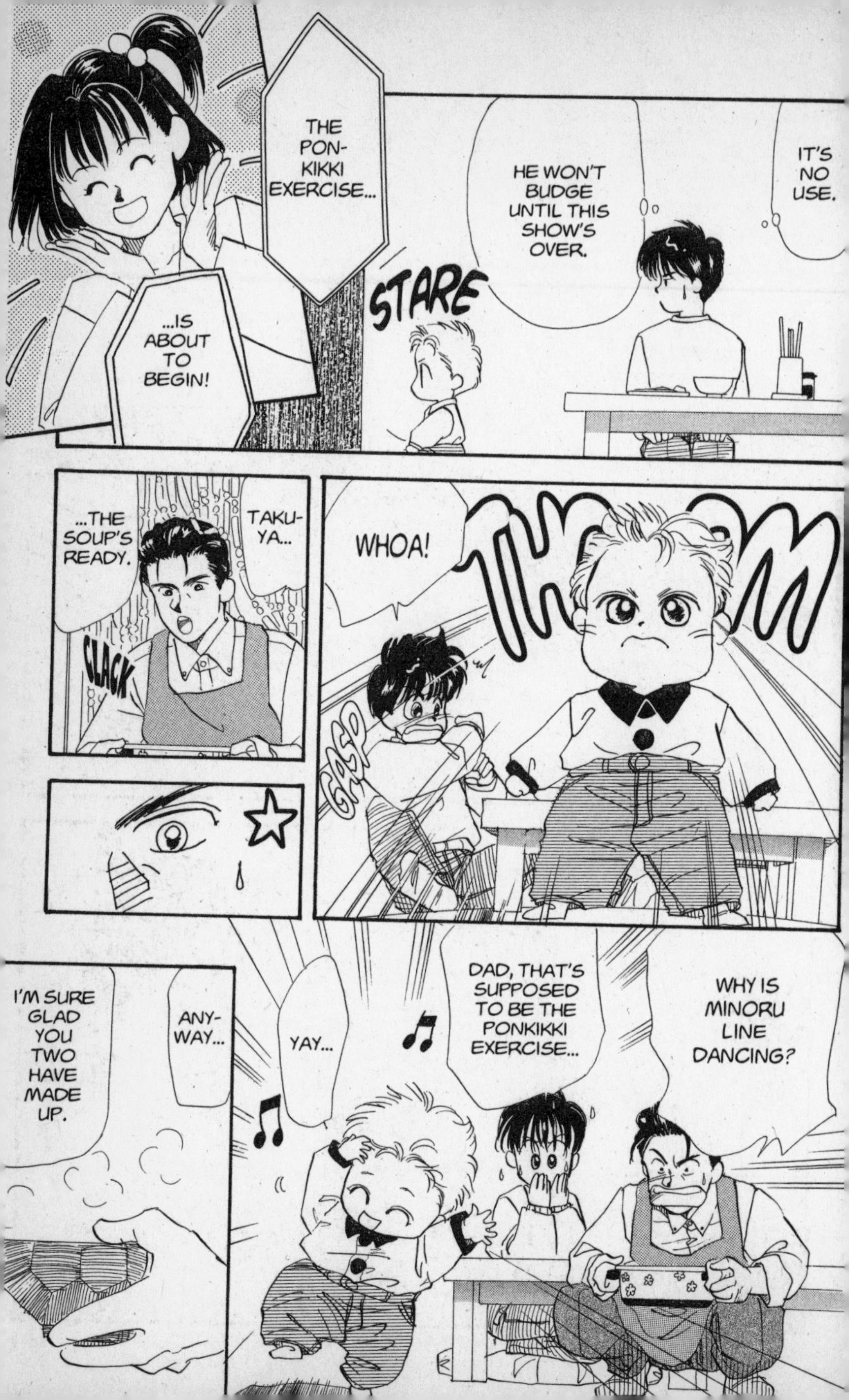
IT'S NO USE.
HE WON'T BUDGE UNTIL THIS SHOW'S OVER.
STARE
THE PON-KIKKI EXERCISE...
...IS ABOUT TO BEGIN!
THOOM
WHOA!
GASP
TAKU-YA...
...THE SOUP'S READY.
CLACK
WHY IS MINORU LINE DANCING?
DAD, THAT'S SUPPOSED TO BE THE PONKIKKI EXERCISE...
YAY...
ANY-WAY...
I'M SURE GLAD YOU TWO HAVE MADE UP.

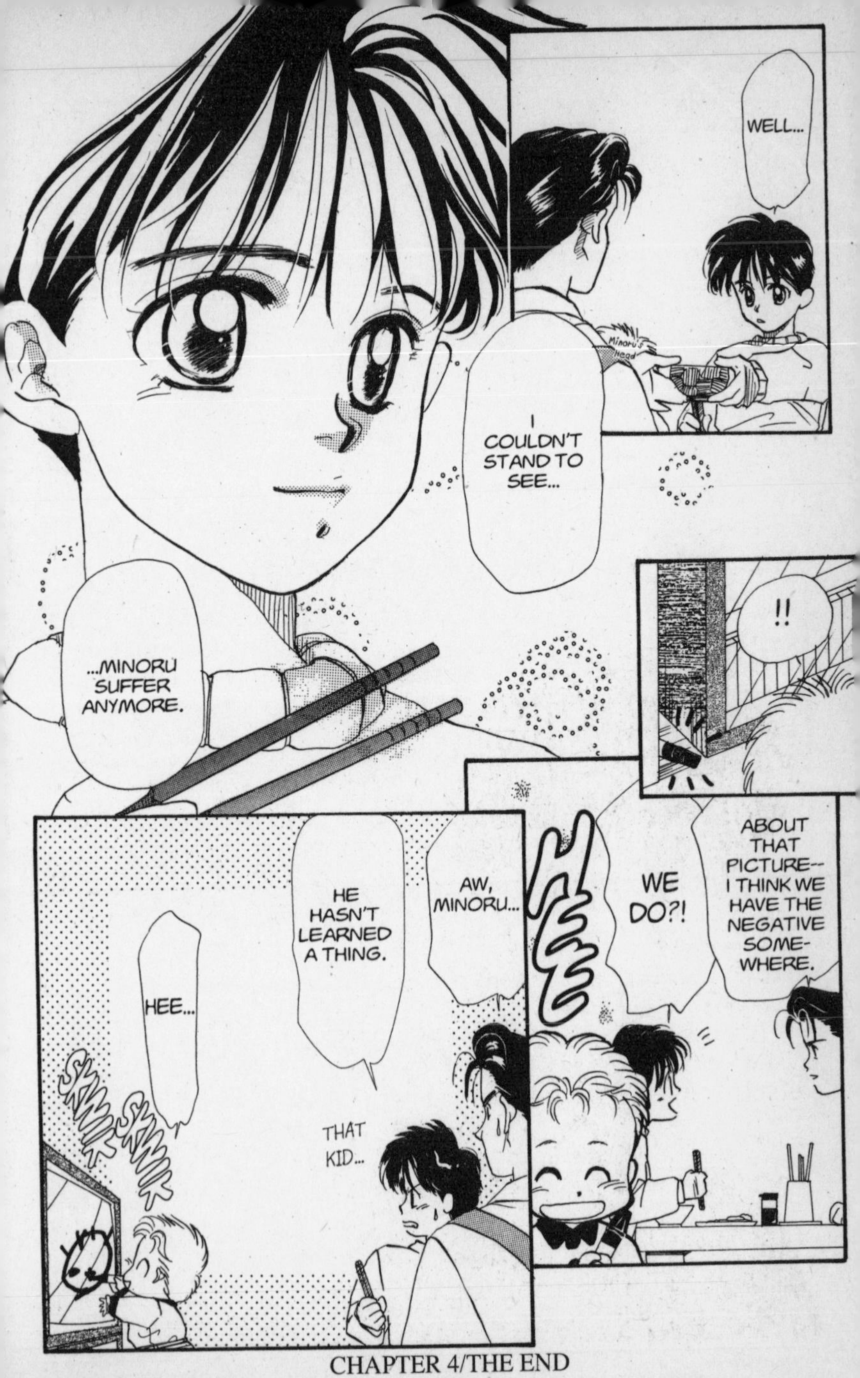
WELL...
Minoru's Head
I COULDN'T STAND TO SEE...
...MINORU SUFFER ANYMORE.
!!
ABOUT THAT PICTURE-- I THINK WE HAVE THE NEGATIVE SOME-WHERE.
WE DO?!
HEE
AW, MINORU...
HE HASN'T LEARNED A THING.
HEE...
THAT KID...
SKWIK
SKWIK

CHAPTER 4/THE END

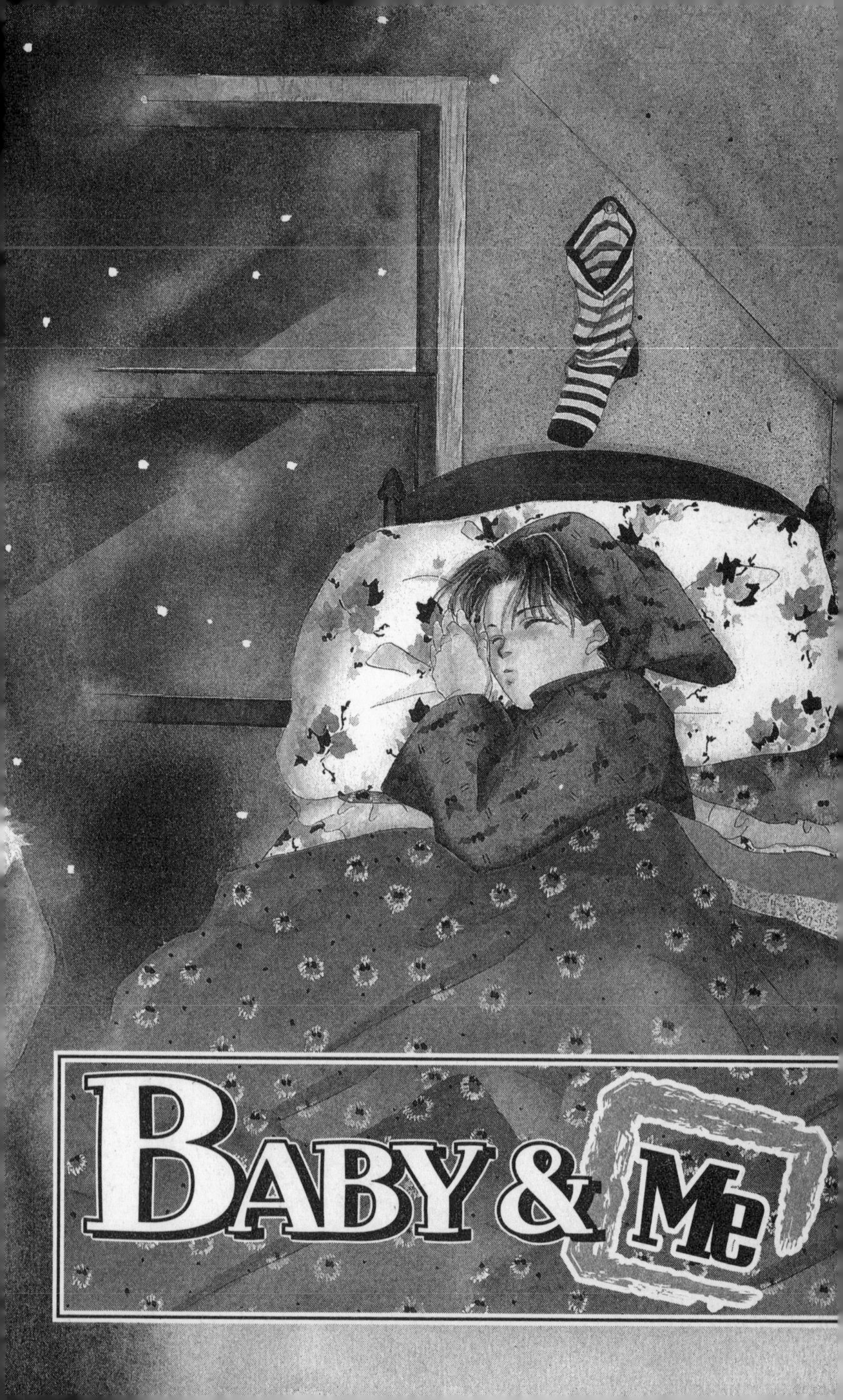
BABY & ME

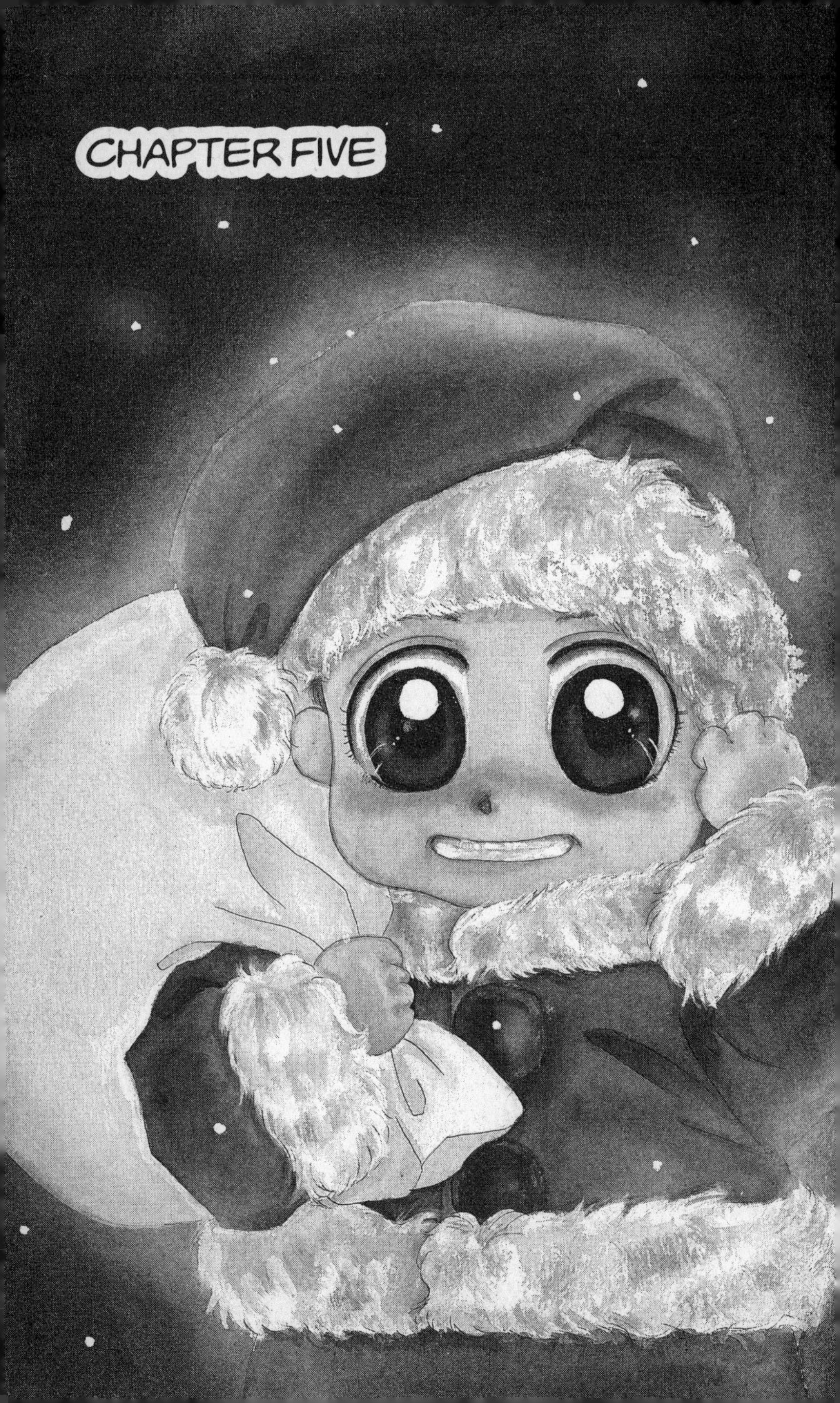
CHAPTER FIVE

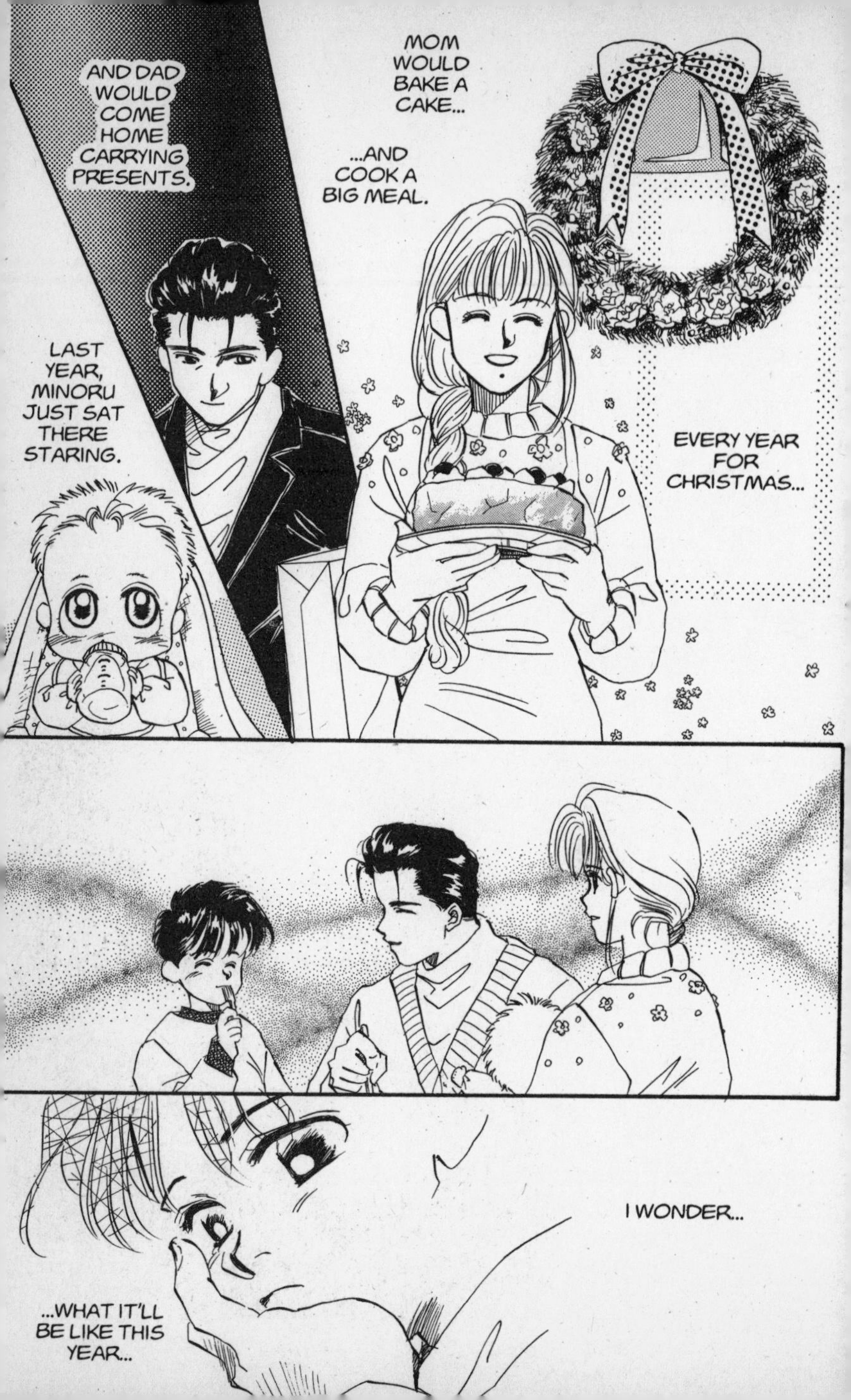
EVERY YEAR FOR CHRISTMAS...
MOM WOULD BAKE A CAKE...
...AND COOK A BIG MEAL.
AND DAD WOULD COME HOME CARRYING PRESENTS.
LAST YEAR, MINORU JUST SAT THERE STARING.
I WONDER...
...WHAT IT'LL BE LIKE THIS YEAR...

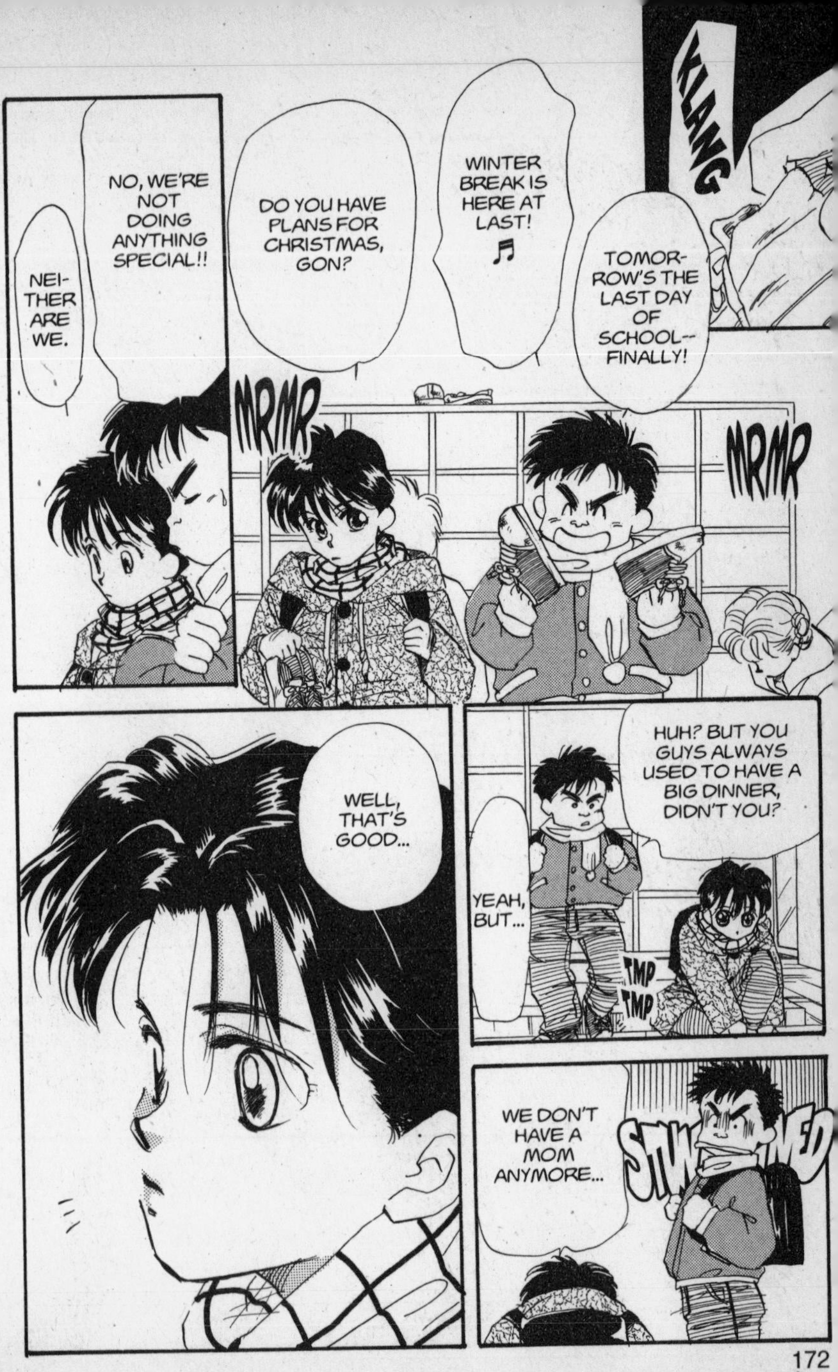
KLANG
TOMORROW'S THE LAST DAY OF SCHOOL--FINALLY!
WINTER BREAK IS HERE AT LAST! ♪
MRMR
DO YOU HAVE PLANS FOR CHRISTMAS, GON?
MRMR
NO, WE'RE NOT DOING ANYTHING SPECIAL!!
NEITHER ARE WE.
HUH? BUT YOU GUYS ALWAYS USED TO HAVE A BIG DINNER, DIDN'T YOU?
YEAH, BUT...
TMP TMP
WE DON'T HAVE A MOM ANYMORE...
WELL, THAT'S GOOD...

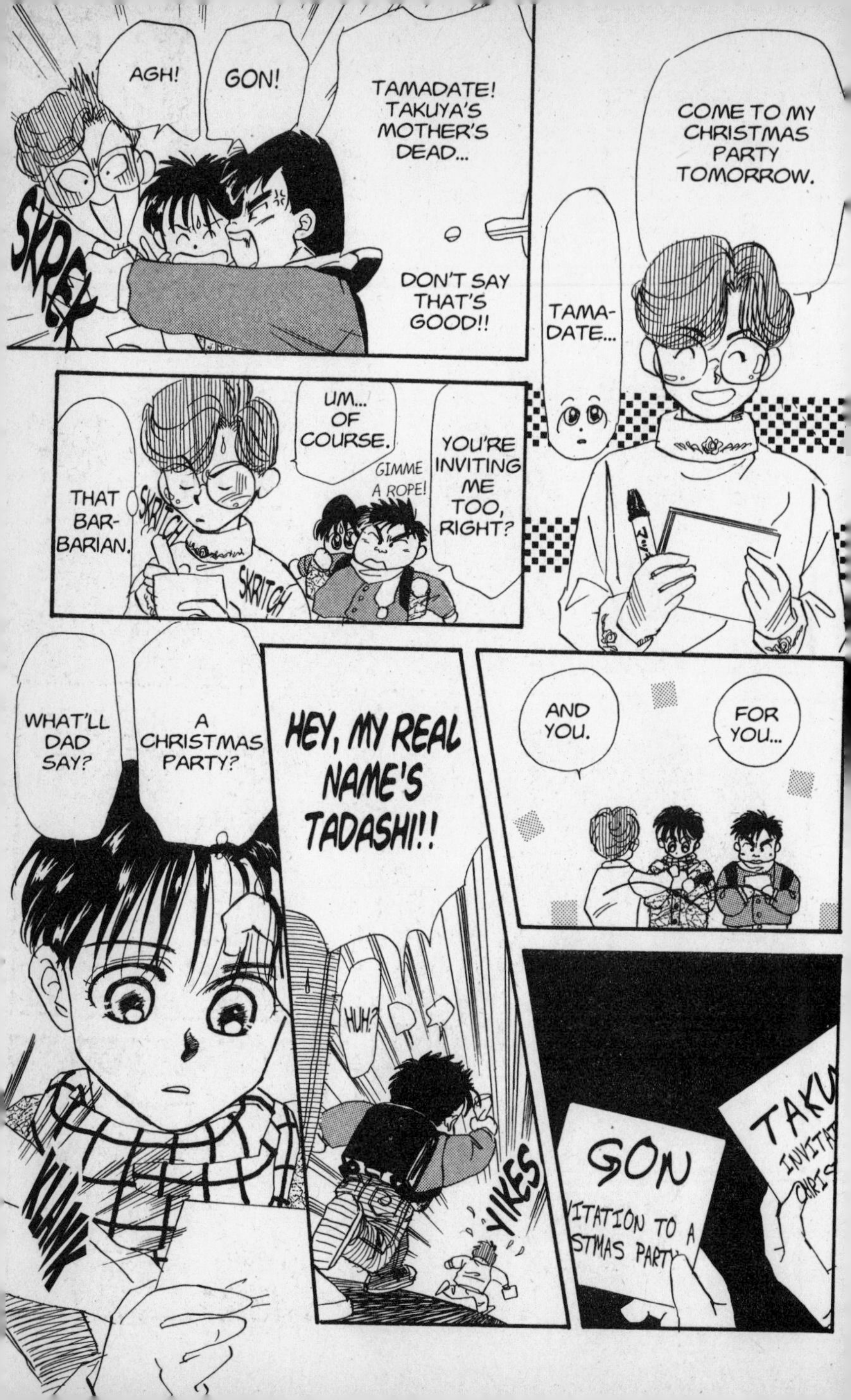
TAMADATE! TAKUYA'S MOTHER'S DEAD...
DON'T SAY THAT'S GOOD!!
GON!
AGH!
SKREK
COME TO MY CHRISTMAS PARTY TOMORROW.
TAMA-DATE...
YOU'RE INVITING ME TOO, RIGHT?
GIMME A ROPE!
UM... OF COURSE.
SKRITCH
SKRITCH
THAT BAR-BARIAN.
FOR YOU...
AND YOU.
GON
VITATION TO A
STMAS PART
TAKU
INVITAT
CHRIS
HEY, MY REAL NAME'S TADASHI!!
HUH?
YIKES
A CHRISTMAS PARTY?
WHAT'LL DAD SAY?
KLANK

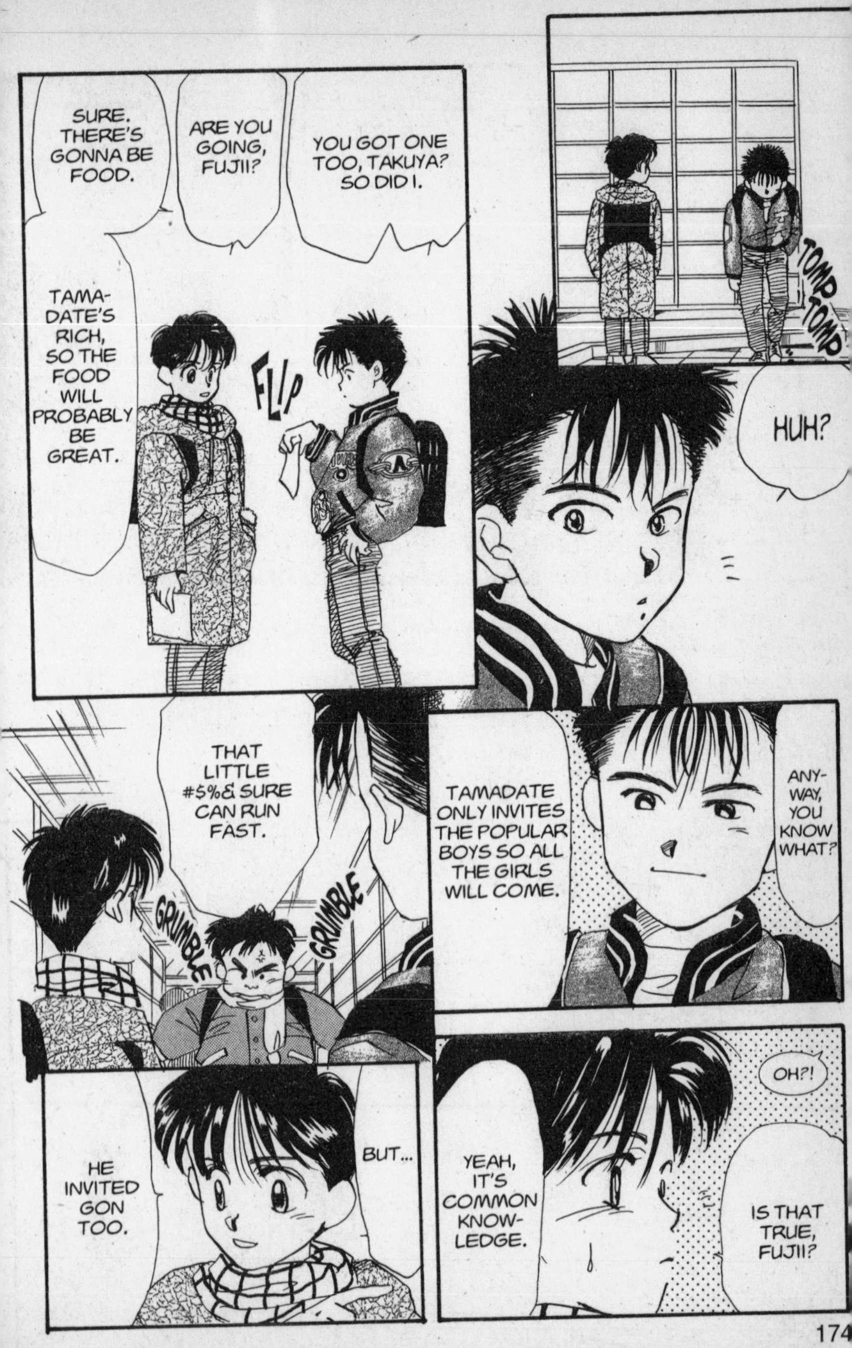
TOMP TOMP
HUH?
YOU GOT ONE TOO, TAKUYA? SO DID I.
ARE YOU GOING, FUJII?
SURE. THERE'S GONNA BE FOOD.
FLIP
TAMA-DATE'S RICH, SO THE FOOD WILL PROBABLY BE GREAT.
ANY-WAY, YOU KNOW WHAT?
TAMADATE ONLY INVITES THE POPULAR BOYS SO ALL THE GIRLS WILL COME.
THAT LITTLE #$%& SURE CAN RUN FAST.
GRUMBLE
GRUMBLE
OH?!
IS THAT TRUE, FUJII?
YEAH, IT'S COMMON KNOW-LEDGE.
BUT...
HE INVITED GON TOO.

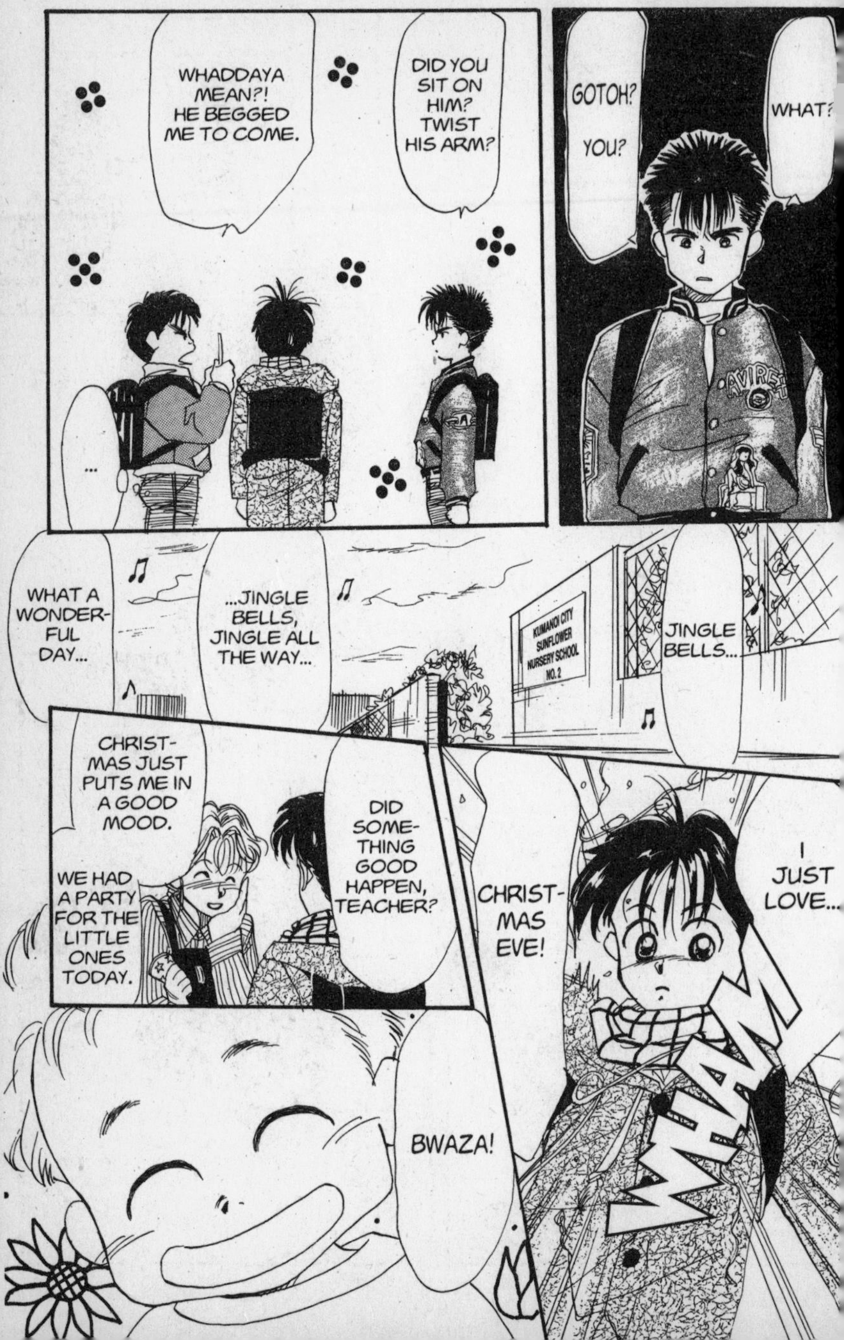
WHAT?
GOTOH? YOU?
DID YOU SIT ON HIM? TWIST HIS ARM?
WHADDAYA MEAN?! HE BEGGED ME TO COME.
...
JINGLE BELLS...
KUMANOI CITY SUNFLOWER NURSERY SCHOOL NO. 2
...JINGLE BELLS, JINGLE ALL THE WAY...
WHAT A WONDER-FUL DAY...
I JUST LOVE...
CHRIST-MAS EVE!
WHAM
DID SOME-THING GOOD HAPPEN, TEACHER?
CHRIST-MAS JUST PUTS ME IN A GOOD MOOD.
WE HAD A PARTY FOR THE LITTLE ONES TODAY.
BWAZA!

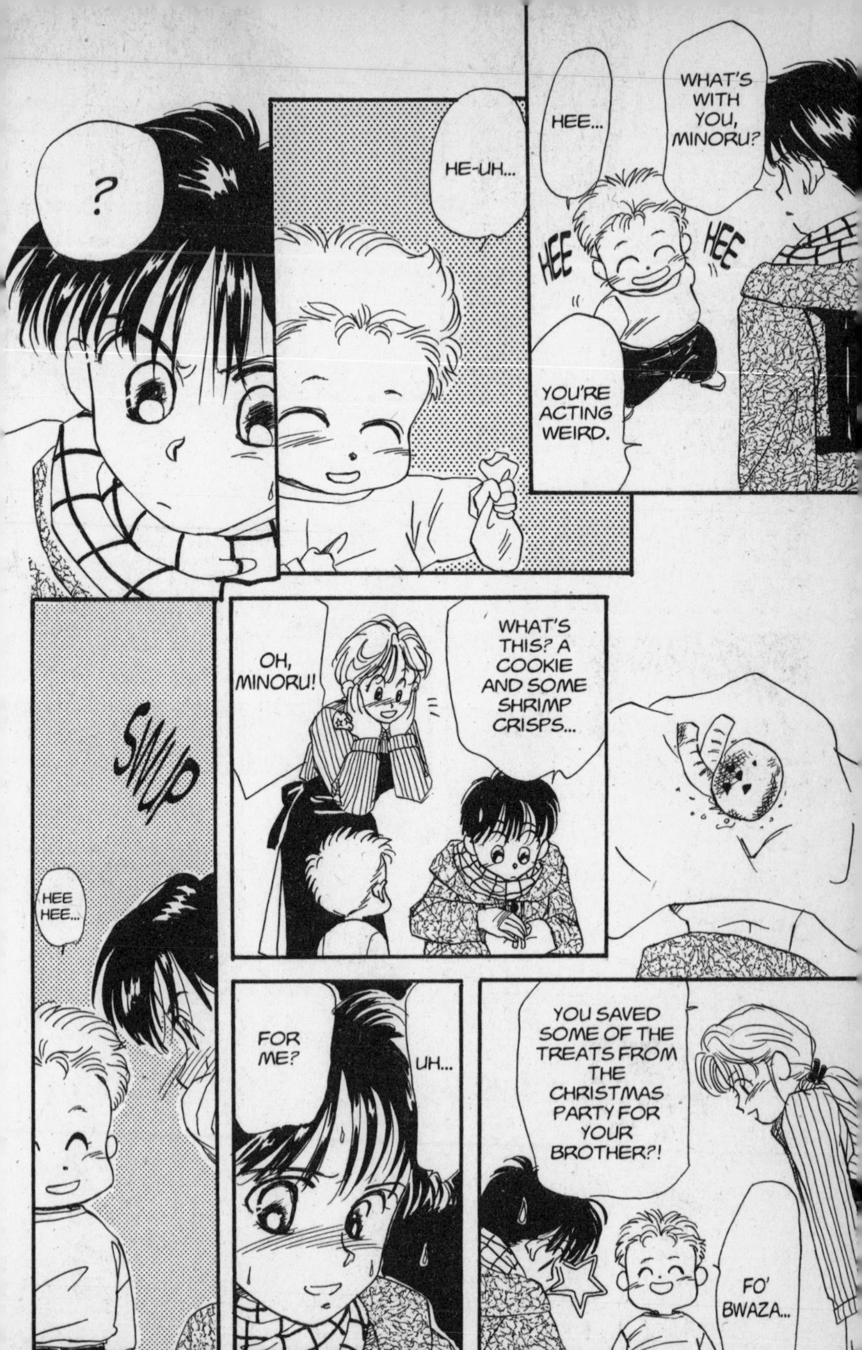
WHAT'S WITH YOU, MINORU?
HEE...
HEE
HEE
YOU'RE ACTING WEIRD.
HE-UH...
?
WHAT'S THIS? A COOKIE AND SOME SHRIMP CRISPS...
OH, MINORU!
YOU SAVED SOME OF THE TREATS FROM THE CHRISTMAS PARTY FOR YOUR BROTHER?!
FO' BWAZA...
UH...
FOR ME?
SNUP
HEE HEE...

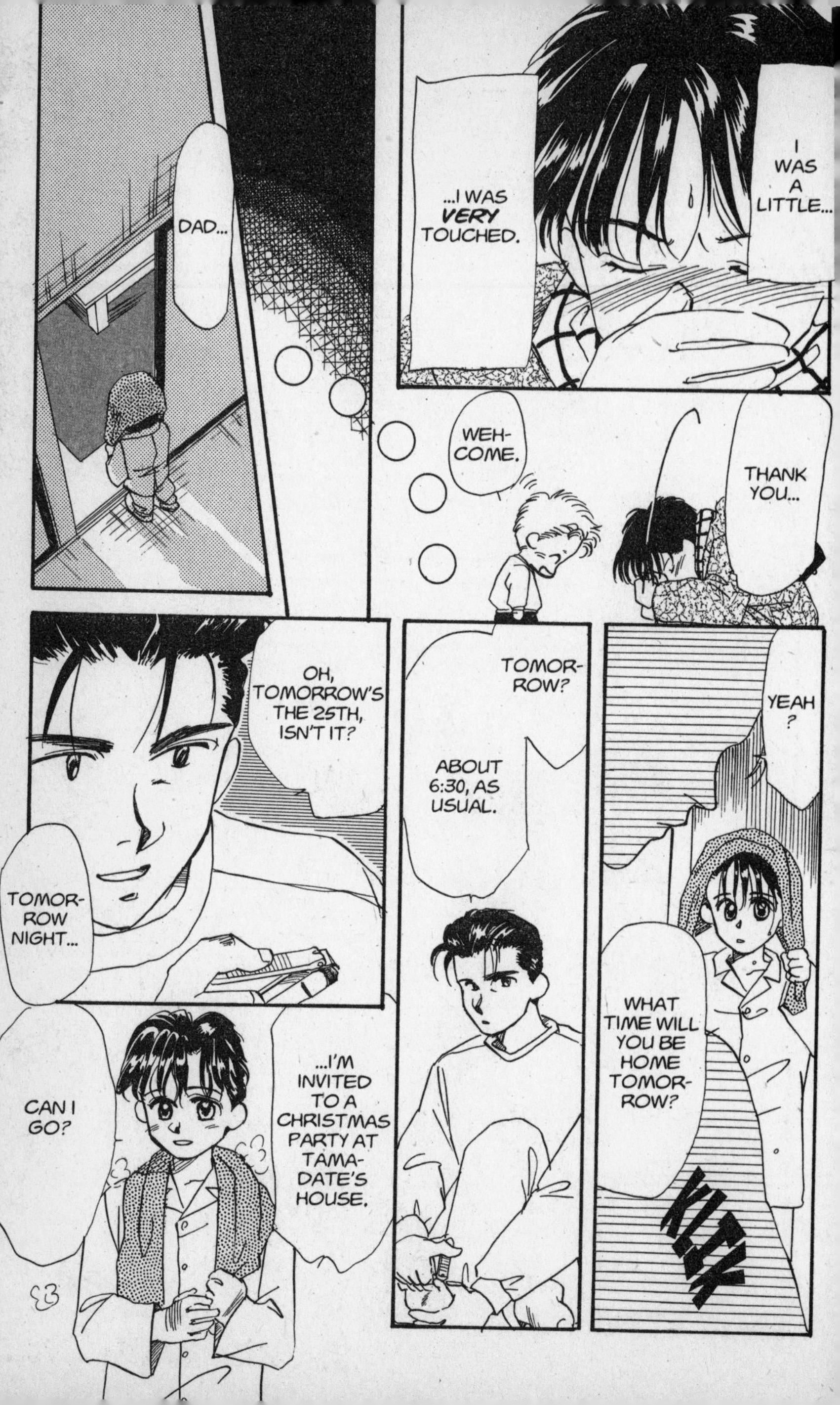
I WAS A LITTLE...
...I WAS *VERY* TOUCHED.
THANK YOU...
WEH-COME.
DAD...
YEAH?
WHAT TIME WILL YOU BE HOME TOMORROW?
KLIK
TOMORROW?
ABOUT 6:30, AS USUAL.
OH, TOMORROW'S THE 25TH, ISN'T IT?
TOMORROW NIGHT...
...I'M INVITED TO A CHRISTMAS PARTY AT TAMADATE'S HOUSE.
CAN I GO?

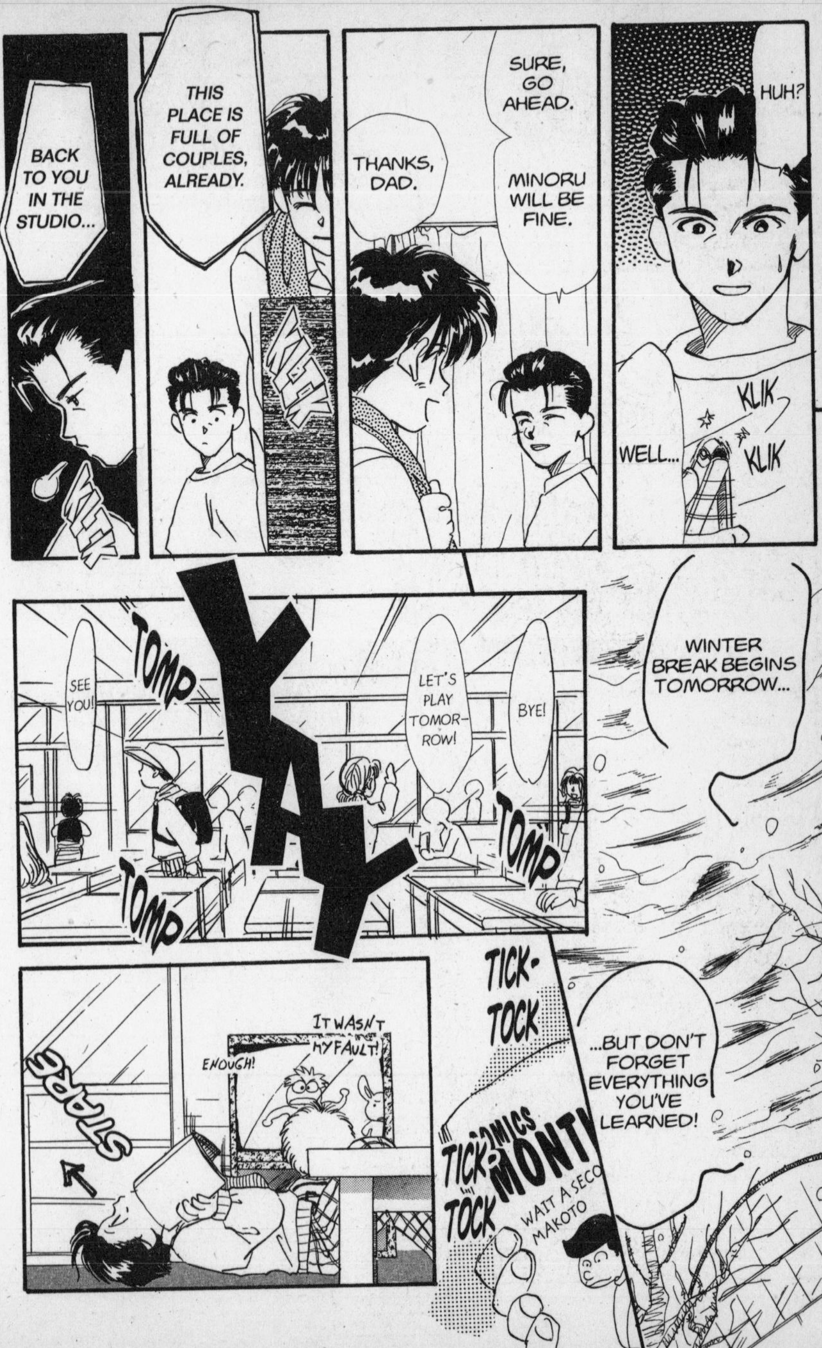
HUH?
KLIK
KLIK
WELL...
SURE, GO AHEAD.
MINORU WILL BE FINE.
THANKS, DAD.
THIS PLACE IS FULL OF COUPLES, ALREADY.
BACK TO YOU IN THE STUDIO...
WINTER BREAK BEGINS TOMORROW...
BYE!
LET'S PLAY TOMORROW!
TOMP
YAY
TOMP
SEE YOU!
TOMP
TOMP
...BUT DON'T FORGET EVERYTHING YOU'VE LEARNED!
TICK-TOCK
TICK-TOCK
IT WASN'T MY FAULT!
ENOUGH!

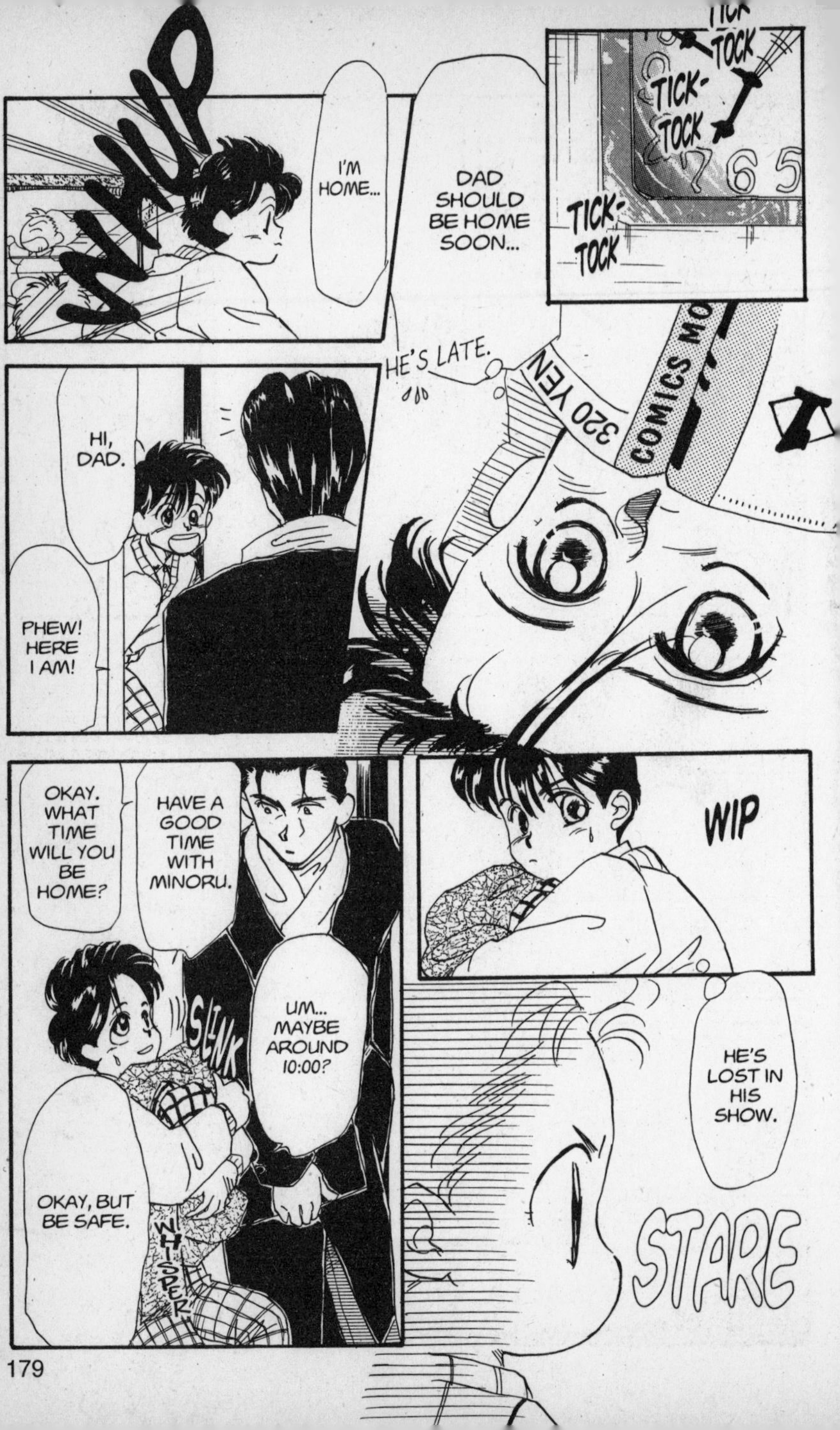
TICK-TOCK
TICK-TOCK
TICK-TOCK
DAD SHOULD BE HOME SOON...
HE'S LATE.
320 YEN
COMICS MO
WHIP
I'M HOME...
HI, DAD.
PHEW! HERE I AM!
WIP
HE'S LOST IN HIS SHOW.
STARE
HAVE A GOOD TIME WITH MINORU.
OKAY. WHAT TIME WILL YOU BE HOME?
UM... MAYBE AROUND 10:00?
SLINK
OKAY, BUT BE SAFE.
WHISPER

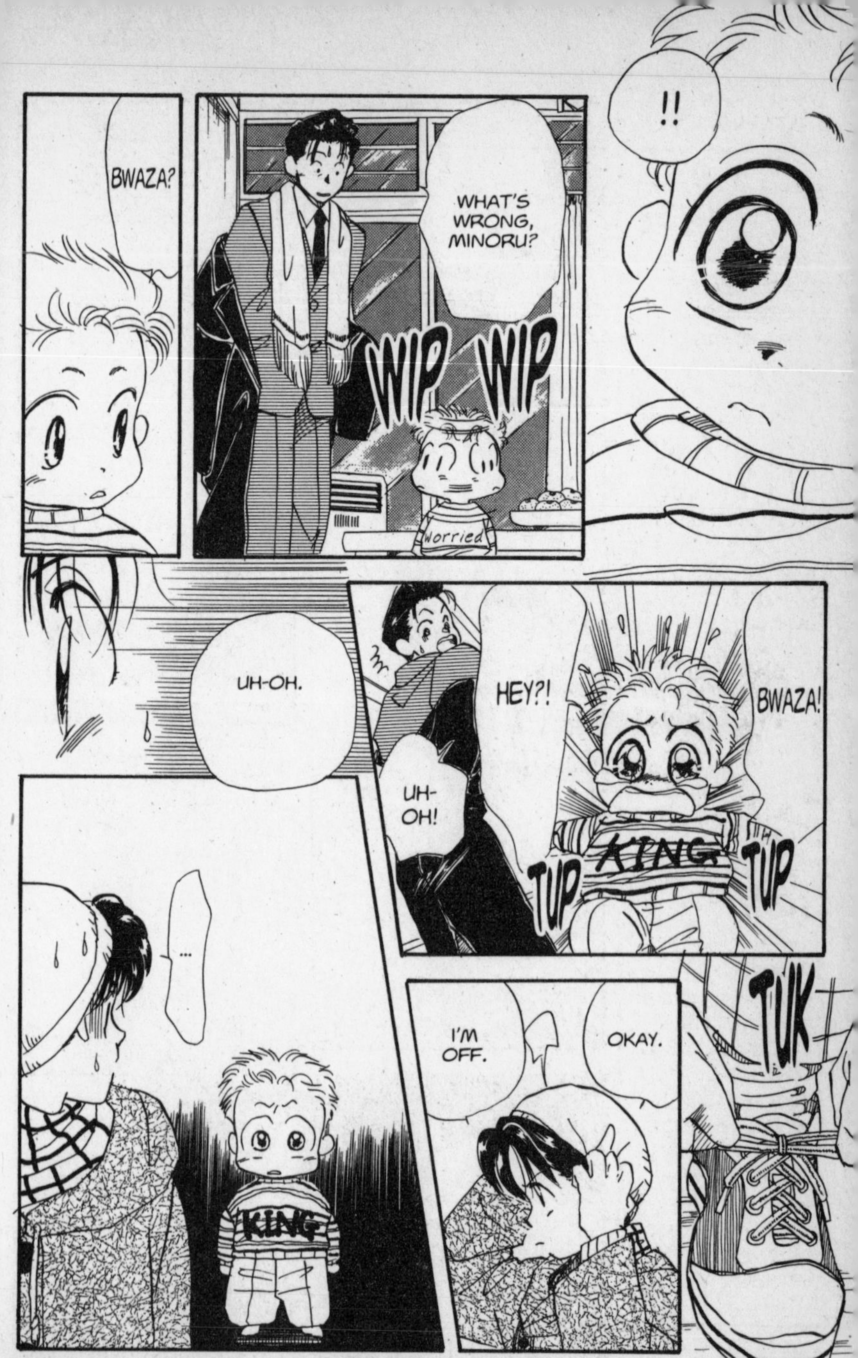
!!
WHAT'S WRONG, MINORU?
WIP WIP
Worried
BWAZA?
BWAZA!
HEY?!
UH-OH!
TUP
KING
TUP
UH-OH.
TUK
OKAY.
I'M OFF.
...
KING

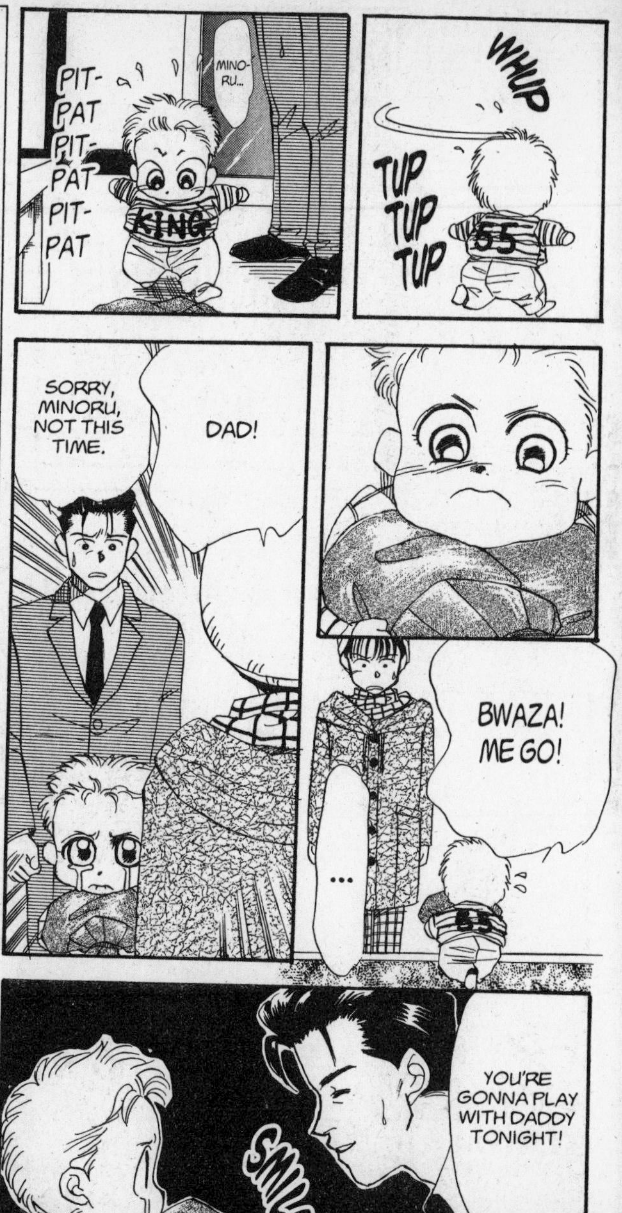
WHUP
TUP TUP TUP
55
MINO-RU...
PIT-PAT PIT-PAT PIT-PAT
KING
DAD!
SORRY, MINORU, NOT THIS TIME.
BWAZA! ME GO!
55
...
YOU'RE GONNA PLAY WITH DADDY TONIGHT!
SMILE

AUTHOR'S NOTE 7

ONE DAY, I SAID TO MY SISTER, "TAKUYA'S THE MAIN CHARACTER, BUT THERE'S NOTHING DISTINCTIVE ABOUT HIS FACE OR HIS PERSONALITY, IS THERE?" SHE SAID, "NOT REALLY." I KNOW I BROUGHT IT UP, BUT I WAS SURPRISED ANYWAY. BUT IT'S TRUE--FOR A MAIN CHARACTER, TAKUYA IS VERY ORDINARY.

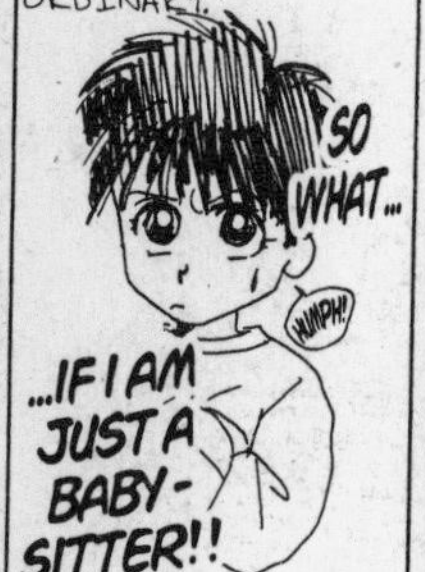
SO WHAT...
HMPH!
...IF I AM JUST A BABY-SITTER!!

SOMEONE ONCE POINTED OUT TO ME THAT YOU DON'T NORMALLY SEE A CHARACTER LIKE GON IN A COMIC BOOK FOR GIRLS. MAYBE, BUT FUJII HAS HIS LIMITATIONS--HE'S REALLY POPULAR, AND HIS HAIRSTYLE'S HARD TO DRAW.

WELL, IF MY LUCK HOLDS, I'LL SEE YOU IN VOLUME 2.

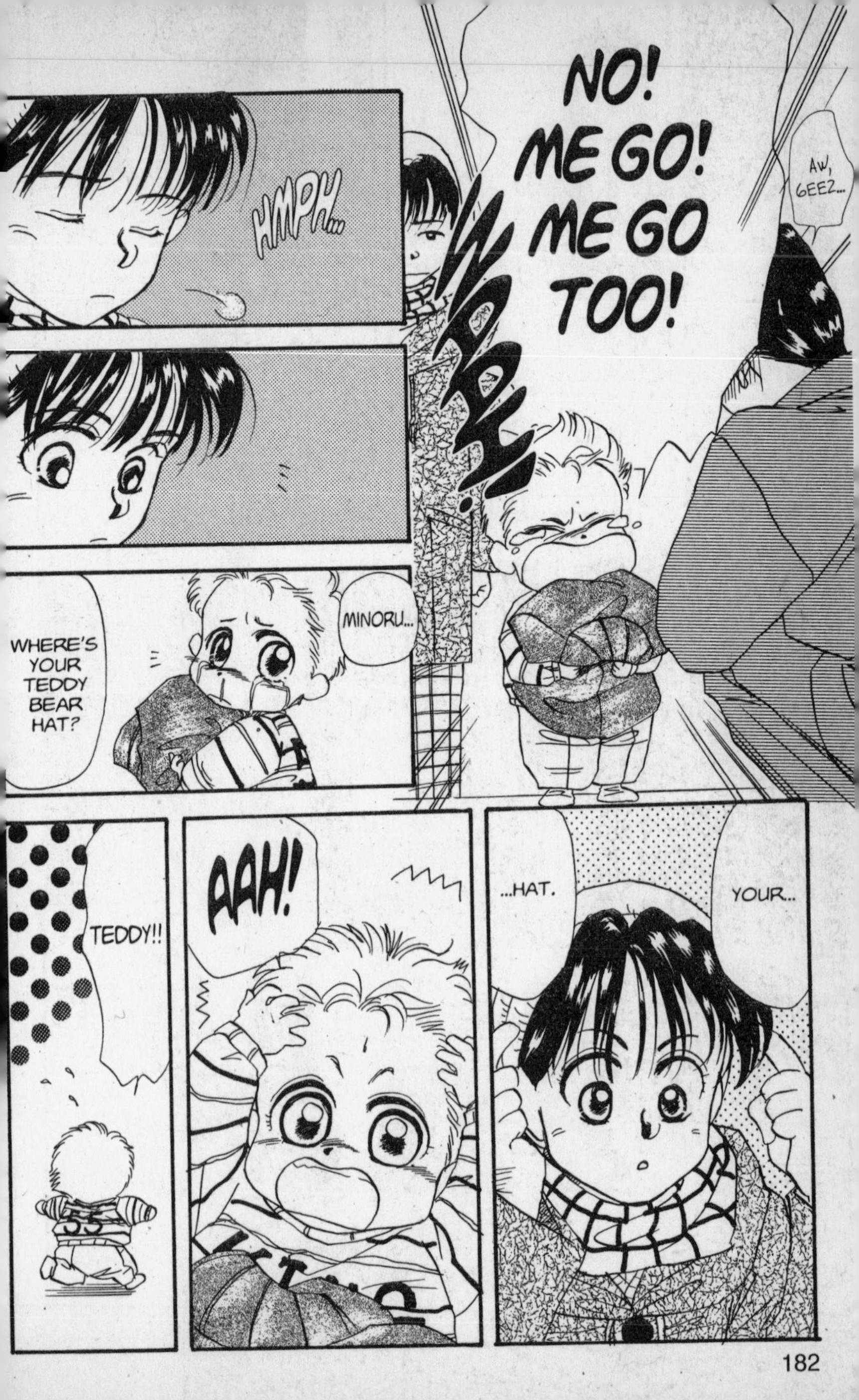
AW, GEEZ...
NO! ME GO! ME GO TOO!
WAAH!
HMPH...
MINORU...
WHERE'S YOUR TEDDY BEAR HAT?
YOUR...
...HAT.
AAH!
TEDDY!!

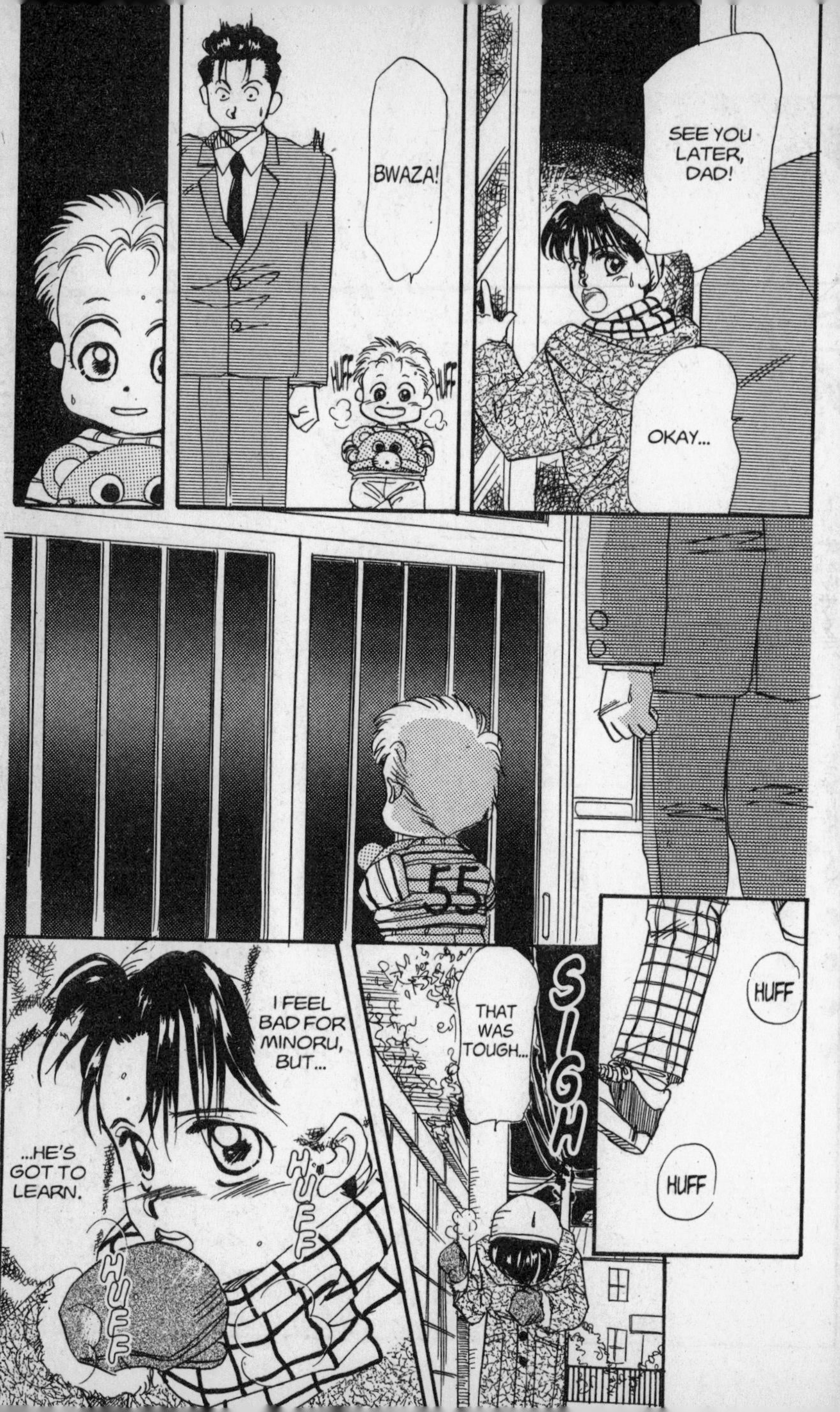
SEE YOU LATER, DAD!
OKAY...
BWAZA!
HUFF HUFF
HUFF
HUFF
SIGH
THAT WAS TOUGH...
I FEEL BAD FOR MINORU, BUT...
...HE'S GOT TO LEARN.
HUFF HUFF

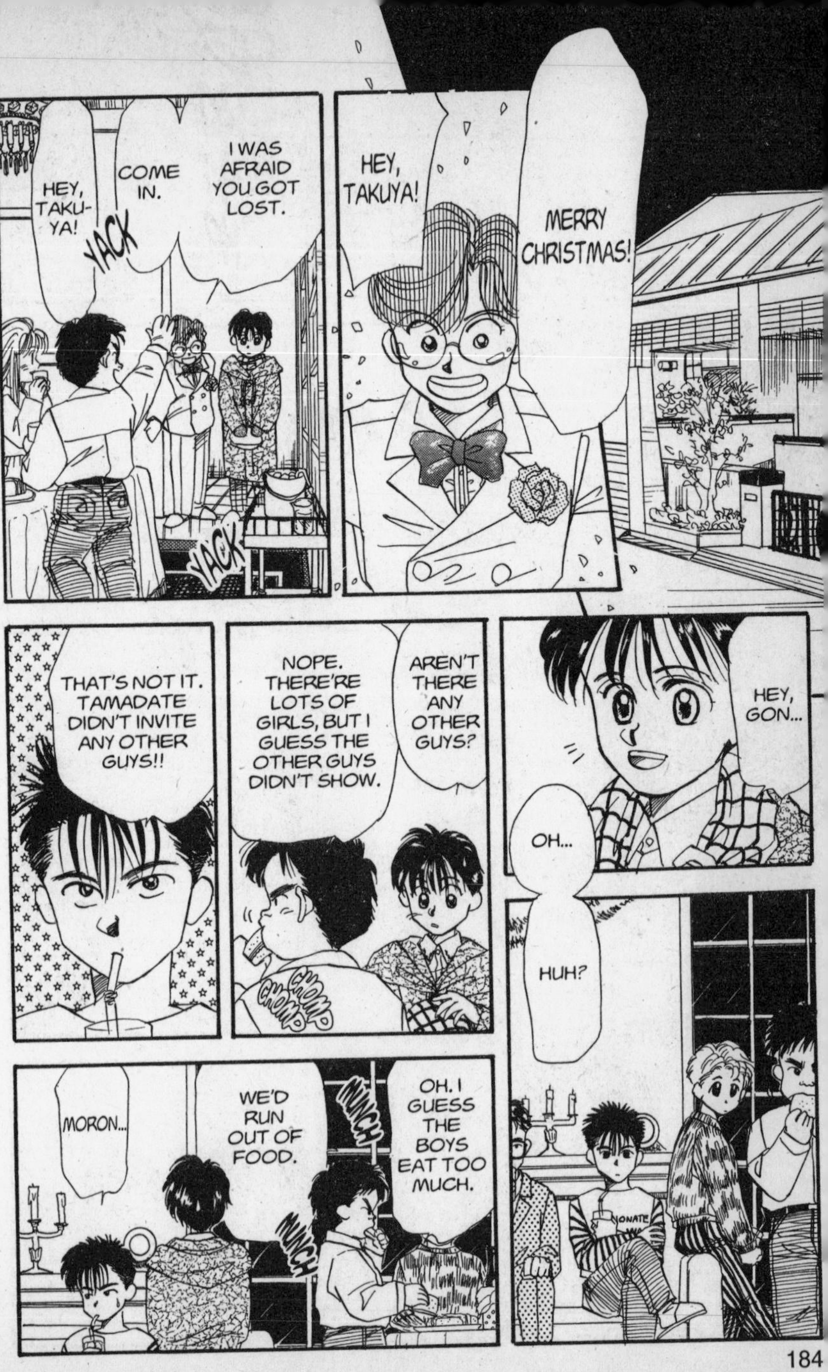
MERRY CHRISTMAS!
HEY, TAKUYA!
I WAS AFRAID YOU GOT LOST.
COME IN.
HEY, TAKU-YA!
YACK
YACK
HEY, GON...
OH...
AREN'T THERE ANY OTHER GUYS?
NOPE. THERE'RE LOTS OF GIRLS, BUT I GUESS THE OTHER GUYS DIDN'T SHOW.
CHOMP CHOMP
THAT'S NOT IT. TAMADATE DIDN'T INVITE ANY OTHER GUYS!!
HUH?
OH. I GUESS THE BOYS EAT TOO MUCH.
MUNCH
WE'D RUN OUT OF FOOD.
MUNCH
MORON...

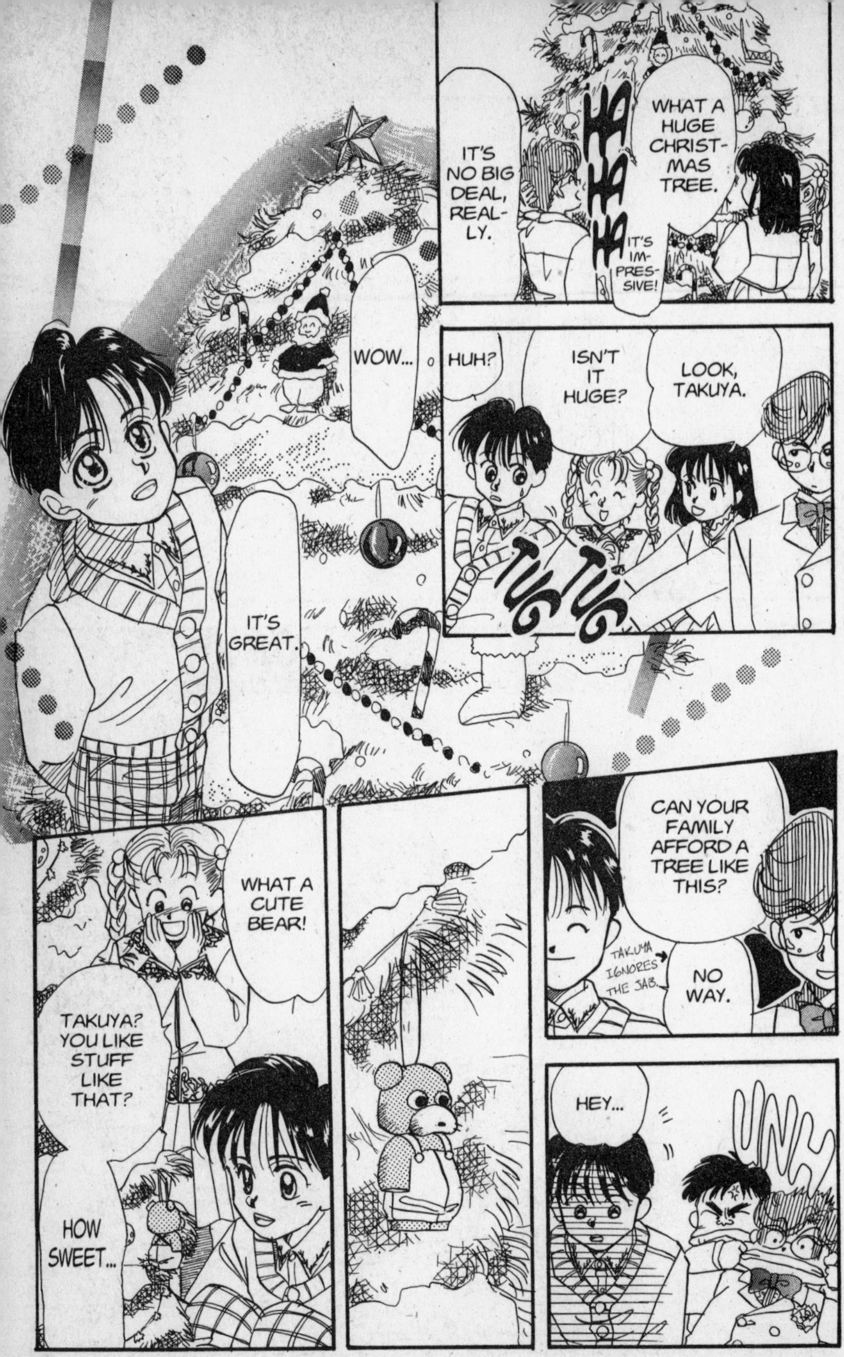
WHAT A HUGE CHRISTMAS TREE.
IT'S IMPRESSIVE!
HA HA HA
IT'S NO BIG DEAL, REALLY.
LOOK, TAKUYA.
ISN'T IT HUGE?
HUH?
TUG TUG
WOW...
IT'S GREAT.
CAN YOUR FAMILY AFFORD A TREE LIKE THIS?
NO WAY.
TAKUYA IGNORES THE JAB.
HEY...
UNH
WHAT A CUTE BEAR!
TAKUYA? YOU LIKE STUFF LIKE THAT?
HOW SWEET...

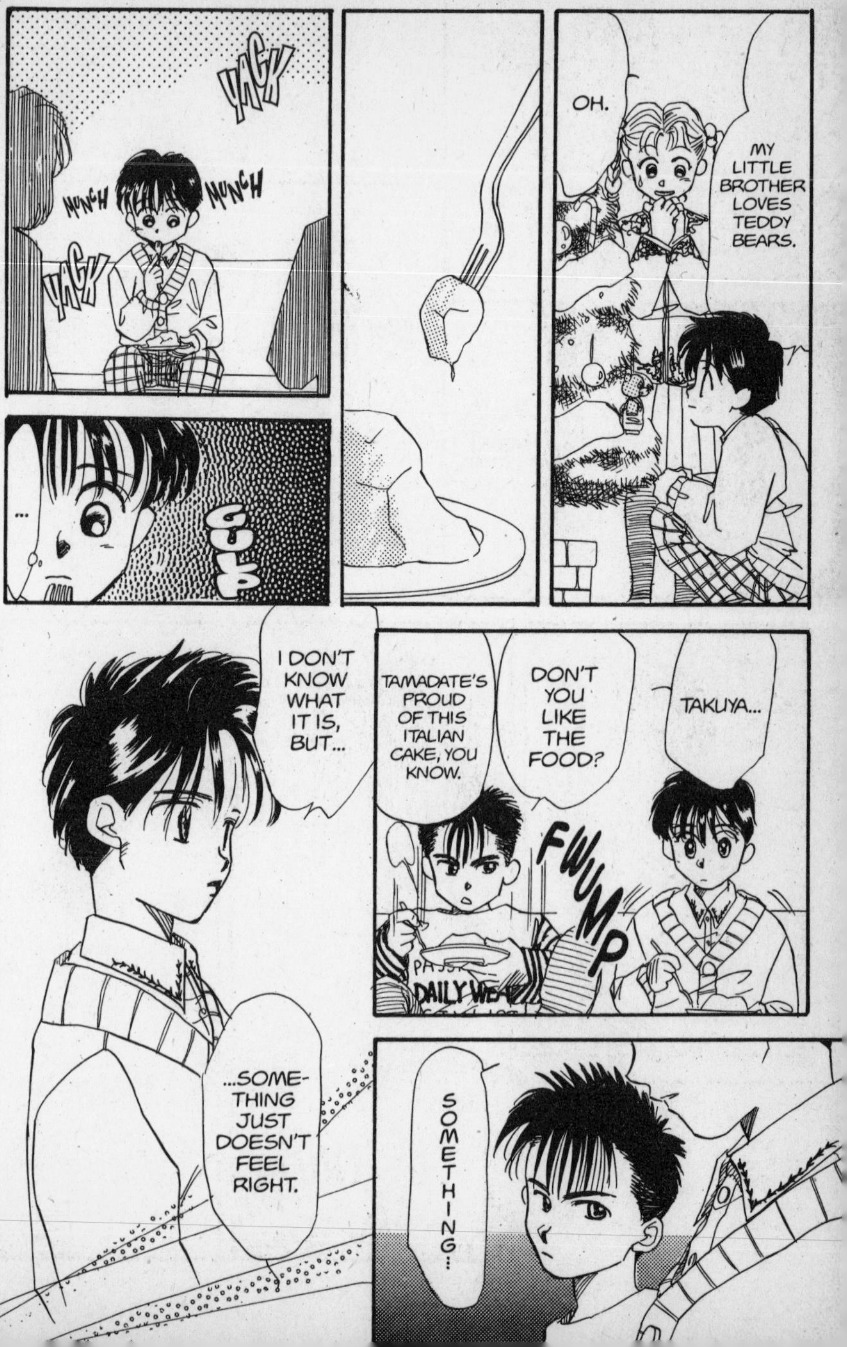
OH.
MY LITTLE BROTHER LOVES TEDDY BEARS.
MUNCH
MUNCH
YACK
YACK
...
GULP
TAKUYA...
DON'T YOU LIKE THE FOOD?
TAMADATE'S PROUD OF THIS ITALIAN CAKE, YOU KNOW.
FWUMP
SOMETHING...
I DON'T KNOW WHAT IT IS, BUT...
...SOME-THING JUST DOESN'T FEEL RIGHT.

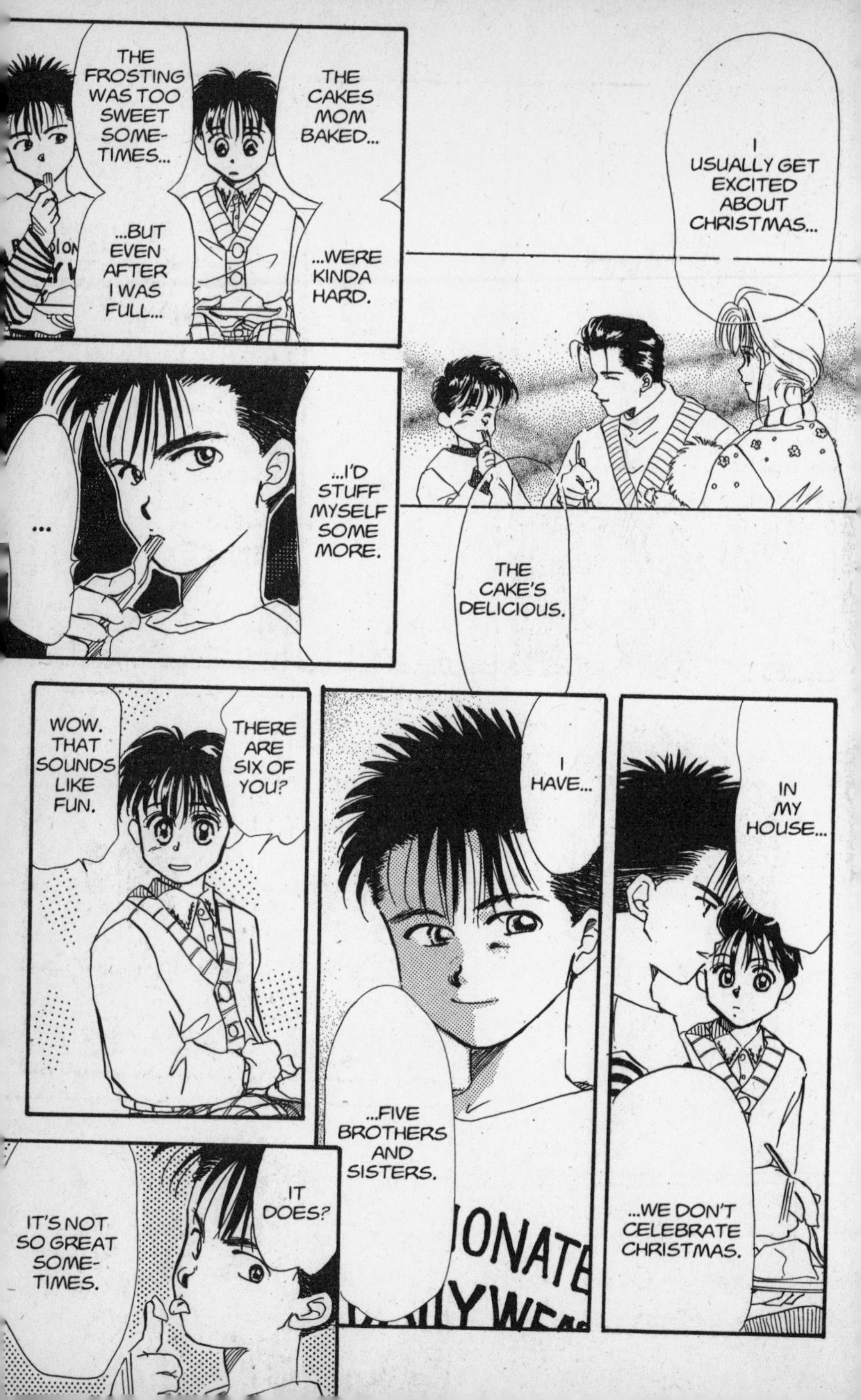
I USUALLY GET EXCITED ABOUT CHRISTMAS...
THE CAKE'S DELICIOUS.
THE CAKES MOM BAKED...
...WERE KINDA HARD.
THE FROSTING WAS TOO SWEET SOME-TIMES...
...BUT EVEN AFTER I WAS FULL...
...I'D STUFF MYSELF SOME MORE.
...
IN MY HOUSE...
...WE DON'T CELEBRATE CHRISTMAS.
I HAVE...
...FIVE BROTHERS AND SISTERS.
THERE ARE SIX OF YOU?
WOW. THAT SOUNDS LIKE FUN.
IT DOES?
IT'S NOT SO GREAT SOME-TIMES.

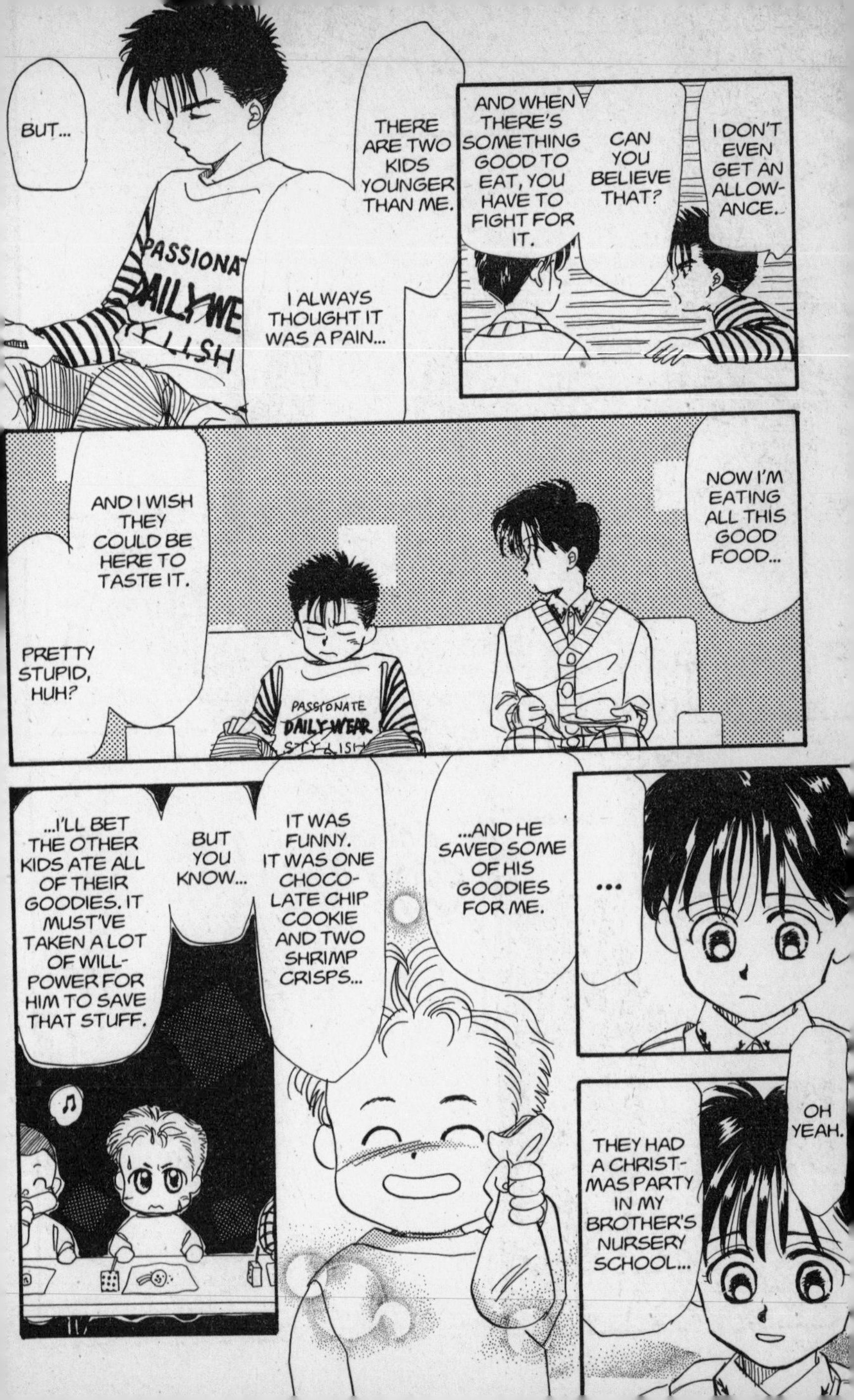
I DON'T EVEN GET AN ALLOW-ANCE.
CAN YOU BELIEVE THAT?
AND WHEN THERE'S SOMETHING GOOD TO EAT, YOU HAVE TO FIGHT FOR IT.
THERE ARE TWO KIDS YOUNGER THAN ME.
I ALWAYS THOUGHT IT WAS A PAIN...
BUT...
NOW I'M EATING ALL THIS GOOD FOOD...
AND I WISH THEY COULD BE HERE TO TASTE IT.
PRETTY STUPID, HUH?
...
OH YEAH.
THEY HAD A CHRIST-MAS PARTY IN MY BROTHER'S NURSERY SCHOOL...
...AND HE SAVED SOME OF HIS GOODIES FOR ME.
IT WAS FUNNY. IT WAS ONE CHOCO-LATE CHIP COOKIE AND TWO SHRIMP CRISPS...
BUT YOU KNOW...
...I'LL BET THE OTHER KIDS ATE ALL OF THEIR GOODIES. IT MUST'VE TAKEN A LOT OF WILL-POWER FOR HIM TO SAVE THAT STUFF.

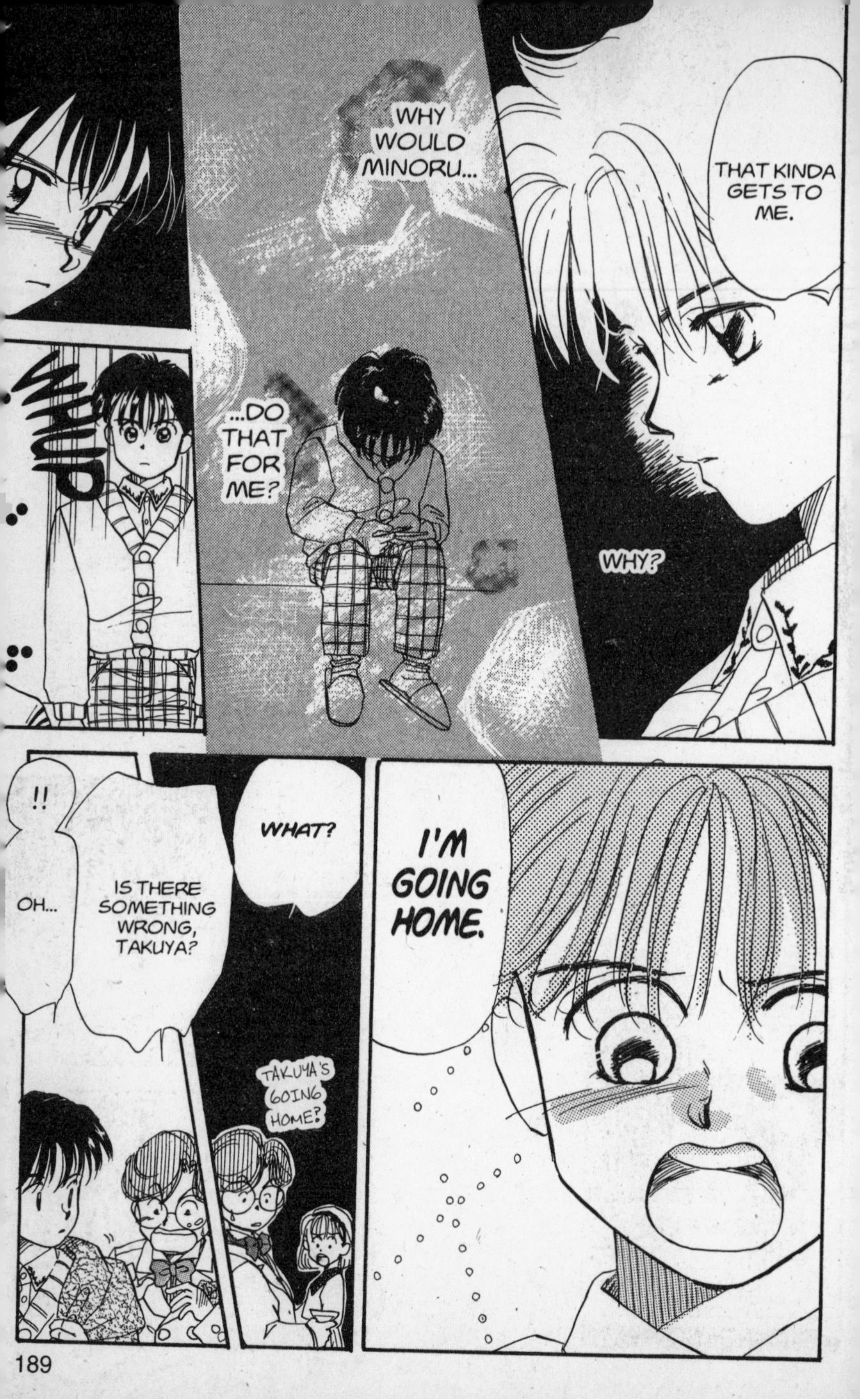
THAT KINDA GETS TO ME.
WHY?
WHY WOULD MINORU...
...DO THAT FOR ME?
WHUP
I'M GOING HOME.
WHAT?
TAKUYA'S GOING HOME?
IS THERE SOMETHING WRONG, TAKUYA?
!!
OH...

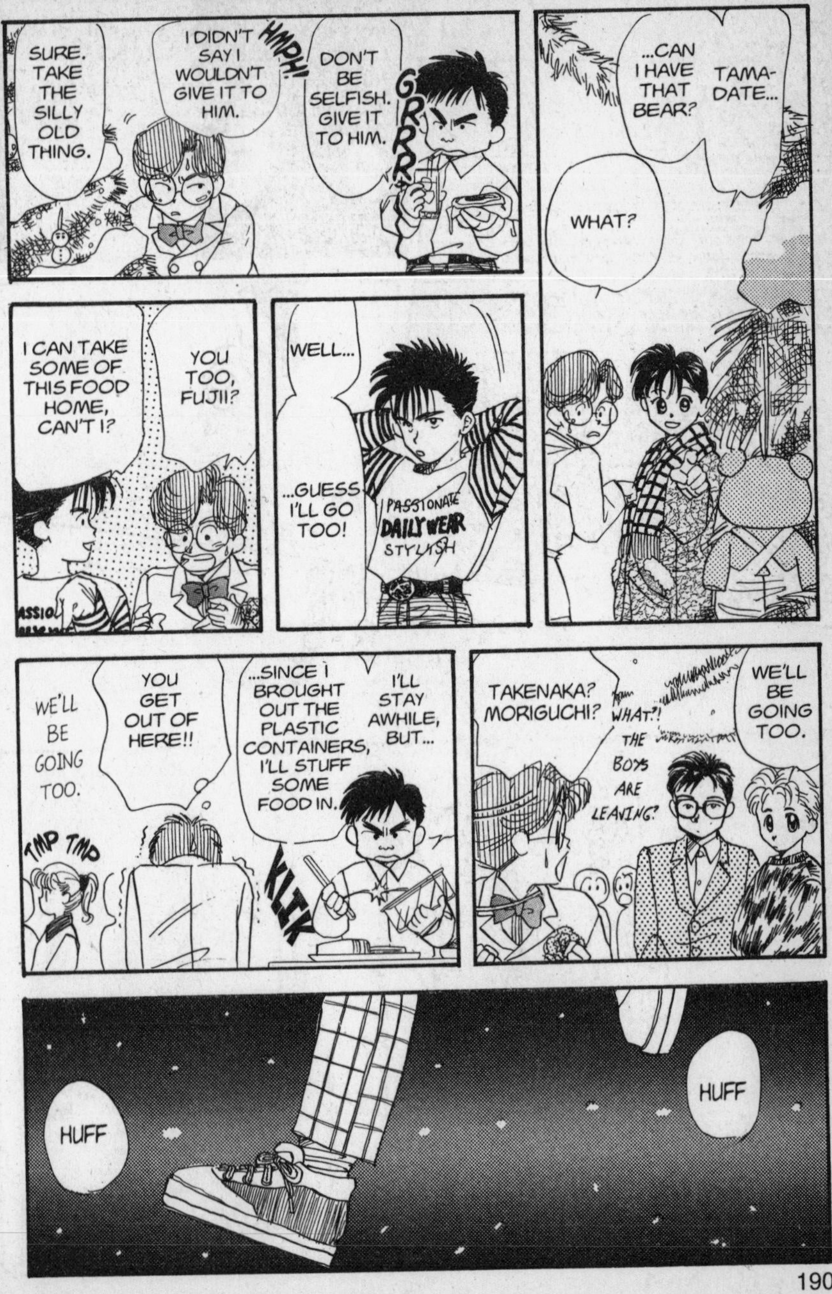
TAMA-DATE...
...CAN I HAVE THAT BEAR?
WHAT?
GRRR
DON'T BE SELFISH. GIVE IT TO HIM.
HMPH!
I DIDN'T SAY I WOULDN'T GIVE IT TO HIM.
SURE. TAKE THE SILLY OLD THING.
WELL...
...GUESS I'LL GO TOO!
PASSIONATE DAILY WEAR STYLISH
YOU TOO, FUJII?
I CAN TAKE SOME OF THIS FOOD HOME, CAN'T I?
WE'LL BE GOING TOO.
WHAT?! THE BOYS ARE LEAVING?
TAKENAKA? MORIGUCHI?
I'LL STAY AWHILE, BUT...
...SINCE I BROUGHT OUT THE PLASTIC CONTAINERS, I'LL STUFF SOME FOOD IN.
KLIK
YOU GET OUT OF HERE!!
WE'LL BE GOING TOO.
TMP TMP
HUFF
HUFF

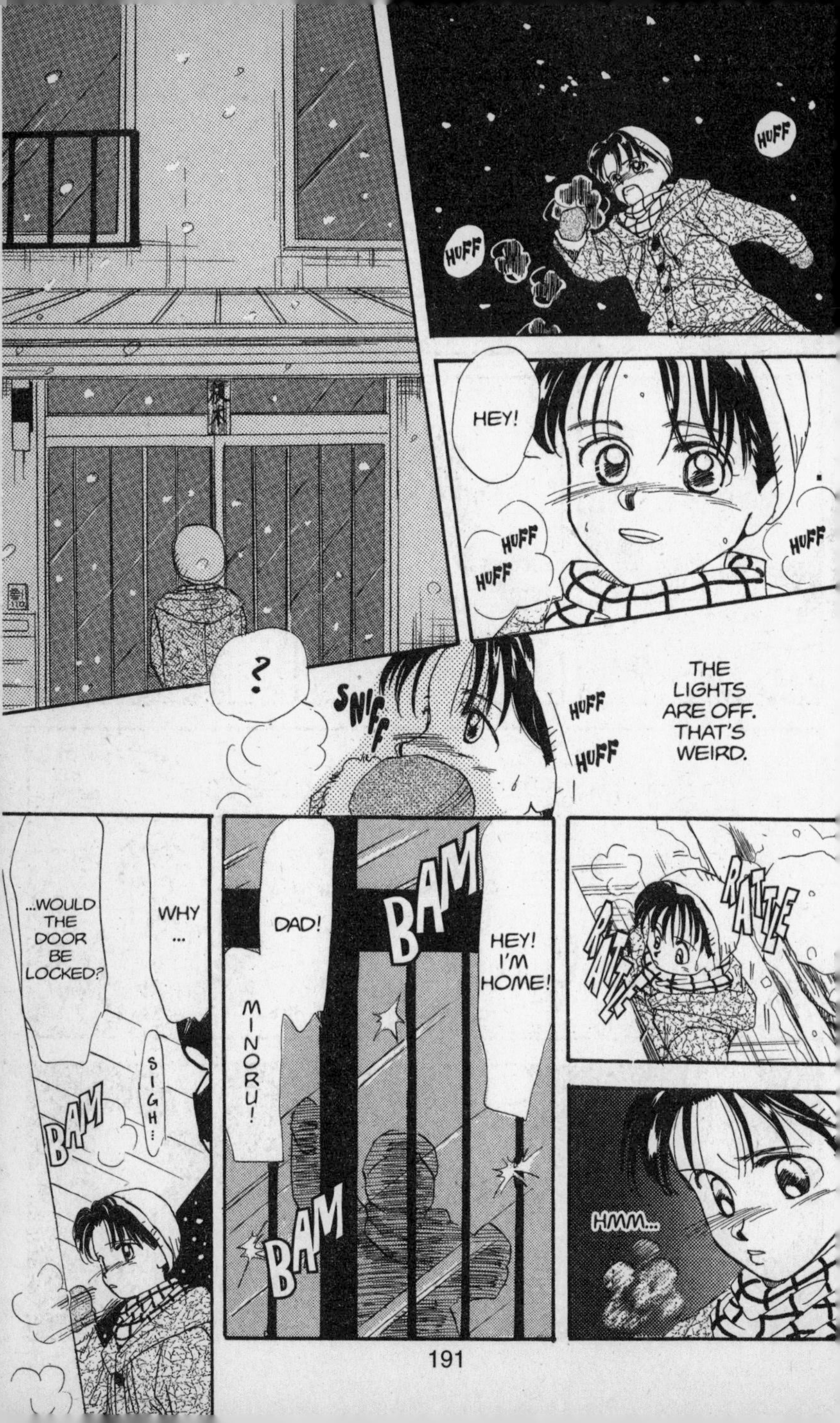
HUFF
HUFF
HEY!
HUFF
HUFF
HUFF
THE LIGHTS ARE OFF. THAT'S WEIRD.
HUFF
HUFF
SNIFF
?
RATTLE
RATTLE
HMM...
HEY! I'M HOME!
BAM
DAD!
MINORU!
BAM
BAM
WHY...
...WOULD THE DOOR BE LOCKED?
SIGH...
BAM

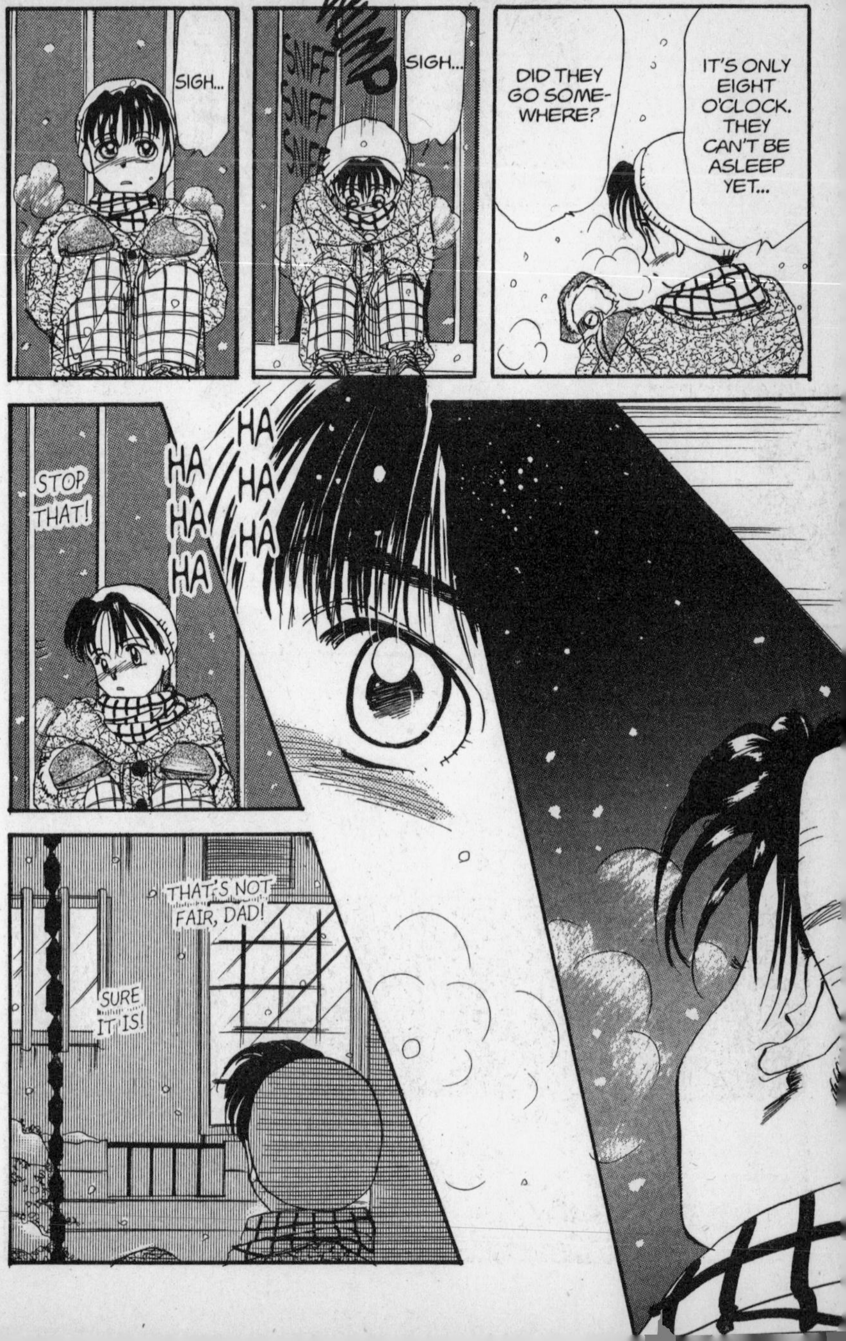
IT'S ONLY EIGHT O'CLOCK. THEY CAN'T BE ASLEEP YET...
DID THEY GO SOME-WHERE?
SIGH...
WUMP
SNIFF SNIFF SNIFF
SIGH...
HA HA HA
HA HA HA
STOP THAT!
THAT'S NOT FAIR, DAD!
SURE IT IS!

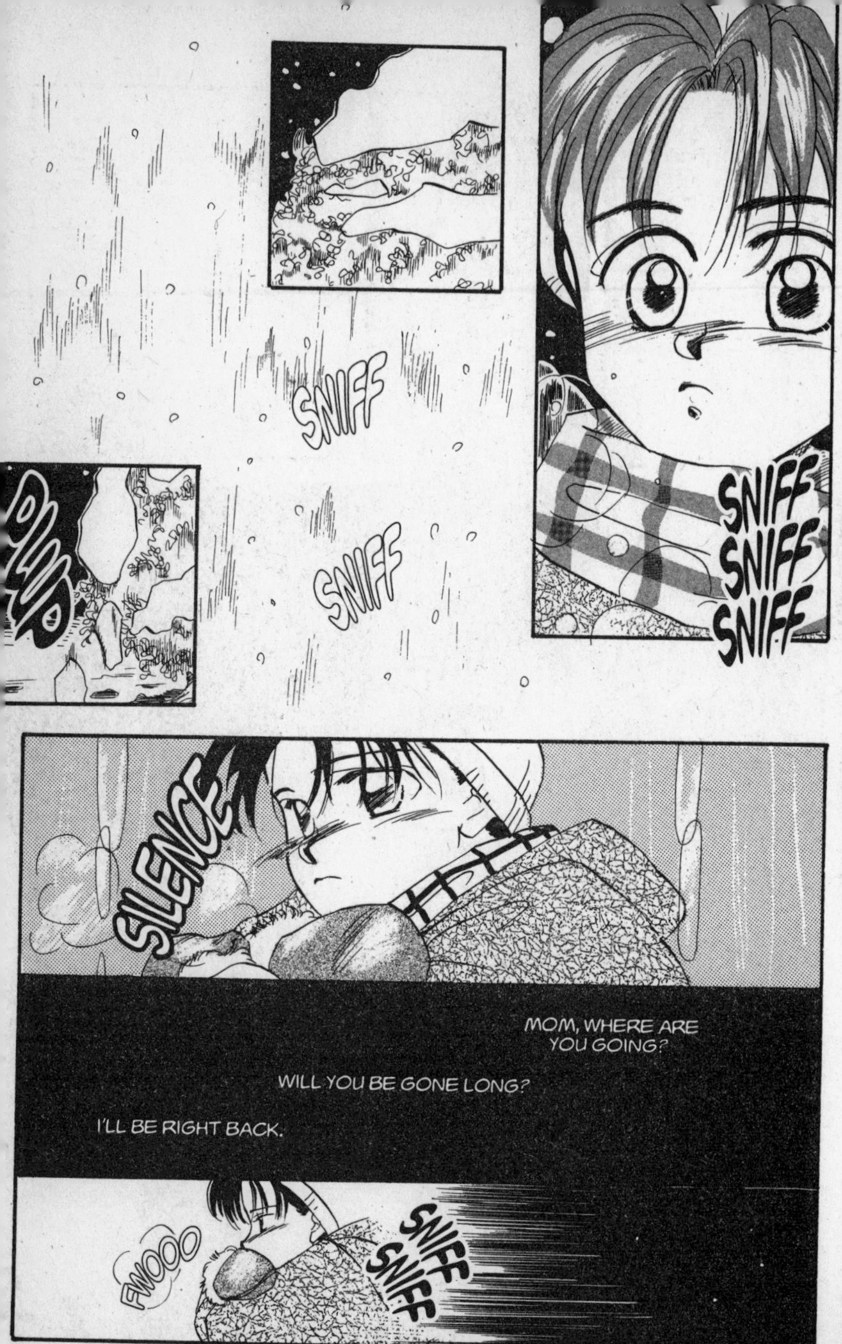
SNIFF
SNIFF
SNIFF
SNIFF
SNIFF
SILENCE
MOM, WHERE ARE YOU GOING?
WILL YOU BE GONE LONG?
I'LL BE RIGHT BACK.
SNIFF
SNIFF
FWOOO

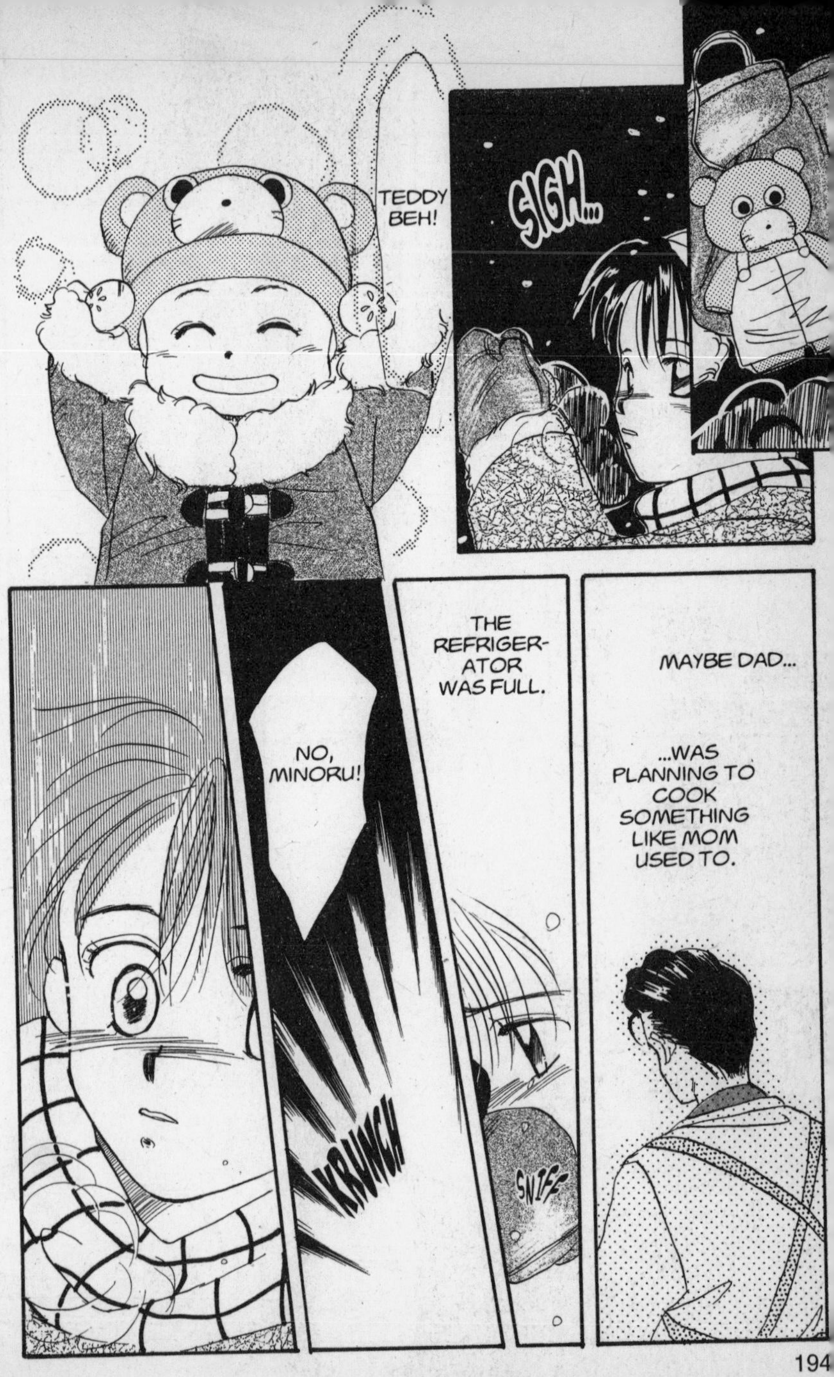
SIGH...
TEDDY BEH!
MAYBE DAD...
...WAS PLANNING TO COOK SOMETHING LIKE MOM USED TO.
THE REFRIGERATOR WAS FULL.
SNIFF
NO, MINORU!
KRUNCH

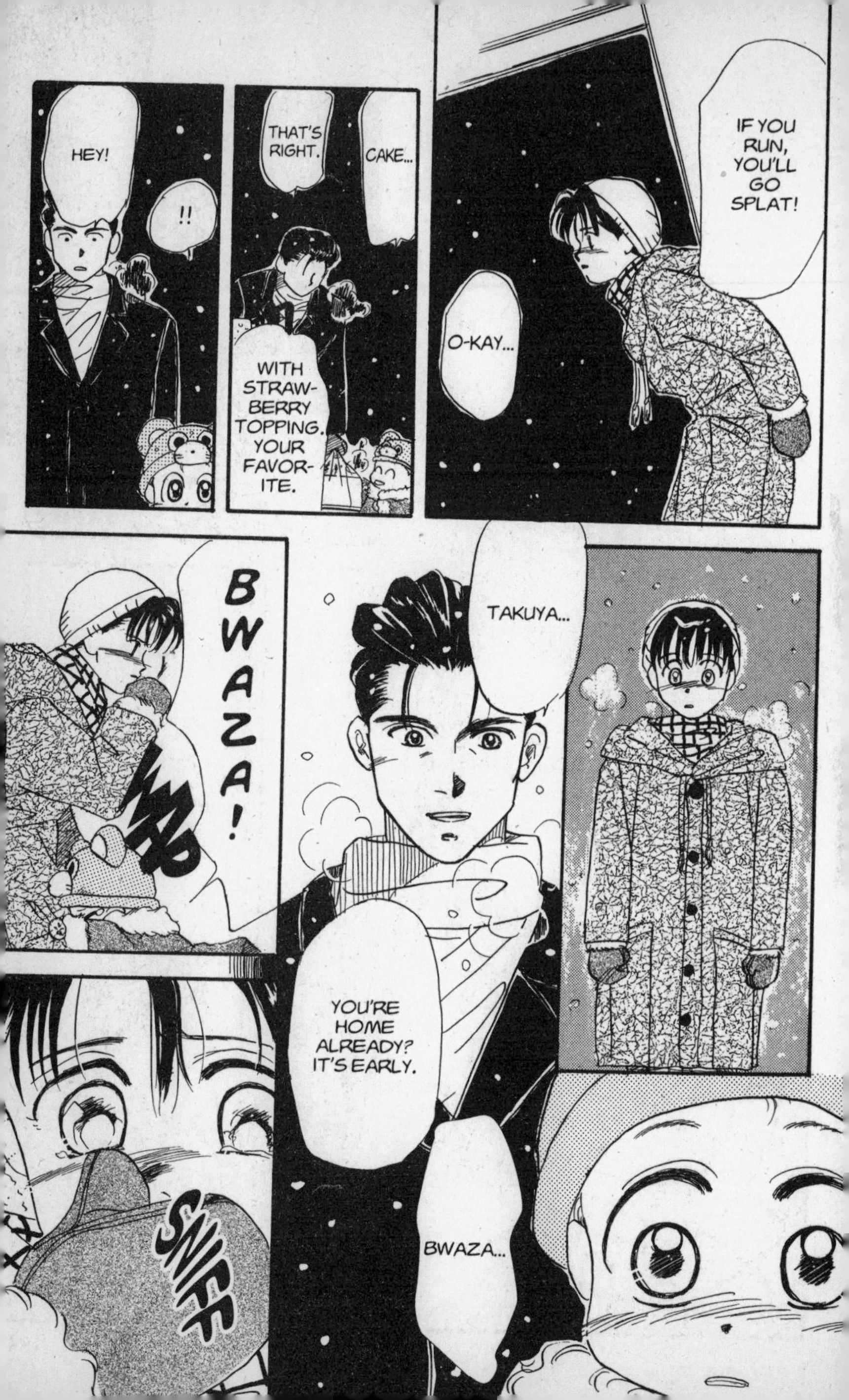
IF YOU RUN, YOU'LL GO SPLAT!
O-KAY...
CAKE...
THAT'S RIGHT.
WITH STRAW-BERRY TOPPING. YOUR FAVOR-ITE.
HEY!
!!
TAKUYA...
YOU'RE HOME ALREADY? IT'S EARLY.
BWAZA...
BWAZA!
WAP
SNIFF

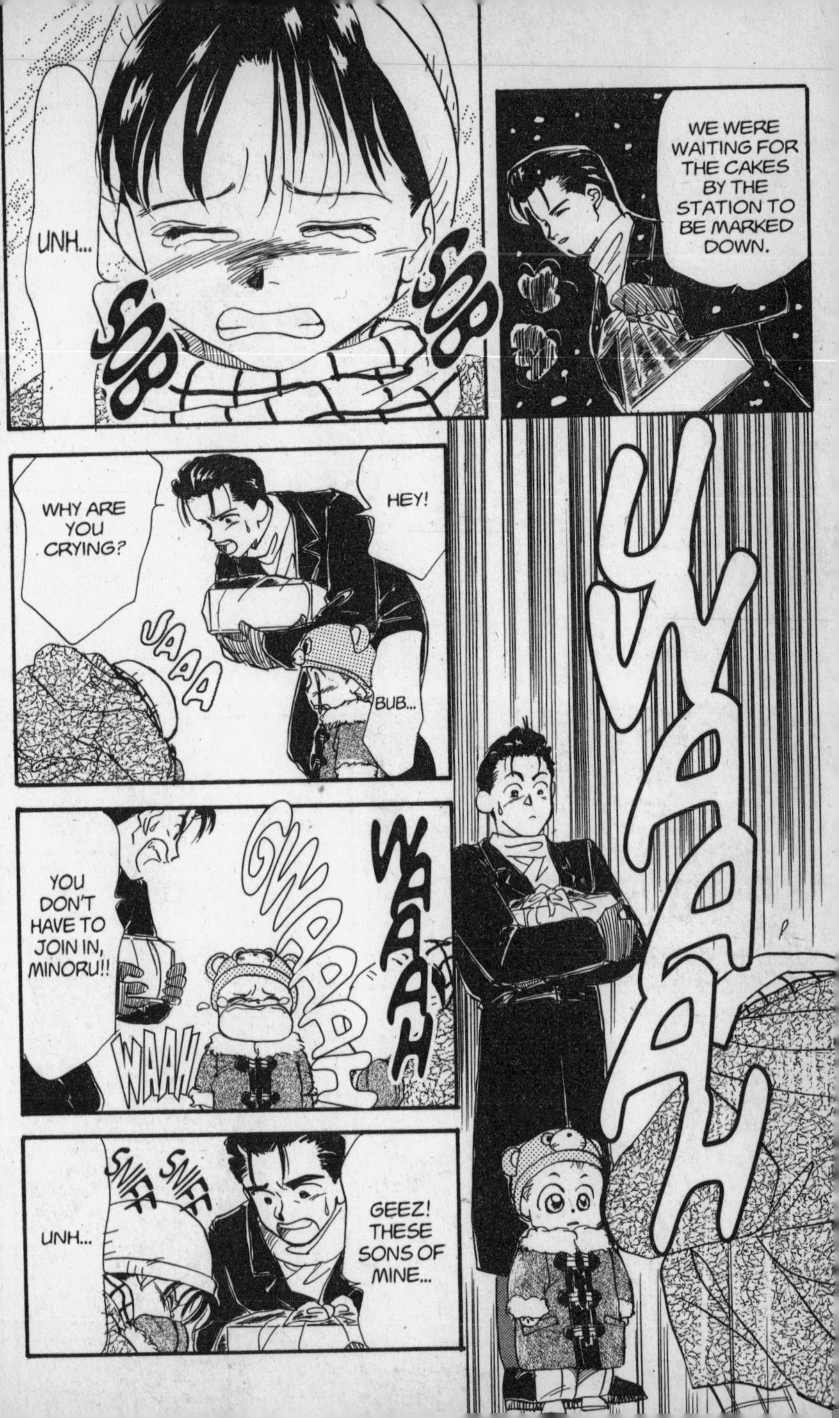

WE WERE WAITING FOR THE CAKES BY THE STATION TO BE MARKED DOWN.
UNH...
SOB
SOB
SOB
UWAAAH
HEY!
WHY ARE YOU CRYING?
JAAA
BUB...
WAAAAH
GWAAAH
YOU DON'T HAVE TO JOIN IN, MINORU!!
WAAH
GEEZ! THESE SONS OF MINE...
SNIFF
SNIFF
UNH...

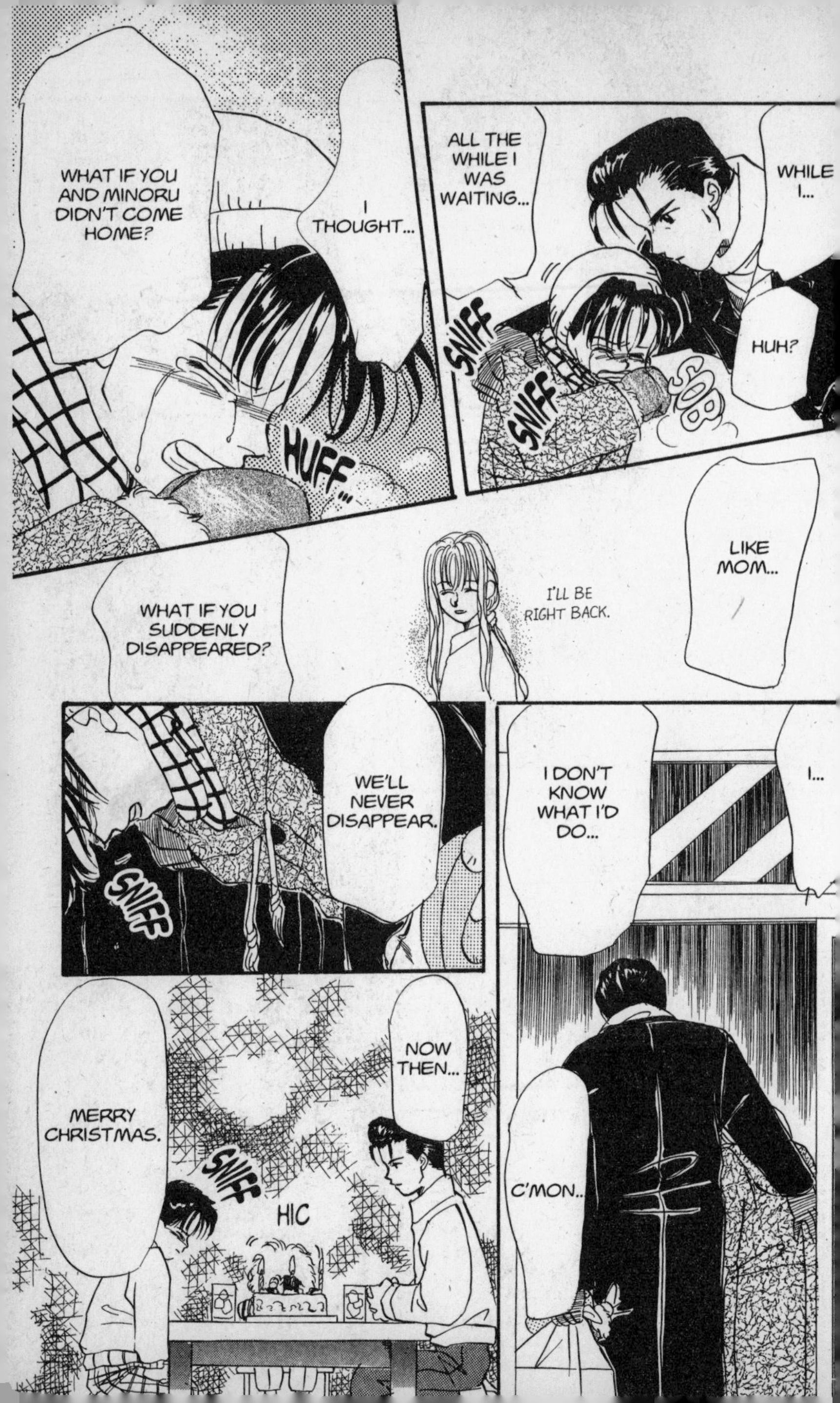
WHILE I...
ALL THE WHILE I WAS WAITING...
HUH?
SOB
SNIFF
SNIFF
I THOUGHT...
WHAT IF YOU AND MINORU DIDN'T COME HOME?
HUFF...
LIKE MOM...
I'LL BE RIGHT BACK.
WHAT IF YOU SUDDENLY DISAPPEARED?
I...
I DON'T KNOW WHAT I'D DO...
C'MON..
WE'LL NEVER DISAPPEAR.
SNIFF
NOW THEN...
MERRY CHRISTMAS.
SNIFF
HIC

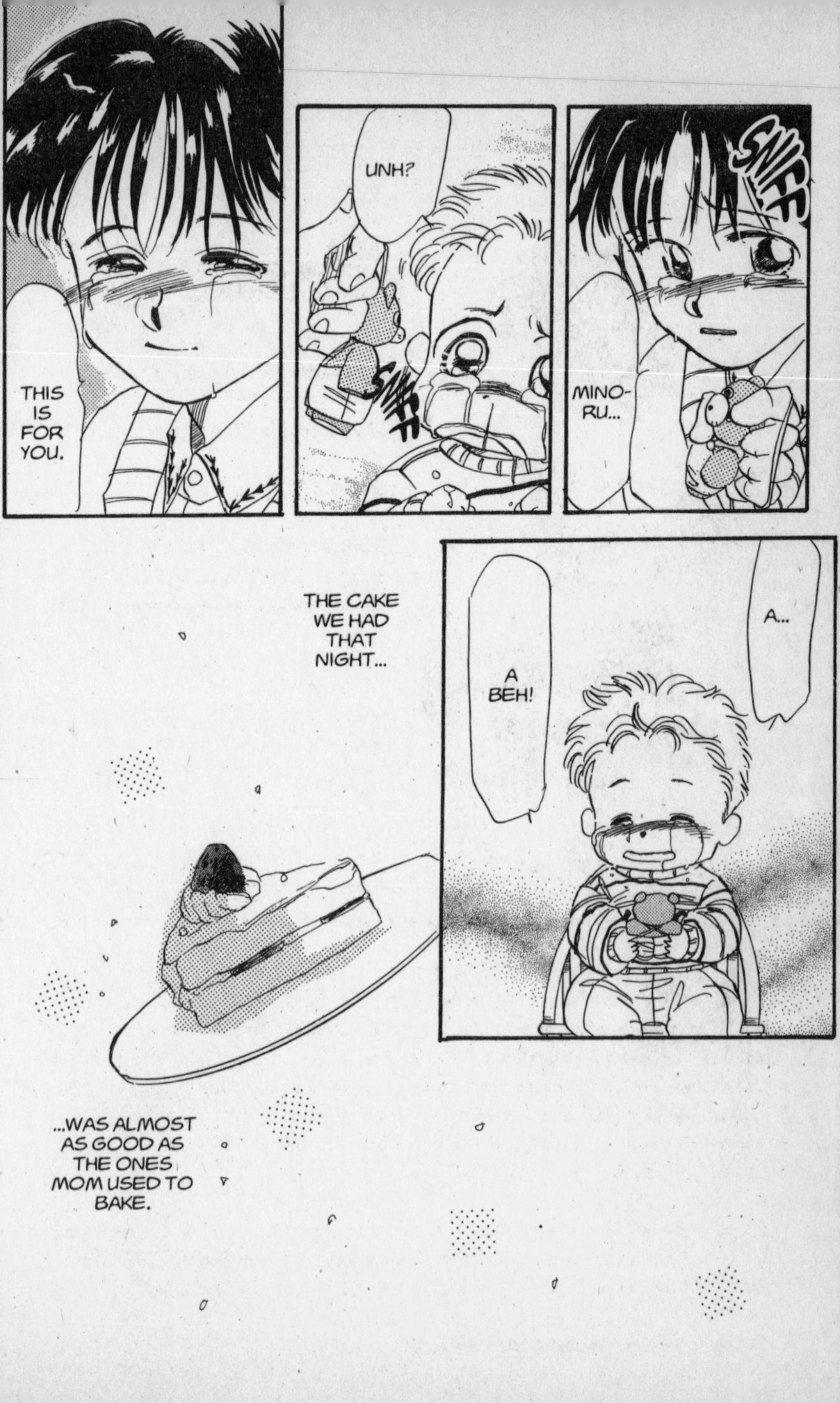
SNIFF
MINO-RU...
UNH?
SNIFF
THIS IS FOR YOU.
A...
A BEH!
THE CAKE WE HAD THAT NIGHT...
...WAS ALMOST AS GOOD AS THE ONES MOM USED TO BAKE.

BABY & Me

Creator: Marimo Ragawa

Date of Birth: September 21

Blood Type: B

Major Works: *Time Limit*, *Baby & Me, N.Y. N.Y.,* and *Shanimuni-Go* (Desperately—Go)

Marimo Ragawa first started submitting manga to a comic magazine when she was 12 years old. She kept up her submissions for four years, but to no avail. She decided to submit her work to the magazine *Hana to Yume*, where she received Top Prize in the Monthly Manga Contest as well as an honorable mention (Kasaku) in the magazine's Big Challenge contest. Her first manga was titled *Time Limit. Baby & Me* was honored with a Shogakukan Manga Award in 1995 and was spun-off into an anime.

Ragawa's work showcases some very cute and expressive line work along with an incredible ability to depict complex emotions and relationships. Some of her other works include *N.Y. N.Y.* and the tennis manga *Shanimuni-Go*.

Ragawa has two brothers and two sisters.

BABY & ME, Vol. 1
The Shojo Beat Manga Edition

This manga volume contains material that was originally published
in English in *Shojo Beat* magazine, #1-5.

STORY & ART BY
MARIMO RAGAWA

English Adaptation/Lance Caseleman
Translation/JN Productions
Touch-up Art & Lettering/Bill Schuch
Design/Courtney Utt
Editor/Ian Robertson

Managing Editor/Megan Bates
Director of Production/Noboru Watanabe
Vice President of Publishing/Alvin Lu
Vice President & Editor in Chief/Yumi Hoashi
Sr. Director of Acquisitions/Rika Inouye
Vice President of Sales & Marketing/Liza Coppola
Publisher/Hyoe Narita

Printed in Canada

Published by VIZ Media, LLC.
P.O. Box 77010
San Francisco, CA 94107

Shojo Beat Manga Edition
10 9 8 7 6 5 4 3 2 1
First printing, February 2006

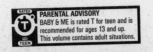

PARENTAL ADVISORY
BABY & ME is rated T for teen and is
recommended for ages 13 and up.
This volume contains adult situations.
RATED TEEN

store.viz.com

Get the Beat online!
Check us out at
www.shojobeat.com!

COMPLETE OUR SURVEY AND LET US KNOW WHAT YOU THINK!

☐ Please do NOT send me information about VIZ Media and Shojo Beat products, news and events, special offers, or other information.

☐ Please do NOT send me information from VIZ Media's trusted business partners.

Name: _____

Address: _____

City: _____ State: _____ Zip: _____

E-mail: _____

☐ Male ☐ Female   Date of Birth (mm/dd/yyyy): ___ / ___ / ___   (Under 13? Parental consent required)

1 Do you purchase *Shojo Beat* magazine?

☐ Yes   ☐ No (if no, skip the next two questions)

If **YES**, do you subscribe?

☐ Yes   ☐ No

If you do **NOT** subscribe, why? (please check one)

☐ I prefer to buy each issue at the store.   ☐ I prefer to buy the manga volumes instead.

☐ I share a copy with my friends/family.   ☐ It's too expensive.

☐ My parents/guardians won't let me.   ☐ Other

2 Which particular Shojo Beat Manga did you purchase? (please check one)

☐ Beauty Is The Beast   ☐ Full Moon   ☐ Fushigi Yûgi: Genbu Kaiden

☐ MeruPuri   ☐ Ouran High School Host Club ☐ Socrates In Love

☐ Tokyo Boys & Girls   ☐ Ultra Maniac   ☐ Other _____

Will you purchase subsequent volumes?

☐ Yes   ☐ No   ☐ Not Applicable

3 How did you learn about this title? (check all that apply)

☐ Advertisement   ☐ Article   ☐ Favorite creator/artist

☐ Favorite title   ☐ Gift   ☐ Recommendation

☐ Read a preview online and wanted to read the rest of the story

☐ Read introduction in *Shojo Beat* magazine   ☐ Special offer

☐ Website   ☐ Other _____

4 Do you plan to purchase Shojo Beat Manga volumes of titles serialized in SB magazine?

☐ Yes ☐ No

If **YES**, which one(s) do you plan to purchase? (check all that apply)

☐ Absolute Boyfriend ☐ Baby & Me ☐ Crimson Hero
☐ Godchild ☐ Kaze Hikaru ☐ Nana

If **YES**, what are your reasons for purchasing? (please pick up to 3)

☐ Favorite title ☐ Favorite creator/artist
☐ I want to read the full volume(s) all at once ☐ I want to read it over and over again
☐ There are extras that aren't in the magazine ☐ Recommendation
☐ The quality of printing is better than the magazine
☐ Other ____________________

If **NO**, why would you not purchase it?

☐ I'm happy just reading it in the magazine ☐ It's not worth buying the graphic novel
☐ All the manga pages are in black and white ☐ There are other graphic novels that I prefer
☐ There are too many to collect for each title ☐ It's too small
☐ Other ____________________

5 Of the titles NOT serialized in the magazine, which ones have you purchased? (check all that apply)

☐ Beauty Is The Beast ☐ Full Moon ☐ Fushigi Yûgi: Genbu Kaiden
☐ MeruPuri ☐ Ouran High School Host Club ☐ Socrates In Love
☐ Tokyo Boys & Girls ☐ Ultra Maniac ☐ Other __________

If you did purchase any of the above, what were your reasons for purchase?

☐ Advertisement ☐ Article ☐ Favorite creator/artist
☐ Favorite title ☐ Gift ☐ Recommendation
☐ Read a preview online and wanted to read the rest of the story
☐ Read introduction in *Shojo Beat* magazine ☐ Special offer
☐ Website ☐ Other ____________________

Will you purchase subsequent volumes?

☐ Yes ☐ No ☐ Not Applicable

6 What race/ethnicity do you consider yourself? (please check one)

☐ Asian/Pacific Islander ☐ Black/African American ☐ Hispanic/Latino
☐ Native American/Alaskan Native ☐ White/Caucasian ☐ Other

THANK YOU! Please send the completed form to:

Shojo Survey
42 Catharine St.
Poughkeepsie, NY 12601

VIZ media™

All information provided will be used for internal purposes only. We promise not to sell or otherwise divulge your information.